网络空间安全系列教材

电子数据取证与 Python 方法

Python Forensics
A Workbench for Inventing and
Sharing Digital Forensic Technology

〔美〕Chet Hosmer 著

张 俊 译
邹锦沛 审校

电子工业出版社
Publishing House of Electronics Industry
北京·BEIJING

内 容 简 介

本书是一本电子数据取证的入门书籍，系统介绍如何应用Python编程语言进行电子数据取证软件开发。第1章和第2章介绍Python基本知识和如何建立一个取证开发环境。第3章到第11章针对电子数字取证的各种需求，详细阐述指导性的解决方法，涵盖哈希计算、关键字搜索、元数据提取、网络分析、自然语言处理以及利用云的多进程等专题，并提供大量的源代码实例供读者学习、改进并应用到实际案例。第12章回顾了全书内容，并就未来的发展进行了探讨。

本书适合网络空间安全、网络安全与执法、信息安全、法学、司法鉴定及相关专业的本科和专科学生作为教材，对于从事数字犯罪调查、计算机司法鉴定、内部调查、软件研发等工作的执法人员、调查分析人员、审计人员，以及取证软件和工具的研发人员，也是提升技能、丰富手段的参考书。

Python Forensics: A Workbench for Inventing and Sharing Digital Forensic Technology
Chet Hosmer
ISBN: 9780124186767
Copyright © 2014 by Elsevier Inc. All rights reserved.
Authorized Simplified Chinese translation edition published by the Proprietor.
Copyright © 2017 by Elsevier (Singapore) Pte Ltd. All rights reserved.
Published in China by Publishing House of Electronics Industry under special arrangement with Elsevier (Singapore) Pte Ltd. This edition is authorized for sale in China Mainland. Unauthorized export of this edition is a violation of Copyright Act. Violation of this Law is subject to Civil and Criminal Penalties.

本书简体中文版由Elsevier (Singapore) Pte Ltd.授予电子工业出版社在中国大陆出版发行与销售。未经许可之出口，视为违反著作权法，将受法律之制裁。

本书封底贴有Elsevier公司防伪标签，无标签者不得销售。

版权贸易合同登记号　图字：01-2016-9444

图书在版编目（CIP）数据

电子数据取证与Python方法 /（美）切特·霍斯默（Chet Hosmer）著；张俊译. —北京：电子工业出版社，2017.9
书名原文：Python Forensics: A Workbench for Inventing and Sharing Digital Forensic Technology
网络空间安全系列教材
ISBN 978-7-121-32131-3

Ⅰ. ①电… Ⅱ. ①切… ②张… Ⅲ. ①计算机犯罪—证据—数据收集—高等学校—教材 Ⅳ. ①D918

中国版本图书馆CIP数据核字（2017）第161153号

策划编辑：马　岚
责任编辑：李秦华
印　　刷：三河市双峰印刷装订有限公司
装　　订：三河市双峰印刷装订有限公司
出版发行：电子工业出版社
　　　　　北京市海淀区万寿路173信箱　邮编：100036
开　　本：787×1092　1/16　印张：15.75　字数：403千字
版　　次：2017年9月第1版
印　　次：2019年1月第2次印刷
定　　价：59.00元

凡所购买电子工业出版社图书有缺损问题，请向购买书店调换。若书店售缺，请与本社发行部联系，联系及邮购电话：(010) 88254888，88258888。
质量投诉请发邮件至zlts@phei.com.cn，盗版侵权举报请发邮件至dbqq@phei.com.cn。
本书咨询联系方式：classic-series-info@phei.com.cn。

中译本序

有幸与湖北警官学院的张俊老师相识，我们经常在学术会议间隙，或者相互访问的交流过程中探讨电子数据取证的问题。张俊老师从事电子数据取证的教学和科研工作多年，培养了很多优秀的学生，他还积极参与电子数据取证的司法鉴定工作，办理了许多重大和复杂的案件。张俊老师一直活跃在电子数据取证领域，并不断关注和跟踪国内外最新的技术发展，所以他有心翻译和出版这样一本书，我觉得一切都是顺理成章的事情。

本书作者Chet Hosmer和技术编辑Gary C. Kessler也是信息网络安全业界的专业人士，他们都是知名的专家，有着长期的专业经历和丰富学识。他们将宝贵的经验和专业知识毫无保留地在书中传授，这将有利于专业人才的成长，有助于立志从事电子数据取证的技术人员和法律人士快速进入这一领域。

电子数据取证是一个发展时间相对较短的领域，还有很多的技术问题、法律问题尚待解决。香港大学计算机科学学系的课程也应用了Python语言编程，我们也鼓励从事信息安全专业的学生学习这门语言，并充分利用其简单易学、第三方库功能强大的特点，与专业知识相结合，针对电子数据取证的不同问题或挑战，开展创造性的工作，提出切实可行的解决方案。

这本书提供了广泛的例子，便于不了解编程或只拥有初级技术的开发人员使用。我们盼望着更多充满智慧和理想的新人的加入，期待你们所有人分享思想、知识和经验，一起推进这一事业的发展。

邹锦沛博士（Dr. CHOW KAM PUI）
香港大学信息安全和密码学研究中心（CISC）
香港大学计算机科学学系
2016年11月18日于香港大学

译 者 序

电子数据取证技术的研究和应用在国内得到了越来越多的关注。全世界的专家和学者在提及信息网络安全时，关注的重点多集中于算法理论的研究、技术方法的对抗以及规范策略的制定等，毫无疑问这些问题极为重要。然而，信息网络安全的最后一道防线必然诉诸法律。最近几年电子数据作为一种独立证据类型，逐渐得到各类法规的认可，例如在深圳快播公司涉嫌传播淫秽物品牟利案的庭审中，关于电子证据的控辩，就引发了司法界对电子证据的广泛关注。作为向法庭呈贡证据的侦查人员、电子数据取证司法鉴定人，他们的知识、水平和能力成为关键。但现实的问题是，由于计算机网络技术的飞速发展，以及案件的复杂和规模化，已有的电子数据取证工具在很多情况下并不能替侦查人员或司法鉴定人自动完成他们所需的全部工作，或者完成更高级的取证调查任务。例如，用现有的工具软件提取一部手机的通话、短信和即时通信记录，通常可以得到数GByte数据，往往一个案件涉及十几部或更多的手机，因此数据量更大。如果侦查人员或司法鉴定人能够快速地编写代码，进行定制的搜索和索引，将极大地提高从这些海量的半结构化数据中高效地得到关键证据的能力。

译者长期从事电子数据取证的科研和教学工作，并作为司法鉴定人，参与了大量重、特大案件的电子数据取证调查工作，在这些过程中一直反复思考上述这些问题。一个偶然的机会，看到了 *Python Forensics: A Workbench for Inventing and Sharing Digital Forensic Technology* 一书，立刻被它的内容所吸引，感觉找到了问题的答案。本书的特点在于，使用Python语言上手快，第三方库丰富，调查员可以方便地编写代码来完成复杂的、特定的取证任务，而且无须过多关注语言细节，从而能将主要精力放到取证任务本身。另外，本书体现了开发过程满足多伯特（Daubert）证据标准的重要性，也就是设计、开发、测试过程符合特定的证据标准。这些特点也是开发普通程序与取证程序的最大区别。

作者Chet Hosmer不仅是信息网络安全、电子数据取证领域的从业人士，也是一名教育工作者，作为Utica学院网络安全研究生课程的客座教授，他擅长从调查员视角讲解如何用Python语言进行电子数据取证。本书在介绍如何建立一个Python取证环境的基础上，首先详细讲解开发一个取证应用的基本框架，然后每一章都针对网络犯罪取证的一个不同问题，讨论能够自由使用、分享和扩展的Python指导性解决方案，包括哈希、关键字搜索、元数据、自然语言处理、网络分析以及利用云的多进程等。最后，对Python应用于网络犯罪调查，以及更广泛领域的网络安全应用，高性能硬件加速和嵌入式解决方案等在未来的机遇进行了展望。作者认为，能否建造自己的取证工具库，是区分初级取证调查员与专业取证调查员的关键。全书贯穿着一个资深调查员通过长期实践得出的理念。作为前辈，他谆谆告诫后来者：只有当我们（调查人员）理解工具如何工作时，它们才真正是我们的工具。他正是以这一核心指导原则展开了本书全部内容。

电子数据取证是计算机科学、法学等的交叉领域，技术开发人员和法律工作者以不同的知识背景进入该领域，他们从各自角度去理解电子数据证据的提取、分析和呈贡，并且在专业词汇、思维过程、解决问题的方式等方面有很大区别，形成了介于一个自然科学和社会科学之间的"沟壑"。所以，本书的另一个目的是试图建立起工程学（如计算机科学、信息科学）与社会科学（如法学）之间的桥梁。技术开发人员和法律工作者通过阅读本书，提升对取证环境和工具的理解，可以轻松交流和平等参与，从而创造出一个协作而不互损的环境，计算机科学与社会科学都能各尽其力。我在阅读和翻译的过程中，深刻体会到作者毫无保留地把自己积累的宝贵经验传授给读者。本书对读者的编程知识（也许根本没有）不做任何预设。只要肯用功，对书中的例子感兴趣，读者就不用担心自己读不懂，甚至可以将其扩展，开发出适应特定情形和问题的进化版本。

以我有限的水平，要翻译好这样一本同时适合技术开发人员和法律工作者阅读的著作，内心难免不安。感谢作者Chet Hosmer对我每次发邮件向他求教或确认问题的耐心解答。感谢我的领导黄凤林教授和张天长教授，他们给予我很多指导和帮助。感谢武汉天宇宁达公司的CEO郭永健先生，他给出了若干非常专业的修改意见。翻译本书时，我还向徐必超和胡壮求证过有关的示例是否有误，他们是湖北警官学院的毕业生，现在战斗在电子数据取证的最前线。感谢湖北警官学院的学生吴沛沛、欧阳桂申、彭洪飞、沈阳、朱俊妍参与部分翻译校对和代码测试工作。最后感谢我的妻子，她承担了所有的家务重任，让我全心投入工作，并以我翻译本书为骄傲。

由于本人学识有限，且时间仓促，书中翻译错误、不当和疏漏之处在所难免，望读者批评指正。

专家荐语

Hosmer不仅为各种层次的取证分析提供了一个出色的Python取证指南，还眼光独到地阐述了如何建立一个意义非凡的协作环境，这种环境将极大地提升个人、组织以及取证社区的取证能力。对于分析人员、调查人员、管理人员、研究人员，以及其他任何对数字取证感兴趣的人来说，这是一本必须读的书！

—— Michael Duren（CISSP）
Cyber Moxie公司创始人

随着当今技术的快速变化，数字取证工具和实践也不得不快速更新，才能保持某种程度的实用性；调查人员昨天还依赖的技术能力，今天就迅速地过时。然而，随着新技术一起到来的也有新的工具和方法，Python语言就是其中最有可能被调查人员利用的事物之一。本书就是走在这一时代前列的一本书。正因为如此，无论对于初学者还是有经验的调查人员，它都是一本绝好的书。Chet Hosmer做了一项伟大的工作，通过循序渐进的指导，帮助读者更新旧的方法，掌握新的技能；通过合理的组织架构，最大限度地促进内容理解和前后贯通。从本书学到的技能，将有助于读者开发灵活而新颖的工具，并在若干年内发挥作用。

—— Greg Kipper
Verizon公司高级安全架构师和战略官

本书展现了Python应用于现代数字取证的崭新和务实的视野，提出了关于这种语言的强项和劣势的有价值的深刻见解。每一个有见识的取证调查员都值得花时间和精力来了解本书。

—— Russ Rogers
Peak Security公司董事长

本书对于Python取证程序员、很少或者没有Python编程经验的人都非常有用，对一个有经验的程序员来说也是一本很棒的参考书。这本书考虑到了与多伯特规则有关的问题，包括测试和验证，这些对于取证案件鉴定是至关重要的。

—— Zeno Geradts
荷兰法政研究所高级取证科学家和研发协同人

一如既往，Chet Hosmer提供了一个适用于数字取证的，具有全面性和突破性的解决方案和现代平台。这本书写得非常棒，很好用，为所有水平的Python取证程序员提供了一个坚实的基础，还包括关于实证检验的十分必要的讨论。这本书确实很简洁，对于所有想拥有一个数字取证库的人来说，本书值得拥有。

—— Marjie T. Britz博士
Clemson大学

序

  2008年6月16日，在2岁的Caylee Anthony家里，有人用谷歌搜索了"防误操作的窒息"的术语。随后还是这位用户，使用Casey Anthony的名字登录了MySpace网站。几个月后悲剧发生，警方发现了这个小女孩腐烂的尸体。检察官以一级谋杀罪指控Casey Anthony，并在3年后对她进行审判。审讯历时6个月，涉及400多份独立证据。遗憾的是，对计算机搜查得到的详细资料却始终没能被提上审讯。检方的计算机取证检查人员使用了一个工具来提取浏览器历史记录。但使用那个工具时，取证检查人员却只搜索了Internet Explorer的历史记录，而没有搜索Firefox浏览器的。这个故事的教训在于，当我们理解工具如何工作时，它们才真正是我们的工具。

  与这个取证检查人员的失败相对比，让我们想想最可怕的武装力量——斯巴达军队。斯巴达军队的强大之处在于其士兵的职业化。优秀士兵从年少时起就只学习一种职业——打仗。在这个行业，士兵严重依赖武器和盔甲的品质。每一个斯巴达士兵的责任就是携带他自己的武器和盔甲上战场，而不是配发的武器。儿辈走上战场前，父辈会把武器传递给他。在接下来的文章里，Chet Hosmer会将现代工具和武器传递下去。但作为取证调查员，你的战场也许是硬盘的未分配空间，但一定不是Thermopylae（希腊东部一个多岩石平原）的道路，无论如何，Chet会像斯巴达长老一样，教你打造自己的工具。能否建造你自己的武器库，是将犯下遗漏浏览器痕迹这种粗劣错误的取证调查员，与专业取证调查员区分开来的关键。

  余下的章节涵盖了广泛的主题，包括哈希、关键字搜索、元数据、自然语言处理、网络分析以及利用云的多进程等。Chet会在利用Python编程语言教你打造自己武器的过程中，涉及这些精彩的话题。作为Utica学院网络安全研究生课程的客座教授，Chet既是一位教育者，也是一位实践者。作为40多项涉及网络安全、数字取证和信息保障研究计划的主要调查人员，他由于出色的工作而获得国际公认和奖项。就像斯巴达长老一样，他的知识会促进专业人才的成长。所以，请尽情享用本书的内容。就像斯巴达人的妻子们曾在战前告诉她们的丈夫："带着你的盾牌回来，不然就战死沙场。"

TJ Oconnor

SANS 红与蓝团队网络卫士（SANS Red & Blue Team Cyber Guardian）

前　　言

在过去的20年中，我有幸能与一些世界上最优秀、最聪明和最专注的取证调查员一起工作。这些女士和先生们为查明真相而不知疲倦——他们通常都工作在条件不理想的环境和严格的最后期限压力下。无论是追查儿童劫犯、有犯罪组织、恐怖分子，或者仅仅是用老旧手段偷取你钱财的犯罪分子，这些调查人员都面临巨大的压力，必须竭尽全力将手边的工作做到最好。

我时常与开发最新取证产品的业界领袖们交流，同时不断提升其当前软件的基线，以满足最广泛的潜在用户的需求。我也时常与设法解决现实困难的客户们打交道，这些困难需要立刻得到答案，然而包含答案的数据量却在分秒间变得更大。

作为一名科学家和教师，我看到了来自学生、执法人员以及信息技术人士的渴求，他们具备强烈的期待、独特的调查技能以及对问题的理解，更重要的是对于手头问题的创新性的想法。然而在许多情况下，他们缺乏有助于其事业，而且必须具备的核心计算机科学技能。

Python编程语言以及整体环境为创新开辟了一条崭新的道路。最重要的是，这种语言广开大门，兼收并蓄，提供了大量免费工具和技术，能够彻底改革取证证据的收集、处理、分析和推理。这本书提供了广泛的例子，不但让那些几乎不了解编程或者零基础的人群容易理解，对于那些已拥有扎实的技术，想进一步探索、跃升并参与到在取证领域中扩展应用Python的开发人员来说，也非常有帮助。我期待你们的参与，分享你们的知识，带着你们的热情，帮助我们推进这一事业。

适合的读者

本书对于那些渴望学习如何将Python语言应用到取证和数字调查的任何人来说，都很容易理解。我一直认为这本书是跳板和起点，希望能激励读者创建一些伟大的东西，并与世界共享。

预备条件

能使用计算机，熟悉操作系统（Windows、Linux或Mac），能访问互联网，并且具有强烈的学习渴望。

阅读方法

本书组织如下，第1章和第2章侧重于引导性的内容，同时建立起一个免费的Python开发环境。第3章到第11章针对数字取证的不同问题或挑战，提供操作指导性的解决方案，聚焦于呈现的关键问题并提出实现的参考。我鼓励读者使用、扩展、改进并提升书中提供的解决方案。最后，第12章回顾了全书内容，并就未来的发展进行了探讨。

支持的平台

　　书中所有例子都是用Python 2.7.x编写，以提供最好的平台兼容性。本书的网站给出了针对Python 2.7.x和Python 3.x的部分代码。当更多的第三方库完全支持Python 3.x时，所有例子都将提供Python 2.7.x和Python 3.x代码。大多数例子都在Windows、Linux和Mac操作系统进行了测试，也将会在完全支持至少Python 2.7.x的其他环境中正常执行。

下载软件

　　读者可以从python-forensics.org网站获得书中例子的源代码（如果可能，将同时提供Python 2.7.x和Python 3.x的版本）。

评论、提问和贡献

　　我鼓励读者们主动参与到这一具有首创精神的活动，你们对python-forensics.org网站的源代码库的评论、提问和贡献会被所有人共享。

　　我鼓励你们所有人分享你们的思想、知识和经验。

致 谢

致以我真诚的感谢：

这本书的技术编辑Gary Kessler博士，你的透彻见解，新鲜观点，深刻的学术理解和指导为这本书增加了极大的价值。你持续不断的鼓励和友情让我十分享受写作的过程。

Elsevier公司的Ben Rearick和Steve Elliot，感谢你们对这个专题的热情以及一直以来的指导和支持。这种精神对我的帮助超出了你们的想象。

我曾经还有很多老师，指导过我多年来的软件开发和取证，正是他们的帮助，我才能构思这本书的内容。这些老师是Ron Stevens，Tom Hurbanek，Mike Duren，Allen Guillen，Rhonda Caracappa，Russ Rogers，Jordon Jacobs，Tony Reyes，Am ber Schroader和Greg Kipper。

Joe Giordano，他在1998年就富于远见地签订了第一个美国空军取证信息战的研究合同。这个合同催生了这个领域中的许多新公司、新发明，并促成了数字取证研究研讨会（DFRWS），以及Utica学院计算机取证研究和发展中心的建立。无庸置疑，你们都是真正的先驱者！

目　　录

第1章　为何使用Python进行取证 ·· 1
 1.1　本章简介 ··· 1
 1.2　网络空间犯罪调查的挑战 ·· 1
 1.3　Python编程环境如何有助于应对这些挑战 ··· 3
  1.3.1　Python的全球支持 ··· 4
  1.3.2　开源和平台独立性 ·· 5
  1.3.3　生命周期定位 ·· 5
  1.3.4　入门的成本和限制 ·· 5
 1.4　Python与多伯特（Daubert）证据标准 ·· 5
 1.5　本书的组织结构 ··· 6
 1.6　章节回顾 ··· 7
 1.7　问题小结 ··· 7
 1.8　补充资料 ··· 7

第2章　建立一个Python取证环境 ·· 8
 2.1　本章简介 ··· 8
 2.2　搭建一个Python取证环境 ·· 8
 2.3　正确的环境 ·· 9
 2.4　选择一个Python版本 ·· 10
 2.5　在Windows上安装Python ··· 10
 2.6　Python包和模块 ·· 15
  2.6.1　Python标准库 ··· 15
 2.7　标准库包含什么 ··· 17
  2.7.1　内建函数 ··· 17
  2.7.2　hex()和bin() ··· 17
  2.7.3　range() ·· 18
  2.7.4　其他的内建函数 ··· 19
  2.7.5　内建常量 ··· 20
  2.7.6　内建类型 ··· 21
  2.7.7　内建异常 ··· 22
  2.7.8　文件和目录访问 ··· 22
  2.7.9　数据压缩和归档 ··· 23

	2.7.10 文件格式	23
	2.7.11 加密服务	23
	2.7.12 操作系统服务	23
	2.7.13 标准库小结	24
2.8	第三方包和模块	24
	2.8.1 自然语言工具包（NLTK）	24
	2.8.2 Twisted matrix（TWISTED）	25
2.9	集成开发环境	25
	2.9.1 有哪些选择	25
	2.9.2 运行于Ubuntu Linux上的Python	30
2.10	移动设备上的Python	32
	2.10.1 iOS中的Python应用	32
	2.10.2 Windows 8 Phone	34
2.11	虚拟机	35
2.12	章节回顾	35
2.13	问题小结	35
2.14	接下来讲什么	36
2.15	补充资料	36
第3章	第一个Python取证应用程序	37
3.1	本章简介	37
3.2	命名惯例和其他考虑	37
	3.2.1 常量	38
	3.2.2 本地变量名	38
	3.2.3 全局变量名	38
	3.2.4 函数名	38
	3.2.5 对象名	38
	3.2.6 模块	38
	3.2.7 类名	38
3.3	第一个应用程序"单向文件系统哈希"	38
	3.3.1 背景	39
	3.3.2 基本需求	40
	3.3.3 设计中的考虑	41
	3.3.4 程序结构	42
3.4	代码遍历	44
	3.4.1 检查Main-代码遍历	44
	3.4.2 ParseCommandLine()	46
	3.4.3 ValidatingDirectoryWritable	48

		3.4.4	WalkPath ···	49
		3.4.5	HashFile ···	50
		3.4.6	CSVWriter ···	53
		3.4.7	pfish.py完整代码清单 ···	53
		3.4.8	_pfish.py完整代码清单 ···	54
	3.5	结果展示 ···		61
	3.6	章节回顾 ···		65
	3.7	问题小结 ···		65
	3.8	接下来讲什么 ··		66
	3.9	补充资料 ···		66
第4章	使用Python进行取证搜索和索引 ···			67
	4.1	本章简介 ···		67
	4.2	关键字上下文搜索 ···		68
		4.2.1	如何用Python轻松完成 ···	69
		4.2.2	基本需求 ···	70
		4.2.3	设计考虑 ···	71
	4.3	代码遍历 ···		73
		4.3.1	分析Main——代码遍历 ···	73
		4.3.2	分析_p-search函数——代码遍历 ···	74
		4.3.3	分析ParseCommandLine ··	74
		4.3.4	分析ValidateFileRead(theFile) ···	76
		4.3.5	分析SearchWords函数 ··	76
	4.4	结果展示 ···		80
	4.5	索引 ···		83
	4.6	编写isWordProbable ··		84
	4.7	p-search完整代码清单 ··		86
		4.7.1	p-search.py ··	86
		4.7.2	_p-search.py ··	87
	4.8	章节回顾 ···		93
	4.9	问题小结 ···		93
	4.10	补充资料 ···		93
第5章	证据提取（JPEG和TIFF） ··			94
	5.1	本章简介 ···		94
	5.2	Python图像库（PIL） ···		95
	5.3	代码遍历 ···		105
		5.3.1	Main程序 ··	105
		5.3.2	logging类 ···	105

	5.3.3	cvs处理器	105
	5.3.4	命令行解析器	106
	5.3.5	EXIF和GPS处理器	106
	5.3.6	检查代码	106
	5.3.7	完整代码清单	114
	5.3.8	程序的执行	121
5.4	章节回顾		123
5.5	问题小结		124
5.6	补充资料		124

第6章 时间取证

6.1	本章简介	125
6.2	给这个环节添加时间	126
6.3	时间模块	127
6.4	网络时间协议	132
6.5	获得和安装ntp库ntplib	132
6.6	全世界的NTP服务器	134
6.7	NTP客户端创建脚本	135
6.8	章节回顾	137
6.9	问题小结	137
6.10	补充资料	137

第7章 在电子取证中使用自然语言工具

7.1	什么是自然语言处理		138
	7.1.1	基于对话的系统	138
	7.1.2	语料库	139
7.2	安装自然语言工具包和相关的库		139
7.3	使用语料库		140
7.4	用NLTK进行实验		140
7.5	从因特网上创建语料库		145
7.6	NLTKQuery应用程序		146
	7.6.1	NLTKQuery.py	146
	7.6.2	_classNLTKQuery.py	148
	7.6.3	_NLTKQuery.py	150
	7.6.4	NLTKQuery例子的执行	150
	7.6.5	NLTK跟踪执行	151
7.7	章节回顾		153
7.8	问题小结		153
7.9	补充资料		153

第8章 网络取证：第1部分 ································· 154
8.1 网络调查基础 ···································· 154
8.1.1 什么是套接字 ······························· 154
8.1.2 最简单使用套接字的网络客户端和服务器连接 ······ 156
8.1.3 server.py的代码 ···························· 156
8.1.4 client.py的代码 ···························· 157
8.1.5 server.py和client.py程序的执行 ·············· 158
8.2 队长雷缪斯：再次核实我们到目标的射程…仅需一个PING ···· 158
8.2.1 wxPython ·································· 159
8.2.2 ping.py ··································· 159
8.2.3 guiPing.py的代码 ·························· 164
8.2.4 ping扫描的执行 ···························· 168
8.3 端口扫描 ······································ 169
8.3.1 公认端口的例子 ···························· 169
8.3.2 注册端口的例子 ···························· 170
8.4 章节回顾 ······································ 176
8.5 问题小结 ······································ 176
8.6 补充资料 ······································ 177

第9章 网络取证：第2部分 ································· 178
9.1 本章简介 ······································ 178
9.2 数据包嗅探 ···································· 178
9.3 Python中的原始套接字 ··························· 180
9.3.1 什么是混杂模式或监控模式 ···················· 180
9.3.2 Linux下Python中的原始套接字 ················ 181
9.3.3 对缓冲区进行解包 ·························· 182
9.4 Python隐蔽式网络映射工具（PSNMT）················ 185
9.5 PSNMT源代码 ··································· 187
9.5.1 psnmt.py源代码 ···························· 188
9.5.2 decoder.py源代码 ·························· 190
9.5.3 commandParser.py源代码 ···················· 192
9.5.4 classLogging.py源代码 ····················· 193
9.5.5 csvHandler.py源代码 ······················· 194
9.6 程序的执行和输出 ······························ 195
9.6.1 取证日志 ·································· 196
9.6.2 CSV文件输出实例 ·························· 197
9.7 章节回顾 ······································ 198
9.8 问题小结 ······································ 198

9.9 补充资料 198

第10章 多进程的取证应用 199
10.1 本章简介 199
10.2 何谓多进程 199
10.3 Python多进程支持 199
10.4 最简单的多进程例子 202
    10.4.1 单核的文件搜索方案 202
    10.4.2 多进程的文件搜索方法 203
10.5 多进程文件哈希 204
    10.5.1 单核方案 204
    10.5.2 多核方案A 205
    10.5.3 多核方案B 208
10.6 多进程哈希表生成 210
    10.6.1 单核口令生成器代码 210
    10.6.2 多核口令生成器 213
    10.6.3 多核口令生成器代码 213
10.7 章节回顾 216
10.8 问题小结 217
10.9 补充资料 217

第11章 云中的彩虹表 218
11.1 本章简介 218
11.2 在云端工作 218
11.3 云端服务的可选资源 220
11.4 在云端创建彩虹表 222
    11.4.1 单核彩虹表 222
    11.4.2 多核彩虹表 224
11.5 口令生成计算 226
11.6 章节回顾 228
11.7 问题小结 228
11.8 补充资料 229

第12章 展望 230
12.1 本章简介 230
12.2 由此我们将走向何方 232
12.3 结束语 235
12.4 补充资料 235

第1章 为何使用Python进行取证

1.1 本章简介

Python编程语言及其环境已经被证明易于学习和使用，并几乎适用于任何领域和问题。这样的例子随手就可以列举，如Google、Dropbox、Disney、ILM[①]以及YouTube等公司，就在它们的业务中使用Python。此外一些组织，如美国航空航天局（NASA）喷气推进实验室（Jet Propulsion Lab）、美国国家气象局（National Weather Service）、瑞典气象水文协会（SMHI）、劳伦斯·利弗莫尔国家实验室（Lawrence Livermore National Laboratories）等，都依靠Python来进行建模、预测、实验，并控制关键的作业系统。

在深入讨论之前，确信你期望对这些问题有更多了解：我将介绍哪些内容，Python编程环境如何适用于数字取证？当然你也许还对这些充满兴趣：知道将会学习哪些东西，此书所涉及的大致范围，以及如何应用书中的思路及实例。

本书的主要目的和适用范围是展示如何应用Python来解决网络空间犯罪和数字取证领域的问题和挑战，为此我将使用真实的例子，并且提供完整的源代码以及详细的解释。因此本书就像一本参考资料或详尽的说明手册，当读完这本书后，你可能会着手开发自己的Python取证应用程序。

在本书逐渐展开的时候，不会对你的编程知识（也许根本没有）做任何设想。我所希望的是你对于使用书中的例子感兴趣，然后将其扩展，或者开发出适应于你的情形和问题的进化版本。另一方面，这不是一本关于如何编程的书籍，这类书籍很多，而且在线资源也极为丰富。

好了，让我们从明确网络空间犯罪和数字取证领域面临的挑战出发。归根结底，这些挑战是本书背后的推动力，并且源自过去20年来，为帮助执法防务、公司机构等收集和分析数字证据而进行的工作。

1.2 网络空间犯罪调查的挑战

在网络犯罪调查中，我们所面临的一些具有挑战性的困难如下。

调查持续变化的性质 过去20年来，大量的工作重点放在了事后的获取、搜索、格式分析和呈现包含于各类媒介的信息。我能清楚地回忆起大约20年前接到的一个电话，来电者是纽约州立警察局的Ron Stevens和Tom Hurbanek。他们当时正在调查涉及一台Linux计算机的案子，他们需要这台计算机上可能已被删除的文件及数据，因为这使得调

[①] 即Industrial Light and Magic公司，中文译为"工业光魔"——译者注。

查无法进行下去。尽管当时已经有了一些针对Windows平台的方法，但针对此问题，还没有提取隐含在被删Linux的inode中的删除文件或者碎片的技术。于是我们合作开发了一些算法，并最终变成了一个名为"extractor"的工具，提供给执法部门免费使用。

在过去几年里，对计算机执行简单的数据提取、删除文件恢复、未分配或松弛空间（slack space）挖掘等的操作已被迅速改变。现在我们关注的重点在于智能移动设备、快速变化的内存、云端应用程序、实时网络取证、自动数据分析以及基于环境的取证，当然还不止如此。新的调查工作正致力于解决直接数字取证的证据与大量转瞬即逝的电子信息存在的关联。无论这些信息来自于文本消息、Facebook帖子、Twitter推文、Linkedin社区、嵌入数字照片或视频的元数据，还是跟踪我们行动的GPS数据，以及每次网上冲浪时留下的数字指纹，皆被关联到甚至应用于民事或刑事案件。问题是，我们如何将这些片段联系起来，还同时确保取证效力呢？

技术开发者与调查员之间不断扩大的鸿沟 调查人员、检查人员、应急响应人员、审计人员以及合规专家等以社会科学的背景进入数字取证领域，与之相反，技术开发人员却具备计算机科学及工程学的背景。显而易见的是，虽然有一些跨越这两个方向的杰出例子，但是专业词汇、思维过程、解决问题的方式还是会有很大的区别。正如图1.1所描述的，我们的目标是使用Python取证解决方案以消除这样的鸿沟，创造出一个协作而不互损的环境，借此，计算机科学与社会科学都能各出其力。

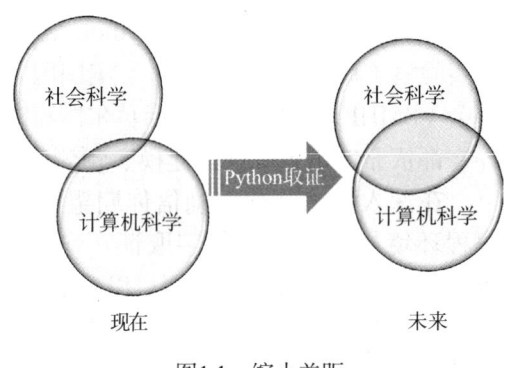

图1.1 缩小差距

困难在于如何开发一个这样的平台或者适宜的环境，使得在研发新的取证方法的过程中，社会科学家和计算机科学家可以轻松交流和平等参与。你将看到，Python环境便提供了这样一个公平竞争的环境或者至少是一个共同的平台，在此所有的创新和想法都可以涌现。这已经被其他科学领域所证明，如太空飞行、气象学、水文学、仿真、互联网技术进步以及实验科学。Python正在这些领域不断地做出宝贵的贡献。

新工具的代价和可用性 除了一些例外（如EnCase App Central），很多来自于供应商渠道的革新和功能需要花费时间去掌握，并会给调查员的工具箱增加极大的代价。在过去调查员只携带少数几个硬件或软件，用来提取并保护数字证据。而今，为了应对可能遇到的各种各样的场合，仅仅是执行数字犯罪现场的获取和基本分析，就需要多达30~40种软件。并且这还只是调查过程的开始而已，分析工具的数量和种类还会继续增加。

这些技术的真实成本以及购置花费同样令人瞠目结舌，尤其当你考虑到教育和培训的时候，进入本领域的费用底限能轻易达到5位数甚至6位数。对于全世界的执法机构而言，这是一个工作量积压持续增长的领域。对于公司和企业界而言亦是如此，他们要处理人力资源问题、企业间谍、内部泄密，甚至大量的管理需求事件。

很明显的是，对于那些对数字取证富有兴趣和天赋的人，我们需要一个更好的捷径以及新的方式，使得他们进入数字调查领域并从事这个行业更加容易和顺畅。随着时间的推移，我们会发现数字犯罪现场越来越像图1.2所描述的那样。

数据与语义　由于资源的限制，我们必须推进新技术和创新，从简单数据分析与搜索向快速语义理解和事件的态势感知发展。调查员需要能帮助他们聚焦到目标或案件中关键点的工具，以便更好地利用资源和快速地发现重要线索。调查下面这些案件时更是如此：频发的诈骗案、拒绝服务攻击、复杂的恶意代码攻击，还有涉及数字证据的暴力犯罪，诸如谋杀、儿童拐卖、强奸以及严重攻击行为等。

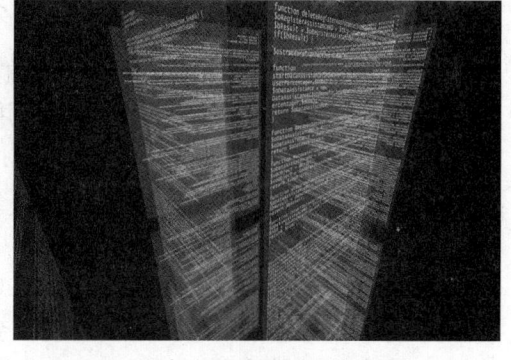

图1.2　未来的数字犯罪现场

此外，在最富有经验的调查员离开岗位之前，我们还必须学习掌握他们的知识和方法。需要一种更好的方式去传承这些知识和经验，因为很多现在利用的数字证据的调查分析方法，就在那些调查员的头脑中。为了表明区别，在图1.3中显示了我们所说的数据与语义或含义。左图描绘的是典型的提取自图像、移动设备或者在线交易的GPS坐标。右图是映射到的地理位置，换言之它是GPS数据的具体表达。GPS数据还包含时间戳，据此我们可以知晓设备的具体位置和时间。

下一代调查员　我们必须使这个研究领域有趣味性，以吸引那些最优秀和聪明的人投身到网络犯罪调查事业。为此，这些新人不仅需要使用工具和技术，还必须在研究、界定、评估甚至开发某些急需且复杂的下一代取证调查能力中起到重要作用（参见图1.4）。

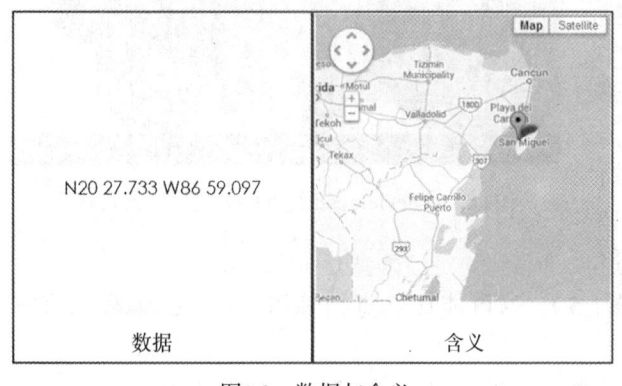

图1.3　数据与含义

图1.4　下一代网络战士

缺乏协作环境　网络犯罪分子的优势是肆虐地相互勾结和强大的资源访问能力，助其实施分布式攻击和复杂的网络犯罪活动。调查员和新方法技术的开发人员同样需要具备这些优势，他们需要一个平台进行协作，联合开发，获得新的创意，并能直接应用于身边的场景。

1.3　Python编程环境如何有助于应对这些挑战

创造一个让社会学家和计算机专家协同工作的环境是困难的。创建一个开发利用新技术，解决前面提到的大量数字调查问题的平台同样困难。考虑到要将这二者结合在一起，更是一个巨大的挑战。无论何时当你遇到类似的问题，要充分考虑利用已有的基础，以便为成功创造最大的机会，这一点十分关键。

对我而言有几个重要的心得体会,多年来都受益于此,所以我十分乐意与你们分享:

1. 你构建平台的基础是否得到广泛的业界支持?
2. 是否能够得到足够的技术资料,并有大量的相关人才和领域专家?
3. 你考虑的技术平台是开源的还是闭源的?
4. 这种技术处于其生命周期的哪一个阶段(也就是太早,太迟,成熟抑或处于评估阶段)?
5. 进入的代价或其他的阻碍是什么(特别是当你准备吸引广泛的参与者时)?
6. 最后,由于我们试图建立连接社会科学与计算机科学之间的桥梁,这个环境是否适合跨学科的合作?

1.3.1　Python的全球支持

Python由Guido van Russom在20世纪80年代后期发明,基本假定是Python适合所有人进行编程。这种理念最终带来了各个方面日益广泛的支持,包括特定领域的研究人员,通用软件开发社区,以及不同背景和水平的程序员。Python是一种通用语言,并且产生的代码易读,能够被不是程序员的人员所理解。而且,由于Python固有的可拓展性,导致存在大量第三方库和模块。数不胜数的网站提供了大量的技巧、提示、代码实例,以及针对希望深入这门语言的那些人的教程。2013年codeeval.com网站显示Python第一次超过Java,成为排名第一的编程语言(参见图1.5),这可能让你觉得惊讶。Python编程语言官方网站python.org是一个绝佳的启程之处。

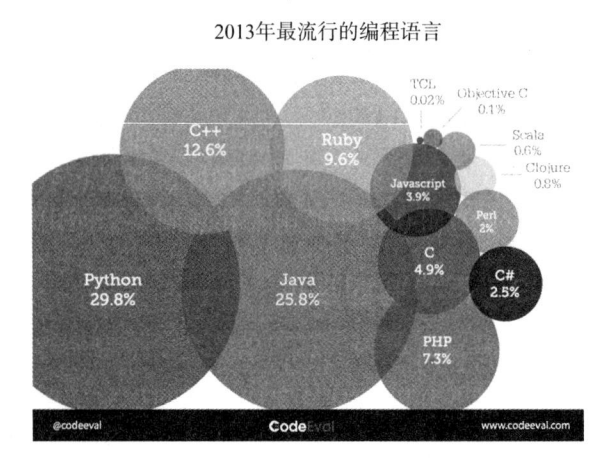

图1.5　codeview.com统计的编程语言流行程度

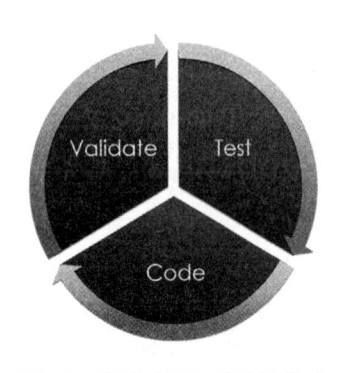

图1.6　测试-编程-检验的模式

最后要提及的是功能丰富的集成软件开发环境,使得即使是新手,也能创造新的理念和设计,直到建立和测试他们的创意发明和原型产品。Python是一种解释型的语言,但编译器也是必须要具备的。如图1.6所示,开发者们采用了测试-编码-验证的思维模式。

无论新手还是老手,都能够利用Python Shell[①],对这种语言及其库、模块和数据结构进行实验,然后试着将它们集成为一个完整的程序或者应用软件。这种先进行实验的方法有助于对编程语言、语言结构、对象等的理解,有助于考虑性能和库的使用,允许用户在将方法投

---

① 指Python命令行模式——译者注。

入使用前进行探索和权衡。一旦用户对这种语言的用法、特点和行为有了足够的自信，集成为一个实用程序的工作就变得更加顺畅。此外，一旦应用程序得以开发完成，这种实验方法还可以测试那些应用于实用程序的问题，于是就完成了测试-编码-验证的循环。

1.3.2 开源和平台独立性

因为Python是一个开源环境，开发者不断创造出能跨多个平台的兼容版本。如你所希望的一样，在当今最流行的平台上都有Python的版本，包括Windows、Linux和OS X，而且对Python语言本身的支持更加广泛。对于移动设备操作系统的支持同样存在，如Andorid、iOS和Windows 8。而且在你未曾想到的平台，如AIX、A/400、VMS、Solaris、PalmOS、OS/2和HP-UX等，Python也获得了支持。对于网络犯罪调查人员，这就意味着这些应用程序在昨天、今天以及未来的平台上都具有良好的可移植性。

2013年3月，英伟达公司（NVIDIA）宣布使用NVIDIA CUDA的GPU加速计算技术（GPU-Accelerated Computing）对Python开发者开放，允许开发者使用并行处理能力，提升几乎所有利用Python开发的应用程序的性能。这将为满足未来计算需求提供巨大能力，如操作处理大数据、执行高级事务分析、完成演绎和归纳推理等。这种广泛用途确保了为建立新的调查方法而产生的投入，也能被使用不同计算平台的同事们所分担，与他们一起利用。

1.3.3 生命周期定位

Python如今是能够用来开发调查类应用程序的首选。这种语言成熟，经验丰富的开发者成千上万，强大支持的团队各就各位，扩展库不计其数，应用程序可移植到各类计算平台，源代码开放并且共享。最重要的是，核心语言总是紧跟着硬件和操作系统的发展而不断进步的。

1.3.4 入门的成本和限制

Python成功之处的关键一点是几乎没有任何入门的限制。开发环境是共享的，语言是平台独立的，代码如同英语一般易读写，而且获得全世界的广泛支持。在我看来，Python语言将会引发一场开发涉及新型网络犯罪、取证、应急响应等解决方案的革命。其中的关键就是促进应用范围的扩展，鼓励和吸引社会学家、计算机科学家，执法部门、取证实验室、应急响应团队及其他组织和机构，以及学者、学生和所有在最广泛定义的网络空间犯罪领域具有专业知识的人群参与到这项工作中来，为他们敞开大门。

1.4 Python与多伯特（Daubert）证据标准

如同我们很多人遇到的那样，在美国的联邦层面以及大约三分之一的州，多伯特标准规定了证据规则，处理包括科学数据在内的专家证言的准入性。"专家"使用取证软件收集和分析的数字证据，其使用会受到置疑，按照非专业人士的说法，多伯特请求是用来对专家以及利用技术产生的证据的效力进行抑制或者置疑的。

在2003年Brian Carrier发表了一篇论文，研究了包括多伯特标准在内的证据标准的规则，并比较和对照了开源和闭源的取证工具。他的主要结论之一就是，"通过使用多伯特测试的指南，我们可以证明，相对闭源工具，开源工具更加清晰和完整地满足了该指南的需求。"

并非因为（开源工具的）源代码是开放的，该结论就理所当然了，而是因为在设计、开发、测试的过程中，下面的特定步骤必须遵循。

1. 程序或算法是否能被合理地解释？这种解释并不是只利用代码，而且还要利用语言。
2. 是否提供足够的信息，以便能开发一个周密的测试方案来测试程序。
3. 是否计算错误率，并经过了独立的验证？
4. 程序是否经过了深入研究和同行评审？
5. 程序是否被社区广泛接受？

真正的问题在于使用Python开发的取证程序如何才能满足这些标准？第3章到第11章构成了本书的操作指导部分，每一个例子都尝试解决多伯特标准的问题，包括：

1. 确定主要问题
2. 需求定义
3. 测试集合开发
4. 设计替代项及其选择
5. 算法描述（可阅读的英语）
6. 代码开发和逐行检查
7. 测试和验证过程
8. 错误率计算
9. 社区的参与

这种组织内容的方法有两个明显的优势。首先，书中操作指导性的实例可以立即使用，以符合甚至超过证据标准的规则。其次，这种明确的流程为有经验的和初学的开发人员提供了一种方法，帮助他们开发数字调查和取证的解决方案。这些操作指导性的实例被设计成为教学和实战的例子，提供了使用Python语言的模型或者实现参考。

1.5 本书的组织结构

为了帮助可能加入新型网络犯罪调查技术领域的最广泛的读者，本书的组织结构既适合于那些很少或没有编程经历的人士，又适合那些有意直接深入更高级的解决办法的人士。

第2章为那些第一次建立Python软件环境的人士提供了循序渐进的介绍，该介绍将涵盖针对Linux和Windows两大平台环境，同时也会探讨是使用Python 2.x还是Python 3.x。还包括高质量的第三方库的安装和设置，这些库在本书的其余部分也会用到。除此之外，还包括使得控制Python和管理项目更容易的集成开发环境。

第3章涵盖一个基本Python应用程序的开发，以描述一个最常见的取证调查应用程序的开发过程，这就是文件哈希（File Hashing），将包括众多在主要的Python发行版本中都直接实现了的单向哈希算法。随后将会展示如何将这个简单的应用程序，转变为一个能够立刻使用的更为复杂的网络安全和调查工具。

从第4章到第11章,每章都将会针对网络犯罪取证的一个不同问题,发布一个能够自由使用、分享和演进的Python指导性解决方法,你还有机会在未来对其进行扩展。

第12章对Python应用于网络犯罪调查、各种网络安全场合,以及高性能硬件加速和嵌入式解决方案等在未来的机遇进行了展望。

最后,每一章都包含章节回顾、问题小结、补充资料,使得本书适合应用于高等学校的教学环境。

1.6 章节回顾

在本章中,我们领略了网络犯罪调查人员、应急响应人员和取证检查人员在处理众多来源的大量数字证据时遇到的难题。讨论了调查和取证技术的使用者与当前解决方案的开发者之间存在的计算机科学和社会科学之间的差异。我们总结了Python编程环境的一些重要特性,正是这些特性使得它能很好地解决上述的难题。这些特性包括Python环境的开源本质、平台独立的操作模式、全球范围支持和技术数据可获得性、当前的生命周期定位等。当然,基于Python开发的解决方案(只要能很好地工作)将会满足甚至超过多伯特证据规则的要求。最后介绍了本书的组织结构,使读者能更好的了解后续章节有哪些内容。

1.7 问题小结

1. 现今的取证调查人员面临的主要挑战有哪些?这些挑战在将来会造成何种深远影响?
2. 从本章展现的内容,或者从自己的研究或经验来看,你相信Python会给取证调查人员带来哪些关键的好处?
3. 现今有哪些其他的组织在使用Python进行科学研究?使用Python对他们的工作产生了怎样的影响?
4. 你认为还有哪些编程语言或者平台是开源、跨平台、有全球支持、入门相对简单、易于理解的,并且能够被计算机科学家和社会科学家用来协同工作呢?
5. 你认为有哪些取证或调查的应用程序是当前缺乏,或者成本高到让你无力承担的呢?

1.8 补充资料

1. 开源数字取证工具:合法性问题争论. Digital-Evidence官方网站,网址http://www.digital-evidence.org/papers/opensrc_legal.pdfhttp;2003
2. Python编程语言. Python.org官方网站,网址http://www.python.org
3. Basu S. Perl与Python: 为什么争论是毫无意义的。The ByeBaker网站
4. 网址http://bytebaker.com/2007/01/29/perl-vs-python-why-the-debate-is-meaningless/;2007 [29.01.07]
5. Raymond E. 为什么是Python? Linux 杂志73期,网址:http://www.linuxjournal.com/article/ 3882;2000 [30.04.03]

第2章 建立一个Python取证环境

2.1 本章简介

几十年前我为一个大型国防承包商工作，作为负责开发一个嵌入式安全设备团队的一员，我最初的任务是建立一个开发环境供团队使用，这看起来似乎是一个相当简单的任务。虽然嵌入式安全硬件完成后交给了我，但是设备本身并不包含操作系统和支持库，它基本上是一个开放的板块。因此，第一个艰巨任务就是开发一个引导装载程序，允许我在这个设备上加载程序。一旦这个任务完成，我需要开发板块的接口功能以便加载其他软件（比如操作系统、共享库、应用程序等），才能让包含在该设备中的安全硬件上线运行。

这个接口软件需要包含一个调试器。当安全硬件在设备上运行时，调试器能够允许我们控制团队开发的操作系统和应用软件，比如启动程序、终止程序、检查变量和寄存器等的能力，以执行单步运行、在代码中设置断点，所有这些都通过一个波特率为19 200的RS232接口完成。

你可能会问，这个20世纪的例子与Python有什么关系呢？答案很简单，对一个稳定且功能多样的开发环境的需求在21世纪依然存在，但是现在我们已经有了现代的工具。如果没有合适的开发环境，要开发高质量、功能丰富的取证或者调查软件的成功几率就会很低。

2.2 搭建一个Python取证环境

在搭建环境之前要考虑很多因素。以下是我自己认为重要的一些考虑因素：

1. 针对你的情况而言，什么样的环境才是合适的？你是一个专业的软件开发者，还是一个具备丰富调查技巧，且想尝试某种调查思路的开发初学者？是在取证实验室工作，还是利用新的方法和工具为应急响应团队提供支持？亦或是任职于一个企业的IT安全团队，需要更好的方法以搜集和分析网络中的问题。
2. 该怎样选择合适的第三方库和模块来增强程序，让你专注于应用程序而不是白费力气做重复的工作。
3. 什么才是合适的集成开发环境（IDE）？在该环境中应该包含哪些功能？
    a. 代码智能，提供自动补齐、内建错误指示器的源代码浏览、代码索引、快捷符号查找。

b. 强健的图形化调试器，允许你在代码中设置断点，单步调试，查看数据，检查变量。
c. 强大的程序员编辑器，充分理解Python语法规则，高级搜索工具，书签，代码高亮显示。
d. 跨平台的支持，使你可以选择平台和环境（即Windows、Linux或者Mac），并在2.x至3.x以及Stackless Python之间选择任意Python版本。

> Stackless Python是一个相对较新的概念，允许Python程序在不受栈内存（C Stack）大小的限制下运行。与堆（heap）内存的数量相比，在许多环境中栈内存的大小是受限的。Stackless Python利用了堆而非栈，为分布式处理提供更大的可行性。例如，这样就可以启动成千上万个独立运行的子任务（tasklet）。在线多人游戏平台就使用了这种方式，支持成千上万的并发用户。我确信地说，如果提前思考，你能为这种环境想象一些数字调查和取证应用的场景。

e. 单元测试功能，使你能够在如unittest、doctesthe和nose等通用测试框架中对代码进行彻底的检验。
f. 针对高级项目的内建版本控制以及直接集成Mercurial、Bazaar、Git、CVS和Perforce等流行的版本控制系统。当构建包含许多移动组件的大型应用程序时，管理多个修订版本变得非常重要。

这种选择将最终决定开发的工具及应用程序是否满足质量标准，这些质量标准对于数字调查和取证应用是不可或缺的。

本书是关于开发符合多伯特标准的取证应用程序的，意识到这一点至关重要。因此，我们要编写的不仅是能在大多时候有效工作的代码，而且应该是能在任何时刻都能有效工作的代码，否则就应视为失败。最重要的是，我们需要开发能够创造出可接受的证据的代码。

2.3 正确的环境

你将做出的最初抉择之一，就是将用于开发Python取证应用程序的平台。正如第1章所述，Python和Python程序能在多种平台上执行，包括最新的桌面、移动甚至传统的系统。然而，这并不意味着必须在这些平台的其中之一上面开发其应用程序。相反，最有可能在一个Windows、Linux或者Mac平台上开发应用程序，只要它支持最新的开发工具。

Python的一个非常好的优点是，如果遵循规则开发出高质量的程序，并确保考虑了跨平台的特性，那么不管选择哪一个平台进行开发，你创造的Python程序都能很容易地运行于各种安装了Python系统的操作系统。

Python Shell

Python Shell提供一种面向对象的高级编程语言，包括内建的数据结构和大量标准库。Python使用了一种几乎任何人都可以学习的简单易用的语法，支持有助于程序代码复用和共享的第三方模块和包，被几乎所有主流平台支持，并可以免费分发。对于数字调查人员或者取证专家，这意味着能够快速开发程序，增强甚至取代当前工具，并即刻在社区分享的能力。解释性环境的好处之一就是可以用标准库、第三方模块、命令、函数和包等进行实验，而无须首先开发出一个程序。这样就能够确认，打算使用的命令、函数和模块是否提供了你所期盼的结果和性能。因为这些函数有很多选择和来源，并且还在不断涌现，解释器允许你在提交最终方案前方便地进行实验。

2.4 选择一个Python版本

和任何一个编程环境一样，当前有很多可用的Python版本。但如今对于Python版本而言，2.x及3.x是两种基本的标准。从Python 2.x到3.x版本的变迁带来了一些移植上的问题，为2.x版本写的程序和库需经过修改才可运行于3.x版本。

Python的一些核心函数已经发生变化，这主要缘于3.x版本对Unicode的完全支持。这不仅影响程序，同样影响先前已开发且尚未针对Python 3.x进行移植或验证的模块。基于此问题，我决定遵循2.x版本来开发本书提供的例子，这样就能使用最为广泛的第三方模块，并具备跨平台兼容性。同时本书中的源代码也可在线获得，在可行的时候，将同时提供代码的2.x及3.x版本。

除此之外，2.x版Python中的类已经经历了考验和验证，并在大量的应用程序中得到部署。因此使用2.x版本开发取证和数字调查应用程序，为我们提供了坚固的基础，以及广泛的部署平台。当然3.x版本一旦被广泛接受，并且第三方库可用并经过验证，我们将得到进行移植所必要的全部信息，进而进一步增强本书中应用程序的性能。

现在我们已经选择了一个版本作为开端，我将引导你在一个Windows桌面系统上安装Python。

2.5 在Windows上安装Python

在本书写作时，如果在Google上搜索"python Installation"，将会得到超过700万个页面的结果。要获得经过测试的标准Python安装包，在我看来最为理想和安全地方就是www.python.org，它是Python编程语言的官方网站，如图2.1所示。在此页面中我选择了Python 2.7.5版本。

接下来浏览到下载页面，根据我的情况选择合适的版本。此处将选择：

Python 2.7.5 Windows x86 MSI installer 2.7.5 (sig)

此处提供下载Windows运行时环境（参见图2.2），还显示了下载文件的哈希值，让你可以验证下载的文件。

如预期的一样，选择此链接将会显示一个Windows对话框，如图2.3所示，以确认你希望保存该安装文件。选择"OK"，开始下载文件并将其保存在默认的下载目录里。

第 2 章 建立一个 Python 取证环境

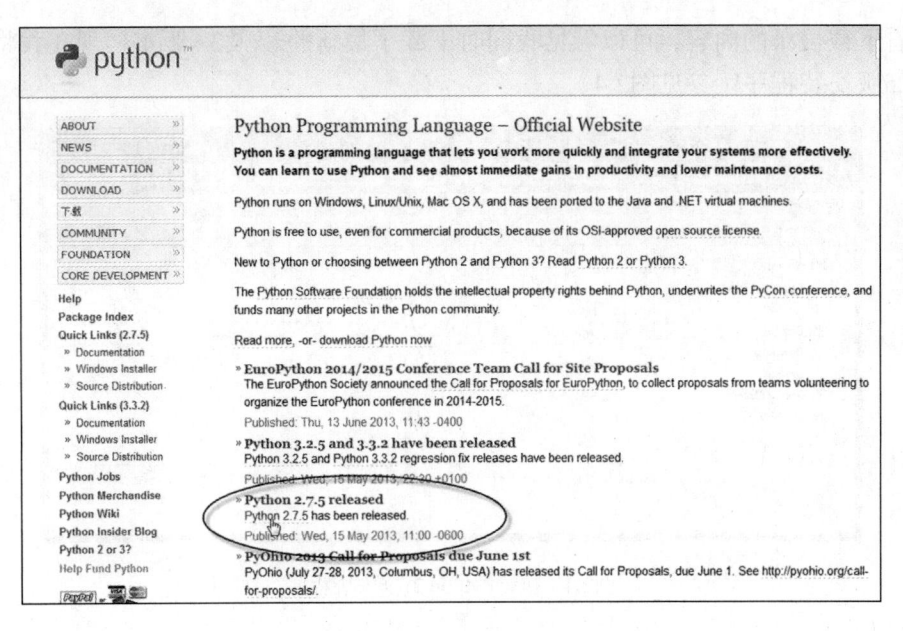

图2.1 Python编程语言官方网站

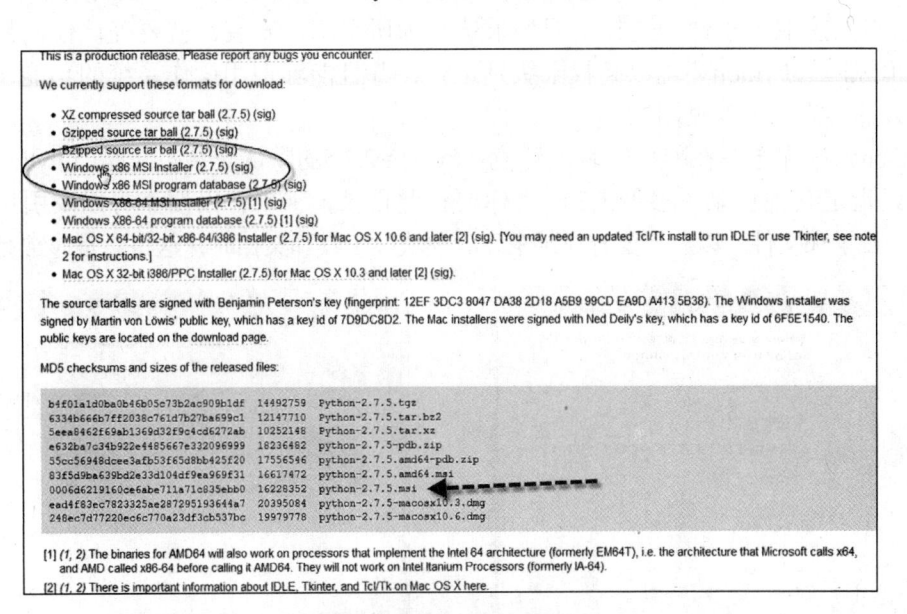

图2.2 下载Windows安装版本

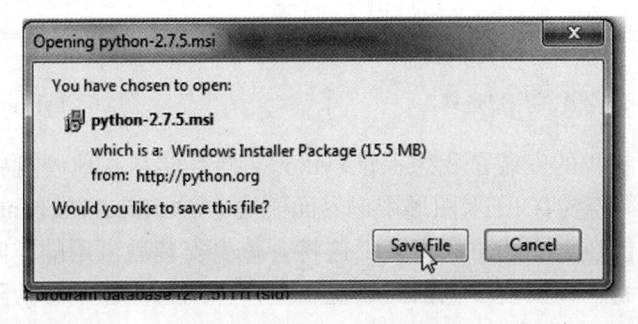

图2.3 Windows系统的下载确认

查看下载目录的内容，可以看见我同时下载了最新的2.x及3.x版本。现在我将选择并执行2.7.5版安装程序（参见图2.4）。

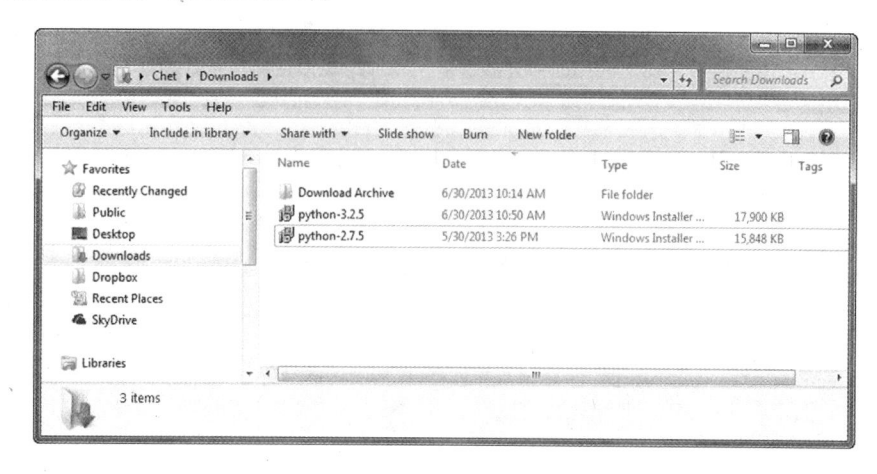

图2.4　执行Python 2.7.5安装程序

在执行过程中，安装程序会询问你是否为当前用户或者本机上的所有用户安装Python。当然这取决于你的选择，但如果选择为所有用户安装，就要确认他们是可信的并且知道风险。Python环境以高权限级别运行，并且能够使用操作系统的功能，这并不是每个人都必需的（参见图2.5）。

Python允许你选择在哪里安装该环境。Python 2.7.5的默认安装目录是C:\Python27，当然也可以指定其他目录（参见图2.6）。你要将此目录记下来，以便查看以及引用存储在那里的子目录和文件。以后当要查找某个库、模块、工具和文档时，这将会是非常有用的。

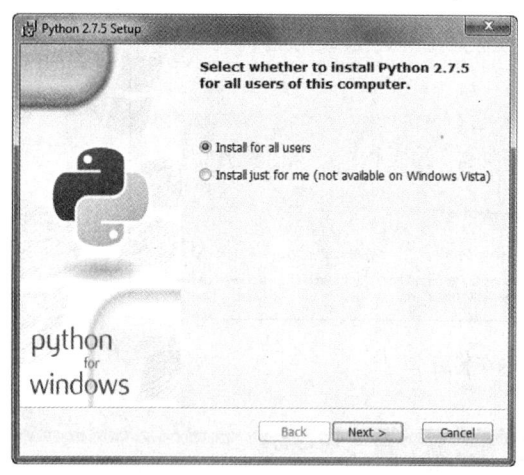

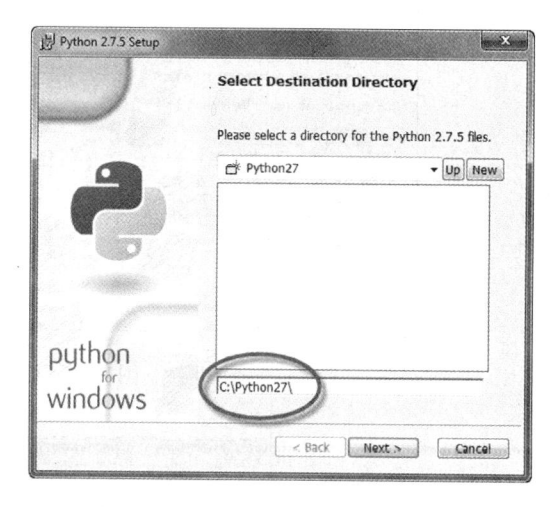

图2.5　Python安装中的用户选择　　　　图2.6　Python安装目录

我决定少许定制我的安装，我想保证Python文档存储在本地硬盘中，以便能随时访问。另外我预期并不需要TCL/TK图形用户界面模块（Graphical User Interface，GUI），因此我设定这一项为仅在需要的时候安装，这将会减少安装后占用的空间。当然如果没有磁盘存储空间的限制，在安装中包括此项也不是一个问题。在本书的随后部分中，将安装其他更为易用的GUI包和模块（参见图2.7及图2.8）。

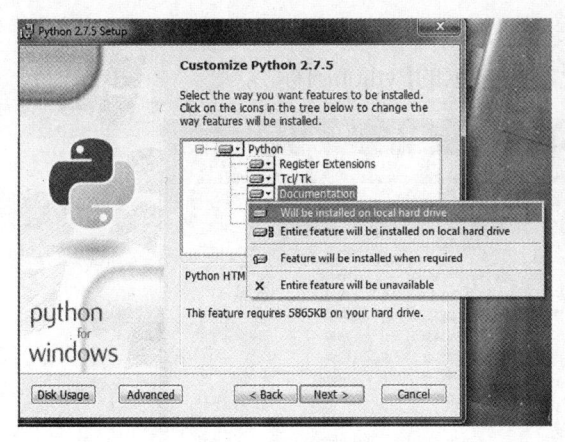

图2.7　Python的用户定制选项 　　　　　　　　图2.8　需要时安装TCL/TK

接下来，Windows将显示标准的用户账户控制（UAC），以帮助维系对计算机的控制，这是通过当程序做出了一个需要管理员级别权限的改变时，向你发出通知来实现的（参见图2.9）。Windows同时也会验证Python的数字签名，并显示与用来签署安装程序的证书相关联的组织名称。选择"Yes"将会安装Python，并且如果该用户拥有管理员权限，则允许对系统做出合适的更改。你可能注意到这张截图是用我的iPhone拍摄的，因为在UAC确认期间，Windows封锁了其他所有的程序访问，直到你选择了"Yes"或者"No"。

最后，Python安装完成，图2.10显示了安装成功的界面。

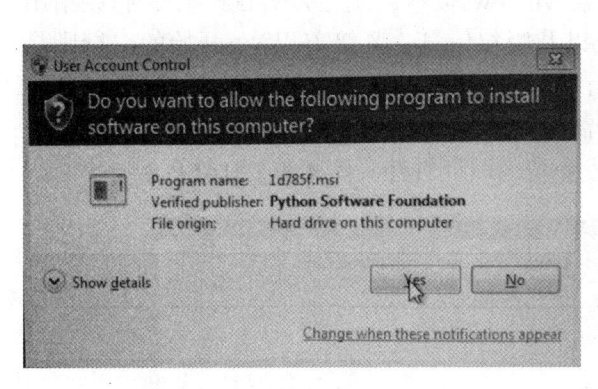

图2.9　Windows用户账户控制 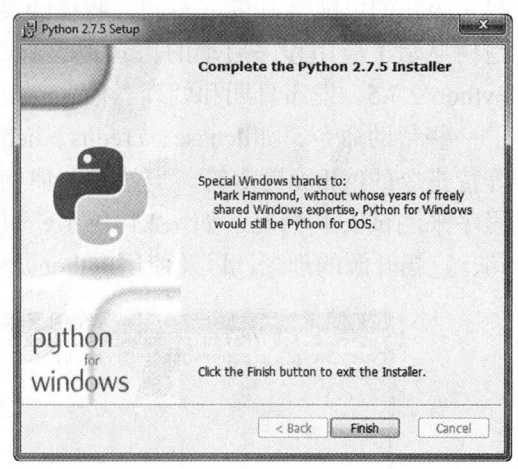　　　　　　　　图2.10　成功安装Python 2.7.5

现在我们可以浏览C:\python27目录（或者在Python安装时指定的目录）并查看内容，如图2.11所示，此处有很多文件夹，包括Docs、Lib、DLL和Tools等，以及重要的文件License、News和ReadMe。最重要的是有两个应用程序文件python和pythonw，它们是Python的可执行文件。

可以双击python来使用Python交互式解释器。如果已经有一个Python程序，并且不想显示解释器窗口，可以执行pythonw，以及对应的python文件来运行（以后将详细介绍）。

我们可以直接运行Python应用程序文件以便快速使用。为方便访问，可以将该应用程序添加到Windows任务栏，可以在图2.12中看见高亮显示的Python图标。

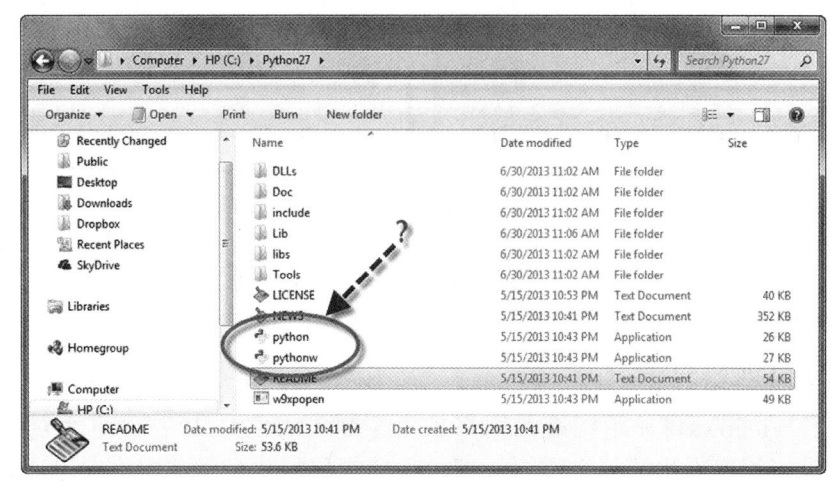

图2.11　Python目录截图

图2.12　带Python图标的Windows任务栏

启动Python的任务栏图标（点击它），Python交互式窗口如图2.13所示。你的窗口看起来跟我的可能会有少许不同，我已经设置我的窗口界面为白底黑字以便图书出版。标题栏显示了应用程序启动的目录是C:\python27。第一行文本列出了Python版本，此处是Python 2.7.5，发布日期和处理器信息，以及Windows版本，此处为win32。下一行则给出了一些帮助命令，如license、credits、help以及版权信息。紧接着以>>>开始的一行则是等待指令的Python提示符。当然按照惯例，我们在这里写入标准的编程语言Hello World程序来测试安装情况，如图2.14所示，只需要一行Python语句。我又添加了一个打印语句，宣扬开源的理念，以及使用Python开发免费的取证软件，而不需要HASP。

图2.13　Python启动时的提示符和消息

图2.14　Python的"Hello World"

> 对于那些不熟悉HASP（Hardware Against Software Piracy，反对软件盗版的硬件，有时亦称加密狗）的人而言，这是一种为特定软件程序提供复制保护的设备。若没有插入HASP，软件将不会运行，这样就只允许得到许可的用户在单个机器或者网络上使用该软件。

现在我们至少已经验证了Python解释器正在运行并接受命令，让我们看一看可用的命令、语言结构、包和模块。

2.6 Python包和模块

在现已有的程序语言中添加核心功能是软件开发的一个标准内容。随着新的方法和改进不断出现，开发者以模块和包的方式提供这些功能组件。在Python网络上，多数模块和包都是共享的，许多还包含完整的源代码，使得你有机会提高这些模块的功能，并独立地对代码进行验证。在正式进入将第三方模块添加到Python的环节之前，需要了解其本身就具备的，更具体地说就是Python标准库里包含哪些模块。我想你会对标准库以及内建语言提供的功能之多而惊讶不已。

2.6.1 Python标准库

Python的标准库相当丰富，提供了广泛的内建功能。为了效率和抽象的需要，这些内建函数主要用C语言编写。因为标准库层面是兼容多种系统的，所以与特定平台API（应用程序接口）的交互作用被抽象化或者规范化，以方便Python程序员的使用。

调查人员执行的基本操作之一就是生成单向加密哈希值。

> 单向加密哈希用于创造一个已有字节串的签名（通常也称为消息摘要），而不考虑这个字节串有多长。单向哈希具有四个基本特征：(1) 一个容易计算并生成信息摘要的函数。(2) 仅有消息摘要值并不会提供原始消息或文件的任何线索。(3) 在不改变消息摘要的前提下，要想改变其关联的消息或文件的内容，是不可行的（或者计算起来很困难）。(4) 找到两个内容不同但产生的消息摘要却相同的消息或文件，是不可行的（或者计算起来很困难）。应该指出的是，在特定受控情况下，对已知的哈希方法如MD5和SHA-1的攻击已经实现。

Python标准库包含了一个名为hashlib的内建模块，能够进行单向加密哈希计算。下面这个简单的哈希计算例子几乎能在任何Python平台上执行（包括Windows、Linux、Mac、iOS、Windows 8 Phone、Android等），并产生同样的结果。

```
#
#Python forensics
#Simple program to generate the SHA-256
#one-way cryptographic hash of a given string
```

```
#Step1
#Instruct the interpreter to import the
    Standard library module hashlib

import hashlib

#print a message to the user

print
print ("Simple program to generate the SHA-256 Hash of the String 'Python forensics'")
print

#define a string with the desired text
myString = "Pythonforensics"

#create an object named hash which is of type sha256
Hash = hashlib.sha256()

#utilize the up date method of the hash object to generate the
#SHA256 hash of myString

hash.update(myString)

#obtain the generated hex values of the SHA256 Hash
#from the object
#by utilizing the hexdigest method

hexSHA256 = hash.hexdigest()

#print out the result and utilize the upper method
#to convert all the hex characters to uppercase

print("SHA-256Hash:" + hexSHA256.upper())
print

print("Processingcompleted")
```

这个简单的示例说明了访问和利用Python标准库是多么容易，以及相同代码运行在不同平台上如何生成正确的SHA256哈希值（如图2.15和图2.16所示）。

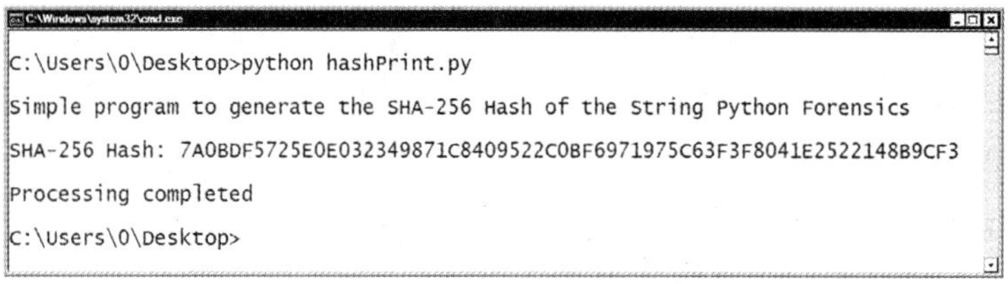

```
C:\Users\0\Desktop>python hashPrint.py
Simple program to generate the SHA-256 Hash of the String Python Forensics
SHA-256 Hash: 7A0BDF5725E0E032349871C8409522C0BF6971975C63F3F8041E2522148B9CF3
Processing completed
C:\Users\0\Desktop>
```

图2.15　Windows环境下执行hashPrint.py

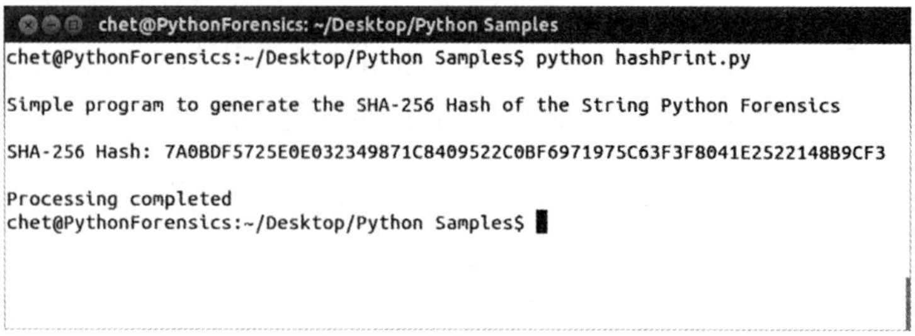

```
chet@PythonForensics:~/Desktop/Python Samples$ python hashPrint.py
Simple program to generate the SHA-256 Hash of the String Python Forensics
SHA-256 Hash: 7A0BDF5725E0E032349871C8409522C0BF6971975C63F3F8041E2522148B9CF3
Processing completed
chet@PythonForensics:~/Desktop/Python Samples$
```

图2.16　Ubuntu Linux环境下执行hashPrint.py

在第3章中，我们将花费比较多的时间，侧重于单向加密哈希算法的应用程序，介绍其在数字调查和取证中的应用。

在下一节，将深入了解Python标准库。

2.7 标准库包含什么

Python标准库可以分为多个类别，下文将简要地总体描述每个类别的内容，并将特别关注到那些我认为很独特，或者具有取证和数字调查价值的类别。它们的描述如下所述。

2.7.1 内建函数

顾名思义，内建函数对Python程序员来说总是可用的，它提供了语言本身附带的基本功能。

2.7.2 hex()和bin()

取证调查员经常需要的一种能力就是用不同的基数显示变量，如基于十进制（基数为10）、二进制（基数为2），以及十六进制（基数为16）。这种显示的能力只是内建函数能力的一部分。在图2.17中，几个简单的Python Shell会话描述了这种功能。在此例中，我们设置变量a等于十进制数字27（默认值是十进制数），然后执行hex(a)函数，它以十六进制形式显示a的值；注意，使用0x前缀表示十六进制。利用二进制转换函数bin(a)将十进制数字27转换成一个由0和1组成的二进制字符串，即11011；注意，使用0b前缀表示二进制。

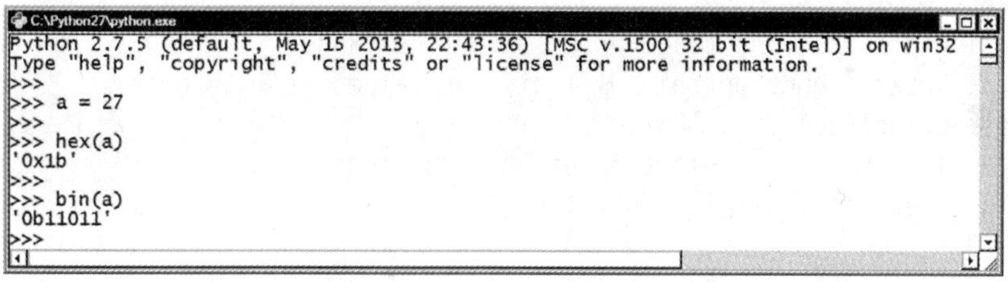

图2.17 使用Python Shell会话的hex()和bin()

如图2.18所示，也可以执行相反的转换，指定一个十六进制的变量，然后以二进制或者十进制的形式显示这个变量。注意，在这两个例子里，存储在变量里的a或者b是单纯的整数值，函数hex()、bin()和str()的功能仅仅是以十六进制、二进制和十进制记号的形式表示这些变量。换言之，变量没有改变，改变的是我们看它的方式。

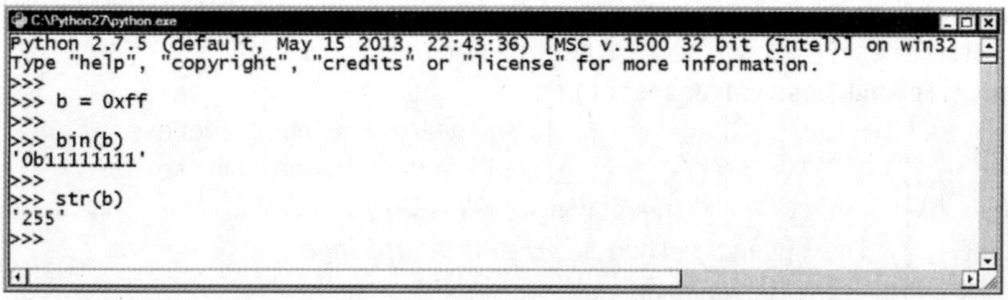

图2.18 输入十六进制值的Python Shell会话

2.7.3 range()

另外一个实用的内建函数是range()。我们经常需要创建一个项目列表，这个内建函数就可以协助我们自动构建这样一个列表。列表（list）、元组（tuple）和字典（dictionary）都是Python中相当强大的结构，我们将会在本书中使用它们来解决问题。现在开始做一个初步介绍。

如图2.19所示，使用Python Shell命令运行了几个例子。第一个例子创建了从0开始的前20个整数的列表。第二个例子给出了一个始于4，止于22的整数列表（注意这个列表结束于22，但列表中不包含22）。最后创建了一个从4~22，步长为3的列表。

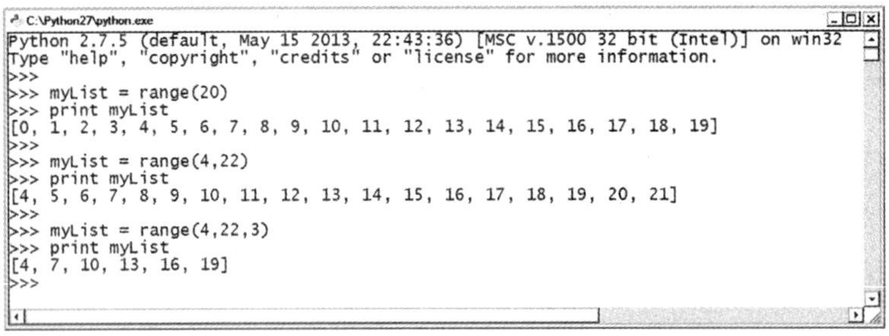

图2.19 Python Shell中使用range()内建标准库函数建立列表

随后将看到如何使用range()函数和列表自动生成一些有用的值的列表。例如，以下程序生成了一个包含前20个主机IP地址的列表，这些地址是从192.168.0起始的C类地址。可以在图2.20中看到程序的输出。

```
#define a variable to hold a string representing the base address
baseAddress = "192.168.0."
#next define a list of host addresses using the range
#standard library function(this will give us values of 1-19 host
Addresses = range(20)
#define a list that will hold the result ip strings
#this starts out as a simple empty list
ipRange=[]
#loop through the host addresses since the list host Addresses
#contains the integers from 0-19 and we can create
#a loop in Python that processes each of the list elements
#stored in hostAddresses,where i is the loop counter value
for i in hostAddresses:
#append the combined ipstrings to the ipRange list
#because ip Range is a list object,the object has a set of
#attributes and methods.We are going to invoke the append method
#each time through the loop and concatenate the base address
#string with the string value of the integer
    ipRange.append(baseAddress+str(i))
#   |       |       |       |   |__value of the host address
#   |       |       |       |__function to convert int to str
#   |       |       |__The string "192.168.0"
#   |       |__The append method of the list ipRange
#   |__The list object ipRange
#
```

第 2 章　建立一个 Python 取证环境

```
#Once completed we want to print out the ip range list
#here we use the print function and instruct it to print out
#the ip Range list object, I wanted to print out each of the
#resulting ip address on a separate line, so I looped
#through the ip Range list object one entry at a time.
for ip Addr in ipRange:
    print ipAddr
```

```
C:\Users\0\Desktop>python ipRange.py
192.168.0.0
192.168.0.1
192.168.0.2
192.168.0.3
192.168.0.4
192.168.0.5
192.168.0.6
192.168.0.7
192.168.0.8
192.168.0.9
192.168.0.10
192.168.0.11
192.168.0.12
192.168.0.13
192.168.0.14
192.168.0.15
192.168.0.16
192.168.0.17
192.168.0.18
192.168.0.19
C:\Users\0\Desktop>_
```

图2.20　ipRange的运行

2.7.4　其他的内建函数

以下是取自Python标准库的完整的内建函数列表。可以从URL:http://docs.python.org/2/library/functions.html中获得每个函数的更多信息。

表2.1中给出了Python 2.x的内建函数。

在第3章到第11章中的详细环节中，将会使用很多个这些函数。

表2.1　Python 2.7内建函数

abs()	divmod()	input()	open()	staticmethod()
all()	enumerate()	int()	ord()	str()
any()	eval()	isinstance()	pow()	sum()
basestring()	execfile()	issubclass()	print()	super()
bin()	file()	iter()	property()	tuple()
bool()	filter()	len()	range()	type()
bytearray()	float()	list()	raw_input()	unichr()
callable()	format()	locals()	reduce()	unicode()
chr()	frozenset()	long()	reload()	vars()
classmethod()	getattr()	map()	repr()	xrange()
cmp()	globals()	max()	reversed()	zip()
compile()	hasattr()	memoryview()	round()	_import_()
complex()	hash()	min()	set()	apply()
delattr()	help()	next()	setattr()	buffer()
dict()	hex()	object()	slice()	coerce()
dir()	id()	oct()	sorted()	intern()

2.7.5　内建常量

在Python中有很多内建常量。顾名思义，常数不同于变量，常量不会发生变化，而变量存储不断变化的值。

Python中两个最重要的内建常量是True和False，都是布尔型的值。如图2.21所示，使用Python Shell定义了两个变量false = 0，true = 1（注意它们均为小写字母）。你可以注意到，当使用Python内建函数type()来识别其变量类型时，对于true及false，都返回了int（整数型）。然而当对True和False（内建常量）使用type()时，返回的则是bool（布尔型）。

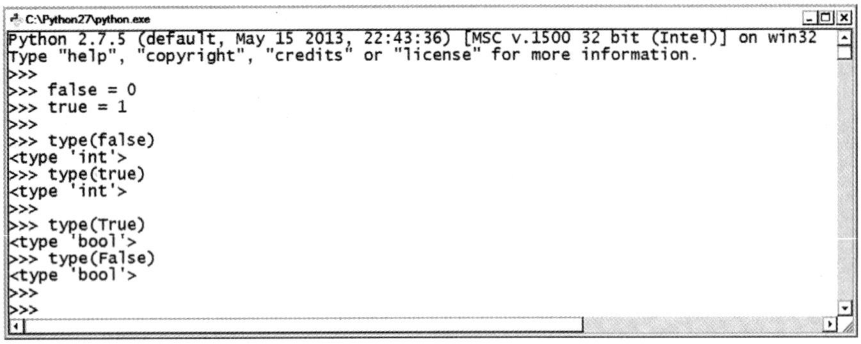

图2.21　内建的True和False常量

使用同样的表示方法，可以创建变量a = True，b = False（如图2.22所示），并用type()检查类型，可以看到它们是bool型。然而切勿对此过于依赖，因为Python并不是一种强类型语言。在强类型语言中，每一个变量都拥有一个声明的类型，且在程序的生命周期中不能改变。Python没有这个限制，可以容易地在下一个紧接着的语句中声明a = range(100,400,2)，将变量a的类型从bool型改为list型。对于强类型语言如Ada、C#、Java或者Pascal的忠实开发者来说，这种结构的缺乏会让他们难以适从，然而如果对命名对象具有合适的训练，就可以控制大多数的混乱状况。

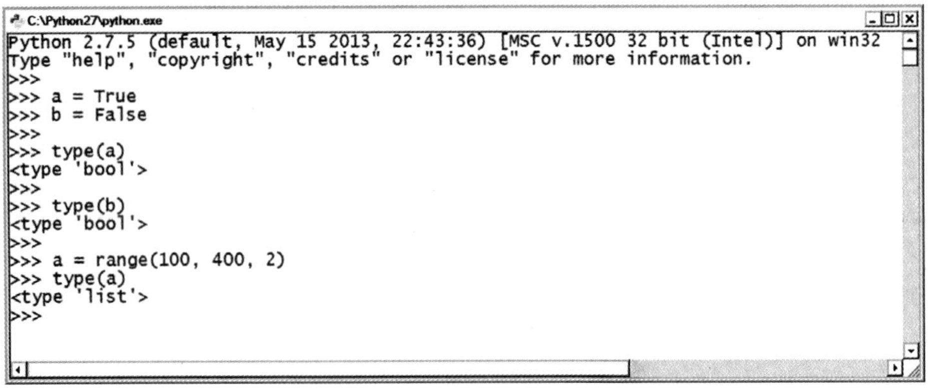

图2.22　Python不是强类型语言

在第3章中，当开发第一个实用的应用程序时，对于如何使用弱类型的语言开发符合取证要求的程序，将给出一些提示。

> 强类型语言必须使用具体的类型来定义变量和对象。这种类型一旦声明了就不得改变，类型规则是由编译器自身，而不是程序员强制执行的。例如，如果一个变量被声明为整数型，那么将值3.14分配给该变量将是不合法的。

2.7.6 内建类型

Python有很多内建类型，我们可以在取证应用程序中加以利用。每一个标准内建类型的详细描述，最新的信息可以在http://docs.python.org/2/library/stdtypes.html得到。

基本的类别包括：

数值类型：int、float、long和complex
序列类型：list、tuple、str、unicode、bytearray和buffer
集合类型：set和frozenset
映射类型：dict或者dictionary
文件对象：file
内存类型：memoryview

我们已经在简单例子中看到了它们中的几个。在我们的示例程序中将大量使用一些高级类型，包括bytearray、list、dictionary、unicode、set、frozenset和memoryview。所有这些类型都有独特的取证用途。

Python中的一些按位运算对于许多取证和调查操作来说是至关重要的。虽然它们已经相当规范化了，但仍有必要介绍，让你感觉有哪些用途。按位运算是几乎任何大小的整数类型数据所独有的。在下面的示例中，x和y的值都是整数。

x|y：变量x及y的按位或
x^y：变量x及y的按位异或
x&y：变量x及y的按位与
x<<n：变量x向左移动n位
x>>n：变量x向右移动n位
~x ：变量x的按位取反

在图2.23中，使用了按位异，或者^操作符，它被用于许多单向哈希和加密运算中。我们首先设定了变量x和y，设定x等于152，y等于103，均为十进制数字，然后设定z等于x和y的异或。随后便可以输出用十进制、十六进制和二进制表示的结果。

如你所见，异或（XOR）不同于单纯的或运算。异或运算需要求两个数字中的每一位数，当且仅当这些位中只有一个位被置为1时才会返回1。例如：

二进制 101
二进制 001
结果：100

每一个二进制值的最低有效位都是1，因此它不符合异或原理，其结果就是0。

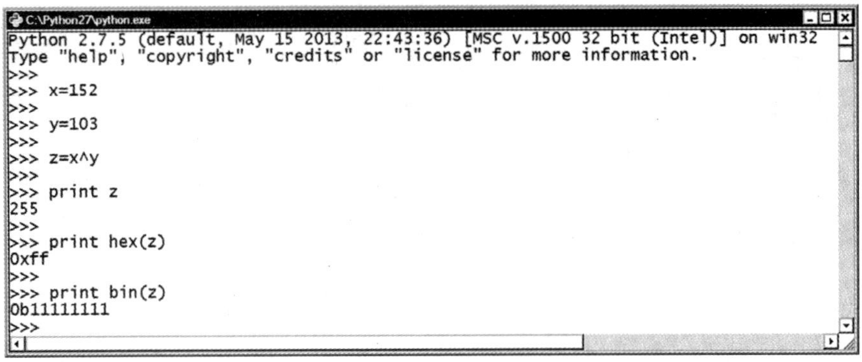

```
C:\Python27\python.exe
Python 2.7.5 (default, May 15 2013, 22:43:36) [MSC v.1500 32 bit (Intel)] on win32
Type "help", "copyright", "credits" or "license" for more information.
>>>
>>> x=152
>>>
>>> y=103
>>>
>>> z=x^y
>>>
>>> print z
255
>>>
>>> print hex(z)
0xff
>>>
>>> print bin(z)
0b11111111
>>>
```

图2.23　应用异或运算

其他更复杂的内建类型如memoryview、bytearray、list、unicode和dict等，为处理复杂数据雕刻、搜索、索引，以及分析最为复杂的数字证据准备了基本构件。随着我们进入示例章节，将大量地使用到这些类型。

2.7.7　内建异常

现代的软件语言大多支持联机异常处理，Python亦不例外。异常处理在大部分应用程序中很重要，但在取证和数字调查应用程序中确实至关重要。能证明你已经处理了所有可能的情况，这一点在开发这些应用时很重要。当开发一个应用程序时，都趋向于使用"快乐模式测试"（happy mode testing）来测试我们的代码。Ronda Caracappa是我所知道的最为优秀的软件质量测试人员之一，多年前创造了"快乐模式测试"这一短语。这意味着我们使用所有输入、事件和第三方模块，测试程序的常规流程，并且程序具有如同我们预期一样的表现。但问题是程序很少，或者几乎不会只遇到这些情况。

为了能够进行异常处理，Python使用了try/except model机制。这里举一个例子，我们将程序设定为两个数字相除，此处用整数27除以0，如果这刚好发生在程序的运行过程中，并且没有设定捕捉这样的错误，程序将会出现故障并崩溃。然而通过使用异常处理，能够避免麻烦并处理故障。在第3章的第一个实用程序中，会遇到一些体现异常处理重要性的实际情况。在Python内建的异常处理的帮助下，可以轻松地应对潜在的缺陷，并使用这些异常来记录所有的运行问题。

```
x = 27
y = 0
try:
    z = x / y
except:
    print("Divide by zero")
```

注意这是一个使用try/except方法，以简洁的方式捕捉执行异常的简单示例。其他的处理操作系统、文件操作和网络异常的例子，将在第3章到第11章演示。

2.7.8　文件和目录访问

Python标准库提供了丰富的文件和目录访问服务。这些服务不仅提供通常的打开、读取和写入文件的能力，也包括了一些很独特的内建功能，如常见的路径名操作。操作系统和平台对目录路径的处理方式是不同的（即Windows使用c:\user\.....标记法，而UNIX环境使用/etc/...标记法）。一些操作环境支持单纯的ASCII的文件和目录命名模式，另一些则支持全部Unicode的命名模式。所有的文件和目录访问函数必须一致地支持这些差异，否则跨平台操作将只是空谈。除此之外，Python标准库文件内建了目录的比较函数、临时目录的自动创建和高级的文件输入处理，无论对于新手还是老手，这些都使得文件系统的处理更加容易。

2.7.9 数据压缩和归档

无须使用如zip和tar之类的第三方库执行标准的压缩和归档功能，这些功能都是内建的。这不仅包括了压缩和解压缩，还包括zip文件的内容信息提取。在调查期间我们经常会遇到加密的zip文件，Python也能对这些文件进行处理（只要有口令，或者还能使用字典或者暴力破解的方法）。

2.7.10 文件格式

Python标准库里也内建了处理特殊文件格式的模块，如逗号分隔值（CSV，comma separated value）文件，超文本标记语言（HTML，Hypertext Markup Language）文件，可扩展标记语言（XML，eXtensible Markup Language）文件，甚至是JavaScript对象符号（JSON，JavaScript Object Notation）格式的文件。我们将会在之后的章节中使用这些模块处理来自网页或者其他互联网内容的数据，并创建标准的XML输出文件来生成报告。

2.7.11 加密服务

在第3章中我们将大量使用hashlib加密模块，以解决数字调查员所面临的一些基本问题。hashlib模块不仅直接支持传统的单向加密哈希算法，如MD5，而且还直接支持现代的单向哈希算法，如SHA1、SHA256和SHA512。集成和利用这些库及其性能优化带来的便利性，使得直接访问这些对于数字取证至关重要的函数成为可能。

2.7.12 操作系统服务

操作系统（OS）服务为访问操作系统核心功能，以及跨平台工作提供了可能。在图2.24中，利用os模块列出了当前工作目录的内容。步骤相当简单：

1. 导入os模块。
2. 调用了os模块的os.getcwd()方法来得到当前工作目录路径，也就是目前所处的路径。
3. 将其值存储在变量myCWD中。
4. 然后使用os.listdir()方法，获取当前工作目录中的文件和目录的名称。
5. 我决定将结果存储到一个名为dirContents的新的列表（list）中，而不是仅仅将os.listdir()打印出来，即print(os.listdir())。
6. 然后通过一个简单的for循环遍历整个列表（list），并使用dirContents在不同的行打印出每一个名称。

将文件置于列表（list）中，就能根据需要处理每个文件或目录。

```
C:\Python27\python.exe
>>> import os
>>>
>>> myCWD = os.getcwd()
>>>
>>> dirContents = os.listdir(myCWD)
>>>
>>> for names in dirContents:
...     print names
...
DLLs
Doc
include
Lib
libs
LICENSE.txt
NEWS.txt
python.exe
pythonw.exe
README.txt
Tools
w9xpopen.exe
>>>
```

图2.24 使用标准库中的os模块的例子

其他操作系统服务，如基于流的io、time、loggin、parsing和platform模块都为访问操作系统服务提供了便利。这就再一次说明在一个跨平台的基础上，应对Windows、Linux、Mac和许多传统的操作系统是很轻松的。

2.7.13 标准库小结

至此，这些对部分直接内建于Python标准库功能的介绍和讨论，还仅是蜻蜓点水而已。对于那些想要走得更远的人来说，还有很多好的专业参考资料和完整书籍。而且在python.org也有可用的在线资源，在此可以找到大量的教程、示例代码，获得每个标准库数据类型、模块、属性和方法的支持。此时我的目标只是给你一种感觉，清楚你能做什么，以及使用标准库是多么容易。

2.8 第三方包和模块

正如之前提到的，可用的第三方包和模块有很多，本书的操作指导章节（第3章到第11章）将就其中的一些进行介绍。但我要在这里首先提及几个，让你有一个基本概念，为什么要利用第三方模块，以及它们给数字取证带来哪些功能。

2.8.1 自然语言工具包（NLTK）

当今在进行调查、电子开示（e-discovery）或应急响应时，很重要的一点是要确认通过电子邮件、短信、文档和其他通信方式交流了哪些内容。眼下利用一些原始的工具和技术去发现和解析这些通信内容，如简单的关键字和短语搜索以及grep。

> grep是全局正则表达式打印（global regular expression print）的简称，允许用户对文本进行检索，以发现一个已定义的正则表达式。正则表达式由元字符组成，通常是代表一个给定模式的一串文本字符序列，它使得计算机程序能执行简单的或高级的模式匹配。

问题是这些技术并不会顾及语言或语义，因此很容易错过某些通信内容或者曲解它们。NLTK模块提供了一种基础设施，用于创造实用的自然语言程序，构建小型甚至大型的语料库。

> 语料库（corpus）是资料的集合，通常是书面资料，但也可以是口语资料。这些资料被数字化采集，用于帮助理解含义的语言学结构研究。

这就给予我们搜索、理解并获得语义的能力。我们将在参考示例的其中之一使用NLTK生成特定的应用程序，以帮助数字取证人员。例如，可以在语言学的协助下，判断某些特定的文档是否出自一个特定的人。

2.8.2　Twisted matrix（TWISTED）

在一个万物互联的世界中，收集和审查证据的能力同时需要事后调查和实时调查的理念。这就意味着我们必须有一个可靠的网络库，它提供异步和基于事件的开发环境，它是开源的并且使用Python编写。这个开发环境包括TCP、UDP、Web服务、邮件服务、验证、安全Shell支持等。

2.9　集成开发环境

就像在本章一开始就提到的，成功的关键之一是IDE的搭建，它能在程序开发过程中提供升值、增强自信、创造效率。对于我们来说，还希望确保我们创造的优良特性胜过证据的标准。你有多个IDE可以选择，其中有些是完全免费的，有些只需要付象征性的入门费用。本节的结尾将透露我的选择。但是你也可以有自己的选择，这在许多方面就像在耐克或阿迪达斯之间做出选择一样，很大程度上取决于你喜欢什么，觉得哪个更舒适。

2.9.1　有哪些选择

事实上回答这个问题可能需要一整本书！这里只是一个可用选项的简单列表，IDLE、PyCharm、PyDev、WingIDE和mDev。我介绍的重点只有两个，IDLE和WingIDE。

IDLE

IDLE特指集成开发环境（Integrated Development Environment），这个名字由Python的创始人Guido Van Russom所挑选。IDLE使用Python编写，具有一系列的优良特性以完成基本的集成开发。它包括了一个用命令进行实验的Python Shell；能高亮显示源代码并提供跨平台支持。IDLE还提供一个调试器，允许用户设置断点和单步执行代码（参见图2.25）。虽然它并非作为一种专业的开发环境而开发，但它确实支持开发简单应用程序的用户，以及正在学习这门语言的学生。它最大的优势是完全免费。注意，我相信有很多使用Python IDLE的Python开发者不同意我的说法，即认为它不是一个专业的开发环境。我也相信你们中的许多人已经使用IDLE开发出了很复杂的应用程序。但是我认为对于当前的数字取证应用程序的开发，有其他许多具备更高级功能的替代选择。

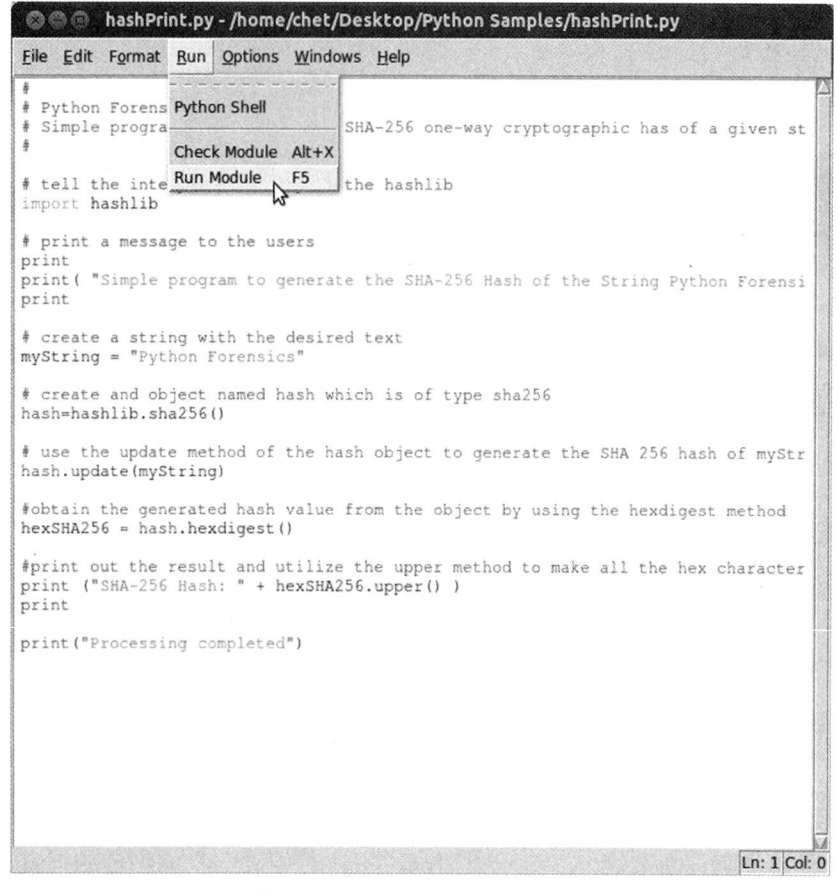

图2.25　Python IDLE集成开发环境

WingIDE

另一方面，虽然WingIDE不是免费的（如果你是一个学生或无报酬的开源开发者，可以获得免费版本），但它确实具有一系列丰富的特性，轻松地支持复杂Python应用程序的开发。根据其意定用途，WingIDE提供了三种版本：

1. 面向学生和无报酬开源开发者的免费版本。
2. WingIDE个人版——顾名思义，限制了一些功能。
3. WingIDE专业版——面向那些希望拥有所有特性和支持的人。例如此版本包含了单元测试、直观的版本控制界面、高级调试和断点设置，以及pyLint的集成。

> pyLint是一个Python源代码分析器分析，帮助识别不当的编程方法，指出潜在错误，对可能的失效提出警告。它还会为代码给出一个总体的评分，以帮助你进行持续改进。

在图2.26中，可以看到我为WingIDE所选择的布局。这个IDE是可配置和可缩放的，用于自定义GUI界面。在每个区域都放置了一个标签，以便在此对其进行介绍。

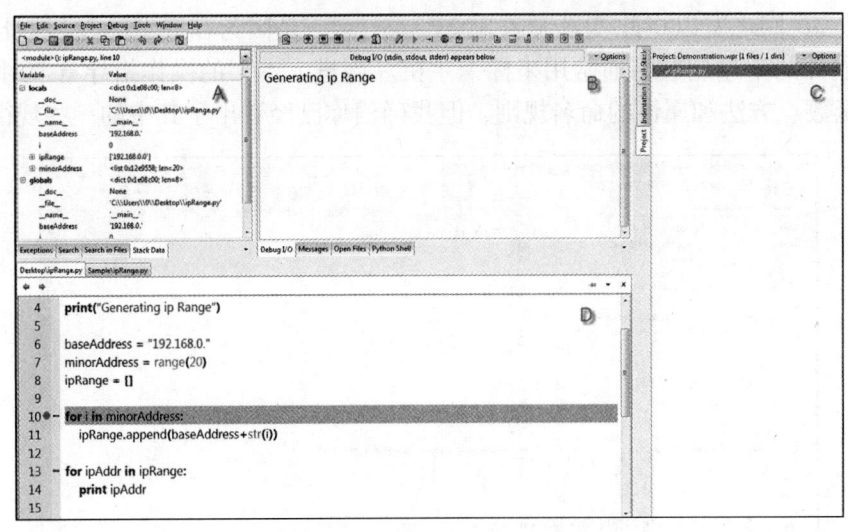

图2.26　WingIDE 4.1个人版截图

区域A：在这个区域中，因为我让程序在断点可以随时停下来，所以可观察到与当前运行程序相关的局部变量以及全局变量。如你所见，顶部的文本框指示ipRange.py模块当前正执行到第10行。在其窗口中，显示baseAddress变量当前包含字符串"192.168.0."。

区域B：显示到目前为止程序的输出。第一条语句已经成功地打印了字符串"Generating ip Range"，在这个窗口的底部还可以看见一些其他的选项，当前的选项为"Debug I/O"。另一个相当有用的选项是"Python Shell"，当选定该选项时，可以执行、研究、试验任一个Python函数，甚至在正式编码前编写一大段语句进行尝试（参见图2.27）。

区域C：这个窗口包含项目信息。由于这是一个非常简单的项目，仅包含了ipRange.py这一个文件，因此这个窗口就只显示这么多。当建立更复杂的应用程序时，这个窗口将帮助我们跟踪程序中的所有组件。

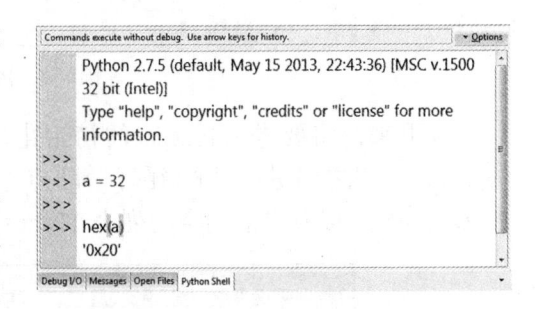

图2.27　WingIDE的Python Shell显示

区域D：这个窗口包含当前程序的源代码，以及调试设定。请注意第10行包含一个点，这里是断点设置的地方，因为当程序执行到该处，断点会停止程序的继续执行，所以该行被突出显示。

现在既然已经有了大致的概念，就让我们通过WingIDE从头到尾走完这个简单的程序，看看变化如何发生。在图2.28中，我们走到下面的代码（我使用F6键做这件事，也可以选择debug菜单下的选项），并在执行ipRange的初始化之前停下。

```
baseAddress = "192.168.0."
minorAddress = range(20)
ipRange = []
```

此时可以检查一下左上方的变量区域（参见图2.28），我们看到，变量baseAddress等于字符串"192.168.0."，变量hostAddress如预期一样，是一个长度为20的列表（list），包括

0到19的值。我们之所以将此变量命名为`hostAddress`，是因为在典型的C类地址中，最后一个逗号隔开的十进制数字通常用来标识主机。当进入本书的操作指导章节时，会考虑到变量、函数、方法和属性的命名规则，但我确信你已经看出了其中的一些规律。

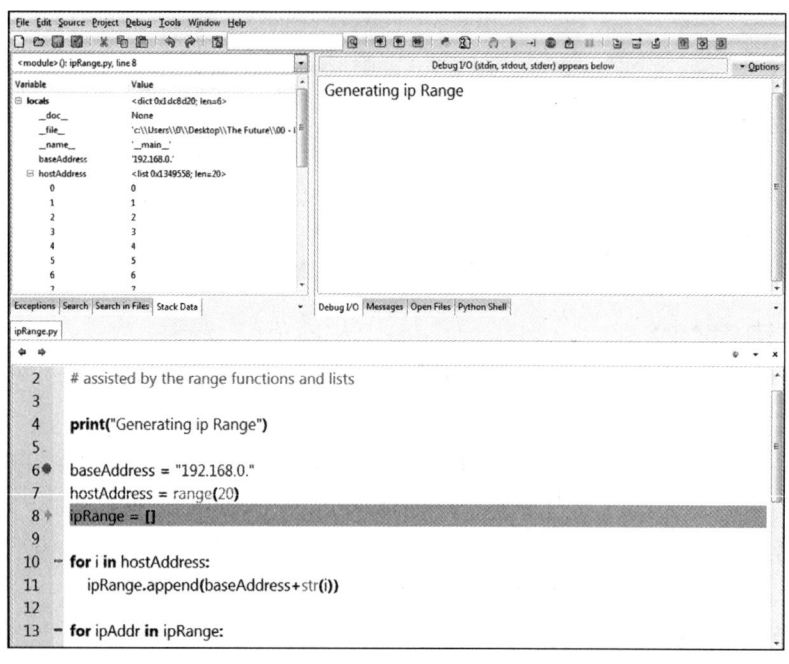

图2.28 运行中的WingIDE

接下来，将要进入`ipRange`的初始化过程（再次用到F6键），在执行第一个`ipRange.append()`方法之前进入"for循环"断点。如图2.29所示，等于0的新变量`i`，也是第一个`hostAddress`，以及目前为空的列表`ipRange`，都显示出来了。

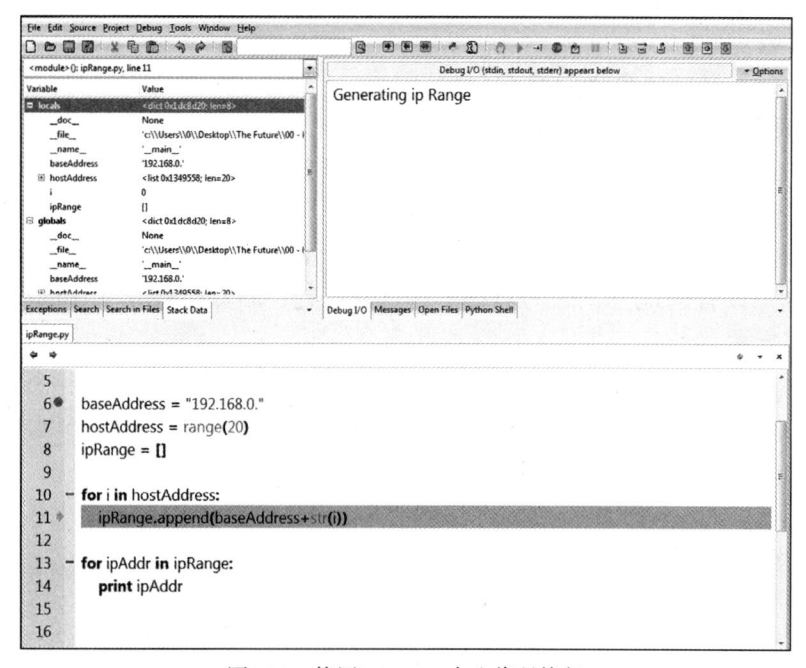

图2.29 使用WingIDE中止代码执行

第 2 章 建立一个 Python 取证环境 29

现在将要遍历这个 for 循环的每一步，本例中有 20 次迭代，并在第二个循环的第一条打印语句处停下。在图 2.30 中的变量区域中，展开了 ipRange 列表的内容，可以看到全部的 ipRange 字符串，此时包含了添加的主机地址。剩下的工作就是逐行打印出 ipRange 列表。

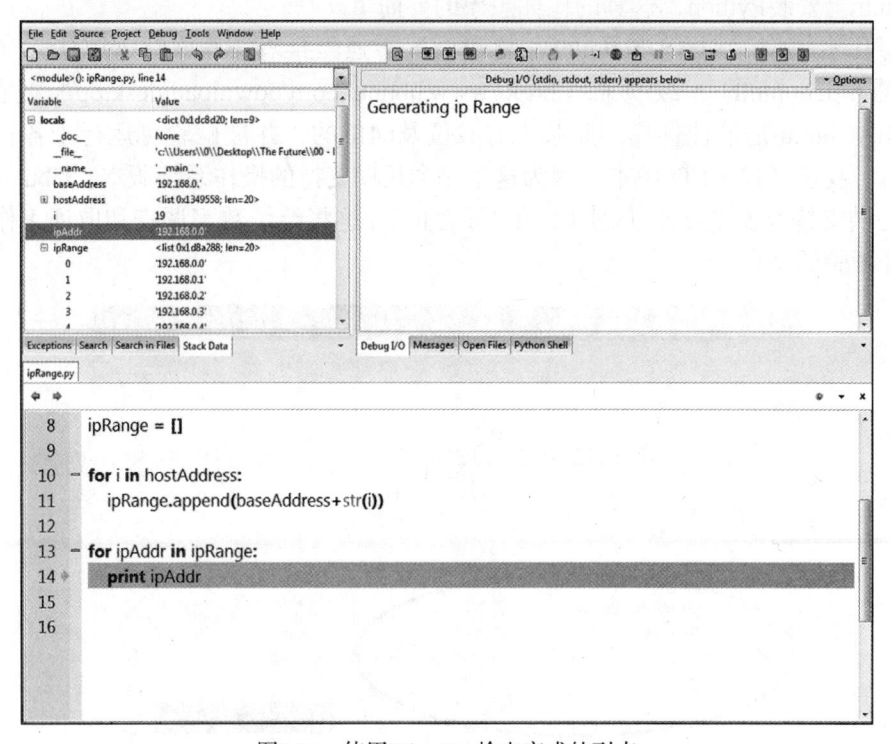

图 2.30 使用 WingIDE 检查完成的列表

至此，关于 WingIDE 的功能，以及如何使用它设置断点、调试代码、查看变量等，已经概述完毕。在本书的余下部分中将会一直使用这个 IDE，并随着内容推进而介绍高级特性。

在编写代码时我使用最多的特性就是自动完成功能。在图 2.31 中，我想看看还有哪些属性和方法与列表 ipRange 相关联。我们已经知道了 append 方法能做什么，但你可能想知道我们还可以做什么。只要简单地添加一行代码，ipRange，输入一个点（即一个句点），一个列表框便会自动出现，并显示出 ipRange 所有可用的属性和方法。注意，因为 ipRange 是一个列表（list）类型，这些

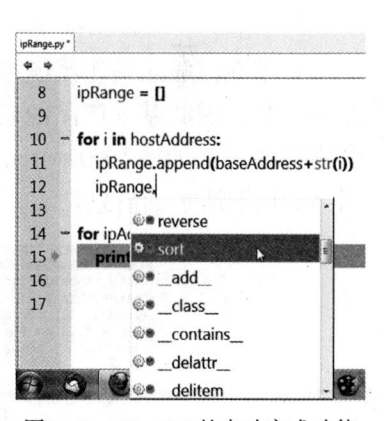

图 2.31 WingIDE 的自动完成功能

方法和属性实际上几乎可以应用到任何列表。你看到的下拉框仅是属性和方法的部分清单。如你所见，向下滚动到了 sort 方法，利用这个方法可以对列表进行排序。传递给 sort 方法的参数将决定列表的实际排序方式。

至此我们一直关注 Windows 平台上的开发及调试。在下一节中，将会探讨 Ubuntu Linux 的安装过程和简单会话。

2.9.2 运行于Ubuntu Linux上的Python

基于Linux的工具在调查和取证上具有很多优势。你可以获得更好性能，安全地挂载多种类型的媒介和镜像，避开操作系统费用，并获得更大的潜在灵活性。接下来就让我们在Ubuntu上安装Python，这真的比你想象的要简单。

在写作本书时，对于Ubuntn的安装和设置，强烈推荐下面的一些方法。在图2.32中，可看到Ubuntu的下载页面（http://www.ubuntu.com/download/desktop）截图。12.x LTS版本的Ubuntn是最佳选择。此版本有32位及64位的，并被检验可运行于各种标准桌面计算机。我选择12.x LTS版本，因为这是一个长期支持的操作系统版本。Ubuntu承诺为此版本提供支持及安全更新（到2017年4月为止），这将给予数字调查和取证工作一个稳定而久经考验的平台。

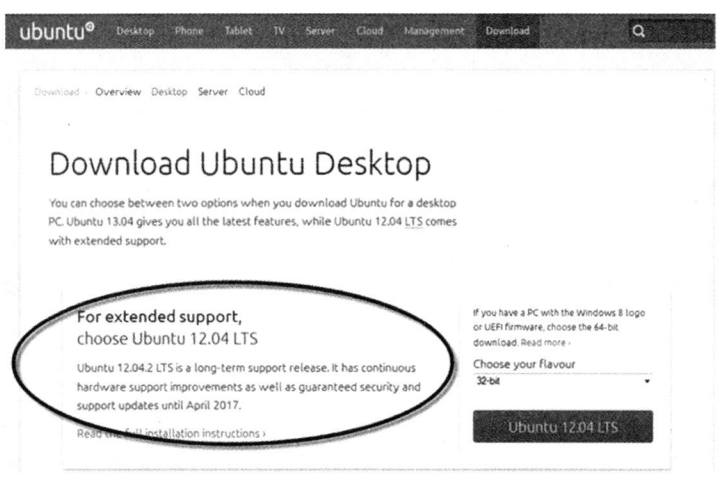

图2.32　Ubuntu 12.04 LTS下载页面

对于在Ubuntu操作系统中安装及运行Python而言，2.7.3版本已经作为操作系统的一部分安装，因此基本产品的安装工作已经为你完成了。若你对此还拿不准，不妨启动一个终端窗口（如图2.33所示），并在提示符处输入python。若正确地安装了Python，则看到类似该图所示的消息。

图2.33　Ubuntu 终端窗口的Python命令

若并没有得到期望的结果，应该重新安装Ubuntu12.x LTS以修复此问题（在进行重新安装前，请确认已将数据备份）。

如果已经长时间未使用Linux，或者这是你首次安装Ubuntu，会发现以往那个安装Linux的痛苦不堪的日子已经结束了，就像大家说的"简直易如反掌"。一旦成功安装了这个操作系统，添加新功能的过程就很简单。例如，如果想在Ubuntu环境中安装一个

第 2 章　建立一个 Python 取证环境　　31

类似于WingIDE或者IDLE的集成开发环境，可以从Ubuntu软件中心（Ubuntu Software Center）获得安装程序。可以通过点击如图2.34所示的任务栏图标以打开Ubuntu软件中心，然后在其中搜索你想要的任何应用程序。

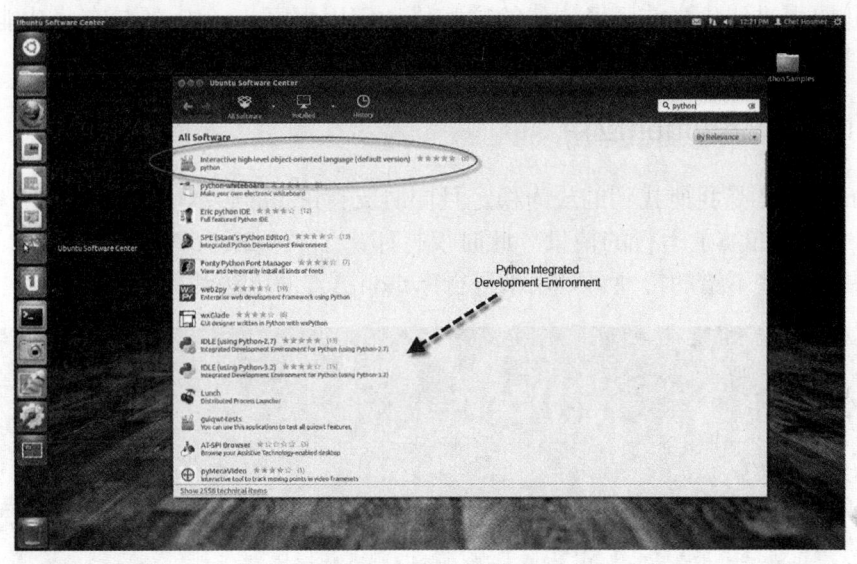

图2.34　Ubuntu软件中心

如你所见，搜索Python，软件中心显示了所有相关的应用程序和服务。可以看到，我圈出的第一个条目就是Python环境。Ubuntu软件中心显示该应用程序已被安装（注意图标上的对勾标记）。而且也可以看到，表中还列出了IDLE集成开发环境的两种不同版本，其中一个支持2.7版本，另一个则支持3.4版本。

继续下去，我为Ubuntu安装WingIDE，Ubuntu，因为这正是我选择的环境。可以在图2.35中看到WingIDE运行于Ubuntu 12.04 LTS的截图，与你在本章较早部分见到的Windows版本相比，其特性集合和操作方式是一样的。

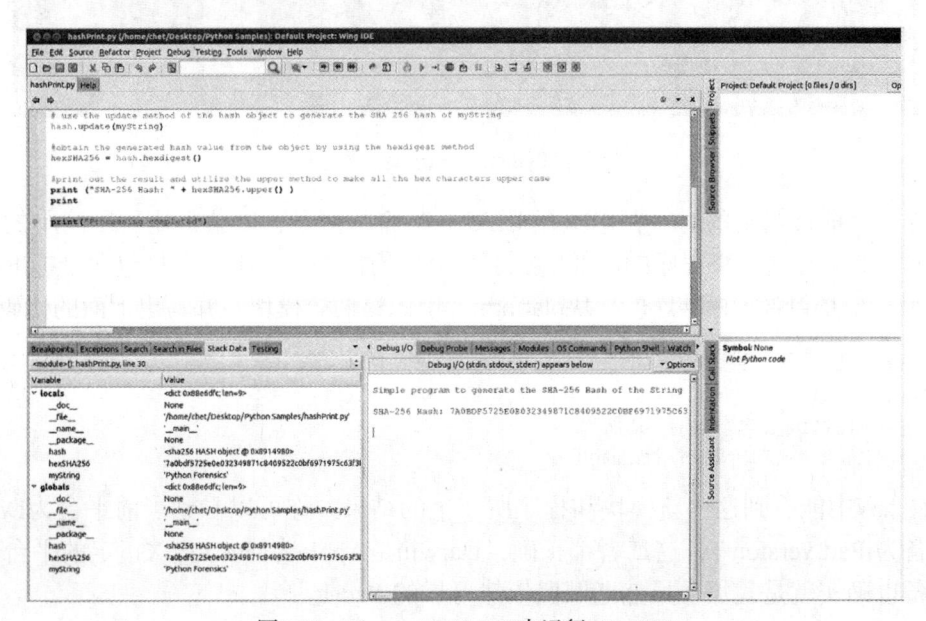

图2.35　Ubuntu 12.04 LTS中运行WingIDE

2.10 移动设备上的Python

将Python版本向智能移动设备（iOS，Windows 8 Phone，当然还有安卓设备）的迁移目前正不断取得进展。当前已经创建的这些移动应用程序（app）还是有些功能限制的，但是它们具有实验和学习的价值。在下一节中，将会简要介绍一下这些应用。

2.10.1 iOS中的Python应用

Python for iOS是我所找到的最为稳定且同时支持iPad的版本。在图2.36中，可以看见Python 2.7 Shell在iOS上运行的情景。此时仅打印出了类似Hello World的消息。这个Shell和编辑器具有一些不错的特性，可用来进行Python语言的语法和模块的实验。

图2.36　Python Shell运行在iOS上

导入一个前面提到的对字符串执行SHA256哈希的例子，以获得比这个简单的例子更多一些的功能。在这个小程序的前部增加了几个新的模块，其中一个是包含于标准库的模块sys，另一个是包含于标准库的模块platform。引入这两个模块，并写出下面的代码：

```
import sys
import platform
print("Platform:"+ sys.platform)
print("Machine:"+ platform.machine())
```

在图2.37中能看到这些新模块和程序所产生的结果。你可以看到当前平台为Darwin，当前设备为iPad version 1，这二者都正确，Darwin是Apple为Mac OS X指定的平台名，并且该设备也确实就是我那台虽然老旧但依然可靠的iPad 1。

第 2 章 建立一个 Python 取证环境

对于那些有兴趣在苹果应用商店（Apple App Store）查找这个iOS应用程序的人，图2.38是来自于这个商店的一个截图，显示了关于Python for iOS的更加详细的信息。

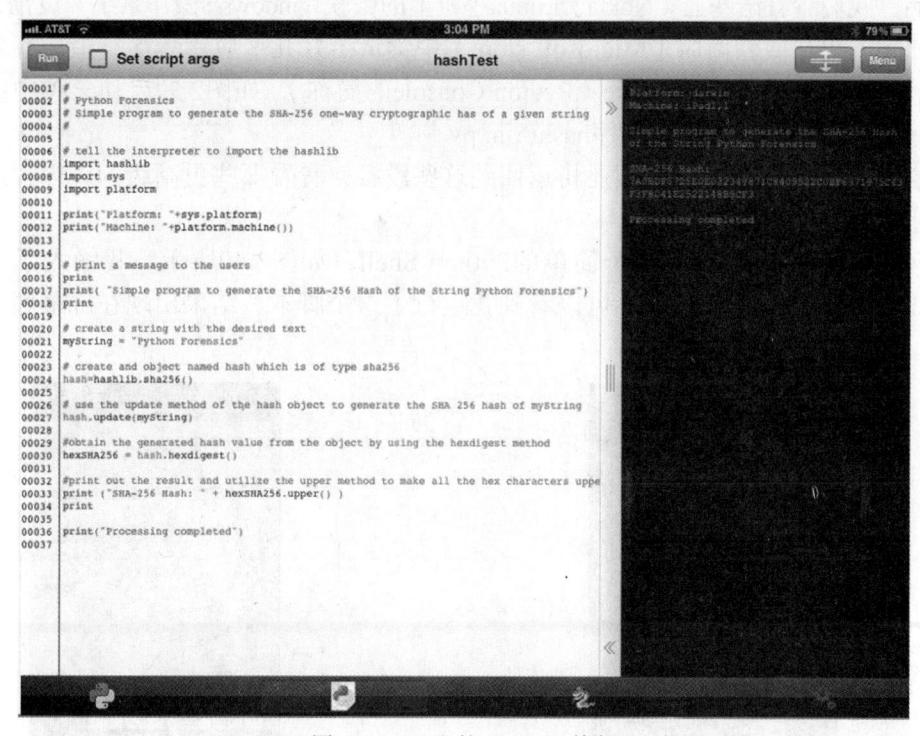

图2.37　iOS上的HashPrint执行

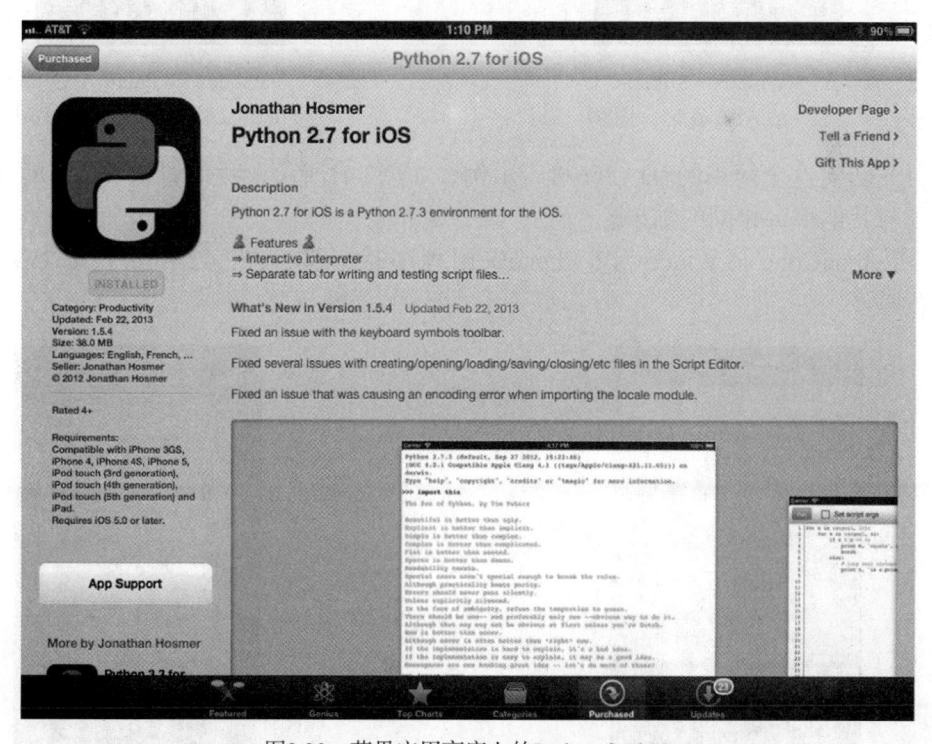

图2.38　苹果应用商店上的Python for iOS

2.10.2　Windows 8 Phone

最后，我们看看诺基亚（Nokia）Lumia手机上的微软Windows 8操作系统。没错，手机上的Python，我在微软商店（Microsoft store）中尝试了好几个应用程序，最后找到了一个工作得相当好的，即PyConsole（Python Console的简称），如图2.39启动菜单中所示的那样，运行与之前相同的例子程序hashPrint.py。

随着本书内容的推进，我们还将返回到这些设备，看看那些更高级的应用程序在这些设备上是如何运行的。

当该应用启动时将开启一个简单的Python Shell，如图2.40所示。我输入了一句简单的hello mobile world消息，你可以看到我运行了这个脚本。结果出现在屏幕底部的显示窗口。

图2.39　Windows 8 Phone上的pythonconsole截图

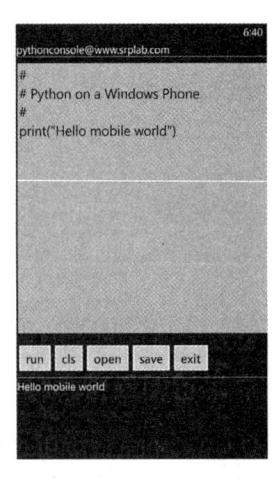

图2.40　在Windows 8 Phone上pythonconsole中的"Hello World"

将目光转向这个简单的SHA256哈希示例，如图2.41所示，我们看到代码，程序的执行产生了与其他平台相同的结果。

若对PythonConsole Windows 8 Phone应用程序感兴趣，图2.42给出了其在Windows Store中的截图。

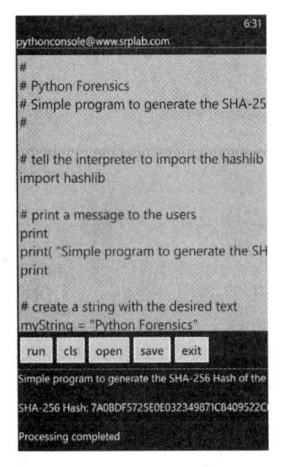

图2.41　在Windows 8 Phone上运行HashPrint应用软件

图2.42　Windows商店的pythonconsole页面

2.11 虚拟机

如今，我们对于任何事情似乎都可以使用虚拟机，从完整的服务器基础设施到特定的应用程序、标准开发环境、数据库、客户服务、桌面等。出于为想要快速入门的人考虑，我创建了一个Ubuntu Python环境，以配合这本书的出版。该环境包括一个标准Ubuntu的安装，以及第3章至第11章中所有的包、模块和详细程序。其中还涵盖了所有的测试数据，以便你能够对书中不管是最简单还是最复杂的数字调查或取证应用程序进行实验。访问www.python-forensics.org即可了解这个虚拟机。

2.12 章节回顾

在本章中，我们对Python环境在微软Windows和Linux环境下的搭建进行了广泛而初步的探讨。我们讨论了哪里才能下载到官方的最新Python环境，一步步地介绍了Windows下的Python环境安装步骤。我们还特别建议选择已经随操作系统安装了2.x版本Python的Ubuntu版本。介绍了Python 2.x与3.x版本间的主要差异。我们还介绍了Python标准库，并探讨了一些重要的内建函数、数据类型和模块。我们还开发了一些利用标准库的示例应用程序，并展示了使用Python所编写的程序如何无须修改即可在Windows，Linux，iOS或者Windows 8 Phone上运行。MacOS同样也是受支持的，并且也有最新版本的Python2.x的标准安装。

我们还测试了两个特定的用于处理自然语言以及网络应用的第三方包。还尝试了在一个IDE中将需要包含的功能，逐步深入地了解了WingIDE的特性，并简要介绍了IDLE IDE。最后，在所有提及的计算平台上尝试了Python Shell。

2.13 问题小结

1. 针对以下情形的人群，你认为最佳的Python开发环境是什么？
    a. 希望进行Python取证实验的学生。
    b. 有意构建和发布Python调查解决方案的开发者。
    c. 一个实验室，能够处理实际问题，但需要一些现有的标准取证软件所缺乏的特定工具和功能。
2. 如果你正在就一些真实案例，或者在实际调查中开发并使用Python取证应用程序，希望一个IDE应该具有哪些重要特性？
3. 你可能会倾向于哪种Ubuntu Linux版本作为所用平台？为什么？
4. 当有一个全功能的Python环境，可用于像iOS，Android或者Windows 8设备等的移动平台时，将会怎样使用这些平台为调查提供服务？
5. 如今在Python 2.x及3.x版本间进行抉择时需考虑哪些因素？
6. 有助于自然语言处理的第三方模块或包是什么？
7. 有助于创建异步网络应用程序的模块和包是什么？

2.14 接下来讲什么

现在我们马上要进入本书的操作指导章节了，每章将分别解决一个特定的取证或数字调查问题。我们将定义问题难点，详细说明需求，设计解决方案，编写方案代码，并对解决方案进行最终的测试及验证。

随着不断深入，在每一章中将逐步介绍新的语言架构、包和模块，以及调试方法和良好的编码方式。所以我希望此时此刻你已经完成了 Python IDE 安装，做好了开始的充分准备。

2.15 补充资料

1. Python 编程语言官方网站 Python.org. http://www.python.org
2. Python 标准库. http://docs.python.org/2/library/
3. 自然语言工具包. nltk.org
4. Python 的 Twisted 网络编程. http://twistedmatrix.com

第3章 第一个Python取证应用程序

3.1 本章简介

在1998年我写了一篇文章，题目是"使用智能卡和数字签名来保护电子证据"（Hosmer，1998）。这篇文章的目的是改进Gene Kim的早期工作。Gene Kim是普渡大学的一名研究生，也是最初的"搭线"技术（Kim，1993）的创立者。我对改进使用单向哈希技术保护数字证据的模型感兴趣，具体地说，我应用将数字签名绑定到智能卡的方法，来提供该签名的双因素认证（参见图3.1）。

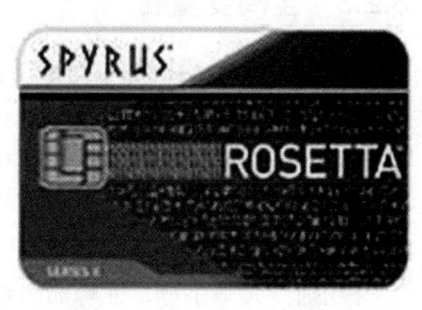

图3.1 具有密码功能的智能卡

几年后，我在提供起源的等式中加入了可信时间戳，或者说是一种准确的签名在"何时"发生的证据。

> 双因素认证将安全物理设备（如智能卡）与具有解锁智能卡功能的口令相结合。这就产生了必须同时具备"持有的事物"和"知道的事物"的效果。为了运行这种实施签名的应用程序，必须持有智能卡，而且还必须知道PIN码（个人识别码），或者知道用来解锁这张卡功能口令。

接下来，将单向哈希方法、数字签名算法以及其他密码学技术应用到数字取证领域的研究兴趣，到目前为止已经有15年的历程了。将这些技术应用到证据保全、证据识别、认证、访问控制决策和网络协议等的工作一直持续到今天。因此我要确信你对于这些基础技术，数字取证的应用，当然也包括Python取证的应用等，都有坚实的理解。

在深入讲解和写代码之前，就像承诺的那样，要为在取证中应用Python编程语言建立一些基本规则。

3.2 命名惯例和其他考虑

在开发Python取证应用程序的过程中，要定义贯穿于本书中操作指导章节的一些规则和命名惯例。这一方面是为了弥补Python对于强类型变量和真实常量的强制执行方面的不足。更为重要的是它定义了一种风格，让程序更易阅读，更易于模仿、理解、修改或者增强。

因此，在这里介绍我将使用的一些命名惯例。

3.2.1 常量

规则：大写字母加下画线分隔符
例：HIGH_TEMPERATRUE

3.2.2 本地变量名

规则：小写字母，驼峰命名法（bumpy cap）（下画线可选）
例：currentTemperature

3.2.3 全局变量名

规则：gl_前缀，加小写字母，驼峰命名法（下画线可选）
注意：全局变量应当包含在一个单一模块中
例：gl_maximumRecordedTemperature

3.2.4 函数名

规则：大写字母，驼峰命名法（下画线可选），具有主动语态
例：ConvertFarenheitToCentigrade(…)

3.2.5 对象名

规则：ob_前缀，加小写字母，驼峰命名法
例：ob_myTempRecorder

3.2.6 模块

规则：下画线加小写字母，驼峰命名法
例：_tempRecorder

3.2.7 类名

规则：class_前缀，驼峰命名法，并且保持简短
例：class_TempSystem
在这一章中将会看到这种命名惯例的很多情形。

3.3 第一个应用程序"单向文件系统哈希"

我们的第一个Python取证应用程序的目标如下：

1. 为取证调查员构建一个实用的应用程序和工具。
2. 按照在本书和将来的应用程序中可复用的原则，开发若干模块。
3. 为开发Python取证应用程序建立一个坚实的方法体系。
4. 开始介绍这种语言的更多高级特性。

3.3.1 背景

在我们能够建立一个执行文件系统单向哈希的应用程序之前,需要更加明确地定义单向哈希运算。在这里很多读者或许会说,"我已经知道什么是单向哈希运算了,赶快继续吧。"然而对于计算机取证来说,这是一个如此重要的基本概念,以至于即使你目前可能已经有较好的理解,仍然值得去做一个更为准确的定义。

单向哈希算法的基本特征

1. 单向哈希算法将二进制数据流作为输入,这个数据流可以是口令、文件、磁盘镜像、固态硬盘镜像、网络数据包、数字记录设备中的1和0,或者几乎任意连续的数字输入。
2. 这个算法生成一个消息摘要,这个摘要是作为输入接收的二进制数据的压缩表示。
3. 仅仅使用摘要来确定产生这个摘要的二进制输入是不可行的。换句话说,不可能逆转这个过程,即根据摘要去恢复生成该摘要的二进制数据流是不可能的。
4. 构造一个新的,能生成给定消息摘要的二进制输入是不可行的。
5. 改变二进制输入数据中的哪怕一个比特,也会产生完全不同的消息摘要。
6. 最后,找到能产生相同摘要的两个完全不同的任意二进制数据流,是不可行的。

有哪些常见的密码学哈希算法

有很多产生消息摘要的算法。表3.1提供了一些最常见算法的基本情况。

表3.1 常见的单向哈希算法

算法	发明者	长度(比特)	相关标准
MD5	Ronald Rivest	128	RFC 1321
SHA-1	NSA,NIST发布	160	FIPS Pub 180
SHA-2	NSA,NIST发布	224	FIPS Pub 180-2
		256	FIPS Pub 180-3
		384	FIPS Pub 180-4
		512	
RIPEMD-160	Hans Dobbertin	160	开放的学术社区
SHA-3	Guido Bertoni,Joan Daemen,Michael Peeters,和Gilles Van Assche	224, 256, 384, 512	FIPS-180-5

单向哈希算法之间有哪些选择权衡

MD5算法现在仍然在使用,对于很多应用程序来说,速度、便利性和互操作性使得它成为算法首选。由于对MD5算法的攻击以及它比较高的碰撞可能性,许多组织转向了SHA-2(256比特和512比特是最常用的大小)。许多组织选择跳过SHA-1,因为它有一些与MD5相同的弱点。

转向SHA-3还仍在未来的考虑中,并且广泛地接受它可能还需要继续若干年。SHA-3是完全不同的,而且为了应用于嵌入式和手持式设备,它被设计得更容易在硬件上实现以提升性能(速度和能量消耗)。我们将会看到手持设备制造商有多么迅速地采用这一新建立的标准。

在取证中单向哈希算法有哪些最佳用途

证据保全　在收集数字数据时（如对机械硬盘或者固态硬盘做镜像），全部内容（换句话说，每一个比特都被收集）组合在一起生成一个唯一的单向哈希值。一旦这个过程完成，就可以重新计算这个单向哈希。如果新的计算结果与原始结果相匹配，就能证明证据没有被修改。当然这是在假设原始结果得到保护且没有被篡改（因为原始结果不会作为秘密来保存），并且这个哈希算法可以得到的情况下。任何人都可以重新计算哈希值，因此数字证据的保管链（chain of custody），包括生成的哈希值在内，都必须妥善维护。

搜索　在传统用法上，单向哈希值被用来执行已知目标文件的查找。例如，如果执法机关有一个确认的儿童色情文件的集合，就可以计算其中每一个文件得到哈希值。然后通过扫描可疑的系统，以查看这些违禁文件是否存在。这是通过计算该系统中每一个文件的哈希值，并将结果与已知的违禁文件的哈希值（即那个儿童色情文件集合的哈希结果）相比较的方式来判断的。如果找到了匹配的，那么这个可疑系统上具有相匹配的哈希值的文件将会被进一步检查。

黑名单　如同搜索中的例子，可以建立一个已知的"坏"文件的哈希值列表。如同儿童色情的例子，它们代表违禁文件，可以用来匹配已知的恶意代码或网络攻击文件，甚至是涉密或专属文档的哈希值。如果发现黑名单上哈希值的匹配项，就能为调查员提供关键的证据。

白名单　通过建立一个好的或良性文件（操作系统或者应用程序可执行文件，供应商提供的动态链接库，或者已知的可信应用程序下载的文件）的哈希值列表，调查员就可以运用这张表过滤掉他们无须审查的文件，因为它们之前就已经被认为是一个"好"文件。使用这种方法，可以显著减少需要审查的文件数量，并将精力集中在那些不属于已知的"好"的哈希列表的文件上。

变化检测　一种流行的防止恶意修改的方法就是通过对"已知正常"的安装或配置文件进行哈希运算，这种恶意修改针对的是网站、路由器、防火墙的配置文件，甚至操作系统的安装文件。然后可以定期地重新扫描这些安装或者配置文件，以确保没有文件发生改变。另外，还可以确认没有文件添加到"已知正常"的文件集合中，或者从中删除。

3.3.2　基本需求

现在已经对单向哈希运算及其用途有了更好的理解，但我们的单向文件系统哈希应用程序有哪些基本需求呢？

当定义任何一个软件或者应用程序的需求时，要把它们定义得尽可能简洁，几乎不使用专业词汇，这样熟悉该领域的任何人都可以理解，即使他们不是软件开发人员。并且每一项需求都应当有一个标识符，方便从定义，直到设计、开发、验证等环节进行跟踪。我想要给设计人员和开发人员留一个创新的空间，因此在需求定义时尽力专注于"什么"而不是"怎样"（参见表3.2）。

表3.2　基本需求

需求编号	需求名称	简单描述
000	总体	我们需要的基本能力是一个取证应用程序，能遍历指定起点的文件系统（如 c:或 /etc），然后为遇到的每个文件生成单向哈希值

（续表）

需求编号	需求名称	简单描述
001	可移植性	应用程序应该支持Windows和Linux操作系统，作为一般的参考，将在Windows 7、Windows 8、Ubuntu 12.04 LTS环境上进行验证
002	主要功能	除了生成单向哈希值，应用程序应该收集每个被哈希的文件的系统元数据，例如，至少包括文件属性、文件名和文件路径等
003	主要结果	应用程序应该以标准输出文件格式提供结果，以满足灵活性
004	算法选择	当指定用到的单向哈希算法时，应用程序应该提供多种选择
005	错误处理	应用程序必须支持操作执行中的错误处理和日志，包括文字描述和时间戳

3.3.3 设计中的考虑

现在已经定义了这个应用程序的基本需求，我将把它们分解到设计考虑中。首先会尽可能利用Python标准库里的内置函数。基于对其核心功能的考察，将这些需求定义映射到将要使用的模块与函数上。这也会揭示出在所有的新的程序模块中，哪些将来源于第三方模块，哪些需要开发（参见表3.3）。

作为设计者的一个重要的步骤，或者说至少是有趣的工作，就是为这个程序命名的。我决定给这第一个程序命名为p-fish，代表Python-file system hashing。

接下来基于对于标准库函数的理解，必须定义我们的第一个应用程序由哪些程序模块构成：

1. 用作用户输入的argparse
2. 用作文件系统操作的os
3. 用作单向哈希运算的hashlib
4. 用作结果输出的csv（其他可选的输出格式将会在以后添加）
5. 用作事件和错误记录的logging
6. 以及其他的各种有用的模块，如time、sys和stat

表3.3 标准库映射

需求	设计考虑	库选择
用户输入（000，003，004）	这些需求的每一个都需要从用户输入以完成任务。例如，000需要用户指定开始目录的路径。003需要用户指定合适的输出格式。004需要我们允许用户指定哈希算法。异常处理或默认设定的细节需要定义（如果允许）	对于这第一个程序，决定使用命令行参数来获得用户输入。基于此种设计决策，就能利用argparse标准库模块
遍历文件系统（000，001）	这个功能需要程序能从指定开始点遍历目录结构。而且，也必须能同时工作于Windows和Linux平台	标准库的os模块提供了遍历路径的关键方法，还提供了跨平台兼容能力的抽象。最后，这个模块的跨平台能力提供了与文件有关的元数据访问
元数据收集（003）	这需要我们收集目录的路径、文件名、所有者，修改/访问/创建时间，权限，属性（如只读，隐藏，系统或归档）	
文件哈希（000）	必须提供用户能够选择哈希算法的灵活性。我决定支持最流行的算法，如MD5以及几种SHA的变体	标准库模块hashlib提供生成单向哈希值的能力。这个库支持常见哈希算法，如md5、sha1、sha224、sha256、sha384和sha512。这就为用户提供了足够的选择余地

（续表）

需求	设计考虑	库选择
结果输出（003）	为满足需要，必须能够组织程序的输出，得到具有灵活性的格式	标准库提供了我能利用的多种选择。如csv模块提供了创建逗号分隔值文件输出的能力，json模块（Java Object Notation）JSON对象的编码器和解码器，XML模块能够用来创建XML输出
日志和错误处理	必须预料到在遍历文件系统过程中将出现的错误。例如，可能不能访问某个文件，某个文件可能是孤立的，某个文件可能被操作系统或其他应用程序锁定。需要处理这些出错情况，记录任何值得注意的事件，例如，应该记录关于调查人员、地点、日期和时间的信息，以及与遍历的文件有关的信息	Python标准库包括logging模块，能用来报告在处理过程中出现的任何事件或错误

3.3.4　程序结构

接下来需要定义程序的结构，换句话说，打算如何将这些程序片段组合在一起。这是很关键的，特别是当我们的目标是在将来的应用程序中复用这个程序的组件时。组合这些组件的一种方法参见图3.2与图3.3的两个简单图解。

上下文图（Context diagram）非常直白而简要地描述了拟编程序的主要输入和输出。用户指定程序参数，p-fish接收这些输入然后处理（哈希、提取元数据等）文件系统，产生一个报告，并将所有值得注意的事件或错误分别送到"p-fish report"和"p-fish event and error log"文件中去。

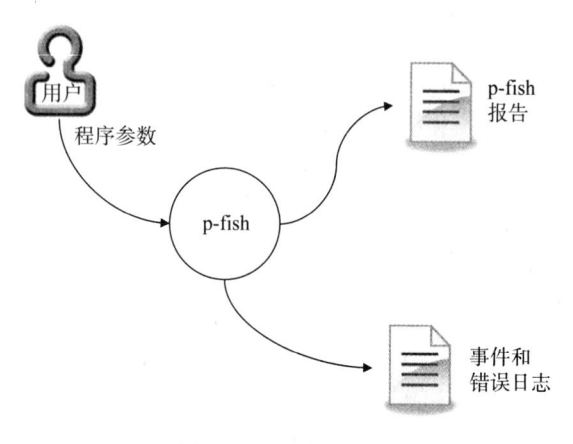

图3.2　p-fish的上下文图

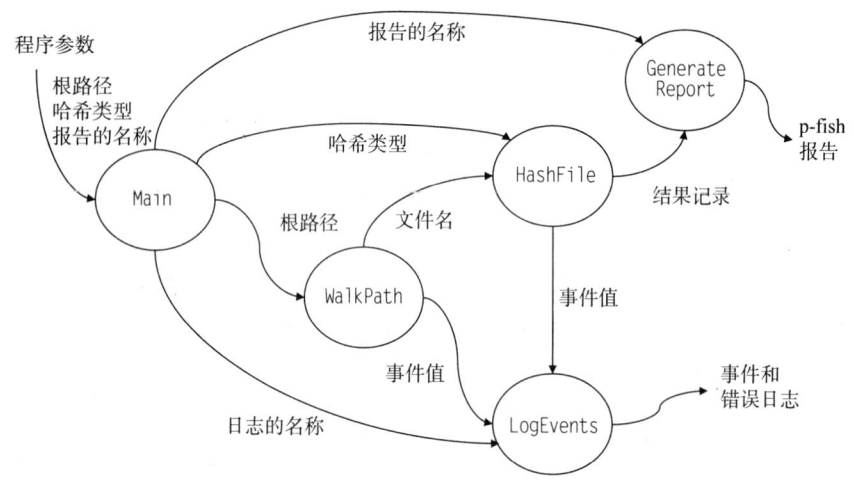

图3.3　p-fish的内部结构

转到内部结构，我已经将这个程序细分成5个主要组件，分别是Main、ParseCommandLine函数、WalkPath函数、HashFile函数、CSVWriter类，以及日志记录器（注意它事实上是Python的日志记录模块），它们都被p-fish的主要功能所使用。下面将简单地描述每个组件的操作，并在代码遍历的环节逐行地给出每个函数运行得更详细的解释。

Main函数

Main函数的作用是控制这个程序的整体工作流。例如在Main里面建立起Python日志记录器，显示开始和完成的消息，并保持对时间的跟踪。另外Main还调用命令行解析器，然后启动WalkPath函数。一旦WalkPath完成，Main会记下完成情况，并给用户显示终止消息，并记入日志。

ParseCommandLine

为了让p-fish流畅运行，利用ParseCommandLine函数来解析和验证用户的输入。一旦完成，与程序的函数（如WalkPath, HashFile, CSVWrite）有关的信息就能从解析器产生的数值中得到。例如，因为hashType是由用户指定的，那么这个必须提供给HashFile。同样地，CSVWriter也需要路径，以写入p-fish产生的报告。WalkPath也需要起点或rootPath来开始其遍历。

WalkPath函数

WalkPath函数必须从目录树或者路径的根开始，遍历所有的目录与文件。对于遇到的每一个有效的文件，它会调用HashFile函数来执行单向哈希操作。一旦所有的文件都被处理，WalkPath会将控制权，以及成功处理的文件数量返还给Main。

HashFile函数

HashFile函数将会对有关的需要调查的文件进行打开、读取、计算哈希并获取元数据等操作。对于每一个文件都有一行数据送到CSVWriter，以添加进p-fish的报告中。一旦这个文件处理完，HashFile会将控制权返回到WalkPath来取出下一个文件。

CSVWriter（类）

为了介绍类与对象使用，我决定将CSVWriter创建成一个类而不是一个简单的函数。接下来的几章将有更多的类似情况，而此处的CSVWriter非常好地建立了一个类/对象的示范。Python标准库中的CSV模块要求对"writer"进行初始化。例如，让产生的csv文件都带有一个由静态的列集合组成的标题行。然后随之对writer的调用将包含填充到每一行的数据。最后，当程序处理完所有的文件，生成的csv报告就必须关闭。注意，当我们遍历完这些程序代码之后，你或许想知道为什么没有在这个程序中更多地使用类和对象。当然这是可以的，但是考虑到这是第一个应用程序，所编写的还是一个更多面向函数的例子。

日志记录器

内置的标准库日志记录器为我们提供了一种向日志文件写消息的功能，这个日志文件与p-fish相关联。这个程序可以写信息类消息、警告类消息和错误类消息。因为我们的目标是要编写一个取证应用程序，日志操作的问题就至关重要。可以扩展这个程序以记录代码中更多的事件，这些扩展代码可以添加到任何一个_pfish函数中。

编写代码

我决定创建两个文件，主要在于展示如何创建你自己的Python模块，并且给你一些如何将程序功能分离的背景知识。对于这第一个简单的应用程序，编写了（1）pfish.py和（2）_pfish.py。正如你可能会回想到的，所有的模块都以一个下画线开头的名字来创建，因为_pfish.py包括了pfish所有的支持函数，所以我简单将其命名为_pfish.py。如果想要拆分出模块以更好地分离功能，可以为HashFile函数、WalkPath函数等创建独立的模块。这个决定通常取决于这些函数间耦合的松紧程度，更确切的表述方式为：取决于是否希望以后独立地复用这些单个的函数。如果是这样，就应将它们分开。

在图3.4中可以看到我的IDE建立了pfish项目。你会注意到最右上方的区域列出了与项目相关联的文件。我把两个文件都打开了，你可以看到在最左边的大约中间位置有两个选项卡，在这里可以查阅每个文件里的源代码。正如你期待的那样，在左上区域可以看到这个程序正在运行并且可以检查变量。最后在屏幕上方正中间的窗口中，可以看到程序的当前显示消息，报告了命令行处理成功，以及pfish的欢迎消息等。

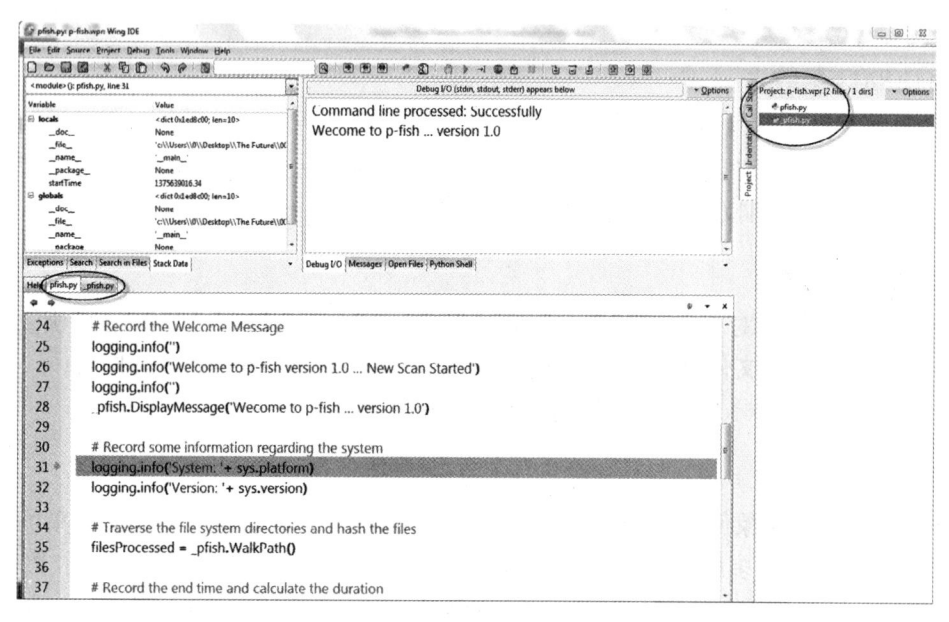

图3.4　WingIDE的p-fish编程

3.4　代码遍历

在讨论每一部分代码时都会插入一些解释。代码的遍历将为你提供程序全部代码的深度视图。我会带你首先把每一个关键函数走一遍，然后提供这两个文件的完整清单。

3.4.1　检查Main-代码遍历

嵌入的注解以楷体字表示，代码本身则以等宽字体显示。

```
# p-fish : Python File System Hash Program
# Author: C. Hosmer
# July 2013
# Version 1.0
#
```

主程序代码非常直观。正如所预期的那样，在最上面你看到了导入语句，这可以让Python标准库模块能够为我们所用。之前没见过的是引用我们自己模块的导入语句，在本例中这个模块就是_pfish。因为我将调用存在于程序组件Main中的函数，这个Main组件必须引入自己的模块_pfish。

```
import logging      #Python Library logging functions
import time         #Python Library time manipulation functions
import sys          #Python Library system specific parameters
import _pfish       #_pfish Support Function Module
if __name__ == '__main__':
    PFISH_VERSION ='1.0'
    # Turn on Logging
```

接下来，可以看见我对Python日志系统进行了初始化。在这个例子中直接指定将日志存储在一个名为pFishLog.log的文件中。我设置了日志记录级别为DEBUG，并且指明我需要对每一个日志事件记录时间及日期。通过把级别设置为DEBUG（这是最低级别），将会确保所有送往日志记录器的消息都是可见的。

```
logging.basicConfig(filename = 'pFishLog.log', level = logging.
DEBUG, format = '%(asctime)s %(message)s')
```

接下来，通过调用_pfish.ParseCommadLine()函数，将控制转到处理命令行参数。我必须为这个函数加上前缀_pfish，因为此函数存在于_pfish模块中。如果解析成功，该函数将返回此处，否则，它将向用户发送一条消息并退出程序。在下一部分，将进一步说明ParseCommandLine()的运作。

```
# Process the Command Line Arguments
_pfish.ParseCommandLine()
```

需要记录应用程序的当前启动时间，以计算出处理所花费的时间。使用标准库函数time.time()来取得自从纪元起所逝去的秒数。请注意从取证角度说，这是我们所运行系统的时间，因此如果在你的调查中时间是一个关键因素，那么应该相应地同步其系统时钟。

```
# Record the Starting Time
startTime = time.time()
```

接下来，这个程序向日志发送一条消息，报告扫描的开始，当且仅当在命令行中选择了verbose选项时（在讲解ParseCommandLine函数时将做进一步说明），会在用户屏幕上显示此消息。值得注意的是我没有简单地嵌入一个魔术数字，而是使用了一个常量来存储版本号。这样在以后需要时，只要修改此常量即可，于是在使用PFISH_VERSION的任何地方，都将显示正确的版本号。我还将系统平台和版本记入日志，以防将来出现对于用来处理这些数据系统的疑问。这里会是一个添加关于组织、调查员姓名、案例编号以及其他案件与相关信息的绝佳地方。

```
# Post the Start Scan Message to the Log
logging.info('Welcome to p-fish version 1.0...New Scan Started')
_pfish.DisplayMessage('Welcome to p-fish...version 1.0')
```

请注意，因为我创建了一个常量PFISH_VERSION，我们可以借此使源代码更加容易维护。就像这样：

_pfish.DisplayMessage('Welcome to p_fish…' + PFISH_VERSION)

```
# Record some information regarding the system
logging.info('System:'+ sys.platform)
logging.info('Version:'+ sys.version)
```

现在Main程序启动了_pfish模块中的WalkPath函数，它会从预先给定的根路径开始遍历目录结构。这个函数会返回WalkPath和HashFile成功处理的文件数量。如你所见，我使用这个值以及结束时间作为整个日志项的结尾。通过从endTime减去startTime，可以确定执行文件系统哈希操作所花费的秒数。当然，也可以将其转化为天、小时、分钟和秒数的形式。

```
# Traverse the file system directories and hash the files
filesProcessed = _pfish.WalkPath()

# Record the end time and calculate the duration
endTime = time.time()
duration = endTime - startTime

logging.info('Files Processed:'+ str(filesProcessed) )
logging.info('Elapsed Time:'+ str(duration) + 'seconds')

logging.info('Program Terminated Normally')

_pfish.DisplayMessage("Program End")
```

3.4.2　ParseCommandLine()

在设计环节，我做出了两个驱动开发过程的决定：

1. 这第一个应用程序是命令行程序。
2. 给用户提供几个选项来控制这个程序的行为。这就决定了命令行选项的设计和实现。

基于这些，我为此程序提供了如下的几种命令行选项。

选项	描述	备注
-v	Verbose，如果指定了此选项，任何对DisplayMessage()函数的调用将会显示到标准输出设备，否则程序将静默运行	
--MD5 --SHA256 --SHA512	哈希类型选择，用户必须指定将会用到的单向哈希算法	选择是互斥的，必须做出至少一个选择，否则程序将终止
-d	rootPath，这里允许用户指定遍历的开始或根路径	这个目录必须存在并且可读，否则程序将终止
-r	reportPath，这里允许用户指定生成的.csv文件将要写入的目录	这个目录必须存在并且可写，否则程序将终止

虽然其中的一些要求初看来可能有些难度，但argparse标准库为处理这些提供了极大的灵活性。这就允许在程序执行前捕获任何可能的用户错误，同时也向我们提供了一种向用户报告问题以处理异常的方法。

```
def ParseCommandLine():
```

使用argparse的关键在于知道如何建立解析器。如果正确地创建了解析器，它将会为你处理所有的麻烦事。首先创建一个新的名为"parser"的解析器，并对它做一个简单的描述。然后增加一个新的参数，本例中是-v或verbose。选项是-v，生成的使用变量是verbose。与参数相关的帮助消息被帮助系统使用，以提醒用户如何使用pfish。-h选项是内建的，无须定义。

```
parser = argparse.ArgumentParser('Python file system hashing ..p-fish')
parser.add_argument('-v', '--verbose' help = 'allows progress messages to
be displayed', action = 'store_true')
```

下一环节定义了一个互斥的参数组，以便选择用户想要产生的特定哈希类型。如果想要加入其他的选项，如sha384，只需要以相同的格式将其他参数添加到组里。因为在add_mutually_exclusive_group中指定了选项required = true，argparse将会确信用户只指定了一个参数，并且至少有一个。

```
# setup a group where the selection is mutually exclusive # # and required.
group = parser.add_mutually_exclusive_group (required = True)
group.add_argument('--md5',    help = 'specifies MD5 algorithm',
action = 'store_true')
group.add_argument('--sha256', help = 'specifies SHA256 algorithm',
action = 'store_true')
group.add_argument('--sha512', help ='specifies SHA512 algorithm',
action = 'store_true')
```

接下来，需要指定遍历的起始点，以及在哪里创建报告。这与之前的设定是一样的，只有添加了type选项这一个不同。这就要求argparse验证我指定的类型。在使用-d选项时，我想确认rootPath是存在并且可读的。对于reportPath，则必须存在而且是可写的。由于argparse没有内置的验证目录的函数，我创建了函数ValidateDirectory()和ValidateDirectoryWritable()。它们大体是相似的，并且都使用了标准库的操作系统函数来验证目录是否与给定的一样。

```
parser.add_argument('-d','--rootPath', type=
ValidateDirectory, required = True, help = "specify the root
path for hashing)"
parser.add_argument('-r','--reportPath', type =
ValidateDirectoryWritable, required = True, help = "specify the
path for reports and logs will be written)"
# create a global object to hold the validated arguments,
# these will be available then to all the Functions
# within the _pfish.py module
global gl_args
global gl_hashType
```

现在解析器可以被调用了。我想在一个全局变量里存储生成的参数（只要经过了验证），以便它们能够被_pfish组件中的函数访问。这将是一个创建类，对付避免使用全局变量的绝佳机会。第4章便是这么做的。

```
gl_args = parser.parse_args()
```

如果解析器是成功的（换句话说，argparse验证了命令行参数），需要确定用户选择了哪个哈希算法。通过检查与哈希类型相关联的每一个值来做到这一点。例如，假设用户选择了sha256，那么gl_args.sha256就会被置为True，并且MD5和sha512会被置为False。因此，通过使用一个简单的if/elif的语句例程，就可以确认选择了哪一个。

```
if gl_args.md5:
    gl_hashType = 'MD5'
elif gl_args.sha256:
    gl_hashType = 'SHA256'
elif gl_args.sha512:
    gl_hashType = 'SHA512'
else:
    gl_hashType = "Unknown"
        logging.error('Unknown Hash Type Specified')

DisplayMessage("Command line processed: Successfully)"
return
```

3.4.3　ValidatingDirectoryWritable

正如上面提到的那样，需要创建函数以验证用户给出的目录，是否可用于报告的存储，以及遍历的起始或者根路径。借助Python标准库模块os完成这个任务。我使用了这个模块的os.path.isdir方法和os.access方法。

```
def ValidateDirectoryWritable(theDir):
```

首先做检查，看看用户提供的目录字符串是否真实存在。如果测试失败，便在argparse里引发一个错误并且给出"Directory does not exist"（目录不存在）的消息。此消息会在测试失败时向用户显示。

```
# Validate the path is a directory
    if not os.path.isdir(theDir):
            raise argparse.ArgumentTypeError('Directory does not exist')
```

接下来，检验是否获得了该目录的写权限。同样，如果测试失败，会引发一个例外并且给出一个消息。

```
# Validate the path is writable
    if os.access(theDir, os.W_OK):
            return theDir
    else:
            raise argparse.ArgumentTypeError('Directory is not writable')
```

现在我已经完成了ParseCommendLine函数的实现。让我们来测试几个例子，看看这个函数如何拒绝不正确的命令行参数。在图3.5中，编造了四个不正确的命令行格式：

(1）将根目录错误键入为TEST_DIR，而不是简单的TESTDIR。

(2）将-sha512参数错误键入为-sha521。

(3）指定了两种哈希类型，-sha512和-md5。

(4）最后，没有指定任何哈希类型。

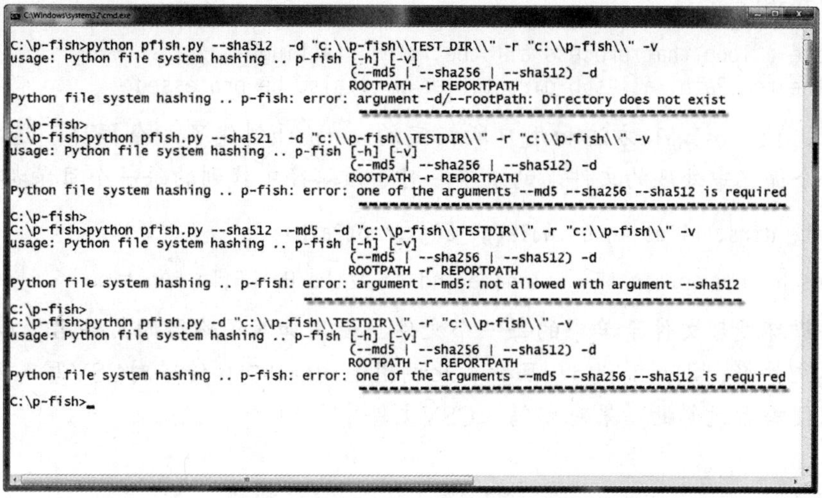

图3.5　ParseCommandLine的演示

正如你在每种情况中看到的那样，ParseCommandLine拒绝了这些命令。

为了让用户回到正确的轨道，只需要利用如图3.6所示的–h或help选项得到正确的命令行参数的说明。

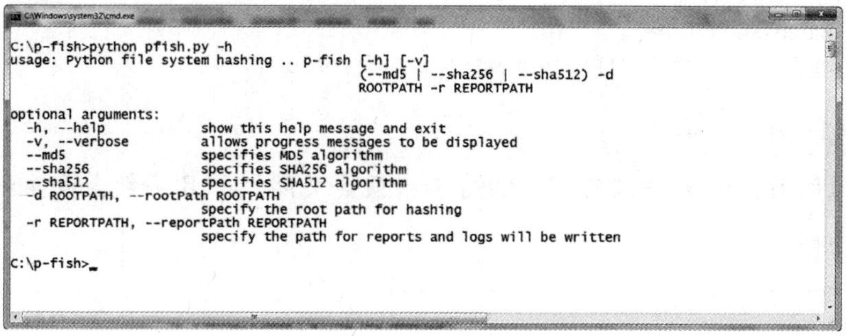

图3.6　pfish的–h命令

3.4.4　WalkPath

现在让我们把遍历目录结构的WalkPath函数遍历一遍，这个函数会对每一个文件调用HashFile函数。我认为你会对这个函数多么简单而感到惊喜。

```
def WalkPath():
```

首先对变量processCount进行初始化，以便对成功处理的文件数量进行计数，然后向日志文件发送一条消息，以记录根路径的值。

```
processCount = 0
errorCount = 0

log.info('Root Path:'+ gl_args.rootPath)
```

接下来利用用户在命令行提供的reportPath对CSVWriter进行初始化。我也给出了用户选择的hashType，以便把它添加到CSV文件的标题行中。本章的稍后部分将会讲到CSVWriter类。

```
oCVS = _CSVWriter(gl_args.reportPath+'fileSystemReport.csv',
gl_hashType)
# Create a loop that process all the files starting
# at the rootPath, all sub-directories will also be processed
```

接下来，使用os.walk方法和用户所指定的rootpath创建了一个循环。这将建立一个将会在下一个循环中处理的文件名的清单。对于该路径中找到的每一个目录都会这么做。

```
for root, dirs, files in os.walk(gl_args.rootPath):
# for each file obtain the filename and call the HashFile Function
```

下一个循环处理文件清单中的每一个文件，使用加入了路径的文件名，以及HashFile使用的简单文件名，调用HashFile函数。此调用还向HashFile传递对CSV写入器（writer）的访问，以便哈希运算的结果可以写入CSV文件中。

```
for file in files:
    fname = os.path.join(root, file)
    result = HashFile(fname, file, oCVS)

    # if successful then increment ProcessCount
```

processCount和errorCount的值也会根据情况相应地增加。

```
    if result is True:
        processCount += 1
    # if not successful, the increment the ErrorCount
    else:
        errorCount += 1
```

一旦所有的目录和文件被处理，CVSWriter便会关闭，并且函数会向主程序返回成功处理的文件数目。

```
oCVS.writerClose()
return(processCount)
```

3.4.5　HashFile

以下为HashFile函数的代码，很明显这是此程序中最长的一段，但同样是简单明了的。让我们把过程遍历一遍。

```
def HashFile(theFile, simpleName, o_result):
```

在试图对文件进行哈希计算之前，对于每一个文件都有几个事项需要验证：

（1）路径存在吗？
（2）路径是一个链接而不是一个真实的文件吗？
（3）文件是真实的吗（确保它不是孤立的）？

对每一项验证都有一个相应的错误记录,并在错误发生时发送到日志文件中。如果一个文件被忽略,程序将会简单地返回至WalkFile,然后处理下一个文件。

```
# Verify that the path is valid
if os.path.exists(theFile):
    #Verify that the path is not a symbolic link
    if not os.path.islink(theFile):
        #Verify that the file is real
        if os.path.isfile(theFile):
```

接下来的一部分需要一点技巧。即便我们已经想尽办法证实文件确实存在,仍然会有文件无法打开或读取的情况。这是由于权限问题、文件被锁住或者可能已损坏等原因造成的。因此在试图打开和读取文件时,运用了try方法。请注意,我十分小心地用"rb"即只读方式来打开文件。这样一旦错误发生,就会生成日志并记录一次报告,程序就会转向下一个文件。

```
            try:
                #Attempt to open the file
                f = open(theFile,'rb')
            except IOError:
                #if open fails report the error
                log.warning('Open Failed:'+ theFile)
                return
            else:
                try:
                    #Attempt to read the file
                    rd = f.read()
                except IOError:
                    #if read fails, then close the file and report error
                    f.close()
                    log.warning('Read Failed:'+ theFile)
                    return
                else:
                    #success the file is open and we can read from it
                    #lets query the file stats
```

一旦文件成功打开并且允许读取,就将与文件相关联的属性提取出来。这些属性包括所有者、分组、大小、MAC时间和模式。这些属性将记录到CSV文件中。

```
theFileStats = os.stat(theFile)
    (mode, ino, dev, nlink, uid, gid, size,
    atime, mtime, ctime) = os.stat(theFile)

#Display progress to the user
DisplayMessage("Processing File: " + theFile)

#convert the file size to a string
fileSize = str(size)

#convert the MAC Times to strings
modifiedTime = time.ctime(mtime)
accessTime = time.ctime(atime)
createdTime = time.ctime(ctime)
```

```
#convert the owner, group and file mode
ownerID = str(uid)
groupID = str(gid)
fileMode = bin(mode)
```

既然文件的属性已经收集,就要正式进行文件的哈希计算。要以用户指定的方法来哈希文件(也就是使用哪一个单向哈希算法)。下面将使用在第2章中就见识过的Python标准库模块hashlib。

```
#process the file hashes
if gl_args.md5:
    #Calcuation the MD5
    hash = hashlib.md5()
    hash.update(rd)
    hexMD5 = hash.hexdigest()
    hashValue = hexMD5.upper()
elif gl_args.sha256:
    #Calculate the SHA256
    hash=hashlib.sha256()
    hash.update(rd)
    hexSHA256 = hash.hexdigest()
    hashValue = hexSHA256.upper()
elif gl_args.sha512:
    #Calculate the SHA512
    hash=hashlib.sha512()
    hash.update(rd)
    hexSHA512 = hash.hexdigest()
    hashValue = hexSHA512.upper()
else:
    log.error('Hash not Selected')
#File processing completed
#Close the Active File
```

既然文件已经处理完成,就应该关闭该文件。接下来使用CSV类将记录写入报告文件中,然后成功地返回到调用函数,在本例中就是WalkPath。

```
f.close()
#write one row to the output file
o_result.writeCSVRow(simpleName,
theFile, fileSize, modifiedTime,
accessTime, createdTime, hashValue,
ownerID, groupID, mode)
return True
```

这一部分发送警告消息到日志文件,这个警告消息与在文件处理过程中遇到的问题有关。

```
else:
    log.warning('['+ repr(simpleName) +', Skipped NOT a File'+']')
    return False
else:
    log.warning('['+ repr(simpleName) +', Skipped Link
```

```
                    NOT a File'+']')
                return False
        else:
            log.warning('['+ repr(simpleName) +', Path does NOT exist'+']')
    return False
```

3.4.6 CSVWriter

在本章最后的代码遍历部分将介绍CSVWriter。正如先前所提到的,将这些代码创建为一个类而非一个函数,使得它更加实用,同时也向你介绍Python中的类概念。这个类只有三个方法,构造器或者init, writeCSVRow和writerClose。让我们逐个看看吧。

```
class _CSVWriter:
```

构造器,也就是ini方法,完成三个基本的初始化工作。

(1)打开输出文件csvFile

(2)初始化csv.writer

(3)写出所有列名组成的标题行。

若在初始化过程中发生了任何差错,将会抛出一个异常,并且产生一个日志项。

```
def __init__(self, fileName, hashType):
    try:
        # create a writer object and write the header row
        self.csvFile = open(fileName,'wb')
        self.writer = csv.writer(self.csvFile,
            delimiter =',', quoting = csv.QUOTE_ALL)
        self.writer.writerow( ('File','Path','Size',
            'Modified Time','Access Time','Created Time',
            hashType,'Owner','Group','Mode') )
    except:
        log.error('CSV File Failure')
```

第二个方法writeCSVRow从HashFile接收一条成功完成了文件的哈希计算后的记录。随后该方法使用csv writer正式地将该记录写入报告文件。

```
def writeCSVRow(self, fileName, filePath, fileSize, mTime,
    aTime, cTime, hashVal, own, grp, mod):
            self.writer.writerow( (fileName, filePath,
                fileSize, mTime, aTime, cTime, hashVal, own, grp, mod))
```

最后如同你预计的,writeClose方法直接关闭了csvFile文件。

```
def writerClose(self):
        self.csvFile.close()
```

3.4.7 pfish.py完整代码清单

```
#
# p-fish : Python File System Hash Program
# Author: C. Hosmer
# July 2013
```

```
# Version 1.0
#
import logging        # Python Standard Library Logger
import time           # Python Standard Library time functions
import sys            # Python Library system specific parameters
import _pfish         # _pfish Support Function Module

if __name__ == '__main__':

    PFISH_VERSION ='1.0'

    # Turn on Logging
    logging.basicConfig(filename='pFishLog.log',level=logging.DEBUG,
    format='%(asctime)s %(message)s')

    # Process the Command Line Arguments
    _pfish.ParseCommandLine()

    # Record the Starting Time
    startTime = time.time()

    # Record the Welcome Message
    logging.info('')
    logging.info('Welcome to p-fish version'+ PFISH_VERSION +'...New Scan Started')
    logging.info('')
    _pfish.DisplayMessage('Welcome to p-fish ... version'+PFISH_VERSION)

    # Record some information regarding the system
    logging.info('System:'+ sys.platform)
    logging.info('Version:'+ sys.version)

    # Traverse the file system directories and hash the files
    filesProcessed = _pfish.WalkPath()

    # Record the end time and calculate the duration
    endTime = time.time()
    duration = endTime - startTime
    logging.info('Files Processed:'+ str(filesProcessed) )
    logging.info('Elapsed Time:'+ str(duration) +'seconds')
    logging.info('')
    logging.info('Program Terminated Normally')
    logging.info('')

    _pfish.DisplayMessage("Program End")
```

3.4.8　_pfish.py完整代码清单

```
#
# pfish support functions, where all the real work gets done
#
# Display Message()        ParseCommandLine()          WalkPath()
# HashFile()               class _CVSWriter
# ValidateDirectory()      ValidateDirectoryWritable()
#

import os                  #Python Standard Library - Miscellaneous
```

```
                              operating system interfaces
import stat                  #Python Standard Library - functions for
                              interpreting os results
import time                  #Python Standard Library - Time access and
                              conversions functions
import hashlib               #Python Standard Library - Secure hashes and
                              message digests
import argparse              #Python Standard Library - Parser for commandline
                              options, arguments
import csv                   #Python Standard Library - reader and writer for
                              csv files
import logging               #Python Standard Library - logging facility

log = logging.getLogger('main._pfish')

#
# Name: ParseCommand() Function
#
# Desc: Process and Validate the command line arguments
#       use Python Standard Library module argparse
#
# Input: none
#
# Actions:
#           Uses the standard library argparse to process the command line
#           establishes a global variable gl_args where any of the functions can
#           obtain argument information
#
def ParseCommandLine():

    parser = argparse.ArgumentParser('Python file system hashing ..p-fish')

    parser.add_argument('-v','--verbose', help='allows progress messages
    to be displayed', action='store_true')

    # setup a group where the selection is mutually exclusive and required.
    group = parser.add_mutually_exclusive_group(required=True)
    group.add_argument('--md5', help ='specifies MD5 algorithm',
    action='store_true')
    group.add_argument('--sha256', help ='specifies SHA256
    algorithm', action='store_true')
    group.add_argument('--sha512', help ='specifies SHA512
    algorithm', action='store_true')

    parser.add_argument('-d','--rootPath', type=
    ValidateDirectory, required=True, help="specify the root
    path for hashing")
    parser.add_argument('-r','--reportPath', type=
    ValidateDirectoryWritable, required=True, help="specify the
    path for reports and logs will be written")

    # create a global object to hold the validated arguments, these will
    be available then
    # to all the Functions within the _pfish.py module

    global gl_args
```

```
        global gl_hashType

        gl_args = parser.parse_args()

        if gl_args.md5:
            gl_hashType ='MD5'
        elif gl_args.sha256:
            gl_hashType ='SHA256
        elif
            gl_args.sha512:
            gl_hashType ='SHA512'
        else:
            gl_hashType = "Unknown"
            logging.error('Unknown Hash Type Specified')

        DisplayMessage("Command line processed: Successfully")

        return
# End ParseCommandLine ====================================
#
# Name: WalkPath() Function
#
# Desc: Walk the path specified on the command line
#           use Python Standard Library module os and sys
#
# Input: none, uses command line arguments
#
# Actions:
#               Uses the standard library modules os and sys
#               to traverse the directory structure starting a root
#               path specified by the user. For each file discovered, WalkPath
#               will call the Function HashFile() to perform the file hashing
#
def WalkPath():

        processCount = 0
        errorCount = 0

        oCVS = _CSVWriter(gl_args.reportPath+'fileSystemReport.csv',
        gl_hashType)

        # Create a loop that process all the files starting
        # at the rootPath, all sub-directories will also be
        # processed

        log.info('Root Path:'+ gl_args.rootPath)

        for root, dirs, files in os.walk(gl_args.rootPath):

        # for each file obtain the filename and call the HashFile Function
            for file in files:
                fname = os.path.join(root, file)
                result = HashFile(fname, file, oCVS)

                # if hashing was successful then increment the ProcessCount
                if result is True:
                    processCount += 1
```

```
                        # if not successful, the increment the ErrorCount
                    else:
                        ErrorCount += 1

            oCVS.writerClose()

            return(processCount)

# End WalkPath ==========================================
#
# Name: HashFile Function
#
# Desc: Processes a single file which includes performing a hash of the file
#            and the extraction of metadata regarding the file processed
#            use Python Standard Library modules hashlib, os, and sys
#
# Input: theFile = the full path of the file
#           simpleName = just the filename itself
#
# Actions:
#            Attempts to hash the file and extract metadata
#            Call GenerateReport for successful hashed files
#
def HashFile(theFile, simpleName, o_result):

        # Verify that the path is valid
        if os.path.exists(theFile):

            # Verify that the path is not a symbolic link
            if not os.path.islink(theFile):

                # Verify that the file is real
                if os.path.isfile(theFile):

                    try:
                        # Attempt to open the file
                        f = open(theFile,'rb')
                    except IOError:
                        # if open fails report the error
                        log.warning('Open Failed:'+ theFile)
                        return
                    else:
                        try:
                            # Attempt to read the file
                            rd = f.read()
                        except IOError:
                            # if read fails, then close the file and
                            report error
                            f.close()
                            log.warning('Read Failed:'+ theFile)
                            return
                        else:
                            # success the file is open and we can read
                              from it
                            # lets query the file stats
```

```python
            theFileStats = os.stat(theFile)
            (mode, ino, dev, nlink, uid, gid, size, atime,
            mtime, ctime) = os.stat(theFile)

            # Print the simple file name
            DisplayMessage("Processing File: " + theFile)

            # print the size of the file in Bytes
            fileSize = str(size)

            # print MAC Times
            modifiedTime = time.ctime(mtime)
            accessTime = time.ctime(atime)
            createdTime = time.ctime(ctime)

            ownerID = str(uid)
            groupID = str(gid)
            fileMode = bin(mode)

            # process the file hashes
            if gl_args.md5:
                # Calcuation and Print the MD5
                hash = hashlib.md5()
                hash.update(rd)
                hexMD5 = hash.hexdigest()
                hashValue = hexMD5.upper()
            elif gl_args.sha256:
                hash=hashlib.sha256()
                hash.update(rd)
                hexSHA256 = hash.hexdigest()
                hashValue = hexSHA256.upper()
            elif gl_args.sha512:
                # Calculate and Print the SHA512
                hash=hashlib.sha512()
                hash.update(rd)
                hexSHA512 = hash.hexdigest()
                hashValue = hexSHA512.upper()
            else:
                log.error('Hash not Selected')
                #File processing completed
                #Close the Active File
                print "==========================="
                f.close()

                # write one row to the output file

                o_result.writeCSVRow(simpleName, theFile,
                fileSize, modifiedTime, accessTime,
                createdTime, hashValue, ownerID, groupID,
                mode)
                return True
        else:
            log.warning('['+ repr(simpleName) +', Skipped NOT a
            File'+']')
            return False
```

```python
            else:
                        log.warning('['+ repr(simpleName) +', Skipped Link
                        NOT a File'+']')
                    return False
    else:
                        log.warning('['+ repr(simpleName) +', Path does NOT
                        exist'+']')
return False
# End HashFile Function ===================================
#
# Name: ValidateDirectory Function
#
# Desc: Function that will validate a directory path as
#           existing and readable. Used for argument validation only
#
# Input: a directory path string
#
# Actions:
#               if valid will return the Directory String
#               if invalid it will raise an ArgumentTypeError within argparse
#               which will in turn be reported by argparse to the user
#
def ValidateDirectory(theDir):

        # Validate the path is a directory
        if not os.path.isdir(theDir):
            raise argparse.ArgumentTypeError('Directory does not exist')

        # Validate the path is readable
        if os.access(theDir, os.R_OK):
            return theDir
        else:
            raise argparse.ArgumentTypeError('Directory is not readable')

# End ValidateDirectory ===================================
#
# Name: ValidateDirectoryWritable Function
#
# Desc: Function that will validate a directory path as
#           existing and writable. Used for argument validation only
#
# Input: a directory path string
#
# Actions:
#               if valid will return the Directory String
#
#               if invalid it will raise an ArgumentTypeError within argparse
#               which will in turn be reported by argparse to the user
#

def ValidateDirectoryWritable(theDir):

    # Validate the path is a directory
```

```python
        if not os.path.isdir(theDir):
            raise argparse.ArgumentTypeError('Directory does not exist')
    # Validate the path is writable
    if os.access(theDir, os.W_OK):
        return theDir
    else:
        raise argparse.ArgumentTypeError('Directory is not writable')
# End ValidateDirectoryWritable ============================
# =========================================================
#
# Name: DisplayMessage() Function
#
# Desc: Displays the message if the verbose command line option is present
#
# Input: message type string
#
# Actions:
#           Uses the standard library print function to display the message
#
def DisplayMessage(msg):

        if gl_args.verbose:
            print(msg)
        return

# End DisplayMessage====================================
#
# Class: _CSVWriter
#
# Desc: Handles all methods related to comma separated value operations
#
# Methods constructor:      Initializes the CSV File
#           writeCVSRow:    Writes a single row to the csv file
#           writerClose:    Closes the CSV File

class _CSVWriter:

    def __init__(self, fileName, hashType):
        try:
            # create a writer object and then write the header row
            self.csvFile = open(fileName,'wb')
            self.writer = csv.writer(self.csvFile, delimiter=',',
            quoting=csv.QUOTE_ALL)
            self.writer.writerow( ('File','Path','Size','Modified Time',
            'Access Time','Created Time', hashType,'Owner','Group',
            'Mode') )
        except:
            log.error('CSV File Failure')

def writeCSVRow(self, fileName, filePath, fileSize, mTime, aTime,
cTime, hashVal, own, grp, mod):

    self.writer.writerow( (fileName, filePath, fileSize, mTime,
```

```
            aTime, cTime, hashVal, own, grp, mod))
    def writerClose(self):
        self.csvFile.close()
```

3.5 结果展示

既然已经将代码完整地走了一遍，而且还进行了深入分析，那就让我们看看结果。在图3.7中，使用如下的选项来运行这个程序。

C:\p-fish>Python pfish.py --md5 –d "c:\\p-fish\\TESTDIR" -r "c:\\p-fish\\" -v

因为使用了-v即verbose选项，程序如同预期的那样，显示了需要处理的每一个文件的信息。

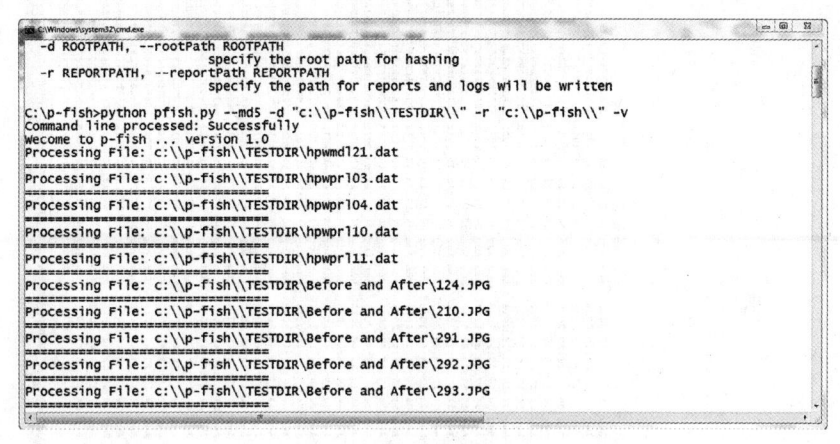

图3.7　pfish.py的测试运行

在图3.8中，查看c:\p-fish目录，会发现在那里生成了两个文件，它们是pfish.py生成的两个文件：

1. fileSystemReport.csv
2. pFishLog.log

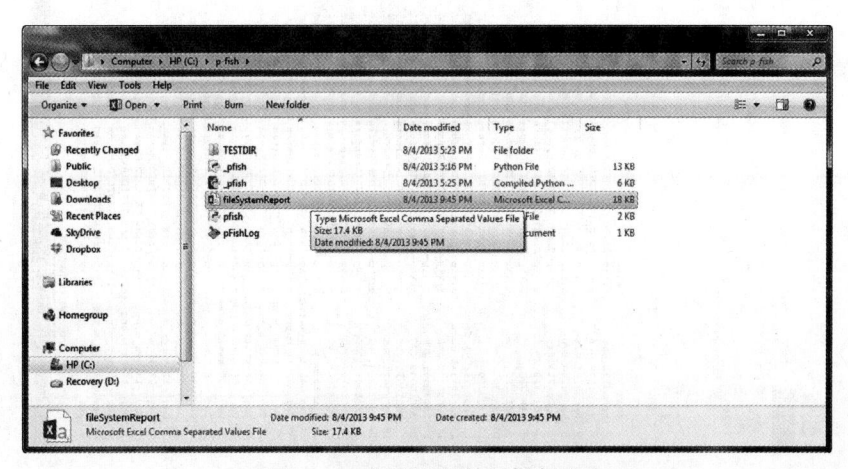

图3.8　pfish运行后的结果保存目录

通过借助Python的csv模块来生成报告文件，Windows已经识别出这是可以通过Microsoft Excel来查看的文件。打开这个文件可以看到如图3.9所示的结果，通过Excel的操作（列排序、寻找特定值、排列日期顺序和逐个查看结果），将会产生一个具有更好的列格式的报告。你会注意到哈希值在名为MD5的列中，之所以显示如此，是因为在csv的初始化中传递了对应的哈希标题值。

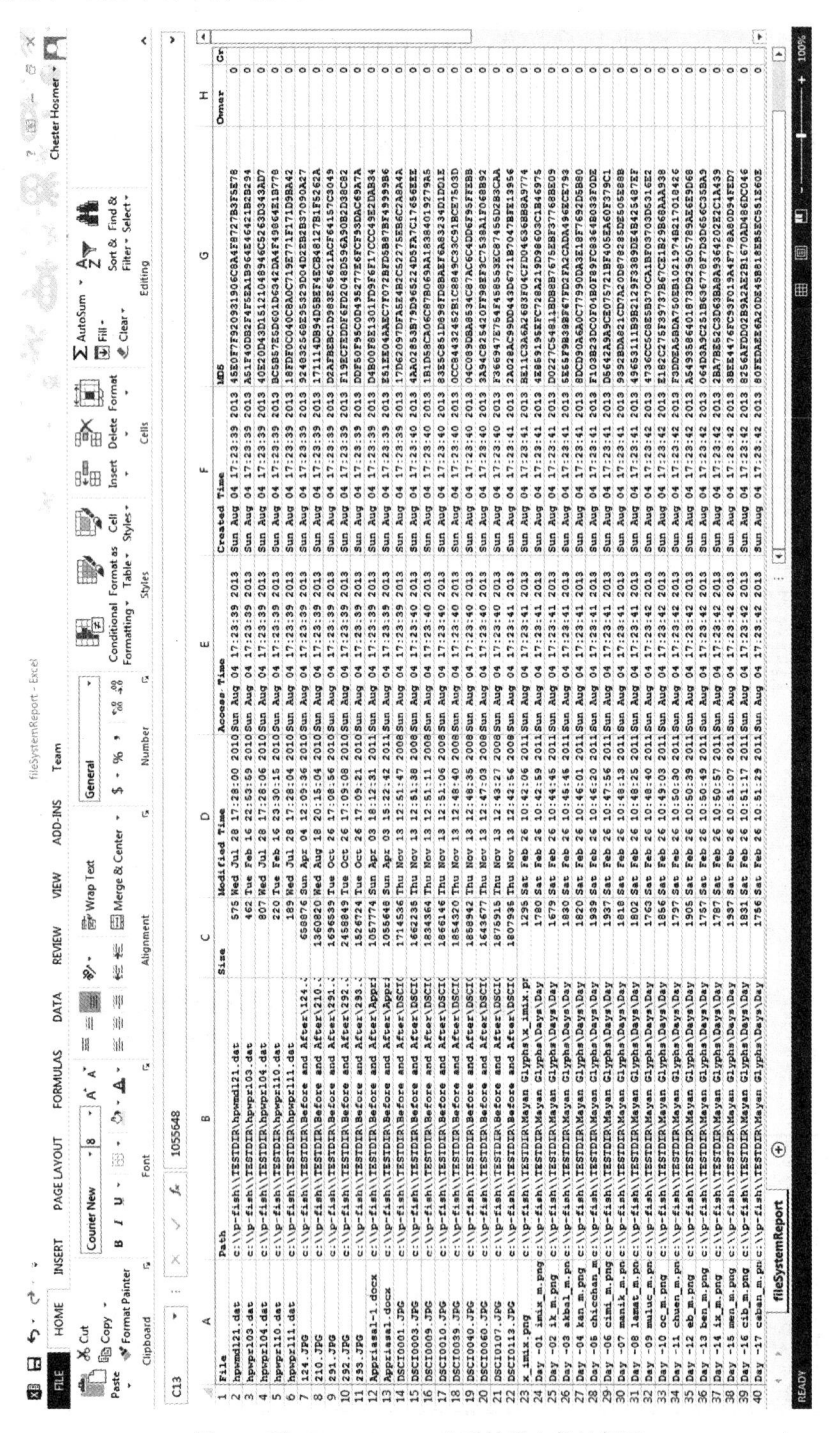

图3.9 用Microsoft Excel查看结果文件的例子

生成的pFishLog.log文件结果描述如图3.10所示。正如所预期的那样，我们找到了那条欢迎消息，还找到了有关Windows环境的细节，用户指定的根路径，处理的文件数量和不超过1 s的运行时间。在这个例子中没有遇到任何错误，程序正常结束。

```
pFishLog - Notepad
File  Edit  Format  View  Help
2013-08-04 21:45:11,042
2013-08-04 21:45:11,042 Welcome to p-fish version 1.0 ... New Scan Started
2013-08-04 21:45:11,059
2013-08-04 21:45:11,059 System: win32
2013-08-04 21:45:11,059 Version: 2.7.5 (default, May 15 2013, 22:43:36) [MSC v.1500 32 bit (Intel)]
2013-08-04 21:45:11,059 Root Path: c:\\p-fish\\TESTDIR\
2013-08-04 21:45:12,042 Files Processed: 82
2013-08-04 21:45:12,042 Elapsed Time: 0.999000072479 seconds
2013-08-04 21:45:12,042
2013-08-04 21:45:12,042 Program Terminated Normally
2013-08-04 21:45:12,042
```

图3.10 pFishLog文件的内容

为迁移到Linux平台运行，只需要复制两个文件。

1. pfish.py
2. _pfish.py

在Linux（本例是Ubuntu 12.04 LTS版本）中的运行无须改变任何Python代码，并且产生了如图3.11到图3.13所示的结果。

```
chet@PythonForensics: ~/Desktop
chet@PythonForensics:~/Desktop$ clear
chet@PythonForensics:~/Desktop$ python pfish.py --sha256 -d /etc/ -r ~/Desktop/ -v
Command line processed: Successfully
Wecome to p-fish ... version 1.0
Processing File: /etc/host.conf
============================
Processing File: /etc/kernel-img.conf
============================
Processing File: /etc/apg.conf
============================
Processing File: /etc/wgetrc
============================
Processing File: /etc/updatedb.conf
============================
Processing File: /etc/crontab
============================
Processing File: /etc/ld.so.cache
============================
Processing File: /etc/gai.conf
============================
Processing File: /etc/blkid.conf
============================
Processing File: /etc/legal
============================
Processing File: /etc/profile
============================
Processing File: /etc/insserv.conf
============================
Processing File: /etc/shells
============================
Processing File: /etc/colord.conf
============================
Processing File: /etc/sysctl.conf
============================
Processing File: /etc/netscsid.conf
============================
Processing File: /etc/fstab
============================
Processing File: /etc/usb_modeswitch.conf
============================
Processing File: /etc/pnm2ppa.conf
```

图3.11 Linux Ubuntu命令行执行

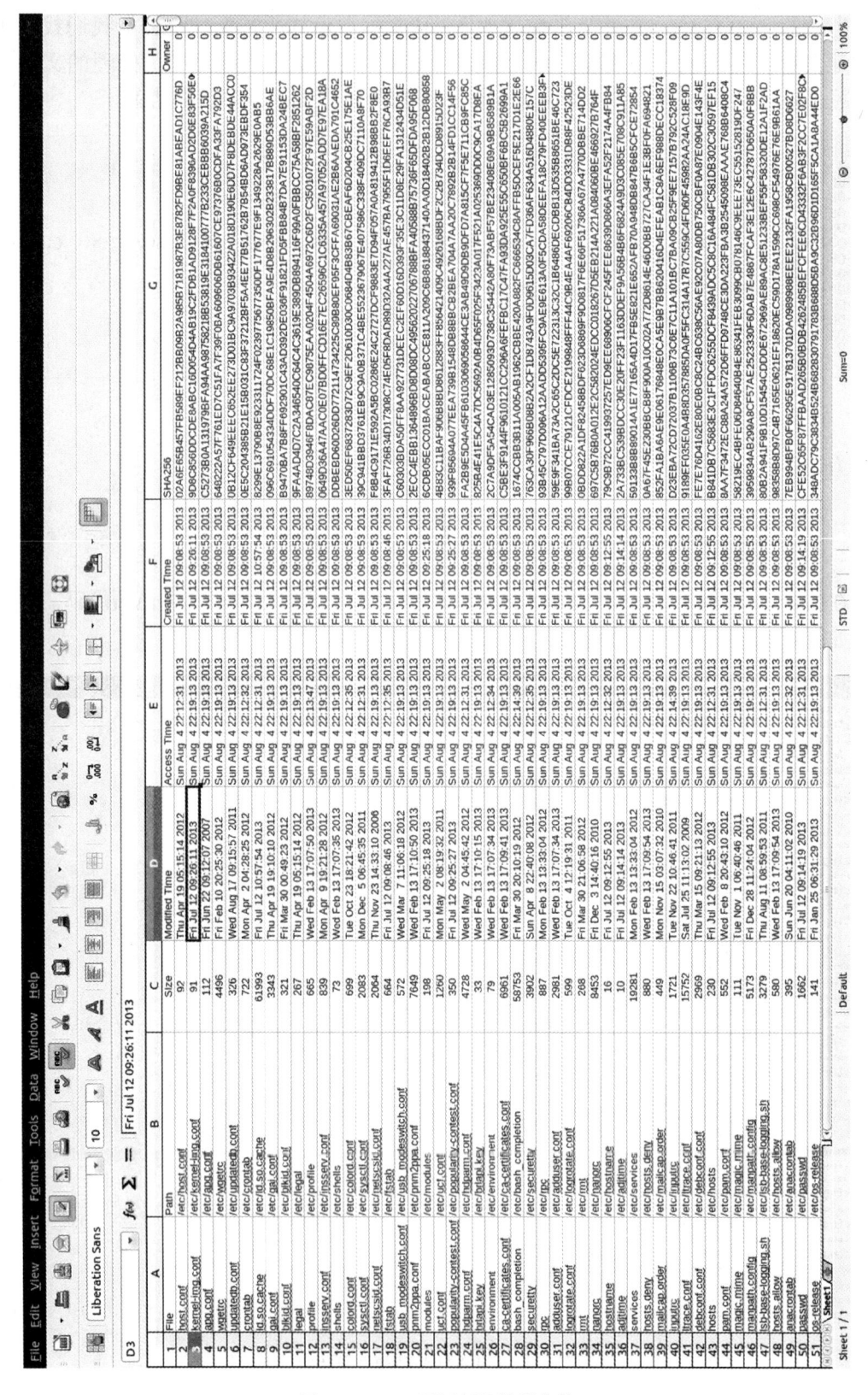

图3.12 Linux下运行的结果文件

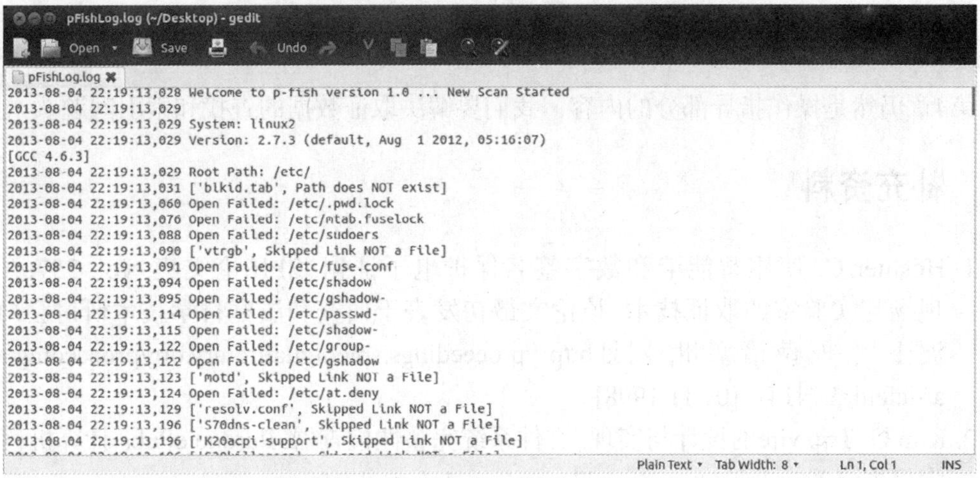

图3.13　Linux下运行产生pFishLog文件

你会注意到在Linux环境下，`pFishLog`文件中有好几个警告，这是由于运行在用户级别的权限下，无法读取/etc目录下的许多文件，以及一些文件由于正在被使用而处于锁定状态。

3.6　章节回顾

在这一章中，创建了我们的第一个实用的Python取证应用程序。这个pfish.py程序可同时运行于Windows和Linux平台。通过巧妙的设计，仅仅使用了Python的标准库模块就完成了我们的代码。我还简要地介绍了argpase，它不仅可以用来解析命令行，还可以在应用程序调用命令行参数之前对其进行验证。

在上述过程中还启用了Python的logger模块，将事件和错误报告给日志记录系统，对我们的操作进行取证意义上的记录。程序还提供给用户在主流哈希算法之间选择的能力，程序提取了每一个处理的文件的主要属性。我还利用CSV模块创建了一个漂亮的格式化输出文件。这个文件能被Windows和Linux的标准应用程序打开和处理。最后实现了我们的第一个Python类，更多的类将在随后章节接踵而至。

3.7　问题小结

1. 如果想添加其他的单向哈希算法，需要修改哪个函数？并且如果只使用Python标准库，还可以使用哪些单向哈希算法？
2. 如果不想使用那两个全局变量，如何通过使用类简单地实现？你将会把哪个函数转换成类，需要创建哪些方法？
3. 你认为还有哪些事件与要素应该记入日志？会怎样去做呢？
4. 还想在报告中看到其他哪些列，应怎样获得这些更多的信息呢？
5. 还应该向记录中添加其他哪些信息（如调查者名或者事件的编号）？如何获取这些信息？

3.8 接下来讲什么

第4章仍然是操作指导部分的内容，我们要解决取证数据的查找和索引问题。

3.9 补充资料

1. Hosmer C. 使用智能卡和数字签名保护电子证据. SPIE论文集, vol. 3576. 犯罪现场与实验室的取证技术. 该论文最初发表于侦查和法庭科学技术研讨会, 1998. 波士顿, 马萨诸塞州, 网址http://proceedings.spiedigitallibrary.org/proceeding.aspx?articleid=974141 [01.11.1998]
2. Kim G. Tripwire的设计与实现: 文件系统完整性检查器. Purdue ePubs 计算机科学技术报告, 1993. 网址http://docs.lib.purdue.edu/cstech/1084/

第4章 使用Python进行取证搜索和索引

4.1 本章简介

搜索绝对是取证调查中的关键性任务之一，如今调查就几乎等同于搜索。知道要搜索什么，在哪里去搜索［在普通文件、删除的文件、松弛空间（slack space）、邮件文件、数据库或者应用程序的数据中］，然后解释搜索的结果，这些都需要经验以及对案情的了解。在过去的几年里证据索引也已经出现，但索引方法的性能遇到窘境。Python编程语言有一些内建的语言机制和标准库模块，有助于进行搜索和索引。

有很多理由要进行搜索和索引，我们要做的不仅仅是单纯的关键字、姓名、哈希等的检查。那么我们进行搜索的背后的动机或理由是什么？当编写一本类似本书这样的著作时，引用虚构的小说或角色通常是要冒风险的，但我相信本书值得这样做。大多数人都或多或少地阅读过柯南·道尔所写的《福尔摩斯探案集》小说和短故事。在这些虚构剧情中，福尔摩斯利用演绎推理和归纳推理的方法建立犯罪理论，并对嫌疑人、受害人甚至旁观者进行画像。

> 演绎推理不用冒风险，也就是说如果有可证明的事实以及一个合理的论据，那么结论必定是确凿的。举例来说：
>
> 1. 所有的男性都属于人类
> 2. 苏格拉底是一个男性
>
> 所以苏格拉底是属于人类。
>
> 另一方面归纳推理具有风险并使用概率，举例来说：
>
> 1. 约翰（John）通常在上午6点离家前往办公室
> 2. 他每天在上午7:30到7:45之间打卡
> 3. 监视摄像头证实约翰今天上午6点迅速地出门，并在上午7:42打卡上班。
>
> 所以，约翰不可能在上午7:05在离办公室三英里外的地方实施谋杀。

不管是基于演绎推理还是归纳推理，这些假设的基础都源自事实。因此我认为进行搜索和索引的理由就是发现事实，然后用它来形成观点和假设。我知道这个过程虽然看起来相当显而易见，但在我们发现可靠的事实之前，有时候会局限于某一种观点。当在数字世界中我们能够快速做出判断时，这一点尤其明显，就像那句话"因为我在互联网上看到它了"。但事实上互联网数据（或数字数据）可能已经被篡改，歪曲了事实。

有经验的调查人员清楚这一点，并且通常在他们的数字犯罪现场调查中非常谨慎。我曾经有机会和很多这样的调查人员一起工作，他们在验证数字证据上非常执着。我已经记不清自己曾有多少次被问到"你对此确定吗？"，或者"你能证明……"，甚至"这件事还会怎样发生？"。最后，当我们进行搜索以发现定罪和无罪证据时需要保持清醒，并且在形成我们的观点和假设之前，确保这两种类型的事实都记录在案。

> 定罪证据支持一个已经形成的假设
> 无罪证据否定一个已经形成的假设

然后这个问题变成了我们希望发现哪些事实？从根本上，答案就是谁、什么、哪里、何时和怎样。为了更加具体些下面列出一些例子。

> 你可能想知道怎样搜索"为什么"。我们趋向于不考虑"为什么"，因为在很多案件中，通过经验、直觉以及对案情的深度了解，这由调查人员自己做出回答。

- 存在哪些文档？其内容以及相互关系是什么？它们何时被创建、修改并最后一次访问，何时被打印以及打印了多少次？这些文件是否被存储或写入闪存设备，亦或是存储在云端？其源头又在哪里？
- 存在哪些多媒体文件，源头是哪里？举例来说，它们是从网络上下载的，还是由嫌疑人或者受害人记录或抓拍的？如果是这样，使用了什么样的照相机或记录设备？
- 谁是我们调查的嫌疑人，我们对其了解多少？我们有照片、电话号码、邮箱地址、家庭住址吗？他们在哪里工作，他们何时到哪里旅行过，他们是否拥有交通工具？如果有，其制造商、车型、年份和车牌号是什么？他们有没有别名（现实世界或者网络世界中的）？
- 谁是和他们有关联的人，对这些人我们了解多少？

我想你已经明白了我的意思，在搜索中可能提出的问题相当广泛，其中有些十分具体，有些则更加一般。在本章中我们肯定不能解决所有这些问题，但是可以从头开始，创建现在就可以帮助我们，并且还能在将来演进的Python程序。

4.2 关键字上下文搜索

关键字上下文搜索具有对像磁盘镜像或者内存快照这样的数据对象进行搜索的能力，以发现与特定上下文和类别相关联的关键字或者短语。例如，想在一个磁盘镜像中搜索下列可卡因毒品代名的所有出现情况：

blow, C, candy, coke, do a line, freeze, girl, happy dust, mama coca, mojo, monster, nose, pimp, shot, smoking gun, snow, sugar, sweet stuff, white powder, base, beat, blast, casper, chalk, devil drug, gravel, hardball, hell, kryptonite, love, moonrocks, rock, scrabble, stones, and tornado.

4.2.1 如何用Python轻松完成

为了使用Python处理关键字搜索，必须先解决几个简单的问题。第一个问题，应该如何存储搜索的单词或短语？Python有一些内建数据类型完美地支持处理这类数据，并有各自不同的性能和规则。基本的类型是集合（set）、列表（list）和字典（dictionary）。我的偏好是创建一个集合来存储这些搜索的单词和短语。Python中的集合为处理这种类型的数据提供了很好的方法，这主要是因为它能够自动消除重复，实现起来简单，对成员的检测也容易。

下面的代码展示了基本用法。从初始化一个名为searchWords的空集合开始，然后代码打开并读取文件narc.txt，它包含与麻醉品有关的单词和短语。当然我将文件操作的异常处理也包含在其中，以确保成功地打开文件并读取其中的每一行。接下来打印出搜索单词和短语的清单，它们是被逐行读取的（注意每行一个单词或短语）。然后在这个清单中搜索单词"kryptonite"，如果在搜索单词清单中存在该单词，就打印出"Found word"，如果不存在该单词，就打印出"not found"。巧妙的一点是，当在searchWords集合里添加单词时指定了line.strip()，这样就去掉了每行结尾的换行符。

```
import sys
searchWords = set()
try:
    fileWords = open('narc.txt')
    for line in fileWords:
        searchWords.add(line.strip())
except:
    print("file handling error)"
    sys.exit()
print(searchWords)
if ('kryptonite' in searchWords):
    print("Found word")
else:
    print("not found)"
```

代码的执行生成了如下的输出：

从集合的内容开始：

{'shot', 'devil drug', 'do a line', 'scrabble', 'casper', 'hell', 'kryptonite', 'mojo', 'blow', 'stones tornado', 'white powder', 'smoking gun', 'happy dust', 'gravel', 'hardball', 'moonrocks', 'monster', 'beat', 'snow sugar', 'coke', 'rock', 'base', 'blast', 'pimp', 'sweet stuff', 'candy', 'chalk', 'nose', 'mama coca', 'freeze girl ' }

随后显示出了针对"kryptonite"产品的搜索结果

Found word

这个简单的代码解决了两个基本难题：

（1）从文件中读入清单放到集合中
（2）对集合进行搜索，确定一个项是否存在于集合中。

然后，我们还必须解决从搜索目标中提取出单词和短语的问题。通常这需要解析二进制文件或者流。这些二进制数据可能是一个内存快照、一个磁盘镜像或者一个网络数据的快照。关键之处是这些数据要么是无格式化的，要么基于数百种标准格式中的一个。这数百种标准格式有的是开源的，有的是专属的，文本和二进制数据混合在一起。因此如果想要开发一个可以提取并比较文本字符串的简单搜索工具，在不考虑其格式或内容的前提下，该怎样实现呢？

我们首先遇到的难题是确定使用哪个Python数据对象存储这些二进制数据。在此选择了Python的字节数组（bytearray）对象，因为它非常符合我们的标准。如同其名，字节数组就是单纯的由字节构成的序列（1字节是8位的无符号值），字节序列从0数组元素开始一直到数组结尾。我将利用几个Python特性的优势，例如将一个文件读入字节数组，此举的核心代码仅需两行。

第一行以二进制方式打开一个文件进行读取，而第二行将文件内容读入一个名为baTarget的字节数组中。你会注意到我给对象"Target"使用了"ba"作为前缀，这样仅是为了使代码更具可读性，任何人都可以立刻辨别出这个对象是字节数组类型的。同样请注意这些代码只是为了举例说明。在真正的程序中，还要检查函数调用的返回值并确保没有任何差错。当我们开始编写真实的程序时，会说明有关的技巧。

```
targetFile = open('file.bin','rb')
baTarget = bytearray(targetFile.read())
```

你可能立即想到一个问题，"我如何知道有多少字节加载到字节数组了？"如同处理其他Python对象一样，这通过使用len函数得到答案。

```
sizeOfTarget = len(baTarget)
```

在图4.1中，可以看到baTarget对象已被创建，以及通过使用len函数，由baTarget决定的sizeOfTarget的值。

Variable	Value
⊟ locals	<dict 0x202e930; len=7>
baTarget	<huge bytearray 0x1f255f0>
baTargetCopy	<huge bytearray 0x1f255f0>
fileWords	<closed file 'c:\\pytest\\narc.txt', mode 'r' at 0x01FAED30>
line	'tornado\n'
⊞ searchWords	<set 0x1fc6120; len=27>
sizeOfTarget	77650
targetFile	<closed file 'c:\\pytest\\capture.raw', mode 'rb' at 0x01FAED88>

图4.1　baTarget对象和baTarget字节数组的字节长度数据截图

4.2.2　基本需求

由于我们已经确定了用于简单文本搜索的新的语言和数据元素，我需要定义程序的基本需求，如表4.1所示。

第4章 使用Python进行取证搜索和索引

表4.1 基本需求

需求编号	需求名称	简单描述
SRCH-001	命令行参数	允许用户指定一个包含关键词的文件（本例使用ASCII码关键字） 允许用户指定一个文件，该文件包含用来搜索的二进制文件 允许用户指定输出的verbose模式，显示搜索进度
SRCH-002	日志	程序必须产生一个符合取证要求的审计日志
SRCH-003	性能	程序应该高效地执行搜索
SRCH-004	输出	程序应该识别出找到的关键词，给出十六进制/ASCII码的打印输出、发现关键词的位置偏移量，以及用来提供上下文环境的前后值
SRCH-005	错误处理	程序必须支持错误处理和操作执行日志，包括文本描述和时间戳

4.2.3 设计考虑

既然已经定义了应用程序的基本需求，就需要将其分解到设计考虑中。针对这个搜索程序，将使用Python的标准库模块和我们开发的专门用于解析目标文件的代码。表4.2描述了从需求到将要利用的模块和函数之间的映射情况。

表4.2 标准库映射

需求	设计考虑	库的选择
用户输入 （001）	用户输入关键词和目标文件	将使用标准库模块的argparse从用户获得输入
性能 （003）	当设计搜索方法时，选择正确的语言和库对象来处理数据是重要的	将使用Python的集合（set）和字节数组（bytearray）和来处理与搜索有关的数据，以提升性能和使得过程可扩展
输出 （004）	必须用容易理解的方式给出搜索结果。亦即描述找到的关键词的偏移量，及其前后值	将使用标准打印函数完成任务，但没有把结果直接写入一个文件，而是将数据写入一个标准输出，这样用户就可以利用管道，将输出导出到一个文件、一个程序或函数
日志和错误处理 （002和005）	错误可能在关键词和目标文件的处理过程中出现，因此必须严格处理这些潜在问题	Python标准库logging模块，可以用它来报告在处理过程中发生的任何事件或错误

接下来将明确搜索功能的整体设计。就像我们在第3章中开发的p-fish程序，这里将使用命令行，命令行参数规定程序的输入。通过使用特别设计的方法，将搜索的结果导出到标准输出设备，这样数据更容易解释。最后将使用内建的日志记录函数，使得这种搜索更具有取证性质（参见图4.2）。

转到内部结构，把程序分成了4个主要组件。分别是Main函数、ParseCommandLine函数、实际的SearchWords函数、用于输出结果的PrintBuffer函数，以及日志记录器

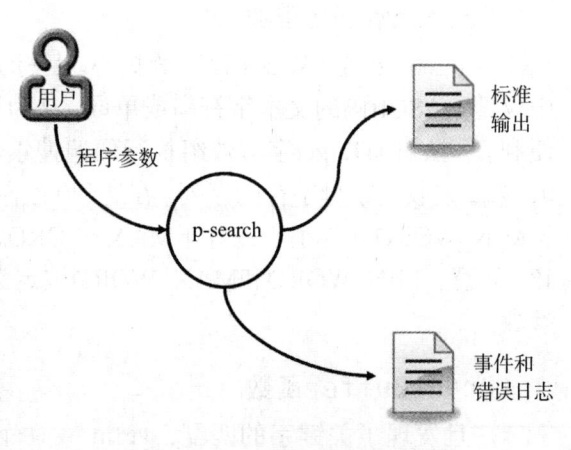

图4.2 p-search的上下文图

（注意它事实上是Python的日志记录模块），它们都被p-search的主要功能所使用。下面我简单地描述每个组件的操作，然后在代码遍历的环节逐行地给出每个函数运行更详细的解释。

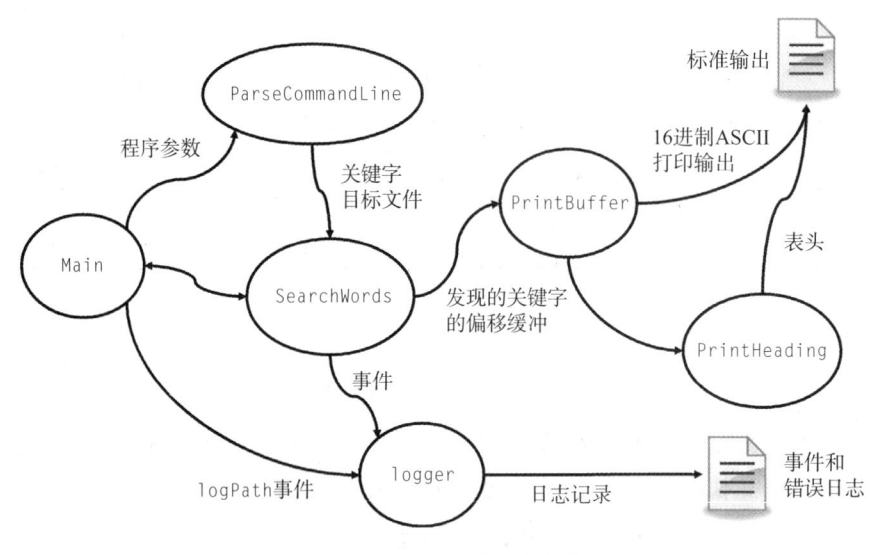

图4.3　p-search的内部结构

Main函数

Main函数的作用是控制这个程序的整体工作流。例如在Main里面我建立起Python日志记录器，显示开始和完成的消息，并保持对时间的跟踪。另外Main还调用命令行解析器，然后启动SearchWords函数。一旦SearchWords完成，Main会记下完成情况，并给用户显示终止消息，并记入日志。

ParseCommandLine函数

为了让p-search流畅运行，利用ParseCommandLine函数来解析和验证用户的输入。一旦完成，核心搜索方法所需的信息就能通过解析器得到。

SearchWords函数

SearchWords是p-search程序的核心。目标是要让这个函数尽可能快速和精确。在本例中仅搜索ASCII码的文本字符串或单词。这为我们创建一个快速高效的搜索提供了极大的便利。算法对baTarget字节数组执行两遍搜索。第一遍将任何不是字母字符的字节转换为0，第二遍收集字母字符的序列。在遇到0之前的连续字母字符序列，如果其长度大于或等于MIN_WORD并且小于或等于MAX_WORD，这些字符将被收集并与关键词集合进行比较。注意，MIN_WORD和MAX_WORD被定义为常量，并且将来可能就是搜索的命令行参数。

PrintBuffer函数

一旦发现了关键字的匹配，PrintBuffer函数将被SearchWords调用。然后文件内的偏移量和Hex/ASCII码内容被发送到标准输出设备。

日志记录器

内建的标准库日志记录器为我们提供了向p-search的日志文件写入信息的能力。程序可以写入信息类消息、警告类消息和错误类消息。由于这将是一个取证应用程序，程序的日志操作就十分重要。可以扩展这个程序以记录代码中更多的事件，这些扩展代码可以添加到任何一个_p-search函数中。

编写代码

再次将代码分割成源文件p-search.py和_p-search.py，其中_p-search.py为p-search提供支持性和关键性的函数。在图4.4中可以看到WingIDE环境下p-search程序的运行。左上角显示的是本地变量和全局变量。在正上方的面板中不难看到程序的输出，显示的是单词"tornado"的匹配情况，以及输出详细的Hex/ASCII码表示。在最右边列出的是程序相关文件。最后在屏幕的底部可以看见程序的源代码。在随后的环节中将会把关键代码要点走一遍，以展示详细的方法和所采用的思路。

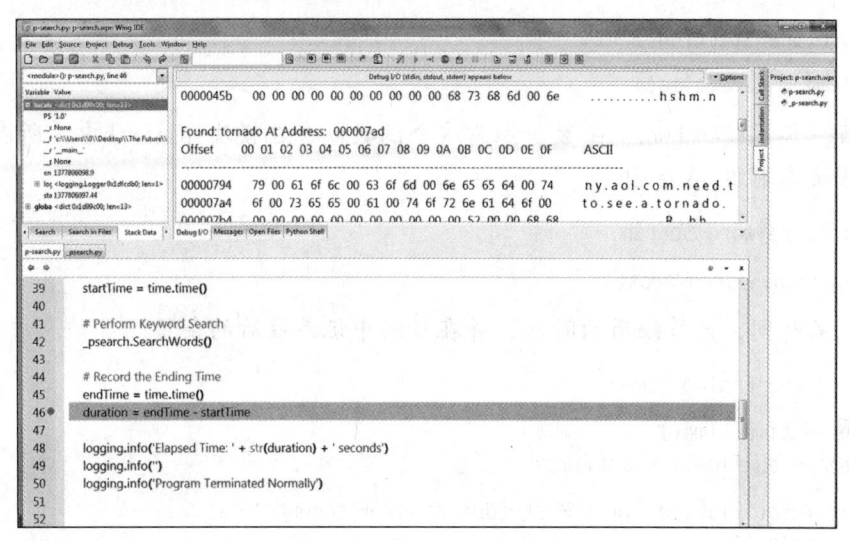

图4.4　WingIDE中运行p-search

4.3　代码遍历

在讨论每一部分代码时会插入一些解释。代码的遍历将为你提供程序全部代码的深度视图。我会带你首先把每一个关键函数走一遍，然后提供p-search.py和_psearch.py这两个文件的完整清单。

4.3.1　分析Main——代码遍历

```
import logging
import time
import _psearch
```

对于main程序，需要从Python标准库导入logging来记录取证事件，导入time来计算程序运行了多久，我们还要导入包含了支持性和核心函数的_psearch模块。

```
if __name__ == '__main__':
    P-SEARCH_VERSION = '1.0'
    # Turn on Logging
    logging.basicConfig ( filename = 'pSearchLog.log',
    level = logging.DEBUG, format = '%(asctime)s %(message)s')
```

下一步调用命令行解析器获得用户传入的程序参数。

```
# Process the Command Line Arguments
_psearch.ParseCommandLine()
```

然后设定日志记录器，并把启动事件发送给日志记录器。

```
log = logging.getLogger('main._psearch')
log.info("p-search started")
```

记录程序运行的开始时间，以便计算当搜索完成时经历的时间。

```
# Record the Starting Time
startTime = time.time()
```

下一步，调用SearchWords函数。注意这个函数包含在模块_psearch中，所以必须在调用时加上模块名前缀_psearch。

```
# Perform Keyword Search
    _psearch.SearchWords()
```

记录结束时间，计算经历的时间，并在日志中记录最后的条目。

```
# Record the Ending Time
endTime = time.time()
duration = endTime - startTime
logging.info('Elapsed Time:'+ str(duration) +'seconds')
logging.info('')
logging.info('Program Terminated Normally')
```

4.3.2　分析_p-search函数——代码遍历

余下的函数包含在文件_p-search.py文件中。该文件由导入所需模块开始，包括处理命令行参数的argparse。os模块是为了处理文件的I/O操作。最后，logging用于实现取证的日志记录功能。

```
import argparse
import os
import logging
```

4.3.3　分析ParseCommandLine

对于p-search程序，只需用户提供2个参数，就是包含搜索关键词的文件的完整路径名，以及我们希望进行搜索文件的完整路径名。verbose模式是可选的，如果未提供该值，程序的消息将被禁止显示（参见表4.3）。

第 4 章　使用 Python 进行取证搜索和索引

表4.3　p-search命令行参数定义

选型	设计的考虑	库的选择
-v	verbose，如果此选项指定，任何对函数DisplayMessage() 的调用将显示到标准输出设备，否则程序将静默运行	
-k	keyword，此选项允许用户指定包含关键词文件的路径	这个文件必须存在并且可读，否则程序将终止
-t	target，此选项允许用户指定被搜索的文件路径	这个文件必须存在并且可读，否则程序将终止

如同所看到的，ParseCommandLine可以接受3个参数：verbose，keywords和srchTarget。其中keywords和srchTarget是必需的参数，它们也会被函数ValidateFileName()验证。

```
def ParseCommandLine():
    parser = argparse.ArgumentParser('Python Search')

    parser.add_argument('-v','--verbose', help = "enables printing of
    program messages", action ='store_true')

    parser.add_argument('-k','--keyWords', type = ValidateFileRead,
    required = True, help = "specify the file containing search words)"

    parser.add_argument('-t','--srchTarget', type = ValidateFileRead,
    required = True, help = "specify the target file to search)"
```

接下来建立一个全局变量来存储parse_args运算的结果。

```
    global gl_args
    gl_args = parser.parse_args()
    DisplayMessage("Command line processed: Successfully")
    return
```

argparse的出色特性之一是为每个选项提供帮助消息的能力。由此无论何时当用户在命令行中指定-h，argparse便自动显示相应的反馈信息。这样就允许开发者提供尽可能多的信息，帮助用户提供正确的回应，这就是所谓的verbose模式。图4.5说明了p-search的-h选项的操作。

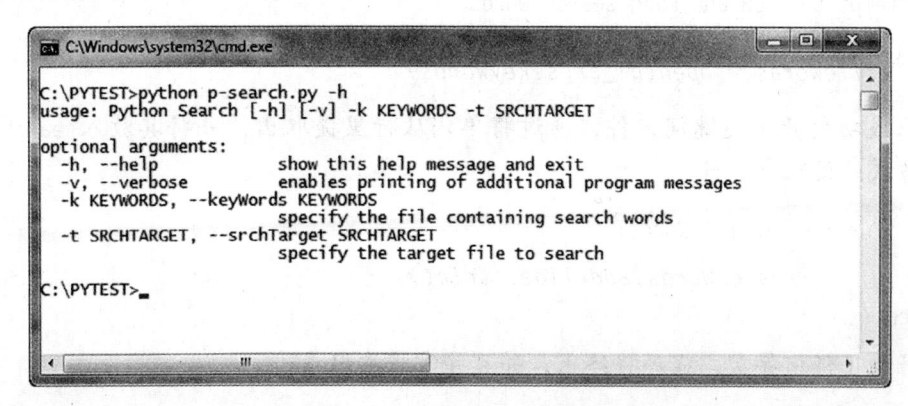

图4.5　p-search的-h选项的操作

4.3.4 分析ValidateFileRead(theFile)

这个函数通过验证用户提供的文件名来支持ParseCommandLine和parser.parse_args()。该函数首先确保文件是存在的，然后证实这些文件是可读的。只要这两个检测中的任何一个未通过，就会导致程序终止并将会引起相应的异常。

```
def ValidateFileRead(theFile):
  # Validate the path is a valid
    if not os.path.exists(theFile):
        raise argparse.ArgumentTypeError('File does not exist')
  # Validate the path is readable
    if os.access(theFile, os.R_OK):
        return theFile
    else:
        raise argparse.ArgumentTypeError('File is not readable')
```

4.3.5 分析SearchWords函数

p-search的核心是SearchWords函数，它将用户提供的关键词与指定目标文件的内容进行比较。我们将逐行地看看SearchWords的代码。

```
def SearchWords():
    # Create an empty set of search words
```

正如在设计考虑中提及的，我决定使用一个Python集合对象保存要搜索的关键词。为此只需要将searchWords赋值为一个集合对象。

```
searchWords = set()
```

接下来需要从用户在命令行参数中指定的文件中载入关键字。通过使用"try, except, finally"的方法确保我们能捕获到所有的错误。

```
# Attempt to open and read search words
try:
    fileWords = open(gl_args.keyWords)
```

一旦成功打开了关键词文件，通过将单词从行里提取出，并将其放入searchWords集合中的方式来处理每一行。

```
    for line in fileWords:
        searchWords.add(line.strip())
except:
```

若产生了任何异常，程序将终止，并且异常将被记录。

```
    log.error('Keyword File Failure:'+ gl_args.keyWords)
    sys.exit()
finally:
```

当成功处理了所有的行后，文件关闭。

```
        fileWords.close()
# Create Log Entry Words to Search For
```

随后，将所有的关键词写入取证日志，以记录要搜索的这些关键字。

```
log.info('Search Words')
log.info('Input File:'+gl_args.keyWords)
log.info(searchWords)

# Attempt to open and read the target file
# and directly load the file into a bytearray
```

既然有了要搜索的关键词，下一步就要读取提供的目标文件，并将数据存储到 Python 的字节数组对象中。

```
try:
    targetFile = open(gl_args.srchTarget,'rb')
    baTarget = bytearray(targetFile.read())
except:
```

所有的异常都会被捕获、记录，同时程序会退出。

```
    log.error('Target File Failure:'+ gl_args.srchTarget)
    sys.exit()
finally:
    targetFile.close()
```

成功后记录了目标文件的大小。

```
sizeOfTarget = len(baTarget)
# Post to log
```

我还将这些信息记录到取证日志文件中。

```
log.info('Target of Search:'+ gl_args.srchTarget)
log.info('File Size:'+str(sizeOfTarget))
```

通过用0替代所有非字母字符的方式对baTarget进行修改。为了确保可以显示目标文件的原始内容，还进行了备份。

```
baTargetCopy = baTarget
# Search Loop
# step one, replace all non characters with zero's
```

搜索的第一步是遍历目标并用0替代所有非字母字符，使得关键词的搜索更为简单而迅速。下面的循环从文件的开头进行替代。

```
for i in range(0, sizeOfTarget):
    character = chr(baTarget[i])
    if not character.isalpha():
        baTarget[i] = 0

# step # 2 extract possible words from the bytearray
# and then inspect the search word list
```

现在字节数组baTarget仅包含有效的字母字符和0,对所有连续字母字符序列的长度计数,如果序列满足定义的字符长度特征,便可以在较小的关键词清单中检查是否出现收集到的字符序列。

create an empty list of not found items

为周密起见,我将创建一个未被找到的字符序列的列表,这种序列满足我们的字符序列条件,但不与用户指定的关键词匹配。

notFound = []

现在开始真正的搜索。直接检查每一个字节,如果其是一个字符便将计数加1。如果遇到0,将停止计数,检查是否遇到了足够多的,有资格作为可能单词的连续字符。如果不是,便会将计数清零并继续搜索。另一方面,如果计数满足最小和最大字符数条件,便得到了一个可能的单词。

```
cnt = 0
for i in range(0, sizeOfTarget):
    character = chr(baTarget[i])
    if character.isalpha():
        cnt += 1
    else:
        if (cnt >= MIN_WORD and cnt <= MAX_WORD):
            newWord = " "
```

如果得到了一个满足条件的序列,就需要收集跳读过的字符。一个小窍门便是在满足条件之前,无须费力地收集和构造可能的字符串。一旦条件满足,就进行回溯,将连续的字符组合在一起并将其存储在变量newWord中。使用变量newWord对关键词集合进行搜索。

```
        for z in range(i-cnt, i):
            newWord = newWord + chr(baTarget[z])
```

为了搜索存储在searchWords中的关键词集合,只需编写一行检测代码。这便是为存储关键字而适当选择正确对象类型的威力所在。

```
        if (newWord in searchWords):
```

如果在searchWord列表中得到一个命中,就用命中的细节作为参数来调用PrintBuffer函数。这些参数包括找到的单词、在缓冲区内的偏移、保存的未被修改的缓冲区,以及从哪里开始打印结果和在哪里结束。

```
            PrintBuffer(newWord, i-cnt, baTargetCopy, i-PREDECESSOR_SIZE,
            WINDOW_SIZE)
                print
            else:
                notFound.append(newWord)
                cnt = 0
    else:
        cnt = 0
```

在处理完整个字节数组之后,还打印出所创建的notFound列表,这将把不在关键词列表中,但疑似的单词提供给调查人员,以供考虑。

```
PrintNotFound(notFound)
# End of SearchWords Function
```

分析PrintBuffer函数

大多数从事网络犯罪调查的专业人士会经常使用十六进制编辑器或者查看器。PrintBuffer函数就是一个使用Python编写的非常简单的Hex和ASCII查看器。它足够简单，可以在几乎任何平台上运行（Windows、Linux、Mac，甚至移动设备）。这并非异想天开之事，而是有着事实强力支撑的。让我们看看此举是如何利用短短的几行Python代码实现的。

```
def PrintBuffer(word, directOffset, buff, offset, hexSize):
```

该函数的输入如下：

word：识别出的字母字符串
directOffset：字母字符串在目标文件内起始处的偏移量
buff：实际缓冲区
Offset：Hex/ASCII区域应该开始的偏移量
hexSize：需要显示的字节长度

从打印基本情况、单词和该字符串找到的偏移量开始。

```
print "Found: "+ word + " At Address: ",
print "%08x " % (directOffset)
```

随后，将打印如下的标题行：

```
Offset 00 01 02 03 04 05 06 07 08 09 0A 0B 0C 0D 0E 0F ASCII
    PrintHeading()
```

然后，只需要打印出在缓冲区中找到的从指定偏移开始的Hex和ASCII值。外层循环连续的分块大小为16，因为每一行将包含接下来的16个值。因为我们是以十六进制的方式打印，所以这就是选择分块大小为16的意义所在。

```
for i in range(offset, offset+hexSize, 16):
    for j in range(0,17):
```

随后内层循环需要以十六进制方式打印出接下来16个字节中的每一个字节。从打印十六进制的偏移值开始，余下的每一行也做同样处理。还需注意，我使用了语法%08x，这就允许显示以0填充高位的8位十六进制地址。对于本演示程序，这已经足够了。

```
        if (j == 0):
            print "%08x " % i,
        else:
            byteValue = buff[i+j]
            print "%02x " % byteValue,
print "      ",
```

然后重复此循环，但是这一次打印的是ASCII字符的内容而非十六进制值。

```
for j in range (0,16):
    byteValue = buff[i+j]
```

为了避开所有特殊字符，仅显示ASCII可打印集合，并用句号代替其他值。

```
    if (byteValue >= 0x20 and byteValue <= 0x7f):
        print "%c" % byteValue,
    else:
        print '.',
print
# End Print Buffer
```

4.4 结果展示

现在把过程遍历一遍，并且深入分析了代码，让我们看看结果。图4.6是包含所有必要文件的目录截图。这里包括两个Python程序文件p-search.py和_p-search.py，以及一个包含搜索单词的narc.txt文件，Capture.raw是包含了我们想要进行搜索的二进制数据的文件。pSearchLog.log是由p-search输出产生的取证日志文件，最后，results.txt是包含了标准输出结果的文件，可以导入其他程序以方便查看。

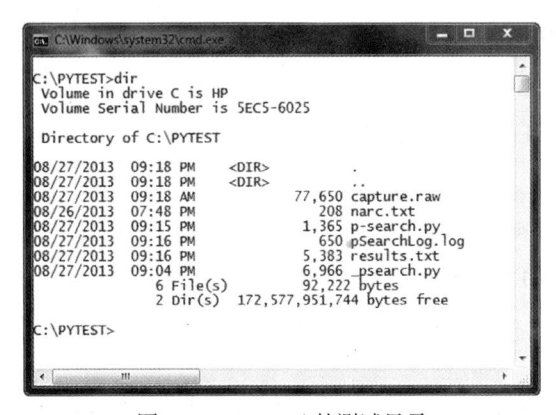

图4.6 p-search的测试目录

图4.7列出了narc.txt文件的内容，它包含我们要搜索的有关毒品的关键词。

图4.7 关键字文件的内容

图4.8是从命令行入口开始的程序的直接输出，该命令行指定结果导出到results.txt文件中。图中也包括results.txt的内容。可以看到在目标文件中找出了3个匹配，包括sugar、tornado和moonrocks。图中同样可以看到程序所产生的Hex/ASCII输出，以及下方的未被识别出的单词。

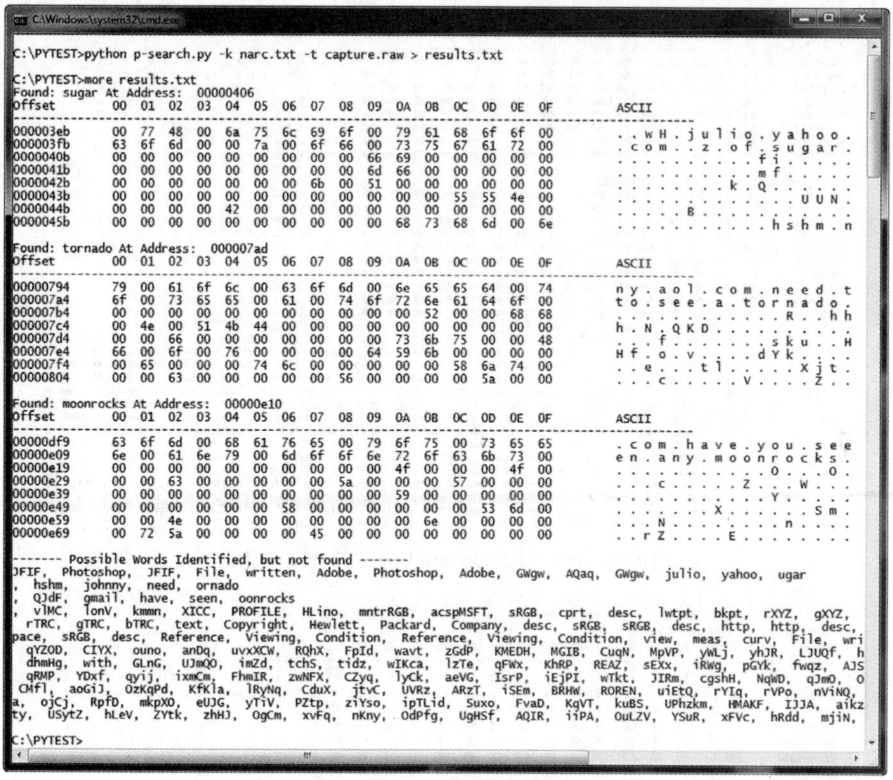

```
C:\PYTEST>python p-search.py -k narc.txt -t capture.raw > results.txt

C:\PYTEST>more results.txt
Found: sugar At Address:   00000406
Offset      00  01  02  03  04  05  06  07  08  09  0A  0B  0C  0D  0E  0F         ASCII
-------------------------------------------------------------------------------------------
000003eb    00  77  48  00  6a  75  6c  69  6f  00  79  61  68  6f  6f  00         . . w H . j u l i o . y a h o o .
000003fb    63  6f  6d  00  00  7a  00  6f  66  00  73  75  67  61  72  00         . c o m . . z . o f . s u g a r .
0000040b    00  00  00  00  00  00  00  00  00  66  69  00  00  00  00  00         . . . . . . . . . . f i . . . . .
0000041b    00  00  00  00  00  00  00  00  00  6d  66  00  00  00  00  00         . . . . . . . . . . m f . . . . .
0000042b    00  00  00  00  00  00  00  6b  00  51  00  00  00  00  00  00         . . . . . . . . k . Q . . . . . .
0000043b    00  00  00  00  00  00  00  00  00  00  00  00  55  55  4e  00         . . . . . . . . . . . . . U U N .
0000044b    00  00  00  00  42  00  00  00  00  00  00  00  00  00  00  00         . . . . . B . . . . . . . . . . .
0000045b    00  00  00  00  00  00  00  00  00  00  68  73  68  6d  00  6e         . . . . . . . . . . . h s h m . n

Found: tornado At Address:   000007ad
Offset      00  01  02  03  04  05  06  07  08  09  0A  0B  0C  0D  0E  0F         ASCII
-------------------------------------------------------------------------------------------
00000794    79  00  61  6f  6c  00  63  6f  6d  00  6e  65  65  64  00  74         n y . a o l . c o m . n e e d . t
000007a4    6f  00  73  65  65  00  61  00  74  6f  72  6e  61  64  6f  00         t o . s e e . a . t o r n a d o .
000007b4    00  00  00  00  00  00  00  00  00  00  00  52  00  00  68  68         . . . . . . . . . . . . R . . h h
000007c4    00  4e  00  51  4b  44  00  00  00  00  00  00  00  00  00  00         h . N . Q K D . . . . . . . . . .
000007d4    00  00  66  00  00  00  00  00  00  00  73  6b  75  00  00  48         . . . f . . . . . . . s k u . . H
000007e4    66  00  6f  00  76  00  00  00  00  64  59  6b  00  00  00  00         H f . o . v . . . . d Y k . . . .
000007f4    00  65  00  00  00  74  6c  00  00  00  00  00  58  6a  74  00         . . e . . . t l . . . . . X j t .
00000804    00  00  63  00  00  00  00  00  56  00  00  00  00  5a  00  00         . . . c . . . . . V . . . . Z . .

Found: moonrocks At Address:   00000e10
Offset      00  01  02  03  04  05  06  07  08  09  0A  0B  0C  0D  0E  0F         ASCII
-------------------------------------------------------------------------------------------
00000df9    63  6f  6d  00  68  61  76  65  00  79  6f  75  00  73  65  65         . c o m . h a v e . y o u . s e e
00000e09    6e  00  61  6e  79  00  6d  6f  6f  6e  72  6f  63  6b  73  00         e n . a n y . m o o n r o c k s .
00000e19    00  00  00  00  00  00  00  00  00  00  4f  00  00  00  4f  00         . . . . . . . . . . . O . . . O .
00000e29    00  00  63  00  00  00  00  00  5a  00  00  00  57  00  00  00         . . . c . . . . . Z . . . W . . .
00000e39    00  00  00  00  00  00  00  00  00  00  59  00  00  00  00  00         . . . . . . . . . . . Y . . . . .
00000e49    00  00  00  00  00  00  58  00  00  00  00  00  00  53  6d  00         . . . . . . . X . . . . . . S m .
00000e59    00  00  4e  00  00  00  00  00  00  00  00  6e  00  00  00  00         . . . N . . . . . . . . n . . . .
00000e69    00  72  5a  00  00  00  00  45  00  00  00  00  00  00  00  00         . . r Z . . . . E . . . . . . . .

------- Possible Words Identified, but not found -------
JFIF,  Photoshop,  JFIF,  File,  written,  Adobe,  Photoshop,  Adobe,  GWgw,  AQaq,  GWgw,  julio,  yahoo,  ugar
,  hshm,  johnny,  need,  ornado
,  QJdF,  gmail,  have,  seen,  oonrocks
,  vlMC,  lonV,  kmmn,  XICC,  PROFILE,  HLino,  mntrRGB,  acspMSFT,  sRGB,  cprt,  desc,  lwtpt,  bkpt,  rXYZ,  gXYZ,
 rTRC,  gTRC,  bTRC,  text,  Copyright,  Hewlett,  Packard,  Company,  desc,  sRGB,  sRGB,  desc,  http,  http,  desc,
pace,  sRGB,  desc,  Reference,  Viewing,  Condition,  Reference,  Viewing,  Condition,  view,  meas,  curv,  File,  wri
 qYZOD,  CIYX,  ouno,  anDq,  uvxXCW,  RQhX,  FpId,  wavt,  zGdP,  KMEDH,  MGIB,  CuqN,  MpVP,  yWLj,  yhJR,  LJUQf,  h
 dhmHg,  with,  GLnG,  UJmQO,  imZd,  tchS,  tidz,  wIKca,  lzTe,  qFWx,  KhRP,  REAZ,  sEXx,  iRWg,  pGYk,  fwqz,  AJS
 qRMP,  YDxf,  qyij,  ixmCm,  FhmIR,  zwNFX,  CZyq,  lyCk,  aeVG,  IsrP,  iEjPI,  wTkt,  JIRm,  cgshH,  NqWD,  qJmO,  O
 CMfl,  aoGiJ,  OzKqPd,  KfKla,  lRyNq,  CduX,  jtvC,  UVRz,  ARzT,  iSEm,  BRHW,  ROREN,  uiEtQ,  rYIq,  rVPo,  nViNQ,
a,  ojCj,  RpfD,  mkpXO,  eUJG,  yTiV,  PZtp,  ziYso,  ipTLid,  Suxo,  FvaD,  KqVT,  kuBS,  UPhzkm,  HMAKF,  IJJA,  aikz
ty,  USytZ,  hLeV,  ZYtk,  zhHJ,  OgCm,  xvFq,  nKny,  OdPfg,  UgHSf,  AQIR,  iiPA,  OuLZV,  YSuR,  xFVc,  hRdd,  mjiN,

C:\PYTEST>
```

图4.8　p-search运行示例

最后在图4.9中，看到了由p-search生成的日志文件的内容，包括了开始消息、搜索单词文件及其内容，还包含目标文件capture.raw的名字和大小。最终，可以看到程序执行所花费的秒数和程序结束的消息。

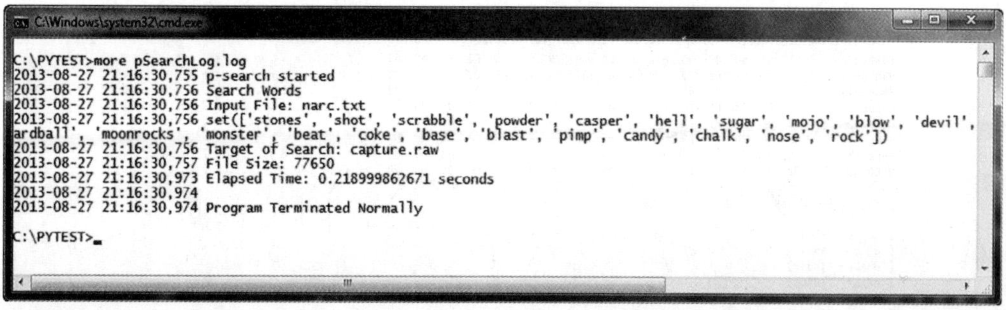

```
C:\PYTEST>more pSearchLog.log
2013-08-27 21:16:30,755 p-search started
2013-08-27 21:16:30,756 Search Words
2013-08-27 21:16:30,756 Input File: narc.txt
2013-08-27 21:16:30,756 set(['stones', 'shot', 'scrabble', 'powder', 'casper', 'hell', 'sugar', 'mojo', 'blow', 'devil',
ardball', 'moonrocks', 'monster', 'beat', 'coke', 'base', 'blast', 'pimp', 'candy', 'chalk', 'nose', 'rock'])
2013-08-27 21:16:30,756 Target of Search: capture.raw
2013-08-27 21:16:30,757 File Size: 77650
2013-08-27 21:16:30,973 Elapsed Time: 0.218999862671 seconds
2013-08-27 21:16:30,974
2013-08-27 21:16:30,974 Program Terminated Normally

C:\PYTEST>_
```

图4.9　列出日志文件内容

为了圆满说明本程序并证明其可移植性，我还涵盖了程序未经修改地在Linux（参见图4.10）和iMac（参见图4.11）平台上的另外两个运行截图。

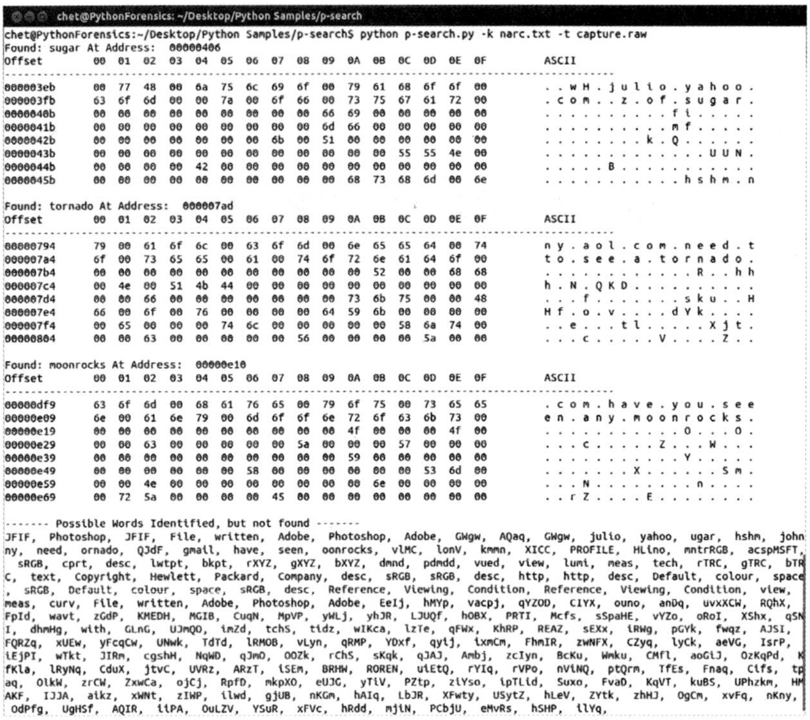

图4.10　p-search在Ubuntu Linux 12.04 LTS上运行

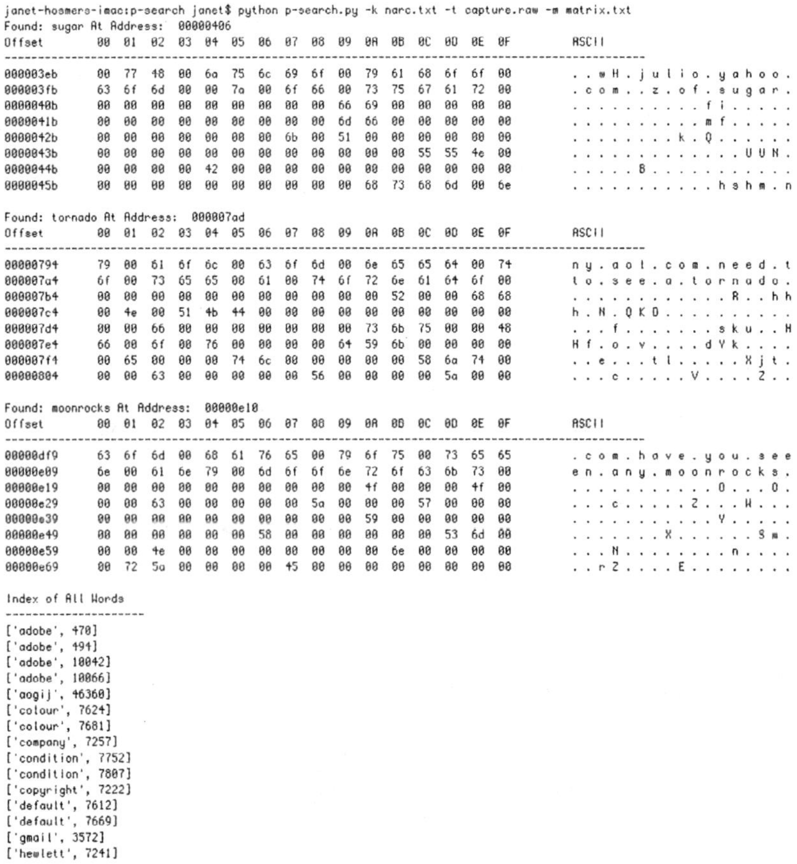

图4.11　p-search在iMac上运行

4.5 索引

索引为调查人员提供一种查看数据和潜在证据的不同视图，潜在证据可能包含于文件、磁盘镜像、内存快照或者网络痕迹中。我们不再是搜索什么关键字，而是需要p-search给我们提供一个满足最小字符串定义的所有单词的列表，并且无须匹配任何关键词定义。然而，我们当前展示的方法缺少两块关键的数据。第一个问题较为简单，只需要确定每一个在目标文件中找到的字符串的偏移。第二个问题则相对更具挑战性，即只打印出可能的合法单词。最后，如果能提供一个排序的单词列表则更好。

为了解决这个更为困难的问题，即找出所有的具有高度可能性是单词的字符串，我设计出一种非常有效且快速的方法，在图4.12中描述了其基本概念。首先使用了一种算法对已知的单词进行处理，即基于每一个单词的内部特征产生其数字权重值。

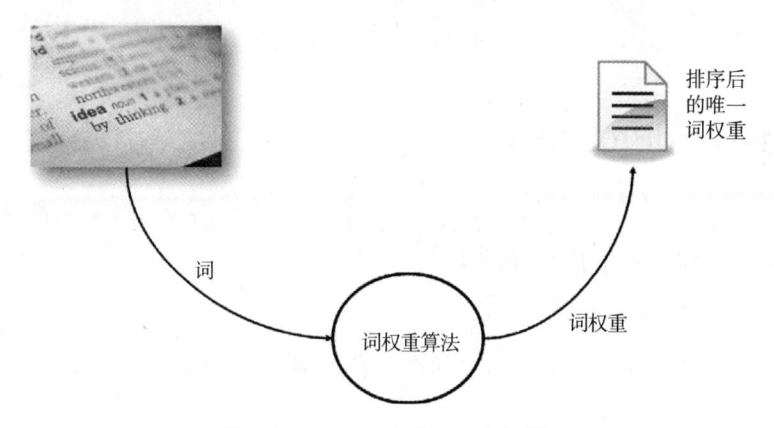

图4.12　p-search在iMac上运行

一旦计算出了单词的数字权重值，这些权重值便被排序，并且去掉所有重复的部分。此处的关键是处理一个庞大的单词列表。就本例而言，使用了一个包含超过六十万单词的字典。这样就产生了一个原始权重值矩阵，可以用来将在原始数据中找到的字符串（采用与构建原始权重值矩阵相同的权重算法进行处理）与此矩阵进行对比。若在该矩阵中找到了所计算出的权重值，我会认为这可能是一个单词，反之，该字符串将被丢弃。图4.13说明了这种方法如何工作。单词中所包含的每一个核心字母（忽略前导字符）将被用于权重的计算。

由于有相当数量的单词，至少在英语语言中，是由其他单词衍生而来的，这便不再需要有一个包含了所有可能单词的字典。而且如果单词出现了拼写错误，或者是新创建或派生的，那么这种权重方法相比较直接匹配方法而言，对于单词的可能性提供了更加宽泛的解释。

> 近似搜索和索引的价值是至关重要的。例如在Casey Anthony案件中，调查人员遗漏了可以作为证据的互联网搜索历史数据，因为他们只查找"他们"正确拼写的各种搜索条目，然而她错误地拼写了几个条目，尽管Google在搜索中纠正了拼写，但并未纠正互联网搜索历史中的拼写错误。

用于权重计算

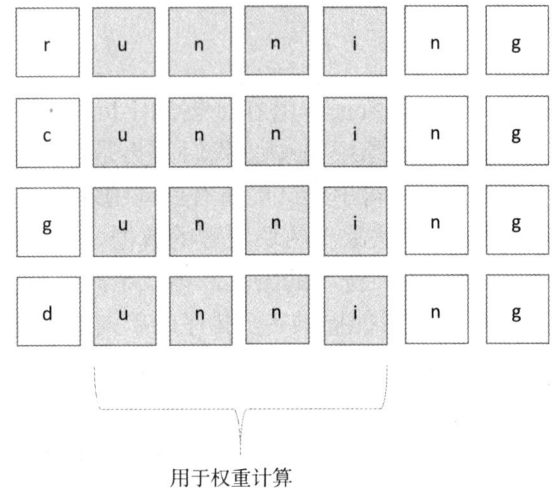

图4.13 权重特征示例

4.6 编写isWordProbable

为了构建isWordProbable(word)方法，我创建了一个命名为Matrix的类。像前面一样，让我们深入地探讨一下这个新的类。

class class_Matrix:

从声明一个命名为weighted matrix的新的集合对象开始。

weightedMatrix = set()

当类被实例化，这个对象将加载包含于矩阵中的值到weightedMatrix集合，为此只需要添加一个新的命令行参数-m或--theMatrix，以允许用户指定一个矩阵文件。就像在前面看到的那样采取了一些预防措施，以捕获在文件操作中出现的任何错误。

```
def __init__(self):
   try:
           fileTheMatrix = open(gl_args.theMatrix,'rb')
           for line in fileTheMatrix:
                   value = line.strip()
                   self.weightedMatrix.add(int(value,16))
   except:
       log.error('Matrix File Error:'+ gl_args.theMatrix)
       sys.exit()
   finally:
       fileTheMatrix.close()

   return
```

接下来定义isWordProbable方法，它将计算传递的字符串的权重值，在weightedMatrix中执行查找，以确定是否获得一个匹配。注意我首先检查传递的theWord是否小于最小大小。

```
def isWordProbable(self, theWord):
    if (len(theWord) < MIN_WORD):
        return False
    else:
        BASE = 96
        wordWeight = 0
```

下面是核心权重计算，产生一个名为wordWeight的无符号长整数值。

```
        for i in range(4,0,-1):
            charValue = (ord(theWord[i]) - BASE)
            shiftValue = (i-1)*8
            charWeight = charValue << shiftValue
            wordWeight = (wordWeight | charWeight)
```

一旦计算出了词的权重，只需要检查该权重值是否存在于weighted matrix。

```
        if ( wordWeight in self.weightedMatrix):
            return True
        else:
            return False
```

为了将这个功能正确地集成到程序中，下面就是所需要的全部代码。

初始化相当简单，创建一个名为wordCheck的对象（执行矩阵代码的初始化，以加载权重值），还创建一个名为indexOfWords的列表，在这里存储发现的可能单词。

```
wordCheck = class_Matrix()
indexOfWords = []
```

接着将下面的代码嵌入已有的搜索循环，检查字符串是否是可能的单词。如果wordCheck返回True，就将该单词加入indexOfWords列表，注意该列表的每一项有两个元素，（1）字符串newWord；（2）在发现它的目标文件中起始位置的偏移量。

```
if wordCheck.isWordProbable(newWord):
    indexOfWords.append([newWord, i-cnt])
```

最后在搜索的结尾处增加一个方法，打印出indexOfWords列表，同时包括了单词和偏移量。在打印之前还要按照字母顺序对列表进行排序。

```
def PrintAllWordsFound(wordList):

    print "Index of All Words"
    print "--------------------"

    wordList.sort()

    for entry in nfList:
        print entry

    print "--------------------"
    print

    return
```

从程序的执行角度，可以看到合并后的搜索和索引的结果，如图4.14所示。

```
Found: moonrocks At Address:   00000e10
Offset      00 01 02 03  04 05 06 07  08 09 0A 0B  0C 0D 0E 0F   ASCII
00000df9    63 6f 6d 00  68 61 76 65  00 79 6f 75  00 73 65 65   .com.have.you.see
00000e09    6e 00 61 6e  79 00 6d 6f  6f 6e 72 6f  63 6b 73 00   en.any.moonrocks.
00000e19    00 00 00 00  00 00 00 00  00 00 4f 00  00 00 4f 00   ..........O...O.
00000e29    00 00 63 00  00 00 00 00  5a 00 00 00  57 00 00 00   ..c.....Z...W...
00000e39    00 00 00 00  00 00 00 00  00 59 00 00  00 00 00 00   .........Y......
00000e49    00 00 00 00  00 58 00 00  00 00 00 00  53 6d 00 00   .....X......Sm..
00000e59    00 00 4e 00  00 00 00 00  00 00 6e 00  00 00 00 00   ..N.......n.....
00000e69    00 72 5a 00  00 00 00 45  00 00 00 00  00 00 00 00   .rZ....E........
Index of All Words
-------------------
['adobe', 470]
['adobe', 494]
['adobe', 10042]
['adobe', 10066]
['aogij', 46360]
['colour', 7624]
['colour', 7681]
['company', 7257]
['condition', 7752]
['condition', 7807]
['copyright', 7222]
['default', 7612]
['default', 7669]
['gmail', 3572]
['hewlett', 7241]
['hlino', 6881]
['johnny', 1936]
['julio', 1008]
['moonrocks', 3600]
['packard', 7249]
['photoshop', 24]
['photoshop', 476]
['photoshop', 10048]
['profile', 6868]
['qyzod', 11694]
['reference', 7734]
['reference', 7789]
['roren', 51038]
['space', 7631]
['space', 7688]
['sspahe', 22967]
['sugar', 1030]
['tornado', 1965]
['viewing', 7744]
['viewing', 7799]
['written', 459]
['written', 10031]
['yahoo', 1014]
-------------------
```

图4.14 具有索引能力的p-search运行

4.7 p-search完整代码清单

4.7.1 p-search.py

```
#
# p-search:PythonWordSearch
# Author:C.Hosmer
# August2013 #Version1.0
#
# Simplep-searchPythonprogram
#
# Read in a list of search words
# Read a binary file into a bytearray
# Search the bytearray for occurrences of any specified search words
# Print a HEX/ ASCII display localizing the matching words
# Print out a list of possible words identified that didn't match
#
# Definition of a word. a word for this example is an uninterrupted sequence of
# 4 to 12 alpha characters
#

import logging
import time
```

```python
import _psearch

if __name__ == '__main__':

    PSEARCH_VERSION = '1.0'

    # Turn on Logging
logging.basicConfig(filename = 'pSearchLog.log',level = logging.DEBUG,
format = '%(asctime)s %(message)s')

    # Process the Command Line Arguments
    _psearch.ParseCommandLine()

    log =logging.getLogger('main._psearch')
    log.info("p-search started")

    # Record the Starting Time
    startTime =time.time()

    # Perform Keyword Search
    _psearch.SearchWords()

    # Record the Ending Time
    endTime = time.time()
    duration = endTime - startTime

    logging.info('Elapsed Time:'+ str(duration) +'seconds')
    logging.info('')

    logging.info('Program Terminated Normally')
```

4.7.2　_p-search.py

```
#
# psearch support functions, where all the real work gets done
#
# Display Message()                 ParseCommandLine()
# ValidateFileRead()                ValidateFileWrite()
# Matrix (class)
#
import argparse                     # Python Standard Library -
                                    Parser for command-line
                                    options, arguments
import os                           # Standard Library OS
                                        functions
import logging                      # Standard Library Logging
                                    functions

log = logging.getLogger('main._psearch')

# Constants
MIN_WORD =5                    # Minimum word size in bytes
MAX_WORD =15                   # Maximum word size in bytes
PREDECESSOR_SIZE =32           # Values to print before match found
WINDOW_SIZE =128               # Total values to dump when match found

# Name: ParseCommand() Function
#
# Desc: Process and Validate the command line arguments
```

```
#                use Python Standard Library module argparse
#
# Input: none
#
# Actions:
#                Uses the standard library argparse to process the command line
#
def ParseCommandLine():

    parser = argparse.ArgumentParser('Python Search')

    parser.add_argument('-v','--verbose', help = "enables printing of additional program messages", action = 'store_true')
    parser.add_argument('-k','--keyWords', type = ValidateFileRead, required = True, help ="specify the file containing search words")
    parser.add_argument('-t','--srchTarget', type=ValidateFileRead, required = True, help ="specify the target file to search")
    parser.add_argument('-m','--theMatrix', type=ValidateFileRead, required = True, help = "specify the weighted matrix file")

    global gl_args

    gl_args = parser.parse_args()

    DisplayMessage("Command line processed: Successfully")

    return

# End Parse Command Line
#
# Name: ValidateFileRead Function
#
# Desc: Function that will validate that a file exists and is readable
#
# Input: A file name with full path
#
# Actions:
#                if valid will return path
#
#                if invalid it will raise an ArgumentTypeError within argparse
#                which will inturn be reported by argparse to the user
#
def ValidateFileRead(theFile):

    # Validate the path is a valid
    if not os.path.exists(theFile):
        raise argparse.ArgumentTypeError('File does not exist')

    # Validate the path is readable
    if os.access(theFile, os.R_OK):
        return theFile
    else:
        raise argparse.ArgumentTypeError('File is not readable')

# End ValidateFileRead =========================================
#
```

```python
# Name: DisplayMessage() Function
#
# Desc: Displays the message if the verbose command line option is present
#
# Input: message type string
#
# Actions:
#              Uses the standard library print function to display the message
#
def DisplayMessage(msg):

    if gl_args.verbose:
        print(msg)

    return

# End DisplayMessage ==========================================
#
# Name SearchWords()
#
# Uses command line arguments
#
# Searches the target file for keywords
#
def SearchWords():

    # Create an empty set of search words
    searchWords = set()

    # Attempt to open and read search words
    try:
        fileWords = open(gl_args.keyWords)
        for line in fileWords:
            searchWords.add(line.strip())
    except:
        log.error('Keyword File Failure:' + gl_args.keyWords)
        sys.exit()
    finally:
        fileWords.close()
    # Create Log Entry Words to Search For
    log.info('Search Words')
    log.info('Input File:'+ gl_args.keyWords)
    log.info(searchWords)

    # Attempt to open and read the target file
    and directly load into a bytearray

    try:
        targetFile = open(gl_args.srchTarget,'rb')
        baTarget = bytearray(targetFile.read())
    except:
        log.error('Target File Failure:'+ gl_args.srchTarget)
        sys.exit()
    finally:
        targetFile.close()
```

```python
        sizeOfTarget = len(baTarget)

        # Post to log

        log.info('Target of Search:'+ gl_args.srchTarget)
        log.info('File Size:' + str(sizeOfTarget))

        baTargetCopy = baTarget

        wordCheck = class_Matrix()

        # Search Loop
        # step one, replace all non characters with zero's

        for i in range(0, sizeOfTarget):
            character =chr(baTarget[i])
            if not character.isalpha():
                baTarget[i] =0

        # step # 2 extract possible words from the bytearray
        # and then inspect the search word list
        # create an empty list of probable not found items

        indexOfWords =[]

        cnt =0
        for i in range(0, sizeOfTarget):
            character = chr(baTarget[i])
            if character.isalpha():
                cnt +=1
            else:
                if (cnt >=MIN_WORD and cnt <=MAX_WORD):
                    newWord =""
                    for z in range(i-cnt, i):
                        newWord =newWord + chr(baTarget[z])
                    newWord =newWord.lower()
                if (newWord in searchWords):
                    PrintBuffer(newWord, i-cnt, baTargetCopy,
                    i-PREDECESSOR_SIZE, WINDOW_SIZE)
                    indexOfWords.append([newWord, i-cnt])
                    cnt =0
                    print
                else:
                    if wordCheck.isWordProbable(newWord):
                        indexOfWords.append([newWord, i-cnt])
                    cnt = 0
            else:
                cnt = 0

        PrintAllWordsFound(indexOfWords)

        return

# End of SearchWords Function

#
# Print Hexidecimal / ASCII Page Heading
#
def PrintHeading():
```

```python
        print("Offset 00 01 02 03 04 05 06 07 08 09 0A 0B 0C 0D 0E 0F    ASCII")
        print("----------------------------------------------------------------")

    return
# End PrintHeading

#
# Print Buffer
#
# Prints Buffer contents for words that are discovered parameters
# 1) Word found
# 2) Direct Offset to beginning of the word
# 3 buff The bytearray holding the target
# 4) offset starting position in the buffer for printing
# 5) hexSize, size of hex display windows to print
#
def PrintBuffer(word, directOffset, buff, offset, hexSize):

    print "Found: "+ word + " At Address: ",
    print "%08x   " % (directOffset)

    PrintHeading()

    for i in range(offset, offset+hexSize, 16):
        for j in range(0,16):
            if (j==0):
                print "%08x " % i,
            else:
                byteValue =buff[i+j]
                print "%02x " % byteValue,
        print " ",
        for j in range (0,16):
            byteValue =buff[i+j]
            if (byteValue >=0x20 and byteValue <=0x7f):
                print "%c" % byteValue,
            else:
                print'.',
        print
    return

# End Print Buffer

#
# PrintAllWordsFound
#

def PrintAllWordsFound(wordList):
    print "Index of All Words"
    print "--------------------"

    wordList.sort()

    for entry in wordList:
        print entry
    print "--------------------"
```

```
            print
        return
# End PrintAllWordsFound
#
# Class Matrix
#
# init method, loads the matrix into the set
# weightedMatrix
#
# isWordProbable method
#    1) Calculates the weight of the provided word
#    2) Verifies the minimum length
#    3) Calculates the weight for the word
#    4) Tests the word for existence in the matrix
#    5) Returns true or false
class class_Matrix:

    weightedMatrix =set()

    def __init__(self):
        try:
                fileTheMatrix =open(gl_args.theMatrix,'rb')
                for line in fileTheMatrix:
                        value =line.strip()
                        self.weightedMatrix.add(int(value,16))
        except:
            log.error('Matrix File Error:'+ gl_args.theMatrix)
            sys.exit()
        finally:
            fileTheMatrix.close()

        return

    def isWordProbable(self, theWord):

        if (len(theWord) < MIN_WORD):
            return False
        else:
            BASE =96
            wordWeight =0

            for i in range(4,0,-1):
                charValue =(ord(theWord[i]) - BASE)
                shiftValue =(i-1)*8
                charWeight =charValue << shiftValue
                wordWeight =(wordWeight | charWeight)

            if (wordWeight in self.weightedMatrix):
                    return True
            else:
                    return False

### End Class Matrix
```

4.8 章节回顾

在本章中开始应用新的Python语言元素，包括集合和字节数组，并且拓展了列表和类的使用。还提供了一些如何打开和读取文件的例子，这些文件包含不同的数值集合，包括关键词、原始二进制数据以及十六进制数据，并将它们直接用到Python的字节数组、列表和集合。本章还演示了如何选用正确的语言元素类型产生简单易读的代码，以实现我们的目标。结果便是p-search成为了一个实用的应用程序，可以为调查人员提供关键字搜索，以及为在文档、磁盘镜像、内存快照甚至网络痕迹中找到的单词生成索引的能力。

此外，再一次演示了Python代码的互操作性，无修改的相同代码运行于Windows、Linux和Mac产生了相同的结果。

4.9 问题小结

1. 内建语言数据类型的优缺点有什么（列表、集合以及字典）？
2. 请解释使用集合存储关键词列表的优势是什么？
3. 与其他语言相比，Python处理大的数据集合（二进制、文本和整型）的能力如何？
4. 如今，很多文件、磁盘镜像、内存快照和网络痕迹都会包含Unicode码数据而不是单纯的ASCII。请对p-search进行修改，以提供对包含简单ASCII码和Unicode码的数据进行搜索和索引功能。
5. 将矩阵进行扩充，以包含更广泛的权重值，包括外语和正确的人名和地名，以及来自于其他领域的词汇，如医学技术。

4.10 补充资料

1. 夏洛克福尔摩斯全集：全部4个小说和56个小故事．高级版．Bantam Classics；1986.10.1
2. Python编程语言．Python.org官方网站，网址http://www.python.org
3. Python标准库．网址http://docs.python.org/2/library/

第5章　证据提取（JPEG和TIFF）

5.1　本章简介

　　以数字形式表达的、简单或是复杂的数据结构，为收集和提取有价值的证据创造了重要条件。文件的简单元数据定义了修改、访问和创建的时间，以及文件的所有者、大小等，文件的其他属性标注文件为只读、系统或者存档。这些信息易于使用常见的桌面工具进行检索和检查。内存快照中包含了结构化和非结构化的数据，对这些数据进行挖掘和重构可以揭示正在运行的进程和线程、用户最近的活动、网络数据，甚至用户键入的口令和密钥加密的资料。

　　其他的复杂文件结构，如包含EXIF（可交换图像文件格式）数据的JPEG文件，包括了与图像本身有关的大量具有潜在价值的信息。这些信息包括拍摄照片的相机型号、拍摄的日期和时间，以及毫不夸张地说，上百个与图像相关的其他大量的不同数据元素。随着Facebook、Instagram、Twitter、Flicker以及其他社交媒体服务的出现，数字照片的分享已经深深融入我们的文化中。如今超过10亿人携带着配备内置摄像头的智能手机或平板电脑，这些设备可以拍摄高质量的照片和视频。使用上述的社交网络应用软件、短信或类似的传统电子邮件，可以将照片和视频立即分享到全球。

　　另外，无论气象频道的人员，还是执法部门的调查人员，都在使用数字照相对真实事件进行报道和分析。美国联邦通信委员会（FCC）已经出台了新的条例，其中就包括在拨打911报警电话时，强制提高发送的位置信息的精度。特别是E911条例要求无线服务提供商提交呼叫者的50~300米内的经度和纬度。这些要求促使智能手机制造商在手机中加入了全球定位系统（GPS）芯片和高质量的照相机，能自动地将位置和时间信息直接嵌入数字图片中。结果是这些发明带来了潜在的有价值的证据，包括"何事：照片内容"，"何时：照片拍摄时间"，"何地：拍照地点"。

　　在此前提下，我将深入探究从数字照片中提取证据，特别是智能手机拍摄的包含EXIF数据的照片。我会将精力主要集中在与JPEG和TIFF图片格式相关的EXIF数据，主要原因是如今大多数智能手机拍摄的照片都支持EXIF嵌入。

　　可能许多人已经使用Hex编辑器和其他简单工具，检测过数字照片中的内容以及EXIF信息，之后的结果可能是需要验光师开具一个升级的处方。为了帮助我们揭开这如洋葱般层层包裹的数字照片之面纱，将引入一个新库为我们完成很多重要而繁琐的工作，它就是Python图像库（PIL）。PIL具有丰富的功能，不仅可以从图片中提取信息，还可以操作这些信息。我打算将重点放在利用PIL提取EXIF信息，但当你学习了怎样正确使用PIL后，还可以使用PIL进行其他图像处理操作。

5.2 Python图像库（PIL）

使用PIL的第一步是安装该库。如果在Windows平台上运行Python，将感到幸运，因为有一个简单的安装程序供你使用，如图5.1所示。

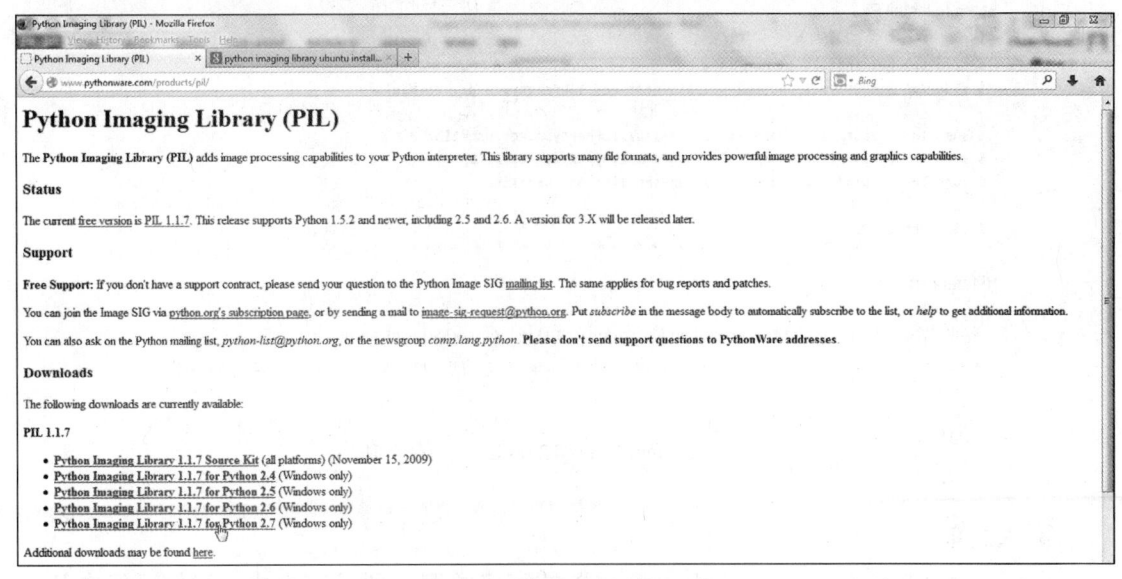

图5.1　下载Windows的PIL库

当根据安装的Python版本成功地下载了合适的安装程序（我使用的是Python 2.7的PIL版本1.1.7）之后，只需要运行下载的文件，并接受由安装向导提供的默认设置，如图5.2所示（这个例子很好地说明了在本书中为什么选择使用Python 2.x，正如同所看到的，PIL库目前还未转换到在Python 3.x版本下工作。一旦转换了，本章的程序可轻松地升级到工作于Python 3.x版本）。

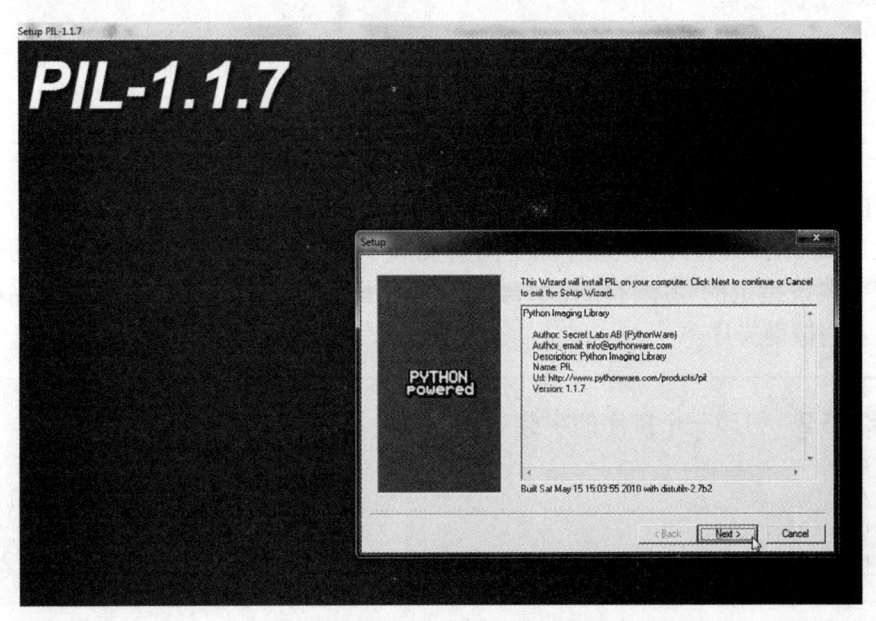

图5.2　PIL库的Windows安装向导

如果使用的是Linux或者Mac，库的安装步骤已经可以在网上找到。针对Ubuntu 12.04 LTS，这里有一个很好的例子，网站是https://gist.github.com/dwayne/3353083（参见图5.3）。

```
installing-pil.md                                                    Markdown

Steps to install PIL

    $ sudo apt-get install python-imaging
    $ sudo apt-get install libjpeg-dev libfreetype6 libfreetype6-dev zlib1g-dev

    $ sudo ln -s /usr/lib/`uname -i`-linux-gnu/libfreetype.so /usr/lib/
    $ sudo ln -s /usr/lib/`uname -i`-linux-gnu/libjpeg.so /usr/lib/
    $ sudo ln -s /usr/lib/`uname -i`-linux-gnu/libz.so /usr/lib/

    $ pip install PIL

References:

    • http://askubuntu.com/questions/156484/how-do-i-install-python-imaging-library-pil
    • http://www.sandersnewmedia.com/why/2012/04/16/installing-pil-virtualenv-ubuntu-1204-precise-pangolin/
```

图5.3　在Ubuntu Linux 12.04 LTS上安装PIL库

深入之前

在深入介绍PIL之前，要介绍Python内置的字典类型。到目前为止，我们已经在几个例子中使用了Python的列表和集合结构。在某些情况下我们需要更灵活、功能更强的结构类型。更加具体地，因为PIL使用了字典，我们需要更好地理解其操作。

如同在代码脚本5.1中所见，字典中的每一项有两个部分，前者为键（key），后面跟着的是值（value）。例如键"fast"有一个对应的值"Porsche"。

代码脚本 5.1　创建一个字典
```
>>> dCars = {"fast": "Porsche", "clean": "Prius", "expensive": "Rolls"}
>>> print dCars
{'expensive':'Rolls','clean':'Prius','fast':'Porsche'}
```

你可能已经注意到，当打印字典中的内容时，顺序发生了改变。这是因为在存储时键被转换成hash值，这样既节省存储空间又提高了对字典进行搜索和索引时的性能。如果你希望字典按指定的顺序打印显示，可以使用下面的代码。这个代码提取字典中的条目，并将它们按键排序。

代码脚本 5.2　打印一个排序的字典
```
>>> dCarsItems = dCars.items()
>>> dCarsItems.sort()
>>> print dCarsItems
[('clean','Prius'), ('expensive','Rolls'), ('fast','Porsche')]
```

如果字典很大，而想找出所有的键，或者在找到了键的情况下，你希望提取其对应的值，该如何处理呢？

代码脚本 5.3　简单的键和值的提取
```
>>> # what keys are available?
>>> dCars.keys()
['expensive','clean','fast']
>>> # what is the value associated with the key "clean"?
>>> dCars.get("clean")
'Prius'
```

最后，可能需要在字典上迭代，提取并显示所有的键值对。

代码脚本 5.4　字典上的迭代
```
>>> for key, value in dCars.items():
...     print key, value
expensive Rolls
clean Prius
fast Porsche
```

如果你并不熟悉Python，但是熟悉其他的编程环境，代码脚本5.4可能看起来有一点奇怪，其原因如下：

1. 我们不需要声明变量key和value，因为Python会自动处理。在这个简单的实例中，key和value都是字符串，但是它们并不是必须如此。
2. 因为我们知道dCars是一个字典，方法items自动返回键和值。在本例中键是"clean"、"expensive"和"fast"，值是车辆的字符串名字"Porsche"、"Prius"和"Rolls"。

因为Python会自动处理数据的归类，让我们来关注一些更复杂的东西。

代码脚本 5.5　更复杂的字典的例子
```
>>> dTemp = {"2013:12:31": [22.0, "F", "High"],
"2013:11:28": [24.5, "C", "Low"], "2013:12:27": [32.7, "F", "High"]}
>>> dTempItems = dTemp.items()
>>> dTempItems.sort()
>>> for key, value in dTempItems:... print key, value
...
2013:11:28 [24.5,'C','Low']
2013:12:27 [32.7,'F','High']
2013:12:31 [22.0,'F','High']
```

正如在代码脚本5.5看到的那样，这些键是表示日期的字符串，而值实际上是一个Python列表，包含时间、时间参照点、温度和温度单位。

现在你对字典（Dictionary）有了一个好的大致理解，就可以创建一些自己的字典，并用合适的方法进行实验。从这个实例开始，我希望你能看到字典类型的威力，并且思考以其他方式应用这个结构。

PIL代码预测试

与其他模块和库一样，熟悉PIL库的最好方法就是用它做实验。记住我们的格言：先测试再编码，这一点特别适用于PIL，主要原因是PIL使用了一个新的Python语言结构，即字典数据结构。另外PIL中的EXIF模块要求在使用之前对其有充分的了解。我将利用Python Shell和以下简短的脚本来说明。

确定可用的EXIF标签

PIL有两类重要的标签（TAGS），提供键以访问字典中的元素，它们是EXIF标签和GPS标签。通过如下的方法，开发了一段脚本用以确定哪些EXIF标签是可用的：

（1）从PIL库中导入EXIFTAGS。
（2）从TAGS中提取字典的条目（键值对）。
（3）对提取的字典条目进行分类排序，以便于识别。
（4）打印排序后的由键值对组成的字典。

代码脚本 5.6　提取EXIF标签
```
>>> from PIL.ExifTags import TAGS
>>> EXIFTAGS = TAGS.items()
>>> EXIFTAGS.sort()
>>> print EXIFTAGS
```

这段代码产生了如下可用标签的打印列表。注意这不是数据，而是EXIF标签的完整列表。

[(256,'ImageWidth'), (257,'ImageLength'), (258,'BitsPerSample'), (259, 'Compression'), (262,'PhotometricInterpretation'), (270, 'ImageDescription'), (271,'Make'), (272,'Model'), (273,'StripOffsets'), (274, 'Orientation'), (277,'SamplesPerPixel'), (278,'RowsPerStrip'), (279, 'StripByteConunts'), (282,'XResolution'), (283,'YResolution'), (284, 'PlanarConfiguration'), (296,'ResolutionUnit'), (301,'TransferFunction'), (305,'Software'), (306,'DateTime'), (315,'Artist'), (318,'WhitePoint'), (319, 'PrimaryChromaticities'), (513, 'JpegIFOffset'), (514,'JpegIFByteCount'), (529,'YCbCrCoefficients'), (530,'YCbCrSubSampling'), (531, 'YCbCrPositioning'), (532,'ReferenceBlackWhite'), (4096, 'RelatedImageFileFormat'), (4097,'RelatedImageWidth'), (33421, 'CFARepeatPatternDim'), (33422,'CFAPattern'), (33423,'BatteryLevel'), (33432,'Copyright'), (33434,'ExposureTime'), (33437,'FNumber'), (34665, 'EXIFOffset'), (34675,'InterColorProfile'), (34850,'ExposureProgram'), (34852,'SpectralSensitivity'), (34853,'GPSInfo'), (34855, 'ISOSpeedRatings'), (34856,'OECF'), (34857,'Interlace'), (34858, 'TimeZoneOffset'), (34859,'SelfTimerMode'), (36864,'EXIFVersion'), (36867, 'DateTimeOriginal'), (36868,'DateTimeDigitized'), (37121, 'ComponentsConfiguration'), (37122,'CompressedBitsPerPixel'), (37377, 'ShutterSpeedValue'), (37378,'ApertureValue'), (37379,'BrightnessValue'),

(37380,'ExposureBiasValue'), (37381,'MaxApertureValue'), (37382, 'SubjectDistance'), (37383,'MeteringMode'), (37384,'LightSource'), (37385, 'Flash'), (37386,'FocalLength'), (37387,'FlashEnergy'), (37388, 'SpatialFrequencyResponse'), (37389,'Noise'), (37393,'ImageNumber'), (37394,'SecurityClassification'), (37395,'ImageHistory'), (37396, 'SubjectLocation'), (37397,'ExposureIndex'), (37398,'TIFF/EPStandardID'), (37500,'MakerNote'), (37510,'UserComment'), (37520,'SubsecTime'), (37521, 'SubsecTimeOriginal'), (37522,'SubsecTimeDigitized'), (40960, 'FlashPixVersion'), (40961,'ColorSpace'), (40962,'EXIFImageWidth'), (40963, 'EXIFImageHeight'), (40964,'RelatedSoundFile'), (40965, 'EXIFInteroperabilityOffset'), (41483,'FlashEnergy'), (41484, 'SpatialFrequencyResponse'), (41486,'FocalPlaneXResolution'), (41487, 'FocalPlaneYResolution'), (41488,'FocalPlaneResolutionUnit'), (41492, 'SubjectLocation'), (41493, 'ExposureIndex'), (41495,'SensingMethod'), (41728, 'FileSource'), (41729,'SceneType'), (41730,'CFAPattern')]

> 时间是一个概念，让社会以一个有序的方式运转，各方都容易理解时间的表示方法，并约定事情的顺序。从1972年起国际时间标准是协调统一时间（Coordinated Universal Time）或者简称UTC。在全球大部分国家UTC作为官方时间源的基础。它受制于一个被世界各国接受的外交条约，各国指派国家级的测量（或计量）机构（NMI）作为UTC时间源。美国的国家标准与技术研究所（NIST）、英格兰的国家物理实验室（NPL）就是两个NMI的例子。大约50个类似的计量机构负责全球的官方时间。此外在检查数字证据时，时区起到关键作用；基于计算机的时区设置，可以对事件和行为进行定位。例如，如果计算机的时区设置为纽约，其本地时间与UTC相差5小时（或者说在UTC后面5小时）。最后，美国的许多州和其他一些国家执行夏时制，多数现代的操作系统自动调整夏时制带来的额外时差并进行UTC的计算，或对跨时区事件进行同步。

在打印出的清单中，高亮显示了感兴趣的标签，包括 `GPSInfo`、`TimeZoneOffset`和`DateTimeOriginal`。

> 值得注意的是，对于任一个图像不能确保所有这些标签都是可用的，这些标签是可能存在于一个图像内的键值对的全部集合。每个制造商自主决定使用哪些键值。因此你必须分析每一个目标图像的键值对，以确定哪些标签被实际用到。我很快就会向你演示如何做到这一点。

当浏览这个标签列表时，可能发现一些对你的调查活动有帮助的其他标签，也可以使用同样的方法，用这些值进行实验。

确定可用的EXIF GPS标签

接下来，我想更深入地讨论一下`GPSInfo`标签，因为本章的目标是提取具体图像的基于GPS的位置数据。在下面的代码中将使用类似的方法确定哪些GPS标签是可用的。

> **代码脚本 5.7 提取GPS标签**
> ```
> >>> from PIL.ExifTags import GPSTAGS
> >>> gps = GPSTAGS.items()
> >>> gps.sort()
> >>> print gps
> ```

[(0, 'GPSVersionID'), (1, 'GPSLatitudeRef'), (2, 'GPSLatitude'), (3, 'GPSLongitudeRef'), (4, 'GPSLongitude'), (5, 'GPSAltitudeRef'), (6, 'GPSAltitude'), (7, 'GPSTimeStamp'), (8, 'GPSSatellites'), (9, 'GPSStatus'), (10, 'GPSMeasureMode'), (11, 'GPSDOP'), (12, 'GPSSpeedRef'), (13, 'GPSSpeed'), (14, 'GPSTrackRef'), (15,'GPSTrack'), (16, 'GPSImgDirectionRef'), (17, 'GPSImgDirection'), (18, 'GPSMapDatum'), (19, 'GPSDestLatitudeRef'), (20, 'GPSDestLatitude'), (21, 'GPSDestLongitudeRef'), (22, 'GPSDestLongitude'), (23, 'GPSDestBearingRef'), (24, 'GPSDestBearing'), (25, 'GPSDestDistanceRef'), (26, 'GPSDestDistance')]

上面高亮显示了一些我们需要的GPS标签，以便精确描述照片拍摄的位置和时间。需要再次指出的是，在一个实际图像中不能确保所有的GPS标签都是可用的。

> 经度和纬度位置提供了精确描述地球上具体位置的能力。全球定位系统GPS（Global Position System）和嵌入智能手机和相机中的GPS接收机能以经度和纬度坐标的形式提供非常精确的地理位置信息。如果设备中配置了GPS，当某个事件发生时这种地理位置信息就会直接嵌入照片、视频和其他数字媒体中。从这些数字媒介中提取地理位置信息，然后将数据输入在线服务，如MapQuest、谷歌地图（Google Map）、谷歌地球（Google Earth）等，就可以得到这些数字媒介在何地何时创建的证据。

如果想利用这些标签精确描述位置，就需要对这些感兴趣的标签的含义与用途有更清晰的定义和更深入的理解。

GPSLatitudeRef　GPS纬度参考值。从赤道向南或向北的度数来标明纬度。赤道以北的地点其范围为0°~90°，赤道以南的地点其范围为0°~90°。因此这个参考值就用来定义纬度与赤道的相对关系。因为在EXIF中用一个正整数规定纬度值，所以如果GPS纬度参考值是"S"（代表"南"），那么该整数值就要转换为一个负数值。

GPSLatitude　指示按度数测量的纬度，EXIF数据规定这是一个纯的度数，接着是分，然后是秒。

GPSLongitudeRef　GPS经度参考值。经度用向东或向西的度数来表示。这个惯例基于通过英格兰格林尼治皇家天文台的本初子午线，规定其经度是0°，本初子午线以西的地点其范围为0°~180°，本初子午线以东的地点其范围为0°~180°，因此这个参考值就用来定义经度值与格林尼治的相对关系。因为在EXIF中用一个正整数规定经度值，所以如果GPS经度参考值是"W"（代表"西"），那么该整数值就要转换为一个负数值。

GPSLongtitude　指示按度数测量的经度，EXIF数据规定这是一个纯的度数，接着是分，然后是秒。

GPSTimeStamp　指定以协调统一时间（UCT）表示的照片拍摄时间。

第 5 章 证据提取（JPEG 和 TIFF） 101

> 由于包含在EXIF结构中的数据是数字形式表示的，这些数据易于操作和伪造。所以保全照片或者直接从智能移动设备获取照片，可以使得欺骗性修改的可能性更小、操作更难实现。

现在对照片中有可能得到的标签有了一个基本理解，让我们检测一个真实的照片。图5.4所示的是一张从互联网上下载的，将作为实验对象的照片。

图5.4　来自互联网的图片cat.jpg

代码脚本 5.8　提取一个简单图片的EXIF标签
```
>>> from PIL import Image
>>> from PIL.ExifTags import TAGS, GPSTAGS
>>>
>>> pilImage = Image.open("c:\\pictures\\cat.jpg)"
... EXIFData = pilImage._getEXIF()
...
>>> catEXIF = EXIFData.items()
>>> catEXIF.sort()
>>> print catEXIF
```

这段脚本导入PIL图像模块，以允许我打开要处理的特定图片并创建对象`pilImage`。然后就可以使用`pilImage`对象的`._getEXIF()`方法获取EXIF数据。我们用与前面同样的方法提取了EXIF标签和GPS标签。在本例中提取了字典项并对它们进行了排序。注意，本例中提取的是实际的EXIF数据（或潜在的证据）而不是TAG的引用。

代码脚本5.8的输出结果显示如下。

```
[(271, 'Canon'), (272, 'Canon EOS 400D DIGITAL'), (282, (300, 1)), (283, (300, 1)), (296,
2), (306, '2008:08:05 23:48:04'), (315, 'unknown'), (33432, 'Eirik Solheim - www.eirikso.
com'), (33434, (1, 100)), (33437, (22, 10)), (34665, 240), (34850, 2), (34853, {0: (2, 2, 0,
0), 1: 'N', 2: ((59, 1), (55, 1), (37417, 1285)), 3: 'E', 4: ((10, 1), (41, 1), (55324, 1253)),
5: 0, 6: (81, 1)}), (34855, 400), (36864, '0221'), (36867, '2008:08:05 20:59:32'), (36868,
'2008:08:05 20:59:32'), (37378, (2275007, 1000000)), (37381, (96875, 100000)), (37383, 1),
(37385, 16), (37386, (50, 1)), (41486, (3888000, 877)), (41487, (2592000, 582)), (41488, 2),
(41985, 0), (41986, 0), (41987, 0), (41990, 0)]
```

上面高亮显示了与这个照片有关的GPSInfo数据。以前面的代码脚本5.6的输出为基础，该输出显示GSPInfo标签有一个大小为34853的键，就能识别出GSPInfo标签。因此这台Cannon EOS 400D DIGITAL照相机，在花括号中的高亮部分提供了GPS数据。对GPS数据的进一步检查表明相应的键值对是可用的。如你所见，嵌入在GPSInfo数据字典中的键值对是0、1、2、3、4、5和6。这些标签就是标准GPS标签。在代码脚本5.7中我打印输出了所有可能的GPS标签。通过查询该输出，我们发现了这台Cannon EOS 400D照相机提供的GPS标签，包括：

```
0 GPSVersionID
1 GPSLatitudeRef
2 GPSLatitude
3 GPSLongitudeRef
4 GPSLongitude
5 GPSAltitudeRef
6 GPSAltitude
```

有了这些信息就可以按照接下来的步骤，借助照片中的EXIF数据计算经度和纬度。但是，第一步我们需要从GPS标签2的键值对提取纬度。

GPSTag 2 : ((59, 1), (55, 1), (37417, 1285))

每一个经度或纬度的值包含三组数值，它们是：

度（Degrees）：**(59, 1)**

分（Minutes）：**(55, 1)**

秒（Seconds）：**(37417, 1285)**

你可能感到奇怪为什么像这样表示它们。答案是EXIF数据不支持浮点数（只能是纯整数）。为了提供高精度的经度和纬度数据，每组数代表一个比值。

接着，需要执行比值计算，以得到精确的小数值，结果如下：

度（Degrees）：59/1=59.0

分（Minutes）：55/1=55.0

秒（Seconds）：37417/1285=29.1182879

或者更加正确的说法是59度55分29.1182879秒。

注意：GPS标签1："N"，表示纬度参考的键值对在赤道以北，不要求将该值转换成一个负数；如果是"S"，就需要做一次额外的转换。

接下来，大部分的在线地图程序（如谷歌地图Google Maps）要求以小数值的方式提供数据，这种转换可以利用下面的公式完成。

Degrees + (minutes/60.0) + (seconds/3600.0)

注意：除数60.0和3600.0分别表示在1度中的分钟数（60.0）或秒数（3600.0）。

因此，这个以浮点数表示的纬度值如下：

Latitude=59.0+(55/60.0)+(29.1182879/3600.0)

Latitude=59.0+.91666667+.00808841=**59.92475508**

用同样的方法计算从GPS标签4中提取的经度值：

((10, 1), (41, 1), (55324, 1253))

GPS标签 3："E"

计算出经度值为**10.6955981201**

得到的纬度值/经度值为**59.92475508**，**10.6955981201**

使用Google Maps，我们可以找到这个地点的确定位置，位于挪威奥斯陆的西北，如图5.5所示。注意挪威奥斯陆确实位于英格兰格林尼治皇家观测台本初子午线的东边。

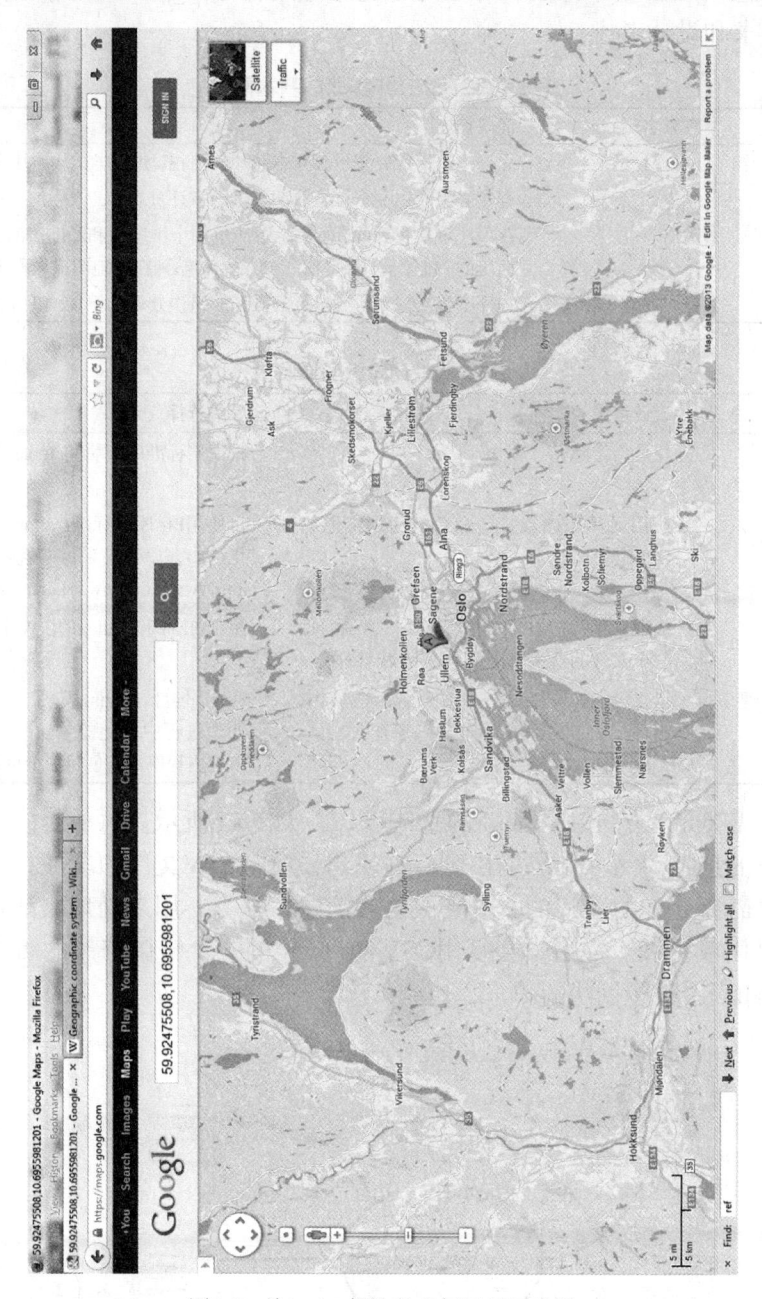

图5.5 从cat.jpg提取的坐标显示于地图

最后再说明一下，这台照相机并没有包含其他的GPS标签，如GPSTimestamp。GPSTimestamp可以给出GPS提供的时间信息。

p-ImageEvidenceExtractor的基本需求

现在我已经使用PIL进行了实验，发现了如何从目标照片提取EXIF标签、GPS标签，以及其他EXIF数据，接下来着手创建我们的第一个完整的提取应用程序。

设计考虑

既然我已经明确了基本方法，那么对于这个应用程序p-gpsExtractor[①]，表5.1和表5.2定义了程序需求和设计考虑。

表5.1 GPS/EXIF提取的基本需求

需求编号	需求名称	简单描述
GPS-001	命令行参数	允许用户指定一个包含样本照片的路径，我们尝试从照片中提取GPS信息
GPS-002	日志	程序必须产生一个符合取证要求的审计日志
GPS-003	输出	程序应该从找到的GPS信息中产生一个维度值和经度值的列表。格式应该是简单的"维度值，经度值"，以便能粘贴到在线地图应用程序
GPS-004	错误处理	程序应该支持对所有执行的操作的错误处理和记录，包括文本描述和时间戳

表5.2 设计考虑和库映射

需求	设计考虑	库的选择
用户输入（001）	用户指定路径	将使用标准库模块的argparse从用户获得输入
输出（003）	使用简单的内置打印命令打印出提取的GPS位置	将使用PIL库和标准Python语言来提取和格式化输出，以便结果可以直接复制粘贴到网页 http://www.darrinward.com/lat-long/
（附加的）	提取附加的EXIF和GPS值，并将遇到的每一个文件的这些值记录到一个CSV文件	使用PIL库和Python的CSV库
日志和错误处理（002和004）	错误可能在文件和EXIF数据的处理过程中出现，因此必须严格处理这些潜在问题	标准库包括logging模块，可以用它来报告在处理过程中发生的任何事件或错误。注意在本应用程序中将创建一个可以复用的日志类

接下来，需要定义p-gpsExtractor的总体设计，如图5.6所示。再一次使用命令行解析器来传达用户的选择。然后结果输出到标准输出设备、CSV文件和取证日志中。用户将指定一个包含需要处理的照片的文件夹。也会创建一个类，用来处理取证日志操作，并可以在将来复用或扩展。最后，会复用CSVWritter类的一个略微修改的版本，该类是在第3章中为pFish应用程序创建的。

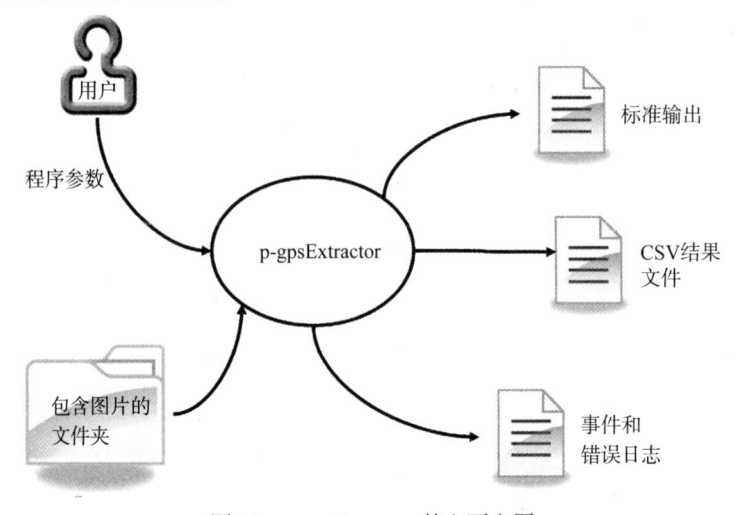

图5.6 p-gpsExtractor的上下文图

[①] 原文此处有误，应为p-gpsExtractor——译者注。

5.3 代码遍历

为了对该程序有感性认识，请看图5.7，该图是WingIDE项目的屏幕截图。注意到在最右边的窗口中的显示，本程序包含了5个Python源程序。

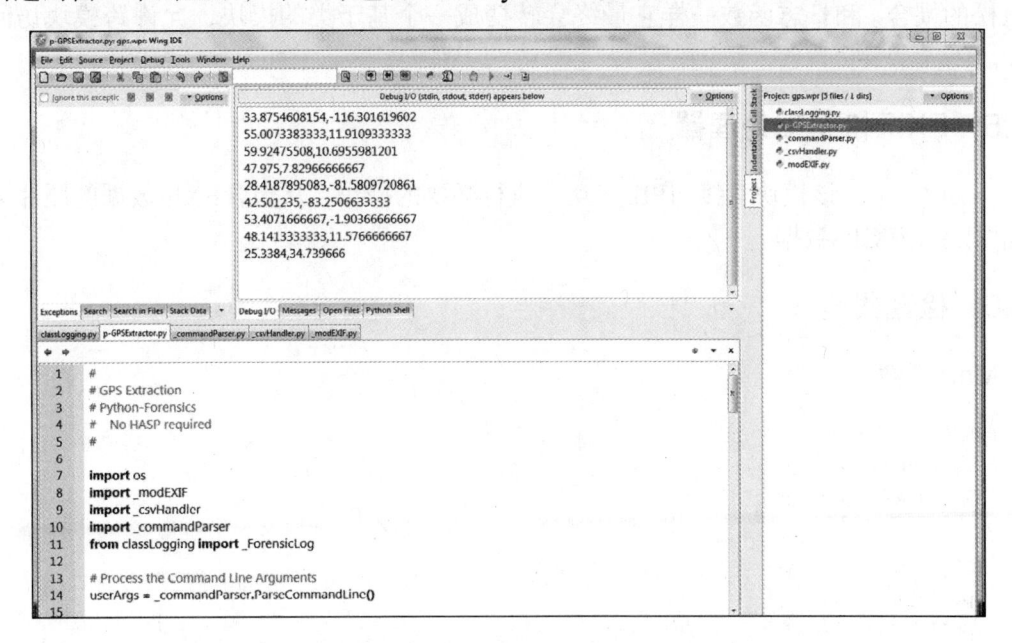

图5.7 WingIDE的项目视图

5.3.1 Main程序

`p-gpsExtracotr.py`：这是本应用的主程序，用来控制程序流程和处理可能是照片的文件。照片文件存放在用户通过命令行指定的文件夹中。主程序将输出数据写入标准输出设备中，以便将数据剪切粘贴到网页中查看地图。主程序还将数据输出到CSV文件中，以保存每一个文件的处理结果，以及所有的取证日志项。

5.3.2 logging类

`classLogging.py`：这个新的日志类将Python类的logging函数进行了抽象，以便实现取证日志功能。这样就允许日志对象继续沿用到以后开发的应用程序中，作为模块或函数，而不再需要任何全局变量。

5.3.3 cvs处理器

`_cvsHandler.py`：这个经修改的用于控制CSV文件的创建和写入的类提供了一个单点接口，用来以CVS格式输出文件。类中函数再一次被抽象化，以使接口更易使用。后面会对这个类做更多的工作，以实现进一步的抽象。

5.3.4 命令行解析器

_commandParser.py：将commandParser.py分离出来成为独立的文件，对本程序或将来的程序都具有更好的移植性。这使得命令行解析器更易处理、修改或者改进，而且与主函数更松的耦合。和日志函数一样它最终会转变成一个基于类的模块，允许跨模块访问和交互。

5.3.5 EXIF和GPS处理器

_modEXIF.py：该模块直接与PIL交互来执行必要的操作，从包含EXIF数据的照片文件中提取EXIF和GPS数据。

5.3.6 检查代码

Main函数

```
# GPS Extraction
# Python-Forensics
# No HASP required
#
import os
import _modEXIF
import _csvHandler
import _commandParser
from classLogging import ForensicLog
```

对于主程序，需要导入完成文件夹处理的os、命令行处理器、cvsHandler，以及新的取证日志类。

```
# Process the Command Line Arguments
userArgs = _commandParser.ParseCommandLine()
```

正如通常所做的，通过处理命令行参数获得用户指定的参数值。如果命令行解析成功，就创建一个新的日志对象来处理所有的取证日志事件，并写入第一个日志事件。

```
# create a log object
logPath = userArgs.logPath+"ForensicLog.txt"
oLog = _ForensicLog(logPath)

oLog.writeLog("INFO", "Scan Started)"
```

接着创建了一个CSV文件对象，用来向CSV结果文件写入数据。该结果文件包含了被处理的文件信息和提取的GPS数据。

```
csvPath = userArgs.csvPath+"imageResults.csv"
oCSV = _csvHandler._CSVWriter(csvPath)
```

对于我们的GPS提取，需要获得用户指定的目标路径，然后才尝试打开和处理目标路径中的每一个文件。如果发生任何错误，都会被采用的try/except模式捕获到，对应的错误信息就被写入取证日志文件中。

```
# define a directory to scan
scanDir = userArgs.scanPath
try:
    picts = os.listdir(scanDir)
except:
    oLog.writeLog("ERROR", "Invalid Directory "+ scanDir)
    exit(0)

for aFile in picts:
    targetFile = scanDir+aFile

    if os.path.isfile(targetFile):
```

当这些初始工作完成后，就可以使用_modEXIF模块处理每一个目标文件，如果处理成功，结果就是一个gpsDictionary对象。该对象将包含文件中可获得的EXIF数据，如果这些数据嵌入EXIF记录中。在使用这些数据之前，要确认gpsDictionary对象是否有数据。

```
gpsDictionary = _modEXIF.ExtractGPSDictionary(targetFile)
    if (gpsDictionary):

        # Obtain the Lat Lon values from the gpsDictionary
        # converted to degrees
        # the return value is a dictionary key value pairs

        dCoor = _modEXIF.ExtractLatLon(gpsDictionary)
```

接着，调用另一个_modEXIF函数进一步处理gpsDictionary。你将会看到，这个函数处理GPS坐标，如果成功就返回原始坐标数据。然后借助在本章前面部分学习过的字典方法，使用get从字典中提取出经度和纬度数据。

```
            lat = dCoor.get("Lat")
            latRef = dCoor.get("LatRef")
            lon = dCoor.get("Lon")
            lonRef = dCoor.get("LonRef")

            if ( lat and lon and latRef and lonRef):
```

在成功提取了经度和纬度数据后，将结果打印到标准输出设备，同时将数据写入CSV文件并更新对应的取证日志。如果没有成功，就向取证日志文件报告相应数据。

```
                    print str(lat)+','+str(lon)

                    # write one row to the output csv file
                    oCSV.writeCSVRow(targetFile, EXIFList[TS], EXIFList [MAKE],
                        EXIFList[MODEL], latRef, lat, lonRef,lon)

                    oLog.writeLog("INFO", "GPS Data Calculated for:" + targetFile)
                else:
                    oLog.writeLog("WARNING", "No GPS EXIF Data for"+ targetFile)
            else:
                oLog.writeLog("WARNING", "No GPS EXIF Data for "+ targetFile)
        else:
            oLog.writeLog("WARNING", targetFile + " not a valid file)"
```

最后，在程序退出前，删除了取证日志和CSV对象，这样就随之关闭了日志和相关的CSV文件。

```
# Clean up and Close Log and CSV File
del oLog
del oCSV
```

EXIF和GPS处理

p-gpsExtractor的核心数据提取部分包含在_modEXIF.py模块中。

```
#
# Data Extraction - Python-Forensics
# Extract GPS Data from EXIF supported Images (jpg, tiff)
# Support Module
#
```

首先导入_modEXIF.py所需要的模块和库，加注释的重要模块是PIL及其对应的功能。

```
import os # Standard Library OS functions
from classLogging import _ForensicLog # Logging Class
```

从PIL导入Image库、EXIF和GPSTags，以便索引到字典结构，这很像在代码脚本5.6到代码脚本5.8所做的工作。

```
# import the Python Image Library along with TAGS and GPS related TAGS

from PIL import Image
from PIL.Exif Tags import TAGS, GPSTAGS
```

现在让我们看看各个函数并进行分析。首先从GPS Dictionary的提取开始。这个函数接受需要进行提取的目标文件的完整路径名。

```
#
# Extract EXIF Data
#
# Input: Full Pathname of the target image
#
# Return: gpsDictionary and extracted EXIFData list
#
def ExtractGPSDictionary(fileName):
```

使用熟悉的try/except模式，试图打开指定的文件，如果成功，就用PIL的getEXIF( )函数提取EXIF数据。

```
try:
    pilImage = Image.open(fileName)
    EXIFData = pilImage._getEXIF()

except Exception:
    # If exception occurs from PIL processing
    # Report the
    return None, None
# Iterate through the EXIFData Searching for GPS Tags
```

接着，通过对EXIFData的标签进行迭代，收集一些基本的EXIF数据。若照片的EXIF数据中还包含了GPS标签，就获得这些GPS标签。

```
imageTimeStamp = "NA"
CameraModel = "NA"
CameraMake = "NA"
if EXIFData:
    for tag, theValue in EXIFData.items():
        # obtain the tag
        tagValue = TAGS.get(tag, tag)
        # Collect basic image data if available
```

在遍历查找照片中的标签的同时，还应检查是否存在DatatimeOriginal，以及照相机生产商和设备型号，以便也将其放入结果文件。

```
        if tagValue == 'DateTimeOriginal':
            imageTimeStamp = EXIFData.get(tag)
        if tagValue == "Make":
            cameraMake = EXIFData.get(tag)
        if tagValue == 'Model':
            cameraModel = EXIFData.get(tag)
```

还应检查GPSInfo标签，如果存在，则通过对GPSInfo标签进行迭代，利用GPSTAGS.get( )函数提取出GPS字典。

```
        # check the tag for GPS
        if tagValue == "GPSInfo":
            # Found it !
            Now create a Dictionary to hold the GPS Data
            gpsDictionary = {}
            # Loop through the GPS Information
            for curTag in theValue:
                gpsTag = GPSTAGS.get(curTag, curTag)
                gpsDictionary[gpsTag] = theValue[curTag]
```

接下来，创建一个简单的Python列表存放EXIF Timestamp、照相机制造商和型号等信息。然后返回收集到的GPSDictionary和basicEXIFData。

```
            basicEXIFData = [imageTimeStamp, cameraMake,
                            cameraModel]
            return gpsDictionary, basicEXIFData
    else:
```

如果目标文件没有包含任何EXIF数据就返回None，以停止对该文件的进一步处理。注意None是内置的Python常量，用来表示空或者数据丢失。

```
        return None, None
# End ExtractGPSDictionary =====================================
```

下一个支持函数是ExtractLatLon。正如本章提及的，需要将EXIF GPS数据转换为浮点数，以便在网络地图应用程序中使用这些数据。

```
#
# Extract the Latitude and Longitude Values from the gpsDictionary
#
```

ExtractLatLon函数接收一个gpsDictionary结构作为输入。

```
def ExtractLatLon(gps):
    # to perform the calculation we need at least
    lat, lon, latRef and lonRef
```

在尝试进行数据转换之前,需要验证gpsDictionary是否包含了恰当的键值对。这些键值对包括纬度、经度、纬度参考、经度参考。

```
    if (gps.has_key("GPSLatitude)" and
        gps.has_key("GPSLongitude)"
        and gps.has_key("GPSLatitudeRef)"
        and gps.has_key("GPSLatitudeRef)"):
```

当我们获得了这些的基本的输入,就可以将这些值单独提取出来。

```
        latitude     = gps["GPSLatitude"]
        latitudeRef  = gps["GPSLatitudeRef"]
        longitude    = gps["GPSLongitude"]
        longitudeRef = gps["GPSLongitudeRef"]
```

然后调用转换函数,计算出经度值和纬度值。

```
        lat = ConvertToDegrees(latitude)
        lon = ConvertToDegrees(longitude)
```

接下来要考虑纬度参考值、经度参考值,如果需要就要设定正确的负数值。

```
        # Check Latitude Reference
        # If South of the Equator then lat value is negative
        if latitudeRef == "S":
            lat = 0 - lat
        
        # Check Longitude Reference
        # If West of the Prime Meridian in Greenwich then the Longitude value is
          negative
        if longitudeRef == "W":
            lon = 0 - lon
```

当这些都处理完成后,创建一个新的字典存放最终的计算值,并返回给调用函数。本例中调用函数就是主程序。

```
        gpsCoor = {"Lat": lat, "LatRef":latitudeRef,
                   "Lon": lon, "LonRef": longitudeRef}
        
        return gpsCoor
    else:
```

同样,若这些最低要求的值不存在,则返回一个内建的Python常量None,表明这是一个空的返回。

```
                return None
```

最后一个支持函数是ConvertToDegrees，它将GPS数据转换为浮点数。这段代码非常简单，仿效了本章介绍的公式。需要指出的唯一重要问题是在两数相除时用到了try/except模式，因为被0除将引发错误，会导致程序终止。因为数据来源不一定可靠，任何情况都有可能，所以我们需要考虑被0除的情况。我曾经遇到过这样的EXIF数据，秒的值为0，那么比值就等于0:0。因为这也是一个合法的值，所以当异常出现时，就简单地设定度、分或秒的值为0。

```
#
# Convert GPSCoordinates to Degrees
#
# Input gpsCoordinates value from in EXIF Format
#
def ConvertToDegrees(gpsCoordinate):
    d0 = gpsCoordinate[0][0]
    d1 = gpsCoordinate[0][1]

    try:
        degrees = float(d0) / float(d1)
    except:
        degrees = 0.0

    m0 = gpsCoordinate[1][0]
    m1 = gpsCoordinate[1][1]
    try:
        minutes = float(m0) / float(m1)
    except:
        minutes = 0.0

    s0 = gpsCoordinate[2][0]
    s1 = gpsCoordinate[2][1]
    try:
        seconds = float(s0) / float(s1)
    except:
        seconds = 0.0

    floatCoordinate = float (degrees + (minutes / 60.0) +
                    (seconds / 3600.0))

    return floatCoordinate
```

logging类

在这个应用程序中，引入了一个新的类logging，该类抽象并简化了跨模块的取证日志事件的操作。

```
import logging
#
# Class: _ForensicLog
#
# Desc: Handles Forensic Logging Operations
#
# Methods
#     constructor:         Initializes the Logger
```

```
#       writeLog:          Writes a record to the log
#       destructor:        Writes an information message
                           and shuts down the logger
class _ForensicLog:
```

init是构造器方法，每当创建一个新的ForensicLog对象时都要被调用。该方法利用Python标准库初始化一个新的Python Logging对象。日志的文件名作为对象实例化的一部分被传递进来。如果出现异常，将会向标准输出设备发送一条消息，程序也会中止。

```
def __init__(self, logName):
    try:
        # Turn on Logging
        logging.basicConfig(filename = logName,
            level = logging.DEBUG,format = '%(asctime)s %(message)s')
    except:
        print "Forensic Log Initialization
            Failure ... Aborting"
        exit(0)
```

接下来的方法是writeLog，该方法接受两个参数，再加上self，第一个参数是日志事件的类型或者说级别（是INFO，还是ERROR或者WARNING），第二个则是字符串，表示要写入日志中的消息。

```
def writeLog(self, logType, logMessage):
    if logType == "INFO":
        logging.info(logMessage)
    elif logType == "ERROR":
        logging.error(logMessage)
    elif logType == "WARNING":
        logging.warning(logMessage)
    else:
        logging.error(logMessage)
    return
```

最后一个方法是del，用来关闭logging对象和日志文件。消息"Logging Shutdown"将在日志关闭前作为关闭信息被送往日志。

```
def __del__(self):
    logging.info("Logging Shutdown")
    logging.shutdown()
```

命令行解析器

命令行解析器处理用户的输入、验证输入的参数、报告错误和帮助文档，以此帮助用户。

```
import argparse     # Python Standard Library - Parser for
command-line options, arguments
import os           # Standard Library OS functions
# Name: ParseCommand() Function
#
# Desc: Process and Validate the command line arguments
#       use Python Standard Library module argparse
```

```
#
# Input: none
#
# Actions:
#                 Uses the standard library argparse
                  to process the command line
#
def ParseCommandLine():
```

gpsExtractor需要三个输入,(1)取证日志的目录路径;(2)要扫描的目录路径;(3)CSV结果文件的目录路径。所有这些目录路径必须是存在并可写入的,以便成功地解析。

```
    parser = argparse.ArgumentParser('Python gpsExtractor)
    parser.add_argument('-v','--verbose', help = "enables
                        printing of additional program messages",
                        action = 'store_true')

    parser.add_argument('-l','--logPath',
                        type = ValidateDirectory, required = True,
                        help = "specify the directory
                        for forensic log output file")

    parser.add_argument('-c','--csvPath',
                        type = ValidateDirectory, required = True,
                        help = "specify the output directory for
                        the csv file)"

    parser.add_argument('-d','-scanPath',
                        type = ValidateDirectory, required = True,
                        help = "specify the directory to scan)"

    theArgs = parser.parse_args()

    return theArgs

# End Parse Command Line ======================================
```

ValidateDirectory函数核实传递的值是否为一个真实目录并且路径确实可写。使用os.path.isdir()方法验证存在性,使用os.access()方法验证可写性。

```
def ValidateDirectory(theDir):

    # Validate the path is a directory
    if not os.path.isdir(theDir):
        raise argparse.ArgumentTypeError('Directory does not exist')

    # Validate the path is writable
    if os.access(theDir, os.W_OK):
        return theDir
    else:
        raise argparse.ArgumentTypeError
            ('Directory is not writable')

# End ValidateDirectory ========================================
```

CSV(逗号分隔值)Writer类

_CSVWriter类提供了基于对象的抽象,以实现将标题和数据写入一个标准的CSV文件。

```
import csv #Python Standard Library - for csv files
#
# Class: _CSVWriter
#
# Desc: Handles all methods related to comma separated value operations
#
# Methods
#     constructor:    Initializes the CSV File
#     writeCVSRow:    Writes a single row to the csv file
#     writerClose:    Closes the CSV File
class _CSVWriter:
```

构造器打开对应文件名的csvFile文件,并将该标题写入该文件。

```
    def __init__(self, fileName):
        try:
            # create a writer object and then write the header row
            self.csvFile = open(fileName,'wb')
            self.writer = csv.writer(self.csvFile,
                          delimiter = ',',
                          quoting = csv.QUOTE_ALL)
            self.writer.writerow( ('Image Path', 'TimeStamp',
                          'Camera Make',
                          'Camera Model',
                          'Lat Ref', 'Latitude',
                          'Lon Ref', 'Longitude') )
        except:
            log.error('CSV File Failure')
```

实际的writeCSVRow方法需将给出的每个列作为输入,并将它们写入csv文件。此外,该函数将浮点数表示的纬度值和经度值转换为规定格式的字符串。

```
    def writeCSVRow(self, fileName, timeStamp, CameraMake,
                   CameraModel,latRef, latValue, lonRef,
                   onValue):
        latStr = '%.8f'% latValue
        lonStr = '%.8f'% lonValue
        self.writer.writerow( (fileName, timeStamp, CameraMake,
                          CameraModel, latRef, latStr,
                          lonRef, lonStr))
```

最后del方法关闭csvFile,以正确地解构对象。

```
    def __del__(self):
        self.csvFile.close()
```

5.3.7 完整代码清单

```
#
# GPS Extraction
# Python-Forensics
```

第 5 章　证据提取（JPEG 和 TIFF）

```
#       No HASP required
#
import os
import _modEXIF
import _csvHandler
import _commandParser
from classLogging import _ForensicLog

# Offsets into the return EXIFData for
# TimeStamp, Camera Make and Model
TS = 0
MAKE = 1
MODEL = 2

# Process the Command Line Arguments
userArgs = _commandParser.ParseCommandLine()

# create a log object
logPath = userArgs.logPath+"ForensicLog.txt"
oLog = _ForensicLog(logPath)

oLog.writeLog("INFO", "Scan Started")

csvPath = userArgs.csvPath+"imageResults.csv"
oCSV = _csvHandler._CSVWriter(csvPath)

# define a directory to scan
scanDir = userArgs.scanPath
try:
    picts = os.listdir(scanDir)
except:
    oLog.writeLog("ERROR", "Invalid Directory "+ scanDir)
    exit(0)

print "Program Start"
print

for aFile in picts:

    targetFile = scanDir+aFile

    if os.path.isfile(targetFile):

        gpsDictionary, EXIFList = _modEXIF.ExtractGPSDictionary
        (targetFile)

        if (gpsDictionary):

            # Obtain the Lat Lon values from the gpsDictionary
            # Converted to degrees
            # The return value is a dictionary key value pairs

            dCoor = _modEXIF.ExtractLatLon(gpsDictionary)

            lat = dCoor.get("Lat")
            latRef = dCoor.get("LatRef")
            lon = dCoor.get("Lon")
            lonRef = dCoor.get("LonRef")
```

```python
            if (lat and lon and latRef and lonRef):
                print str(lat)+','+str(lon)
                # write one row to the output file
                oCSV.writeCSVRow(targetFile, EXIFList[TS], EXIFList
                [MAKE], EXIFList[MODEL],latRef, lat, lonRef, lon)
                oLog.writeLog("INFO", "GPS Data Calculated for :" +
                targetFile)
            else:
                oLog.writeLog("WARNING", "No GPS EXIF Data for "+
                targetFile)
        else:
            oLog.writeLog("WARNING", "No GPS EXIF Data for "+ targetFile)
    else:
        oLog.writeLog("WARNING", targetFile + " not a valid file")
# Clean up and Close Log and CSV File
del oLog
del oCSV
import argparse                     # Python Standard Library - Parser
for command-line options, arguments
import os                           # Standard Library OS functions
# Name: ParseCommand() Function
#
# Desc: Process and Validate the command line arguments
#       use Python Standard Library module argparse
#
# Input: none
#
# Actions:
#            Uses the standard library argparse to process the command line
#
def ParseCommandLine():

    parser = argparse.ArgumentParser('Python gpsExtractor')

    parser.add_argument('-v','--verbose', help="enables printing of
    additional program messages", action='store_true')
    parser.add_argument('-l','--logPath', type= ValidateDirectory,
    required=True, help="specify the directory for forensic log output file")
    parser.add_argument('-c','--csvPath', type= ValidateDirectory,
    required=True, help="specify the output directory for the csv file")
    parser.add_argument('-d','--scanPath', type= ValidateDirectory,
    required=True, help="specify the directory to scan")

    theArgs = parser.parse_args()

    return theArgs

# End Parse Command Line ==============================

def ValidateDirectory(theDir):

    # Validate the path is a directory
    if not os.path.isdir(theDir):
        raise argparse.ArgumentTypeError('Directory does not exist')
```

```python
        # Validate the path is writable
        if os.access(theDir, os.W_OK):
            return theDir
        else:
            raise argparse.ArgumentTypeError('Directory is not writable')
# End ValidateDirectory ====================================

import logging
#
# Class: _ForensicLog
#
# Desc: Handles Forensic Logging Operations
#
# Methods constructor:      Initializes the Logger
#         writeLog:         Writes a record to the log
#         destructor:       Writes an information message and
#                           shuts down the logger

class _ForensicLog:

    def __init__(self, logName):
        try:
            # Turn on Logging
logging.basicConfig(filename=logName,level=logging.DEBUG, format='%(asctime)s %(message)s')
        except:
            print "Forensic Log Initialization Failure . . . Aborting"
            exit(0)

    def writeLog(self, logType, logMessage):
        if logType == "INFO":
            logging.info(logMessage)
        elif logType == "ERROR":
            logging.error(logMessage)
        elif logType == "WARNING":
            logging.warning(logMessage)
        else:
            logging.error(logMessage)
        return

    def __del__(self):
        logging.info("Logging Shutdown")
        logging.shutdown()
#
# Data Extraction - Python-Forensics
# Extract GPS Data from EXIF supported Images (jpg, tiff)
# Support Module
#
import os                               # Standard Library OS functions
from classLogging import _ForensicLog   # Abstracted Forensic Logging Class

# import the Python Image Library
# along with TAGS and GPS related TAGS

from PIL import Image
```

```python
from PIL.EXIFTags import TAGS, GPSTAGS
#
# Extract EXIF Data
#
# Input: Full Pathname of the target image
#
# Return: gps Dictionary and selected EXIFData list
#
def ExtractGPSDictionary(fileName):
    try:
        pilImage = Image.open(fileName)
        EXIFData = pilImage._getEXIF()

    except Exception:
        # If exception occurs from PIL processing
        # Report the
        return None, None

    # Iterate through the EXIFData
    # Searching for GPS Tags

    imageTimeStamp = "NA"
    CameraModel = "NA"
    CameraMake = "NA"

    if EXIFData:

        for tag, theValue in EXIFData.items():

            # obtain the tag
            tagValue = TAGS.get(tag, tag)
            # Collect basic image data if available

            if tagValue =='DateTimeOriginal':
                imageTimeStamp = EXIFData.get(tag)

            if tagValue == "Make":
                cameraMake = EXIFData.get(tag)

            if tagValue =='Model':
                cameraModel = EXIFData.get(tag)
            # check the tag for GPS
            if tagValue == "GPSInfo":

                # Found it !
                # Now create a Dictionary to hold the GPS Data

                gpsDictionary = {}

                # Loop through the GPS Information
                for curTag in theValue:
                    gpsTag = GPSTAGS.get(curTag, curTag)
                    gpsDictionary[gpsTag] = theValue[curTag]
```

```
                    basicEXIFData = [imageTimeStamp, cameraMake, cameraModel]
                return gpsDictionary, basicEXIFData
    else:
        return None, None
# End ExtractGPSDictionary ==============================
#
# Extract the Latitude and Longitude Values
# From the gpsDictionary
#
def ExtractLatLon(gps):
    # to perform the calculation we need at least
    # lat, lon, latRef and lonRef

    if (gps.has_key("GPSLatitude") and gps.has_key("GPSLongitude")
    and gps.has_key("GPSLatitudeRef") and gps.has_key
    ("GPSLatitudeRef")):

        latitude     = gps["GPSLatitude"]
        latitudeRef  = gps["GPSLatitudeRef"]
        longitude    = gps["GPSLongitude"]
        longitudeRef = gps["GPSLongitudeRef"]

        lat = ConvertToDegrees(latitude)
        lon = ConvertToDegrees(longitude)
        # Check Latitude Reference
        # If South of the Equator then lat value is negative

        if latitudeRef == "S":
            lat = 0 - lat

        # Check Longitude Reference
        # If West of the Prime Meridian in
        # Greenwich then the Longitude value is negative

        if longitudeRef == "W":
            lon = 0- lon

        gpsCoor = {"Lat": lat, "LatRef":latitudeRef, "Lon": lon,
        "LonRef": longitudeRef}

        return gpsCoor

    else:
        return None
# End Extract Lat Lon ====================================
#
# Convert GPSCoordinates to Degrees
#
# Input gpsCoordinates value from in EXIF Format
#
def ConvertToDegrees(gpsCoordinate):

    d0 = gpsCoordinate[0][0]
    d1 = gpsCoordinate[0][1]
```

```python
        try:
            degrees = float(d0) / float(d1)
        except:
            degrees = 0.0

        m0 = gpsCoordinate[1][0]
        m1 = gpsCoordinate[1][1]
        try:
            minutes = float(m0) / float(m1)
        except:
            minutes=0.0

        s0 = gpsCoordinate[2][0]
        s1 = gpsCoordinate[2][1]
        try:
            seconds = float(s0) / float(s1)
        except:
            seconds = 0.0

        floatCoordinate = float (degrees + (minutes / 60.0) + (seconds / 3600.0))
        return floatCoordinate

import csv    # Python Standard Library - reader and writer for csv files
#
# Class: _CSVWriter
#
# Desc: Handles all methods related to comma separated value operations
#
# Methods constructor: Initializes the CSV File
#               writeCVSRow:     Writes a single row to the csv file
#               writerClose:     Closes the CSV File

class _CSVWriter:
    def __init__(self, fileName):
        try:
            # create a writer object and then write the header row
            self.csvFile = open(fileName,'wb')
            self.writer = csv.writer(self.csvFile, delimiter=',',
                quoting=csv.QUOTE_ALL)
            self.writer.writerow( ('Image Path','Make','Model','UTC Time',
'Lat Ref','Latitude','Lon Ref','Longitude','Alt Ref','Altitude') )
        except:
            log.error('CSV File Failure')

    def writeCSVRow(self, fileName, cameraMake, cameraModel, utc,
    latRef, latValue, lonRef, lonValue, altRef, altValue):
        latStr ='%.8f'% latValue
        lonStr='%.8f'% lonValue
        altStr ='%.8f'% altValue
        self.writer.writerow(fileName, cameraMake, cameraModel, utc,
        latRef, latStr, lonRef, lonStr, altRef, AltStr)

    def __del__(self):
        self.csvFile.close()
```

5.3.8 程序的执行

p-gpsExtractor分别产生三个输出结果：（1）标准输出，显示从目标文件提取的纬度值和经度值；（2）CSV文件，包含提取的EXIF和GPS的详细数据；（3）取证日志文件，包含程序执行中产生的日志。程序的执行是通过使用下面的命令行选项完成的。

```
c:\pictures\Program>Python p-GPSExtractor.py -d c:\pictures\ -c
  c:\pictures\Results\ -l c:\pictures\Log\
```

图5.8给出了程序执行的结果。我已经选择了输出结果并复制到剪贴板缓冲中，以便在在线地图程序中描绘所有的点。

图5.8是在Windows下执行p-gpsExtractor的屏幕截图。

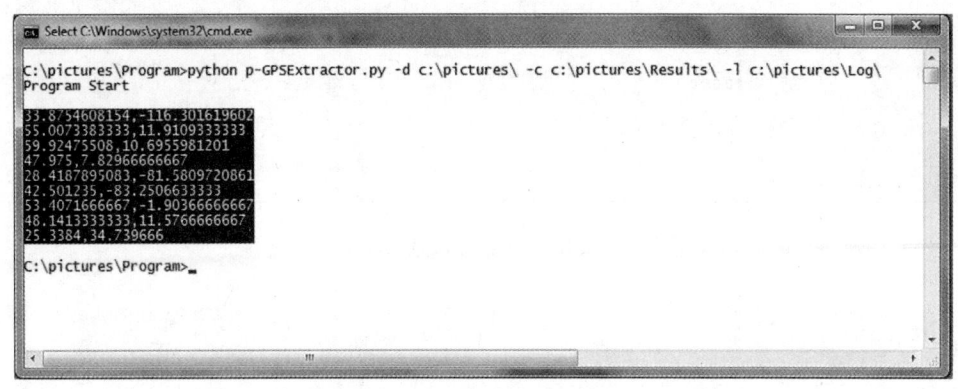

图5.8　p-gpsExtractor程序执行

在图5.9中，从程序执行结果中选择坐标，粘贴到一个在线网站http://www.darrinward.com/lat-long/ [Ward]，然后提交这些坐标。该网页在地图上以图钉的形式标绘出每一个坐标点。图5.10和图5.11给出了地图放大后的位置，从图中可知其位置在德国。

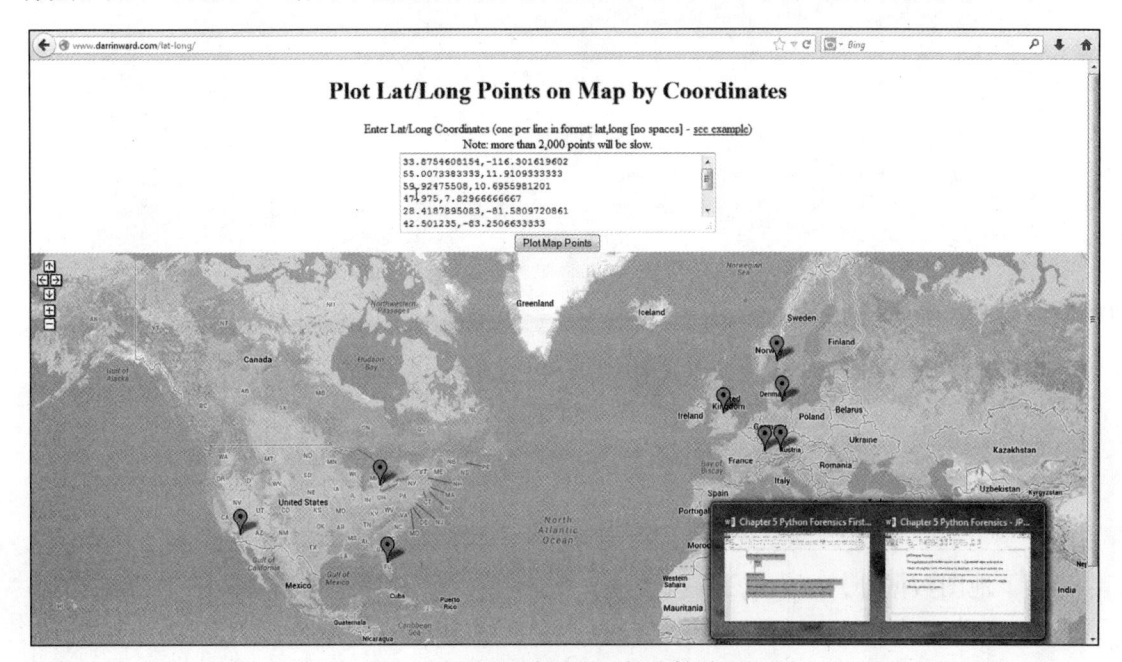

图5.9　把从照片提取的坐标映射到地图

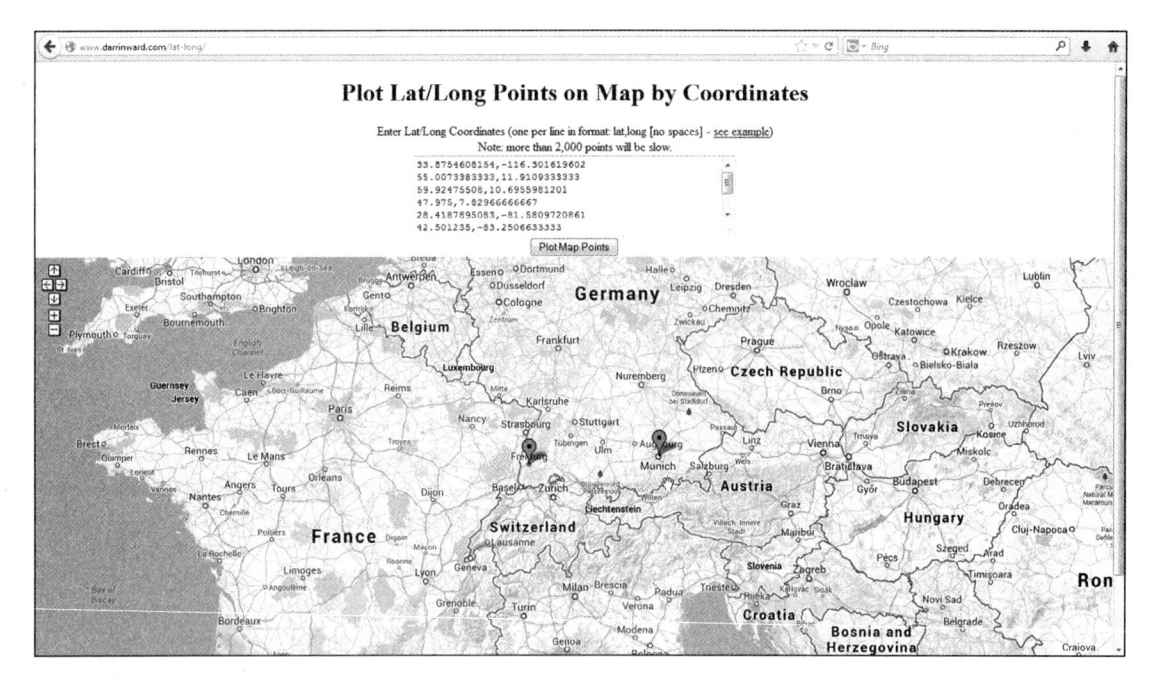

图5.10　地图缩放到西欧

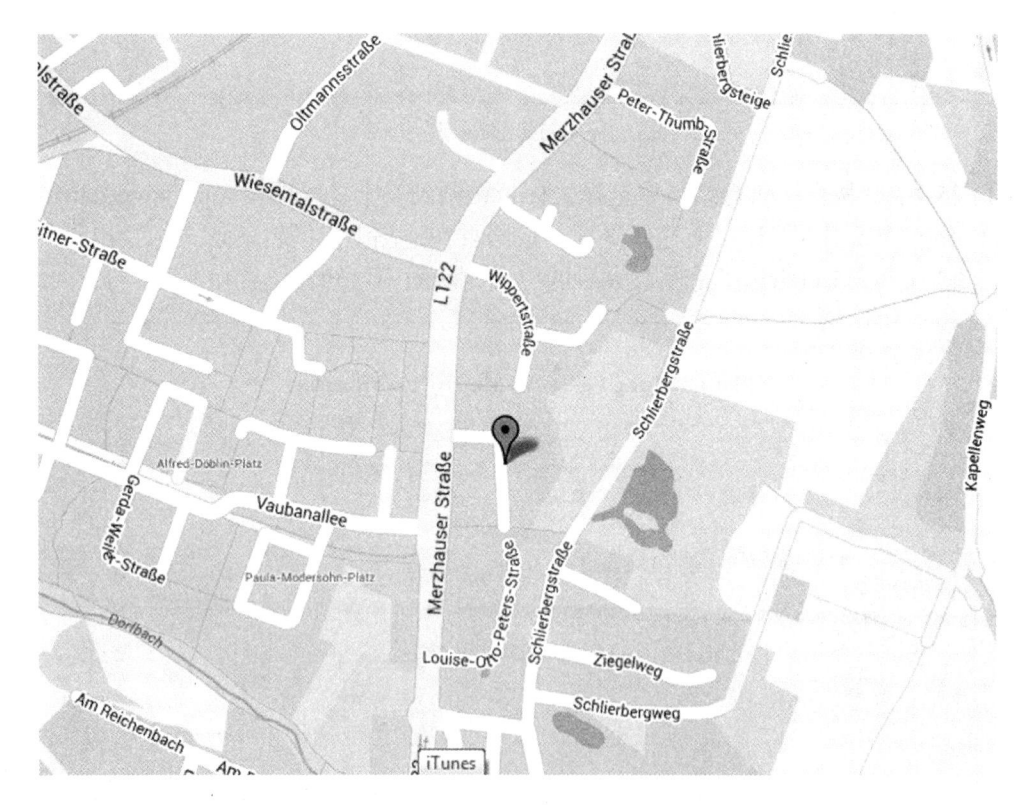

图5.11　地图缩放到德国的街道级别

除了地图数据外，还生成了一个.csv结果文件，用于保存扫描结果。图5.12展示了得到的.csv文件。

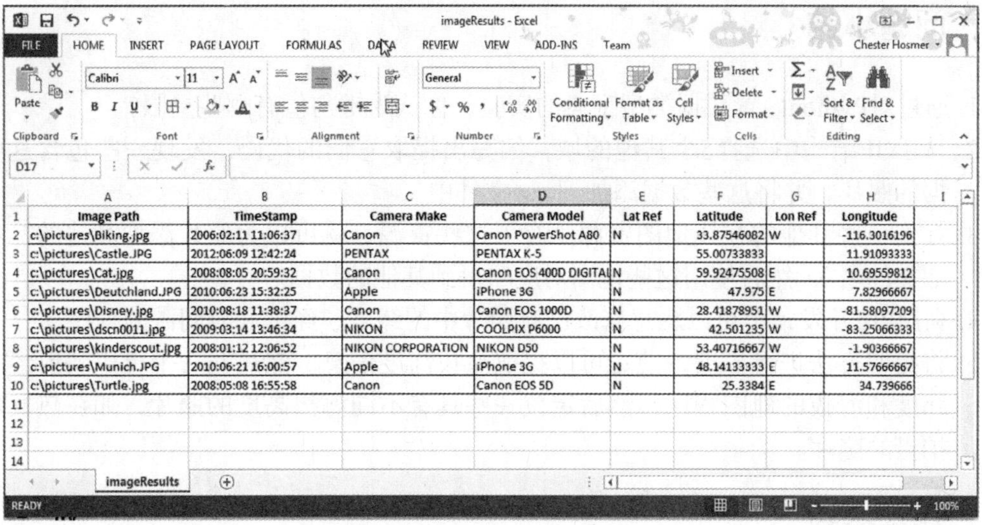

Image Path	TimeStamp	Camera Make	Camera Model	Lat Ref	Latitude	Lon Ref	Longitude
c:\pictures\Biking.jpg	2006:02:11 11:06:37	Canon	Canon PowerShot A80	N	33.87546082	W	-116.3016196
c:\pictures\Castle.JPG	2012:06:09 12:42:24	PENTAX	PENTAX K-5		55.00733833		11.91093333
c:\pictures\Cat.jpg	2008:08:05 20:59:32	Canon	Canon EOS 400D DIGITAL	N	59.92475508	E	10.69559812
c:\pictures\Deutchland.JPG	2010:06:23 15:32:25	Apple	iPhone 3G	N	47.975	E	7.82966667
c:\pictures\Disney.jpg	2010:08:18 11:38:37	Canon	Canon EOS 1000D	N	28.41878951	W	-81.58097209
c:\pictures\dscn0011.jpg	2009:03:14 13:46:34	NIKON	COOLPIX P6000	N	42.501235	W	-83.25066333
c:\pictures\kinderscout.jpg	2008:01:12 12:06:52	NIKON CORPORATION	NIKON D50	N	53.40716667	W	-1.90366667
c:\pictures\Munich.JPG	2010:06:21 16:00:57	Apple	iPhone 3G	N	48.14133333	E	11.57666667
c:\pictures\Turtle.jpg	2008:05:08 16:55:58	Canon	Canon EOS 5D	N	25.3384	E	34.739666

图5.12　Result.csv文件截图

最后，还创建了关于程序执行情况的取证日志文件。该文件包含取证日志内容，如图5.13所示。

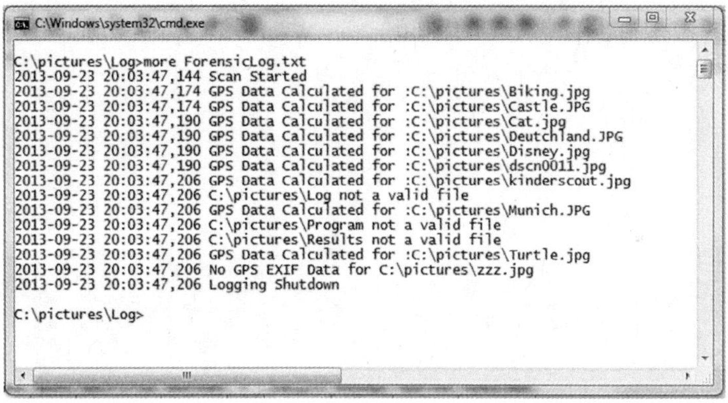

```
C:\pictures\Log>more ForensicLog.txt
2013-09-23 20:03:47,144 Scan Started
2013-09-23 20:03:47,174 GPS Data Calculated for :C:\pictures\Biking.jpg
2013-09-23 20:03:47,174 GPS Data Calculated for :C:\pictures\Castle.JPG
2013-09-23 20:03:47,190 GPS Data Calculated for :C:\pictures\Cat.jpg
2013-09-23 20:03:47,190 GPS Data Calculated for :C:\pictures\Deutchland.JPG
2013-09-23 20:03:47,190 GPS Data Calculated for :C:\pictures\Disney.jpg
2013-09-23 20:03:47,190 GPS Data Calculated for :C:\pictures\dscn0011.jpg
2013-09-23 20:03:47,206 GPS Data Calculated for :C:\pictures\kinderscout.jpg
2013-09-23 20:03:47,206 C:\pictures\Log not a valid file
2013-09-23 20:03:47,206 GPS Data Calculated for :C:\pictures\Munich.JPG
2013-09-23 20:03:47,206 C:\pictures\Program not a valid file
2013-09-23 20:03:47,206 C:\pictures\Results not a valid file
2013-09-23 20:03:47,206 GPS Data Calculated for :C:\pictures\Turtle.jpg
2013-09-23 20:03:47,206 No GPS EXIF Data for C:\pictures\zzz.jpg
2013-09-23 20:03:47,206 Logging Shutdown

C:\pictures\Log>
```

图5.13　取证日志文件截图

5.4　章节回顾

在这一章中，开始使用包括字典在内的一些新的Python语言元素，以便处理更复杂的数据类型并与PIL交互。利用PIL，系统地从照片中提取EXIF数据，包括可用的GPS数据。不仅演示了如何提取GPS原始数据，还演示了如何计算经度和纬度位置，并将程序的输出输入一个在线地图程序中绘出相片的拍摄位置。此外还演示了如何从EXIF数据结构中提取数据，并将这些值保存到一个产生的.cvs文件中。这些值包括文件、照相机、时间戳和位置等信息。

5.5 问题小结

1. 通过对Python内置数据类型字典的实验，你认为键与值有哪些局限？
2. 从EXIF结构中选择5个其他的域，编写出提取它们的代码，发现一些包含这些数据的照片，并将这些数据添加到.csv文件中。
3. 找到一些其他的在线地图资源（有了这些资源，就可以为照片添加其他的标签，如文件名），然后使用这些地图对应项得到其他的数据。
4. 利用PIL开发一个可以恶意修改已有照片中的纬度、经度和时间戳的程序。
5. 将提取方法进行扩展，使之可以提取海拔高度信息。然后找一个可以映射经度、纬度和海拔的地图程序，然后定位一些具有不同海拔高度的照片，如在热气球上拍摄的照片。

5.6 补充资料

1. FCC 911 无线服务指南. 网址http://www.fcc.gov/guides/wireless-911-services
2. Python图像库.网址 https://pypi.python.org/pypi/PIL
3. Python标准库. 网址http://docs.python.org/2/library/
4. 基于Web的多坐标绘图网站. 网址http://www.darrinward.com/lat-long/

第6章 时间取证

6.1 本章简介

在可以从证据的观点进一步探讨时间之前,需要更好地理解什么是时间。下面从摘录于一本我喜欢的书《经度》中的故事说起,书的作者是Dava Sobel。

"生活于18世纪的人应该都知道经度问题是那个时代最棘手的科学难题,并且几个世纪以来一直都是。由于没有能力来测量其经度,在整个大探索时代的水手们只要看不到陆地,就会彻底地迷失在海洋。对于解决方案的需求让科学家以及他们的赞助人忙碌了将近两个世纪,终于,在1714年英格兰议会提高了悬赏,提供相当于一个国王赎金(2万英镑,约合现在的货币1200万美元)的巨奖,给能提出可行方法或装置的任何人。整个欧洲的科学机构,不论是伽利略还是牛顿爵士建立的,都通过绘制两个半球的天空,试图从天上找到答案。与之形成鲜明对比的是,有一个人,约翰·哈里森(John Harrison),大胆地设想了一个机械的方案——一个能在海上保持精确计时的时钟,精确到甚至还没有一个时钟能在陆地上做到。哈里森先生的发明解决了这个时代最重要的科学问题。"

哈里森时钟的基本原理和解决方案仍然指导着当今的航海,因为GPS(全球定位系统)内的时间以及其他导航体系的使用,仍然作为关键的基础组件,让我们能计算我们在哪里。图6.1描述了第一个哈里森海洋时钟H1。

哈里森先生毕生的工作就是推动建立格林尼治标准时间或简称GMT。在全球经济和通信设施高速发展的今天,精确的、准确的、可靠的、不可伪造的和不可否认的时间几乎和18世纪一样难以获得。当然,基于原子、铷、铯的时钟能保证发出准确的时间,甚至一千多年不误差分毫。但是把这种精确性传递给数字证据却是棘手的。我最喜欢的一句话是,"任何人都可以告诉你现在是什么时间,但是要证明过去是什么时间,仍然困难重重"。

时间是一个概念,使得社会以一个有序的方式运转,各方都容易理解时间的表示方法,并约定事情的顺序。从1972年起国际时间标准是协调统一时间(Coordinated Universal Time)或者简称UTC。在全球大部分国家UTC作为官方时间源的基础。它受制于一个被世界各国接受的外交条约,各国指派国家级的测

图6.1 约翰哈里森H1时钟

量（或计量）机构（NMI）作为UTC时间源。美国的国家标准与技术研究所（NIST）、日本的通信研究实验室、英国的国家物理实验室（NPL）都是NMI的例子。大约有50个类似的计量机构负责全球的官方时间。

几百年来时间已经成为商业的关键要素。时间（通过一个机械来记录）建立并提供类似商业交易和事件的有关"何时"的证据（通常记录在纸上，这些时间记录提供了证据的踪迹，这要归功于一些独特的属性——渗入纸中油墨的可辨别性，打字的风格和方式，是机械或是手写，对修改、插入或删除的可检测性）。在电子世界里文件和时间戳仅仅是比特和字节，事件的权威性时间证据很难固定。由于时间的正确性必须绝对追溯到来自官方源的起点，所以依赖于易被操纵的时间源（如典型的计算机系统时钟）是有问题的。

精度和可靠性一直是推动电子计时技术设计的主要因素。下一个技术浪潮给数字时间戳增加了真实性、安全性和可审查性三个维度。当这三个属性应用到文档、事务，或任何其他数字实体时，会提供以下胜于传统的基于计算机时钟时间戳的优点：

保证时间来源于官方时间源
保证时间没有被篡改
证据上的踪迹，用于审计和不可否认

可鉴别性（知道发起人的身份）和完整性（保护内容不被修改）是可信交易的基本要素。但是一个人如果不能相信时间，交易是否真的可以信任？安全时间戳给可信交易过程添加上了一个缺失的环节：它是"何时"发生的？然而，为了让时间戳给这个问题提供一个可靠的答案，那么它基于的时间必须来自可信的源。

6.2 给这个环节添加时间

实践为我们提供了最好的经验，今天的数字签名能够成功地把"谁"（签名者）与"什么"（数字数据）绑定。然而数字签名也有不足之处，留下两个没有解决的关键问题：

1. 数字证据的签名在什么时候发生？
2. 对于签名的数字证据，我们能否证明其完整性保持了多长时间？

对于这些问题，时间成为证明数字证据完整性的关键因素。通过因特网工程任务组（IETF）和民营企业的工作，时间戳已经提升到了实际部署阶段。

要理解这一点，必须首先对时间本身有一点了解。另外，如果选择利用时间作为数字证据的信任机制，那么还有哪些方面是必需的。从古代社会到今天，对时间存在多种解释。本质上时间是一个协议，使得社会全体有序地运作，所有各方都很容易理解时间的表示方法。一些时间测量方法的例子参见图6.2。

如图6.2所示，人类所熟知的第一个计时系统基于月球，因为每个人都容易就这个通用的时间尺度达成一致。再往后，埃及人首先理解了太阳年，基于地球绕太阳的旋转，他们得以建立了一个计时系统。1967年，一个国际协议规定时间单位为秒，使用称为原子钟的精密仪器测量铯的衰减来获得。1972年，米制公约（也称为米制会议，1875年建立）进行扩展，包含了称为UTC的通用时间基准，取代GMT作为世界的官方时间。

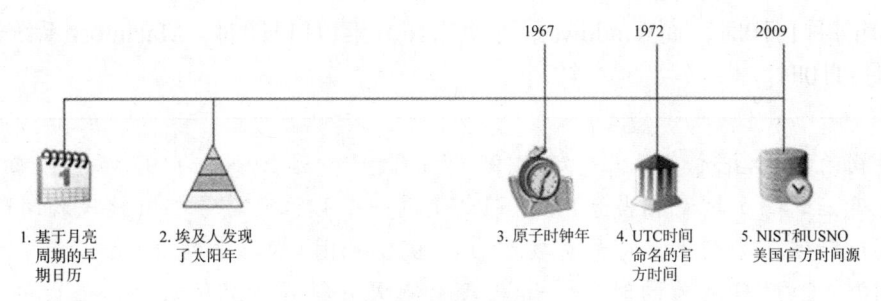

图6.2 时间简史

今天，超过50个国家实验室运行着超过300个原子钟，以提供一致和精确的UTC。因此为了创造一个可信时间源，必须首先引用一个官方时间源。在美国有两个官方时间源：位于科罗拉多州博尔德（Boulder）的美国国家标准与技术研究所（NIST）提供商业时间，以及美国海军气象天文台（USNO）提供军事时间。

尽管有很多方法可以得到精确的时间（手表、计算机的时钟、时间服务器等），在系统中融入可信时间还是需要一个安全和可审计的数字日期/时间戳。除非直接连到NMI，其实如今最值得信赖的来源还是利用GPS作为时间源。如果恰当地调校铷时间服务器，GPS信号提供的准确度可以满足大多数交易和记录保存所需的准确度和精度的要求。当且仅当遵循以下要求、标准和过程时，这种准确度就可以实现。

精确性 表示的时间来自一个权威的源，满足交易所需的精度要求，无论是天、小时，还是毫秒。

可认证性 时间源认证为一个可信的时间源，如NMI计时实验室、GPS信号，或NIST的长波标准时间信号（在美国是WWVB）。

完整性 时间应该是安全的，在正常的"处理"中不容易破坏。如果被破坏了，无论是无心的还是故意的，第三方应该容易察觉。

不可否认性 一个事件或文件应当与其时间绑定，这样事件或文件与时间之间的联系就不能在之后被否认。

可追责性 获取时间，添加可认证性和完整性，以及绑定时间到主体事件等过程应当具有可追责性，这样第三方就可以确定，实施了正确的处置方法，并且没有损坏发生。

阅读本书的大多数人将很快认识到，从现实的角度来看，在数字调查过程中所收集的时间戳很少满足上述标准。然而我们努力建立的关于这些标准的学问是至关重要的。这会使你怀疑与时间相关的任何事。让我们从深入了解Python标准库的time、datetime和calendar模块开始学习。

6.3 时间模块

时间模块具有许多属性和方法来协助处理与时间相关的信息。运用成熟的技术——"代码前测试"，从用time模块进行实验开始起步。

我们遇到的第一个问题是"纪元"的定义，一个纪元被定义为一个显著的事件，标志着一段时期的开始。现代数字计算机引用特定的历史点，如大多数基于UNIX的系统选择了1970年1月1日0时,而Windows系统使用1601年1月1日0时,Macintosh系统通常引用1904年1月1日0时。

> 最初的UNIX纪元实际上是定在1971年1月1日,后来修正为1970年1月1日。如果从纪元开始的每个增量相当于1秒,那么使用一个32位无符号整数就代表约136年。因此通过指定一个32位无符号整数作为自1970年1月1日以来的秒数,就可以标记任何在2106年2月7日之前的时刻。如果只能使用有符号的32位数字,最大的日期是2038年1月19日。

正如前面的描述,大多数系统的纪元开始于1970年1月1日。问题是你怎么知道的?简单的答案是要求Python的time模块gmtime()方法告诉我们,gmtime转换秒数(将其作为参数传递给gmtime()方法)为等效的GMT。举例说明,让我们传递0作为参数,看看该方法返回什么纪元日期。

```
>>>import time
>>> print time.gmtime(0)
time.struct_time(tm_year=1970, tm_mon=1, tm_mday=1, tm_hour=0,
tm_min=0, tm_sec=0, tm_wday=3, tm_yday=1, tm_isdst=0)
```

类似地,如果想知道最大时间值(由于无符号32位数的最大限制),我执行以下代码。

```
>>>import time
>>>time.gmtime(0xffffffff)
time.struct_time(tm_year=2106, tm_mon=2, tm_mday=7, tm_hour=6,
tm_min=28, tm_sec=15, tm_wday=6, tm_yday=38, tm_isdst=0)
```

此外,你可能会想,自从纪元以来已经过了多少秒?为了证实这一点,我使用time模块提供的time()方法。该方法计算自纪元以来的秒数。

```
>>>time.time()
1381601236.189
```

你可以看到,在Windows版本下执行time()方法的这个命令,time()方法返回一个浮点数而不是一个简单的整数,提供了亚秒级精度。

```
>>>secondsSinceEpoch= time.time()
>>>secondsSinceEpoch
1381601264.237
```

然后可以利用这个时间(首先被转换为一个整数)作为gmtime()方法的输入来确定格林尼治的日期和时间。

```
>>>time.gmtime(int(secondsSinceEpoch))
time.struct_time(tm_year=2013, tm_mon=10,tm_mday=12, tm_hour=18,
tm_min=7, tm_sec=44, tm_wday=5, tm_yday=285, tm_isdst=0)
```

结果是2013年10月12日的18时7分44秒,周时间为5(假设周开始于0 = 星期一,该值将代表星期六);这是2013的第285天;我们目前没有发现夏令时。为完整清晰起见应该进一步注意到,这个时间代表UTC/GMT时间而不是当地时间。另外需要注意的是,time

模块使用计算机的系统时间和时区设置计算自纪元以来的秒数,不是神奇的时间上帝。因此如果想改变当前的时间,只需改变自己的系统时钟,然后重新运行前面的脚本。

```
>>>secondsSinceEpoch= time.time()
>>>secondsSinceEpoch
1381580629.793
>>>time.gmtime(int(secondsSinceEpoch))
time.struct_time(tm_year=2013, tm_mon=10, tm_mday=12, tm_hour=12,
tm_min=23, tm_sec=49, tm_wday=5, tm_yday=285, tm_isdst=0)
```

结果就是我们第一个成功的时间伪造。

现在,如果要比较GMT/UTC与本地时间,则利用gmtime()和localtime()方法。

```
>>> import time

>>> now= time.time()

>>> now

1381670992.539

>>> time.gmtime(int(now))

time.struct_time(tm_year=2013, tm_mon=10, tm_mday=13, tm_hour=13,
tm_min=29, tm_sec=52, tm_wday=6, tm_yday=286, tm_isdst=0)

>>> time.localtime(int(now))
time.struct_time(tm_year=2013, tm_mon=10, tm_mday=13, tm_hour=9,
tm_min=29, tm_sec=52, tm_wday=6, tm_yday=286, tm_isdst=1)dst=0)
```

将能看到结果如下:

Local Time: Sunday October 13, 2013 **09:29:52**

GMT Time: Sunday October 13, 2013 **13:29:52**

localtime()和gmtime()都考虑到了确定日期和时间的许多因素,其中一个重要的考虑就是我的系统目前配置的时区。

通过使用下面的脚本,可以用Python来提供自己的系统的当前时区设置。注意time.timezone是一个属性而不是一个方法,它可以直接读取。

```
>>> import time
>>> time.timezone
18000
```

那么,18000是什么意思?我们倾向于认为时区是一个特定的区域或地带,它确实是。我们也倾向于认为每个时区正好是相隔1小时,这并不总是正确的。

例如,全球的有些地方利用相对于UTC/GMT的30分钟偏移值。它们有:

阿富汗

澳大利亚(包括北部和南部地区)

印度

伊朗

缅甸

斯里兰卡

其他地方使用相对于UTC/GMT的15分钟偏移值。这些例子包括：

尼泊尔
新西兰的查塔姆群岛
西澳大利亚的部分地区

18000代表UTC以西的秒数，而UTC以东的地点记录成负秒。因为18000代表UTC以西的秒数，我可以很容易地计算UTC以西的小时，就是18000秒除以60（1分钟有60秒），然后再除以60（1小时有60分钟）：

$$18\,000/60/60 = 5小时$$

这意味着我的当地时间是UTC/GMT以西5小时。然后回到比较的地方，我们的本地时间和GMT时间应该有5小时的差异吗？

Local Time: Sunday October 13, 2013 **09:29:52**
GMT Time: Sunday October 13, 2013 **13:29:52**

完全不是！本例中localtime()和gmtime()的不同是只差4个小时。原因在于Sunday October 13处于美国东部时区的夏令时，正如在本地时间例子中发现的tm_indst=1，因此在这个特定的日期，时间差就是从GMT/UTC通过这两种方式正确报告的4小时。

接下来，你可能想知道如何确定当前系统的时区设置的名称。time模块规定的一个附加属性time.tzname提供了一个元组，第一个值是标准时区名称，而第二个值是本地夏令时时区名称。

```
>>>import time
>>>time.tzname
('Eastern Standard Time','Eastern Daylight Time')
```

请注意，此信息是基于本地操作系统内部表示的。例如在Mac上，就会返回（"EST"，"EDT"）。

因此，如果希望打印本地系统当前时区名称，下面的代码可以用到。

```
import time
# Get the current local time
now=time.localtime()
# if we are observing daylight savings time
# tm_isdst is an attribute that can be examined,
# if the value is 0 the current local time is in
# standard time observations and if tm_isdst is 1
# then daylight savings time is being observed
if now.tm_isdst:
    # print the daylight savings time string
    print time.tzname[1]
else:
```

```
# Otherwise print the standard time string
print time.tzname[0]
```
Eastern Daylight Time

time模块里另一个很有用的方法是strftime()。此方法为从基础时间结构生成自定义字符串提供了极大的灵活性。这使我们能够格式化输出，而无须手动提取单个时间属性。例如：

```
import time
print time.strftime("%a, %d %b %Y %H:%M:%S %p",time.localtime())
time.sleep(5)
print time.strftime("%a, %d %b %Y %H:%M:%S %p",time.localtime())
```

这个简短的脚本使用strftime方法打印出本地时间值，然后使用sleep()方法延迟（本例为5秒），然后打印另一个时间字符串。结果产生以下输出：

```
Sun, 13 Oct 2013 10:38:44 AM
Sun, 13 Oct 2013 10:38:49 AM
```

strftime方法在可用的选项中提供很大的灵活性，如表6.1所示。

表6.1　strftime输出规范

参数	描述
%a	缩写的星期几的名称
%A	完整的星期几的名称
%b	缩写的月名称
%B	完整的月名称
%c	本地相应的日期表示和时间表示
%d	01~31 十进制的月中的天
%H	00~24 十进制的小时
%I	00~12 十进制的小时
%j	001~356 十进制的年中的天
%m	01~12 十进制的月
%M	00~59 十进制的分
%p	本地的上午或下午表示
%S	00~59 十进制秒数
%U	一年中的星期00~53，假定星期天为星期的开始
%w	星期日为0的星期几
%W	一年中的星期00~53，假定星期一为星期的开始
%x	本地的日期表示
%X	本地的时间表示
%y	00~99 不带世纪十进制的年
%Y	带世纪十进制的年
%Z	时区名

正如所看到的，time模块有大量直观的方法和属性。有关time模块的更多信息，可以查看Python标准库。

6.4 网络时间协议

今天，最被广泛接受的同步时间的做法是使用网络时间协议（NTP）。NTP使用用户数据报协议（UDP），在服务器（包含一个高度精确的时间源）和希望与时间源同步的客户端之间，传输简单的定时数据包（NTP协议默认的服务器端口号是123）。NTP模型包括不止一个，而是许多同步到国家实验室的易于访问的时间服务器。NTP的要点是通过互联网从这些服务器向客户端传送或分发时间。NTP协议标准由IETF管理，推荐的标准是RFC 5905，名为"网络时间协议版本4：协议与算法规范"[NTP RFC]。许多程序、操作系统和应用软件被开发出来，以利用此协议来同步时间。可能你已经猜到了我们要开发一个简单的时间同步Python程序，并使用此程序来同步取证操作。我并不是从零开始实现这个协议，而是准备利用一个第三方Python库ntplib来处理一些繁琐操作的，然后把结果与我的本地系统时钟进行对比。

6.5 获得和安装ntp库ntplib

ntplib可供下载地址是https://pypi.python.org/pypi/ntplib/，如图6.3所示，在写这本书时，它的当前版本为0.3.1。这个库提供了一个访问NTP服务器的简单接口，以及能将NTP协议域转换成文本的方法，以便能容易地访问其他关键值，如闰秒和特殊指示符等。

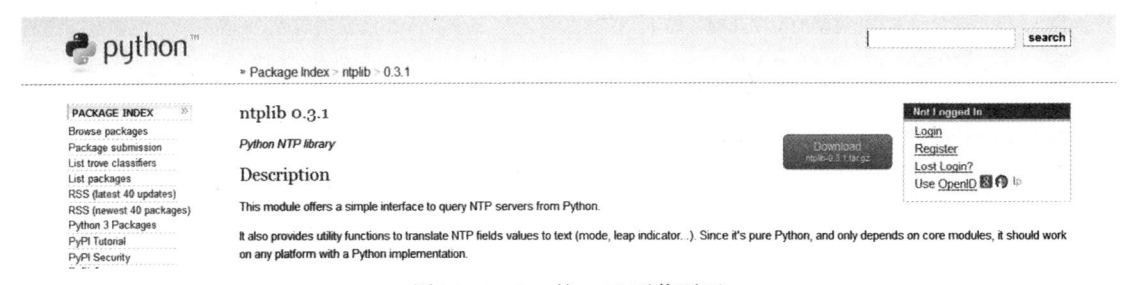

图6.3　Python的ntplib下载页面

目前该库仍是手动安装的，但还是相当直截了当的。因为ntplib完全用原生python编写，具备跨平台兼容性（Windows，Linux和Mac OS X）。

第一个安装步骤是下载安装包，在本例中是一个tar.gz文件，如图6.4所示。

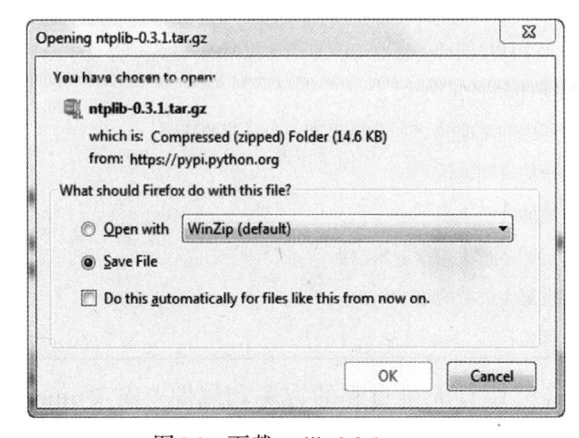

图6.4　下载ntplib-0.3.1.tar.gz

一旦下载，必须解压缩tar.gz到本地目录。解压该文件到C:\python27\lib\ntplib-0.3.1（参见图6.5）。因为我正使用Python 2.75，在此目录中解压缩下载的文件，与其他安装的库组织在一起，便于今后访问和更新。

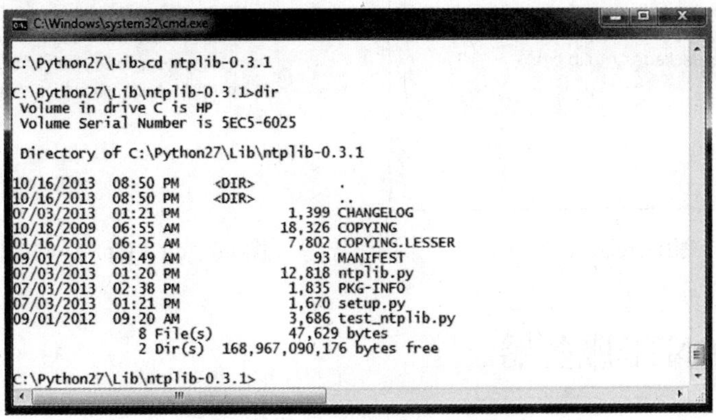

图6.5　解压ntplib-0.3.1.tar.gz

类似ntplib的手动安装库的安装过程，是通过执行包含在该目录中的安装程序setup.py来完成的。要执行安装，只需要打开一个命令窗口，如图6.6所示，输入命令

Python setup.py install

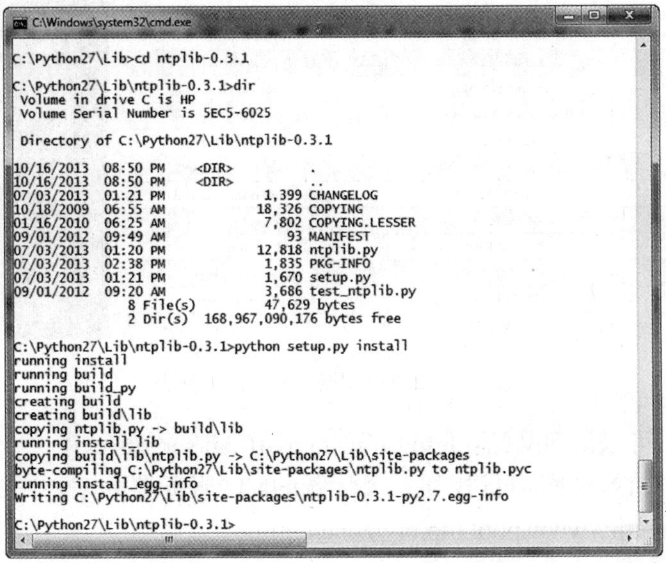

图6.6　安装ntplib

Setup.py程序执行所有必要的安装步骤。接下来，我总是喜欢打开一个Python Shell，然后导入库，再后通过简单地键入库的名称，来验证新库的安装。Python提供了有关证实该库可用的基本信息（参见图6.7）。

对于任何模块，总是可以输入内置函数dir(objName)，以获得与该对象有关的可用属性、类和方法的细节（参见图6.8）。若想获取更多信息，可以使用help(objName)的内置函数。

图6.7　验证安装

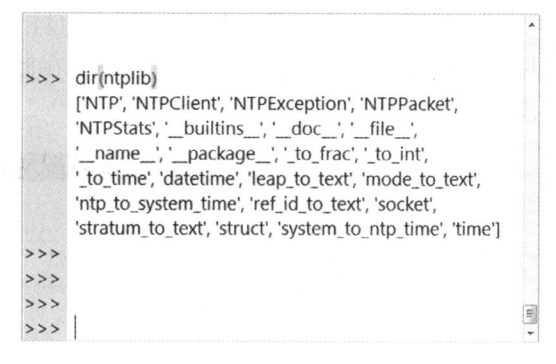

图6.8　dir（ntplib）的结果

6.6　全世界的NTP服务器

查看方法和属性时，第一眼看起来可能有点令人迷惑，但是使用库模块其实相当容易。简单地说，我们要创建一个能够访问指定的NTP服务器的NTP客户端，以获得一个第三方时间源。在美国，NIST管理着一个时间服务器列表，它们可以被访问并获得"根"时间（参见图6.9）。

Name	IP Address	Location	Status
nist1-ny.ustiming.org	64.90.182.55	New York City, NY	
nist1-nj.ustiming.org	96.47.67.105	Bridgewater, NJ	all services available
nist1-nj2.ustiming.org	165.193.126.229	Weehawken, NJ	all services available
nist1-ny2.ustiming.org	216.171.112.36	New York City, NY	All services available
nist1-pa.ustiming.org	206.246.122.250	Hatfield, PA	All services available
time-a.nist.gov	129.6.15.28	NIST, Gaithersburg, Maryland	All services busy, not recommended
time-b.nist.gov	129.6.15.29	NIST, Gaithersburg, Maryland	All services busy, not recommended
time-c.nist.gov	129.6.15.30	NIST, Gaithersburg, Maryland	All services available
time-d.nist.gov	2610:20:6F15:15::27	NIST, Gaithersburg, Maryland	All services via IPV6
nist1.aol-va.symmetricom.com	64.236.96.53	Reston, Virginia	All services available
nist1-macon.macon.ga.us	98.175.203.200	Macon, Georgia	All services available
nist1-atl.ustiming.org	64.250.177.145	Atlanta, Georgia	All services available
wolfnisttime.com	207.223.123.18	Birmingham, Alabama	All services available
nist1-chi.ustiming.org	216.171.120.36	Chicago, Illinois	All services available

图6.9　NIST时间服务器的部分列表

要更新列表，可以访问网站：http://tf.nist.gov/tf-cgi/servers.cgi。

在欧洲，可以在NTP库项目找到一个活跃的NTP服务器列表。图6.10显示了一个截图，来自于其主页http://www.pool.ntp.org/zone/europe。

对于那些希望从美国海军气象天文台或USNO获得时间的人，可能会非常兴奋地了解到，USNO提供NTP服务器访问已经有很长时间了，这个访问被形象地命名为"滴答滴答"（tick and tock）。有关美国海军气象天文台的更多信息，可以访问：http://www.usno.navy.mil/usno。

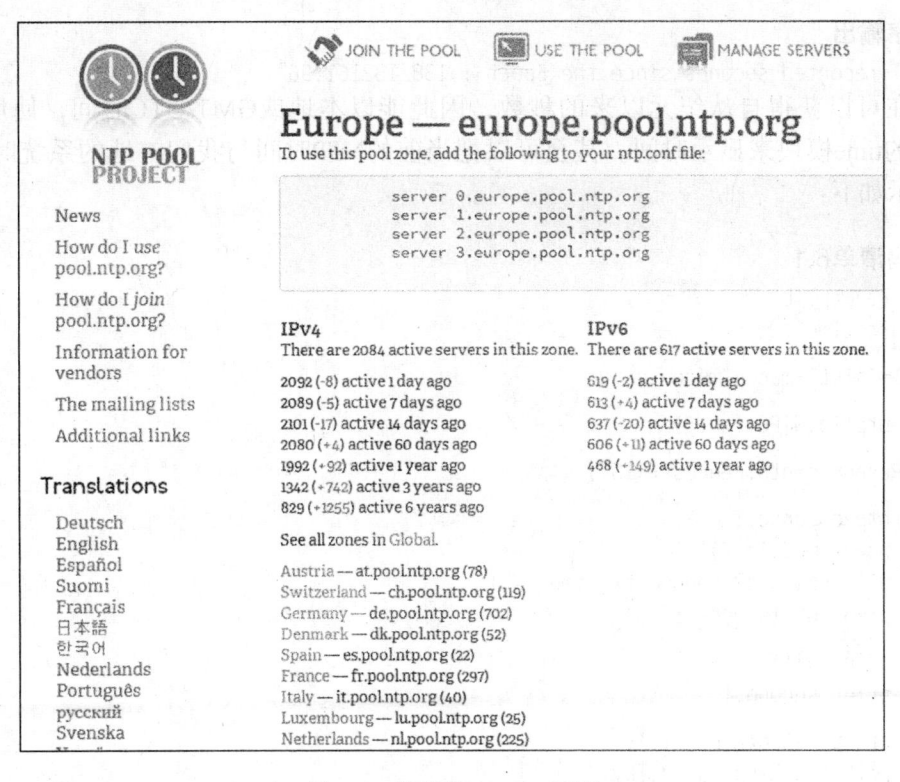

图6.10　欧洲的NTP Pool项目

6.7　NTP客户端创建脚本

用ntplib创建一个Python NTP客户端是一个较为简单的过程：

```
import ntplib         # import the ntplib
import time           # import the Python time module
# url of the closest NIST certified NTP server
NIST='nist1-macon.macon.ga.us'
# Create NTP client object using the ntplib
ntp= ntplib.NTPClient()
# initiate an NTP client request for time
ntpResponse= ntp.request(NIST)
# Check that we received a response
if ntpResponse:
    # obtain the seconds since the epoch from response
    nistUTC= ntpResponse.tx_time
    print'NIST reported seconds since the Epoch :',
    print nistUTC
else:
    print'NTP Request Failed'
```

程序输出

```
NIST reported seconds since the Epoch : 1382132161.96
```

现在可以获得自从纪元以来的秒数,因此能以本地或GMT/UTC时间,使用Python标准库的time模块来显示时间。甚至可以把当前的NTP时间与我们本地的系统时钟做比较,显示如下:

代码清单6.1

```
import ntplib
import time

NIST='nist1-macon.macon.ga.us'

ntp=ntplib.NTPClient()

ntpResponse=ntp.request(NIST)

if (ntpResponse):
    now=time.time()
    diff=now-ntpResponse.tx_time
    print'Difference :',

    print diff,
    print'seconds'

    print'Network Delay:',
    print ntpResponse.delay

    print'UTC: NIST :'þtime.strftime("%a, %d %b %Y %H:%M:%S +0000",
    time.gmtime(int(ntpResponse.tx_time)))

    print 'UTC: SYSTEM : 'þtime.strftime("%a, %d %b %Y %H:%M:%S
    +0000", time.gmtime(int(now)))

else:
    print'No Response from Time Service'
```

程序输出

```
Difference   : 3.09969758987 seconds
Network Delay : 0.0309739112854
UTC NIST     : Fri, 18 Oct 2013 21:48:48 +0000
UTC SYSTEM   : Fri, 18 Oct 2013 21:48:51 +0000
```

注意观察:

(1)在从时间服务器(本例是从NIST)那里获得时间之后,立刻获取本地系统时间,这一点很重要。

```
ntpResponse= ntp.request(NIST)
if (ntpResponse):
    now= time.time()
```

这能确保与我们的系统时钟维持的本地时间做比较时,受到处理延迟的影响最小。

(2)考虑NTP客户端存在的网络延迟也很重要。在这个例子中延迟超过30多毫秒,当然在某些情况下,由于在一天的不同时刻,网络连接速度以及其他的潜在网络问题,延迟可能会更久一点。

（3）在这个例子中，计算出了3.09969758987秒的差异。这意味着我的系统时钟运行比NIST服务器快3秒多。

diff= now-ntpResponse.tx_time

如果结果是负的而不是正的，可以得出结论，我的系统时钟运行得比NIST报告的时间慢。

（4）最后，ntplib客户端的操作是同步的。换句话说，一旦发出如下请求：

ntpResponse= ntp.request(NIST)

就像任何方法或函数调用一样，在请求完成或失败之前，代码不会继续执行。

6.8 章节回顾

在本节中，解释了时间及其计算的基础知识。这包括对纪元的更深入理解，现代时间协调机制的起源，以及一些关于时间的历史知识。然后深入Python标准库的time模块，解释并演示了与该模块相关的许多方法和属性。我开发了几个简短的Python脚本，让你感受如何去应用和解释时间处理的结果。

然后对NTP进行了概述，它提供了与国家计量源同步的能力。接着，带领你把Python的NTP库ntplib的安装和设置过程遍历了一遍。然后用该模块进行实验，建立了一个能与网络时间源交互的NTP客户端。我写了一个脚本，来比较和计算我的本地系统时钟与NIST时间服务器之间的差异。

6.9 问题小结

1. 在第3章中，开发了一个程序，遍历文件系统，对文件哈希，记录每个文件的修改、访问和创建时间（MAC时间）。使用time模块修改该程序，把MAC时间从本地时间转换到GMT / UTC时间。
2. 扩展代码清单6.1的代码，在全球另外选择5个时间服务器，并设计一个方法，将其报告的时间与你的本地系统时钟的关系逐个进行比较和对照。同时记录每一个的网络延迟值。注意，你应该执行多次运行并取平均结果。
3. 在取证调查的时候，有哪些其他的时间源需要仔细检查或规范化？

6.10 补充资料

1. 使用时间证明数字证据的完整性. Int J Digital Evid 2002;1(1) 1–7
2. Python标准库. 网址http://docs.python.org/2/library/time.html?highlight=time#time
3. 网络时间协议版本4: 协议和算法详述. 网址http://tools.ietf.org/html/rfc5905
4. 经度. 经度: 解决了他所处时代最大科学难题的寂寞天才的真实故事. 纽约, NY: Walker & Co.; 1995

第7章　在电子取证中使用自然语言工具

7.1　什么是自然语言处理

在开始之前，需要对自然语言进行定义。回退到1987年，作为研究项目的一部分，我读过一本书*Introduction to Natural Language Processing*。当时我与伊利诺伊理工学院研究所（IITRI）的James Cook博士合作进行一个项目研究。我的妻子Janet当时也在IITRI与Larry Jones博士一起研究一个自然语言项目。作为判断并更好地解释家畜行为的决策引擎的一部分，她的工作利用了自然语言。我们参考的这本书给出了我见过的最好的关于自然语言的定义，所以在此与你分享这一部分内容。

"自然语言是人类从环境当中学习并且用于与其他人交流的任何语言。无论交流的形式如何，自然语言用来表达我们的知识与情感，并传达我们对于周遭事物的回应。"[Harris]

显然，就像所有的好的定义一样，这个定义经受了时间的考验。因为直到20世纪80年代末期，互联网还没有真正地发展成为一个被认可的形态，以数字形式表达知识与情感的方式还不包含Facebook、Twitter、表情符号（Emoticons）、博客（Blogging）、短信息（Texting）、Sexting、BitStrips，甚至互联网邮件！然而这个定义确实涵盖了这些自然语言表达的最新形式。从自然语言中提取含义（语义）远非看上去那般简单。

判断自然语言系统在尝试解释、理解和应答方面的有效性的任务相应地交给了图灵测试（Turing Test），此名称起源于Alan Turing在1950年的论文"计算机器与智能"。在他的论文当中，Turing提出了一个前瞻性的问题，"机器会思考吗？"[Turing]

7.1.1　基于对话的系统

基于对话的系统的目标是自然地回答用户的提问，意味着我们无法区分是人的回答还是机器的回答。很多人对接近这种能力的系统不会陌生。例如下面是我与我的车载Sync系统的一段对话：

我：我肚子饿了。
Sync：好的，你想在哪里找餐馆呢？附近、沿路还是在城里？
我：附近。
Sync：你想怎么找？按照名字还是类型？
我：按照类型。
Sync：好的，什么类型？

我：意大利风味的。
Sync：好的，请从屏幕上的清单中进行选择，例如，可以说"第1行"。
我：第4行。
Sync：好的，罗西餐馆。你是电话预约还是将其设为目的地？
我：打电话。
Sync：好的，正在呼叫罗西餐馆…

尽管很实用，但是它显然没有满足图灵标准，因为我清楚与我对话的是一台计算机而不是一个人。然而，Sync确实能够将口语词翻译成文本并能够及时地回复，结果便是，这个系统通常都会把我带到我想去的地方，或者为我提供一些我寻找的信息。

7.1.2 语料库

实现自然语言处理（NLP）关键的要因素之一就是语料库。语料库是一个与特定主题相关的庞大的语言样本集合。例如，在http://www.gutenberg.org/中可以访问的"古登堡项目"（Gutenberg Project），便包含了四万多本电子书。

在本章中，创建出具有含义的实例的难题之一便是语料库的构建。所以需要演示如何使用语料库创建这些实例，这些实例对于在取证科学领域开发新的NLP应用程序将起到极大的促进作用。请牢记，取决于你打算利用NLP的应用场景，可能需要多个主题。

7.2 安装自然语言工具包和相关的库

与其他的第三方库和模块一样，在Windows、Linux和Mac上都可以安装。自然语言工具包（NLTK）库是免费的，很容易从nltk.org上在线获得。NLTK的安装需要其他依赖库的安装，包括Numpy和PyYAML。图7.1描述了nltk.org的安装页面，该页面还有易于学习的安装指导。一旦安装了所有的内容，就可以使用熟悉的Python Shell来验证安装结果，键入：

```
import NLTK
```

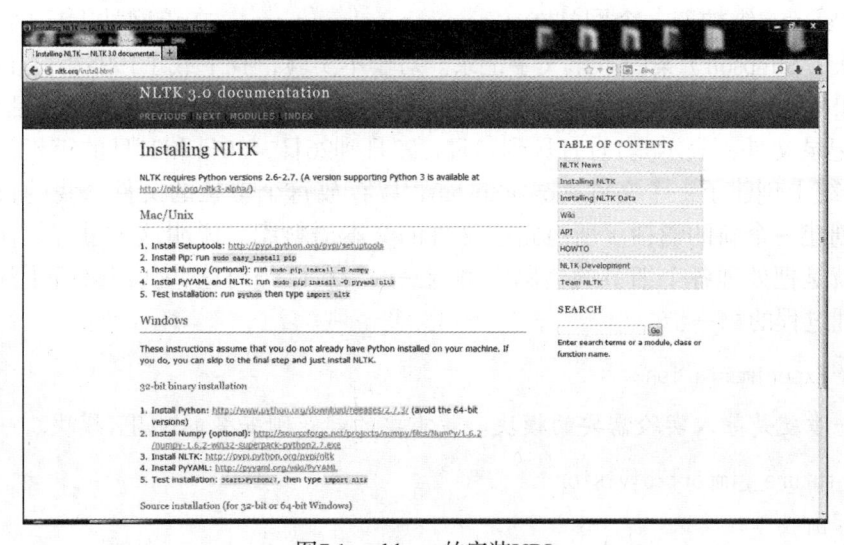

图7.1 nltk.org的安装URL

7.3 使用语料库

使用语料库的第一步是要么加载一个NLTK已有的语料库，要么从本地文件或从互联网上创建一个自己的语料库。此工作一旦完成，就可以对语料库执行一系列的强大操作。而如果不借助NLTK这样的工具集的帮助，这些操作将会是复杂且费时的。表7.1给出了一些在语料库上可以执行的关键操作，在这一章稍后部分，将在代码中详细说明这些操作。

表7.1 NLTK操作介绍性列表

方法	描述
raw()	提取语料库原始内容，本方法返回类型：Python的"str"
word_tokenize()	去掉空格和标点符号，创建一个独立词块（token，基本上是单词）的列表，本方法返回类型：Python的"list"（即列表）
collocations()	单词通常顺序地出现在文本中，这就为调查员提供了有用的信息。而且，一旦检测到这种词语搭配，就可以用来发现单词出现之间的关联。这是通过计算单词的频率以及它们与其他单词的连接关系来完成的。collocations()这一个方法会执行所有这些操作
concordance()	这个方法提供一种能力，生成一个特定单词在上下文环境中的每一个出现频率（如在一个特定的句子中单词如何使用）
fiandall(search)	这个方法能用来简单地，甚至以正则表达式的方式对语料库文本进行搜索
index(word)	这个方法为给定单词的首次出现提供一个索引
similar(word)	注意这不是同义词的意思，而是一个计算分布相似度的方法。简单地说，这个方法能识别出与给定的单词出现在相同上下文中的其他单词
vocab()	对提交的文本生成一个完整的词汇列表

7.4 用NLTK进行实验

在本节中，将调用表7.1中的方法创建一个简单的程序，这个程序首先建立一个新的文本语料库，然后使用这些方法调查该语料库。下面，介绍一下我要建立的语料库的背景。

Jack Walraven维护着一个网站http://simpson.walraven.org/。在该网站上Jack收集整理了辛普森（O. J. Simpson）案的审讯文字记录。对于本实验，我下载了1995年1月的审讯文字记录（如果你愿意，当然也可以下载更多）。网站上存有在1995年1月的诉讼活动中的9个审讯文字记录文件，表示是1月11日到13日，23日到26日，30日和31日的审讯记录。我在Windows系统上创建了一个文件夹c:\simpson\，以存放每个单独的文件。我的目标是使用这些文件创建一个新的囊括了所有这些文件的文本语料库。说明这个过程如何工作的最好方法，就是把处理各个细节的代码实例走一遍。我已经对这些代码进行了注释，确保你理解处理过程的每一步。

```
# NLTK Experimentation
```

这第一步就是导入实验需要的模块。最重要的就是刚安装的NLTK模块。

```
from __future__ import division
import nltk
```

第7章 在电子取证中使用自然语言工具   141

接下来，要从NLTK模块导入PlaintextCorpusReader。此方法将允许读入并最终创建所能用到的文本语料库。

from nltk.corpus import PlaintextCorpusReader

需要指定的第一件事就是将会包含在语料库中文件的位置。我已经将这些文件放在c:\simpson\中。这9个文件都放在那里，每一个都是文本文档。

rootOfCorpus = "c:\\simpson\\"

现在要使用PlainTextCorpusReader方法来收集目录中所有的文件，该目录是我在变量rootOfCorpus中指定的。我使用第二个参数".*"表明指定了所有的文件。如果你的目录中有多个文件类型，并且只想包含文本文档，那么可以将其指定为".txt"。这个调用返回的结果是一个名为newCorpus的NLTK语料库对象。

newCorpus = PlaintextCorpusReader(rootOfCorpus,'.*')
print type(newCorpus)

Print type(newCorpus)产生的输出如下。告诉我newCorpus的NLTK类型。

< class'nltk.corpus.reader.plaintext.PlaintextCorpusReader' >

也可以使用fileids()方法，打印出构成新的语料库的每个文件的名称。

print newCorpus.fileids()

['Trial-January-11.txt','Trial-January-12.txt','Trial-January-13.txt',
'Trial-January-23.txt','Trial-January-24.txt','Trial-January-25.txt',
'Trial-January-26.txt','Trial-January-30.txt','Trial-January-31.txt']

还可以使用abspaths()方法，确定包含于新的语料库的每个文档的绝对路径。

print newCorpus.abspaths()

[FileSystemPathPointer('c:\\simpson\\Trial-January-11.txt'),
FileSystemPathPointer('c:\\simpson\\Trial-January-12.txt'),
FileSystemPathPointer('c:\\simpson\\Trial-January-13.txt'),
FileSystemPathPointer('c:\\simpson\\Trial-January-23.txt'),
FileSystemPathPointer('c:\\simpson\\Trial-January-24.txt'),
FileSystemPathPointer('c:\\simpson\\Trial-January-25.txt'),
FileSystemPathPointer('c:\\simpson\\Trial-January-26.txt'),
FileSystemPathPointer('c:\\simpson\\Trial-January-30.txt'),
FileSystemPathPointer('c:\\simpson\\Trial-January-31.txt')]

现在就能借助newCorpus对象提取原始文本，它代表了包含于指定目录rootOfCorpus中的文件的完整集合，随后可以确定这9个审讯文字记录文件合并后的大小或长度。

rawText = newCorpus.raw()
print len(rawText)

这会产生输出

2008024

现在可以使用nltk.Text模块的方法，以便更好地理解和解释语料库里的内容，通过对语料库的rawText进行词块化来开始这一过程。这将生成词块（主要是单词，当然也包括数字和识别出的特殊字符序列）。

```
tokens = nltk.word_tokenize(rawText)
```

词块化创建了一个标准的Python列表，现在就可以使用标准Python语言操作方法以及与列表对象有关的任何方法来使用它，例如能用len(tokens)方法来确定从文本中提取的词块数量。

```
print len(tokens)
```

这个语句生成了语料库有401032个词块的结果。

401032

因为这就是一个单纯的列表，所以能显示部分内容。在本例中打印出开头的100个列表元素，代表词块化处理后返回的前100个词块。

```
print tokens[0:100]
```

['*LOS','ANGELES',',',',','CALIFORNIA',';','WEDNESDAY',',','JANUARY','11',',',','1995','9:05','A.M.*','DEPARTMENT','NO.','103','HON.','LANCE','A.','ITO',',',',','JUDGE','APPEARANCES',':','(','APPEARANCES','AS','HERETOFORE','NOTED',',','DEPUTY','D-ISTRICT','ATTORNEY','HANK',';','ALSO','PRESENT','ON','BEHALF','OF','SOJOURN',',','MS.','PAMELA','W.','WITHEY',',','ATTORNEY-AT-LAW.',')','(','JANET','M.','MOXHAM',',',',','CSR','NO.','4855',',','OFFICIAL','REPORTER.',')','(','CHRISTINE','M.','OLSON',',',',','CSR','NO.','2378',',','OFFICIAL','REPORTER.',')','(','THE','FOLLOWING','PROCEEDINGS','WERE','HELD','IN','OPEN','COURT',',','OUT','OF','THE','PRESENCE','OF','THE','JURY',':',')','*THE','COURT',':','*','ALL','RIGHT.','THE','SIMPSON']

接下来要使用NLTK.text方法创建一个文本。为此，对经过词块化处理而提取到的词块使用Text()方法，来创建NLTK Text对象textSimpson。

```
textSimpson = nltk.Text(tokens)
```

```
print type(textSimpson)
```

如预期一致，该对象的类型是nltk.text.Text。

< class'nltk.text.Text' >

我想要知道语料库中使用的词汇量的大小。我知道词块的数量，但是当然会有重复的情况。因此使用Python的set( )方法，获得审讯文字记录的文本中的词汇表的唯一集合。

```
vocabularyUsed = set(textSimpson)
```

```
print len(vocabularyUsed)
```

12604

从共计401032个词块中产生了12604个唯一的词块，这个数字更易管理了。接着想看一看所有这些唯一的词块，通过排序这个集合来实现。

```
print sorted(set(textSimpson))
```

'ABERRANT','ABIDE','ABIDING','ABILITIES','ABILITIES.','ABILITY','ABILITY.','ABLAZE','ABLE','ABOUT','ABOUT.','ABOVE','ABRAHAM','ABROGATE','ABROGATED','ABRUPT','ABRUPTLY','ABSENCE','ABSENCE.','ABSENT','ABSOLUTE','ABSOLUTELY','ABSOLUTELY.','ABSORB','ABSTRACT','ABSTRACT.','ABSURD.','ABSURDITY','ABUDRAHM','ABUDRAHM.','ABUNDANCE','ABUNDANT','ABUNDANTLY','ABUSE','ABUSE.','ABUSE/BATTERED','ABUSED','ABUSER',

'ABUSER.','ABUSES','ABUSES.','ABUSING','ABUSIVE','ABUSIVE.',

...

... 此处略过大约10000个词块

...

'WRITTEN','WRITTEN.','WRONG','WRONG.','WRONGFULLY','WRONGLY','WROTE','X','X-RAYS','XANAX','XEROX','XEROXED','XEROXED.','XEROXING','XEROXING.','Y','YAMAUCHI','YAMAUCHI.','YARD','YARD.','YARDS','YEAGEN','YEAH','YEAH.','YEAR','YEAR.','YEARS','YEARS.','YELL','YELLED','YELLING','YELLING.','YELLOW','YEP.','YES','YES.','YESTERDAY','YESTERDAY.','YET','YET.','YIELD','YORK','YORK.','YOU','YOU'LL',"YOU'RE","YOU'VE",'YOU.','YOUNG','YOUNGER','YOUNGSTERS','YOUR','YOURS.','YOURSELF','YOURSELF.','YOURSELVES','YOUTH','YUDOWITZ','YUDOWITZ.','Z','ZACK','ZACK.','ZEIGLER','ZERO','ZLOMSOWITCH',"ZLOMSOWITCH'S",'ZLOMSOWITCH.','ZOOM'

接下来，就可以确定在审讯文字记录中某个特定词的出现次数。调用NLTK.Text对象类型的count()方法来完成这一任务。

myWord = "KILL"

textSimpson.count(myWord)

84

这就产生了一个84次的计数，这就是此语料库包含的，在1995年1月期间9天的审讯文字记录中，单词"KILL"的出现次数。

至此，这些操作都极为直接明了。下面让我们看看几个NLTK.Text模块中包含的更高级的方法。我将从collocations( )方法开始，这将会提供统计意义上在文本中经常一同出现的单词清单。

```
print textSimpson.collocations()
Building collocations list
*THE COURT; *MS. CLARK; *MR. COCHRAN; MR. SIMPSON; NICOLE BROWN;
*MR.DARDEN; OPENING STATEMENT; LOS ANGELES; MR. COCHRAN; DETECTIVE FUHRMAN;
DISCUSSION HELD; WOULD LIKE; *MR. DOUGLAS; BROWN SIMPSON;THANK YOU.;
MR. DARDEN; DEPUTY DISTRICT; FOLLOWING PROCEEDINGS; DISTRICT ATTORNEYS.;
MISS CLARK
```

如你所见，生成的单词搭配（collocation）清单具有重要意义。在文档中这些单词搭配的出现比与其他单词搭配自然更为频繁。

接下来，想为记录中可能感兴趣的特定单词生成一个用语索引（concordance）。NLTK将生成单词的所有出现情况及其上下文（换句话说，就是包围该索引单词的句子）。第二个可选的参数指定你希望看到的包围单词的窗口的大小。我将会展示一些例子。

下面将从单词KILL开始，这个操作生成了84个匹配结果，我列出了前面6个。

myWord = "KILL"

print textSimpson.concordance(myWord)

显示84个匹配结果中的6个：

```
WAS IN EMINENT DANGER AND NEEDED TO KILL IN SELF-DEFENSE. BUT THE ARIS COURT
R OCCURRED.''I KNOW HE'S GOING TO KILL ME. I WISH HE WOULD HURRY UP AND GET
FLICTED HARM WAY BEYOND NECESSARY TO KILL THE VICTIM. AND THIS IS A QUOTE FROM
```

'M GOING TO HURT YOU, I'M GOING TO KILL YOU, I'M GOING TO BEAT YOU.''THO
HAVE HER AND NO ONE ELSE WILL IS TO KILL HER. THAT IS CLEAR IN THE RESEARCH.
WAS A FIXED PURPOSE, FULL INTENT TO KILL, WHERE THE DEFENDANT LITERALLY WENT

如果使用单词GLOVE, 这段代码产生了92个匹配结果, 我列出了前6个。

myWord = "GLOVE"

print textSimpson.concordance(myWord)

显示92个匹配结果中的6个:

CE DEPARTMENT PLANTED EVIDENCE, THE GLOVE AT ROCKINGHAM. NOW, THAT OF COURSE
HAT A POLICE DETECTIVE WOULD PLANT A GLOVE, AND IT MADE HOT NEWS AND THE DEFEN
R THIS POLICE DETECTIVE PLANTED THIS GLOVE AT ROCKINGHAM. NOW, YOUR HONOR, BE
DETECTIVE FUHRMAN'S RECOVERY OF THE GLOVE AND AS - INSOFAR AS IT RELATES TO T
HEY SAW THE LEFT-HANDED BULKY MAN'S GLOVE THERE AT THE FEET OF RONALD GOLDMAN.
E BUNDY CRIME SCENE. THEY SAW A LONE GLOVE, A SINGLE GLOVE AT THE FEET OF RONA

NLTK还提供了更多的操作文本语料库的复杂方法, 例如能够识别单词使用的相似性。这个方法可以识别出还有哪些单词出现在相似的上下文中。

myWord = "intent"

print textSimpson.similar(myWord)

Building word-context index . . .
time cochran court evidence and house it blood defense motive that jury
other people the this witnesses case defendant discovery

如果将这个单词改成victim, 输出的结果就是

Building word-context index . . .
court defendant jury defense prosecution case evidence and people record
police time relationship house question statement tape way crime glove

也可以利用NLTK来产生完整的词汇清单, 以及语料库中所有词块的频率分布。通过在文档中使用这个方法, 我们能派生出一个文档的作者或创建者的行文偏好。vocab()方法返回一个基于nltk.probablity.FreqDist类的对象, 如下所示。

simpsonVocab = textSimpson.vocab()

type(simpsonVocab)

< class'nltk.probability.FreqDist' >

从而我们就可以利用simpsonVocab对象, 来测试文本当中任意一个或者所有词块的频率分布。只需使用其中的任何一个方法, 例如simpsonVocab.item( ), 就可以得到一个排序的每个词汇表条目的使用清单 (越是常用的则越是处于靠前的位置)。

simpsonVocab.items()

< bound method FreqDist.items of < FreqDist with 12604 samples and 401032 outcomes >>

[('THE', 19386), (',', 18677), ('TO', 11634), ('THAT', 10777), ('AND', 8938), (':', 8369), ('OF', 8198), ('*', 7850), ('IS', 6322), ('I', 6244), ('A', 5590), ('IN', 5456), ('YOU', 4879), ('WE', 4385), ('THIS', 4264), ('IT', 3815), ('COURT', 3763), ('WAS', 3255), ('HAVE', 2816), ('–', 2797), ('?', 2738), ('HE', 2734), ('"S', 2677), ('NOT', 2417), ('ON', 2414),

('THEY', 2287), ('*THE', 2275), ('BE', 2240), ('ARE', 2207), ('YOUR', 2200), ('WHAT', 2122), ('AT', 2112), ('WITH', 2110),

为简洁起见，直接跳到输出的结尾部分。

('WRENCHING', 1), ('WRESTLING.', 1), ('WRISTS.', 1), ('WRITERS', 1), ('WRONGLY', 1), ('X-RAYS', 1), ('XANAX', 1), ('XEROXED.', 1), ('XEROXING.', 1), ('YAMAUCHI.', 1), ('YARD.', 1), ('YARDS', 1), ('YEAGEN', 1), ('YELL', 1), ('YELLING.', 1), ('YEP.', 1), ('YIELD', 1), ('YOUNGSTERS', 1), ('YOURS.', 1), ('YUDOWITZ', 1), ('YUDOWITZ.', 1), ('Z', 1), ('ZEIGLER', 1),('ZERO', 1), ("ZLOMSOWITCH'S", 1)]

注意：vocab()方法的一个附带好处是，当不同的词汇条目具有相同的出现次数时，它们按字母顺序排序。

7.5 从因特网上创建语料库

在很多情况下，我们要检查的文本可在互联网上发现。通过结合使用Python、Python标准库urllib和NLTK，可以对在线文档进行同样类型的分析。我从下载于Gutenberg Project的一个简单文本文档开始说明。

首先导入必要的模块，本例中就是NLTK和urllib中的urlopen模块。注意：如你所见，可以选择性地从库中导入指定的模块而不用加载整个库。

```
>>> import nltk
>>> from urllib import urlopen
```

接下来，指定想要访问的URL，并调用urlopen.read方法。

```
>>> url = "http://www.gutenberg.org/files/2760/2760.txt"
>>> raw = urlopen(url).read()
```

如同预期的那样，它返回的类型是"str"。

注意：因为从Python Shell界面键入这些命令并直接检查输出，所以并没有用到try/except模式，但如果这个例子是真实的程序执行，就会用到这个模式。当然，如果你愿意，也可以自行添加。

```
>>> type(raw)
```

<type 'str'>

现在已经确认结果是一个字符串，可以检查返回的长度，本例中是3.6 MB。

```
>>> len(raw)
```

3608901

为了使你能够了解这个在线资源包含了什么，简单地运用标准Python字符串功能打印出它的前两百个字符，产生以下输出：

```
>>> raw[:200]
```

'CELEBRATED CRIMES, COMPLETE\r\n\r\n\r\nThis eBook is for the use of anyone anywhere at no cost and with almost\r\nno restrictions whatsoever. You may copy it, give it away or re-use it\r\n'

现在可以执行NLTK模块的任何功能，我已经在这里应用了几个，使你对我下载的文本有所了解。

```
>>> tokenList = nltk.word_tokenize(raw)
>>> type(tokenList)
< type'list' >
>>> len(tokenList)
707397
>>> tokenList[:40]
['CELEBRATED','CRIMES',',',',','COMPLETE','This','eBook','is','for','the','use','of','anyone','anywhere','at','no','cost','and','with','almost','no', 'restrictions','whatsoever.','You','may','copy','it',',','give','it','away','or','re-use','it','under','the','terms','of','the','Project','Gutenberg']
```

还有许多其他的NLTK方法、对象和函数可以让你探究自然语言。现在你已经学会了"先测试后编码"方法的基本用法。现在还将创建一个简单的应用程序，它使得利用这些同样的方法访问NLTK功能变得更加容易，而且为你拓展功能提供了一个基线。

7.6　NLTKQuery应用程序

为了使与NLTK的交互更为简单和可拓展，建立了NLTKQuery应用程序它，它有三个源文件（参见表7.2）。

表7.2　NLTKQuery应用程序的源文件

源文件	描述
NLTKQuery.py	作为与NLTK交互的主程序循环
_classNLTKQuery.py	这个模块定义了一个新的类，当正确地安装和使用，将允许以一个可控的方式访问NLTK方法
_NLTKQuery.py	这个模块为NLTKQuery主程序循环提供支撑函数，主要用来处理用户输入和菜单显示

这个程序提供了一个简化的访问NLTK方法的用户界面，而无须让用户理解NLTK库是如何工作的。用户要做的全部工作就是建立一个包含一个或多个文件的目录，这些文件将被引入一个语料库。这个应用程序将基于提供的目录创建语料库，并允许用户与之交互，更准确地说，应查询语料库。

这三个源文件的内容如下所述。

7.6.1　NLTKQuery.py

```
#
# NLTK QUERY FRONT END
# Python-Forensics
#    No HASP required
#
```

```
import sys
import _NLTKQuery

print "Welcome to the NLTK Query Experimentation"
print "Please wait loading NLTK . . . "

import _classNLTKQuery

oNLTK = _classNLTKQuery.classNLTKQuery()

print
print "Input full path name where intended corpus file or files are stored"
print "Note: you must enter a quoted string e.g. c:\\simpson\\ "
print
userSpecifiedPath = raw_input("Path: ")

# Attempt to create a text Corpus
result = oNLTK.textCorpusInit(userSpecifiedPath)

if result == "Success":

    menuSelection = -1

    while menuSelection != 0:

        if menuSelection != -1:
            print
            s = raw_input('Press Enter to continue...')

        menuSelection = _NLTKQuery.getUserSelection()
        if menuSelection == 1:
            oNLTK.printCorpusLength()

        elif menuSelection == 2:
            oNLTK.printTokensFound()

        elif menuSelection == 3:
            oNLTK.printVocabSize()

        elif menuSelection == 4:
            oNLTK.printSortedVocab()
        elif menuSelection == 5:
            oNLTK.printCollocation()

        elif menuSelection == 6:
            oNLTK.searchWordOccurence()

        elif menuSelection == 7:
            oNLTK.generateConcordance()

        elif menuSelection == 8:
            oNLTK.generateSimiliarities()

        elif menuSelection == 9:
            oNLTK.printWordIndex()

        elif menuSelection == 10:
            oNLTK.printVocabulary()

        elif menuSelection == 0:
            print "Goodbye"
            print
```

```
            elif menuSelection == -1:
                continue
            else:
                print "unexpected error condition"
                menuSelection = 0
    else:
        print "Closing NLTK Query Experimentation"
```

7.6.2 _classNLTKQuery.py

```
#
# NLTK QUERY CLASS MODULE
# Python-Forensics
#    No HASP required
#

import os                          # Standard Library OS functions
import sys
import logging                     # Standard Library Logging functions
import nltk                        # Import the Natural Language Toolkit
from nltk.corpus import PlaintextCorpusReader     # Import the PlainText
                                                  #   CorpusReader Module

# NLTKQuery Class

class classNLTKQuery:

    def textCorpusInit(self, thePath):
        # Validate the path is a directory
        if not os.path.isdir(thePath):
            return "Path is not a Directory"
        # Validate the path is readable
        if not os.access(thePath, os.R_OK):
            return "Directory is not Readable"
        # Attempt to Create a corpus with all .txt files
        found in the directory
        try:
            self.Corpus = PlaintextCorpus
            Reader(thePath,'.*')
            print "Processing Files : "
            print self.Corpus.fileids()
            print "Please wait ..."
            self.rawText = self.Corpus.raw()
            self.tokens = nltk.word_tokenize
            (self.rawText)
            self.TextCorpus = nltk.Text(self.
            tokens)
        except:
            return "Corpus Creation Failed"

        self.ActiveTextCorpus = True

        return "Success"
```

```python
def printCorpusLength(self):
        print "Corpus Text Length: ",
        print len(self.rawText)
def printTokensFound(self):
        print "Tokens Found: ",
        print len(self.tokens)
def printVocabSize(self):
        print "Calculating..."
        print "Vocabulary Size: ",
        vocabularyUsed = set(self.TextCorpus)
        vocabularySize = len(vocabularyUsed)
        print vocabularySize
def printSortedVocab(self):
        print "Compiling..."
        print "Sorted Vocabulary ",
        print sorted(set(self.TextCorpus))
def printCollocation(self):
        print "Compiling Collocations..."
        self.TextCorpus.collocations()
def searchWordOccurence(self):
        myWord = raw_input("Enter Search Word : ")
        if myWord:
                wordCount = self.TextCorpus.count
                (myWord)
                print myWord+" occured: ",
                print wordCount,
                print " times"
        else:
                print "Word Entry is Invalid"
def generateConcordance(self):
        myWord = raw_input("Enter word to Concord : ")
        if myWord:
                self.TextCorpus.concordance
                (myWord)
        else:
                print "Word Entry is Invalid"
def generateSimiliarities(self):
        myWord = raw_input("Enter seed word : ")
        if myWord:
                self.TextCorpus.similar(myWord)
        else:
                print "Word Entry is Invalid"
def printWordIndex(self):
        myWord = raw_input("Find first occurrence of
        what Word? : ")
        if myWord:
                wordIndex = self.TextCorpus.index
                (myWord)
                print "First Occurrence of: " +
```

```
                                    myWord + "is at offset: ",
                                    print wordIndex
                    else:
                                    print "Word Entry is Invalid"

            def printVocabulary(self):
                    print "Compiling Vocabulary Frequencies",
                    vocabFreqList = self.TextCorpus.vocab()
                    print vocabFreqList.items()
```

7.6.3　_NLTKQuery.py

```
#
# NLTK Query Support Methods
# Python-Forensics
#    No HASP required
#

# Function to print the NLTK Query Option Menu
def printMenu():
        print"==========NLTK Query Options =========="
        print "[1] Print Length of Corpus"
        print "[2] Print Number of Token Found"
        print "[3] Print Vocabulary Size"
        print "[4] Print Sorted Vocabulary"
        print "[5] Print Collocation"
        print "[6] Search for Word Occurrence"
        print "[7] Generate Concordance"
        print "[8] Generate Similarities"
        print "[9] Print Word Index"
        print "[10] Print Vocabulary"
        print
        print "[0] Exit NLTK Experimentation"
        print

# Function to obtain user input
def getUserSelection():
        printMenu ()

        try:
            menuSelection = int(input('Enter Selection (0-10) >>'))
        except ValueError:
            print'Invalid input. Enter a value between 0 -10 .'
            return -1

        if not menuSelection in range(0, 11):
            print'Invalid input. Enter a value between 0 - 10.'
            return -1

        return menuSelection
```

7.6.4　NLTKQuery例子的执行

NLTKQuery在Windows、Linux或者Mac中的命令行的执行是一样的。在命令行中简单地输入命令Python NLTKQuery.py，然后根据屏幕上的说明和菜单提示操作。

7.6.5　NLTK跟踪执行

注意，为简洁起见，部分输出内容经过了编辑，并在该处做出了标识。我还省略了菜单选项的重复显示。

```
C:\Users\app\Python NLTKQuery.py
Welcome to the NLTK Query Experimentation
Please wait loading NLTK ...
Input full path name where the intended corpus file or files are stored
Format for Windows e.g. c:\simpson\
Path: c:\simpson\
NLTKQuery Application 199
Processing Files:
['Trial-January-11.txt','Trial-January-12.txt','Trial-January-13.txt',
'Trial-January-23.txt','Trial-January-24.txt','Trial-January-25.txt',
'Trial-January-26.txt','Trial
-January-30.txt','Trial-January-31.txt']

========== NLTK Query Options =====
[1]     Print Length of Corpus
[2]     Print Number of Token Found
[3]     Print Vocabulary Size
[4]     Print Sorted Vocabulary
[5]     Print Collocation
[6]     Search for Word Occurrence
[7]     Generate Concordance
[8]     Generate Similarities
[9]     Print Word Index
[10]    Print Vocabulary

[0] Exit NLTK Experimentation

Enter Selection (0-10) >> 1
Corpus Text Length: 2008024

Enter Selection (0-10) >> 2
Tokens Found: 401032

Enter Selection (0-10) >> 3
Calculating...
Vocabulary Size: 12604

Enter Selection (0-10) >> 4
Compiling... Sorted Vocabulary
'ABYSMALLY','ACADEMY','ACCENT','ACCEPT','ACCEPTABLE','ACCEPTED','ACCEPTING',
'ACCESS','ACCESSIBLE','ACCIDENT','ACCIDENT.','ACCIDENTAL','ACCIDENTALLY',
'ACCOMMODATE',
.
.（为简洁起见，此处省略部分输出）
.
'YOUNGER','YOUNGSTERS','YOUR','YOURS.','YOURSELF','YOURSELF.','YOURSELVES',
'YOUTH','YUDOWITZ','YUDOWITZ.','Z','ZACK','ZACK.',
"ZLOMSOWITCH'S",'ZLOMSOWITCH.','ZOOM','' '']

Enter Selection (0-10) >> 5
Compiling Collocations...
```

```
Building collocations list
*THE COURT; *MS. CLARK; *MR. COCHRAN; MR. SIMPSON; NICOLE BROWN; *MR.
DARDEN; OPENING STATEMENT; LOS ANGELES; MR. COCHRAN; DETECTIVE FUHRMAN;
DISCUSSION HELD; WOULD LIKE; *MR. DOUGLAS; BROWN SIMPSON; THANK YOU.;
MR. DARDEN; DEPUTY DISTRICT; FOLLOWING PROCEEDINGS; DISTRICT
ATTORNEYS.; MISS CLARK

Enter Selection (0-10) >> 6
Enter Search Word: MURDER
MURDER occurred: 125 times

Enter Selection (0-10) >> 7
Enter word to Concord: KILL
Building index...
Displaying 15 of 84 matches:
WAS IN EMINENT DANGER AND NEEDED TO KILL IN SELF-DEFENSE. BUT THE ARIS
COURT
R OCCURRED.' 'I KNOW HE'S GOING TO KILL ME. I WISH HE WOULD HURRY UP AND GET
FLICTED HARM WAY BEYOND NECESSARY TO KILL THE VICTIM. AND THIS IS
A QUOTE FROM
'M GOING TO HURT YOU, I'M GOING TO KILL YOU, I'M GOING TO BEAT YOU.' 'THO
HAVE HER AND NO ONE ELSE WILL IS TO KILL HER. THAT IS CLEAR IN THE RESEARCH.
ELLED OUT TO HIM,' 'HE'S GOING TO KILL ME.' 'IT WAS CLEAR TO OFFICER EDWAR
NNING OUT SAYING,' 'HE'S GOING TO KILL ME,' 'THEN THE DEFENDANT ARRIVES I
NS OUT AND SAYS,' 'HE'S TRYING TO KILL ME.' 'SHE'S LITERALLY IN FLIGHT. S
HERDURINGTHE BEATING THATHEWOULDKILLHER, AND THE DEFENDANT CONTINUED TH
TATEMENT OF THE DEFENDANT,' 'I'LL KILL YOU,' 'CONSTITUTES COMPOUND HEARSA
FFICER SCREAMING,' 'HE'S GOING TO KILL ME.' 'I CA N'T IMAGINE A STRONGER C
''HE'S GOING CRAZY. HE IS GOING TO KILL ME.' 'THIS IS VERY SIMILAR TO THE S
NNER THAT SHE BELIEVED THAT HE WOULD KILL HER. NOW , MR. UELMEN HAS TALKED
ABO
OF A DOMESTIC VIOLENCE, A MOTIVE TO KILL, THE FINAL ACT OF CONTROL. THERE IS
CTIMTHATTHEDEFENDANTHADTRIEDTOKILLHER PREVIOUSLYWASUSEDTOSHOWTHAT

Enter Selection (0-10) >> 8
Enter seed word: MURDER
Building word-context index...
court and case evidence defendant time jury crime motion relationship
statement witness issue so that trial blood defense person problem

Enter Selection (0-10) >> 9
Find first occurrence of what Word? : GLOVE
First Occurrence of: GLOVE is at offset: 93811

Enter Selection (0-10) >> 10
Compiling Vocabulary Frequencies Building vocabulary index...
[('THE', 19386), (',', 18677), ('TO', 11634), ('THAT', 10777), ('AND', 8938),(':',
8369), ('OF', 8198), ('*', 7850), ('IS', 6322), ('I', 6244), ('A', 5590),('IN',
5456), ('YOU', 4879), ('WE', 4385), ('THIS', 4264), ('IT', 3815), ('COURT',3763),
('WAS', 3255), ('HAVE', 2816), ('-', 2797), ('?', 2738),
.
. (为简洁起见, 此处省略部分输出)
.
('WORLDWIDE', 1), ('WORRYING', 1), ('WORSE.', 1), ('WORTHWHILE', 1), ('WOULDBE', 1),
(' 'WOULDN'T ', 1), ('WOUNDS.', 1), ('WRECKED.', 1), ('WRENCHING', 1),('WRESTLING.',
```

1), ('WRISTS.', 1), ('WRITERS', 1), ('WRONGLY', 1), ('X-RAYS',1), ('XANAX', 1), ('XEROXED.', 1), ('XEROXING.', 1), ('YAMAUCHI.', 1), ('YARD.',1), ('YARDS', 1), ('YEAGEN', 1), ('YELL', 1), ('YELLING.', 1), ('YEP.', 1),('YIELD', 1), ('YOUNGSTERS', 1), ('YOURS.', 1), ('YUDOWITZ', 1), ('YUDOWITZ.',1), ('Z', 1), ('ZEIGLER', 1), ('ZERO', 1), (' 'ZLOMSOWITCH'S' ', 1)]

现在你有了一个NLTK的工作实例。为了进一步探索自然语言实验的发展潜力，建议你利用这个应用程序进行实验，并着手在NLTKQuery类中添加新的NLTK操作。

7.7 章节回顾

在本章中引入了NLP的概念，以扩展你的思维，超越简单的获取、格式化和显示的取证应用程序的限制。探讨了NLP的一些历史，以及Alan Turing的有趣的提问。然后介绍了NLTK，它能完成很多繁重的工作，并允许我们可以立即在Python中对NLP进行实验。同时也介绍了基于文本的语料库的概念与应用，并借助辛普森（O. J. Simpson）案件的审讯文字记录中的小部分样本，创建了一个简单的实验用语料库。初步介绍了一些基本的NLTK方法和操作的细节，以便不仅可以创建我们的语料库，还可以进行查询。当适应了这些基本内容，便创建了NLTKQuery应用程序，它通过一个菜单驱动的界面抽象了NLTK函数。NLTKQuery的关键就是NLTKQuery类，这个类易于拓展以执行更复杂的操作，并能用来深入研究NLTK。

7.8 问题小结

1. 通过增加以下的功能来拓展NLTKQuery类：
   a. 创建一个新的类方法，它能为辛普森审判生成一个频率分布图，显示在审讯全程文字记录中的语言是如何细微变化的（提示：用 dispersion_plot 方法进行实验，它能用于 self.textCorpus 对象）。
   b. 创建一个生成不常用单词的清单的新方法。这可能是一些不一般的长，或在标准字典中找不到的单词（提示：在http://nltk.org/data.html下载NLTK Data，并借助word list语料库滤去常用词语）。
   c. 创建一个能识别名称或者地点的新方法（提示：利用names语料库匹配在辛普森语料库中发现的名字）。
2. 从自己的参考资源中收集一些文本文件，就某个领域或主题创建自己的语料库，它将对取证行业有所帮助。

7.9 补充资料

1. Gutenberg项目. 网址http://www.gutenberg.org/
2. Harris MD. 自然语言处理入门. Reston, VA: A Prentice-Hall Company: Reston Publishing Company, Inc.; 1985
3. Turing A. 计算机器与智能. 网址http://www.csee.umbc.edu/courses/471/papers/turing.pdf; 1950.10

第8章 网络取证：第1部分

8.1 网络调查基础

调查现代网络环境充满着困难。无论是响应网络入侵、调查内部活动、执行漏洞评估、监控网络流量，还是验证合规情况，困难都无处不在。

许多专业工具和技术都源自McAfee、Symantec、IBM、Saint、Tenable以及其他很多类似的主流供应商。然而这些工具究竟做了什么，怎么做的以及调查结果是否彻底，对这些疑问的深入了解还多少是一个谜团。当然也还有些像Wireshark之类的免费工具，可以执行网络数据包的截获和分析。

为了揭示这些技术之下的一些基础，本章将仔细审查这些网络调查方法的基本技术。利用Python标准库加上几个第三方库，可以完成这些操作指导性的例子。我将非常细致地把这些例子遍历一遍，因此如果这是你第一次接触到网络编程，将会得到足够多的细节，从而可以扩展这些例子。

8.1.1 什么是套接字

当与网络打交道时，套接字（socket）是绝对必要的组件，它允许我们利用底层操作系统的功能与网络进行对接。套接字为网络终端（如客户端与服务器）之间的通信提供了一个信息通道。可以把套接字当成客户端与服务器之间连接的端点。使用像Python、Java、C++和C#开发的应用程序都利用应用程序接口（API）与网络套接字进行对接。现在大多数系统的套接字API都基于伯克利套接字（Berkeley socket）。伯克利套接字是在1983年随着UNIX BSD 4.2版本而首次提供的。在之后的1990年左右，伯克利发布了一个免许可的版本，这就是现在大多数操作系统（Linux, Mac OS和Windows）中使用的套接字API的基础。这种标准化为跨平台实现提供了一致性。

图8.1描述了一个简单的网络，其中多个主机（终端）连接到一个集线器。每一个主机都有一个唯一的互联网协议（IP，Internet Protocol）地址，对于这个简单的网络而言，我们看到每一个主机都拥有一个唯一的IP地址。

这些IP地址在局域网设置里是最常见的。这些特定的地址都基于第四版网络协议（IPv4）标准，并且代表着一个C类网络地址。

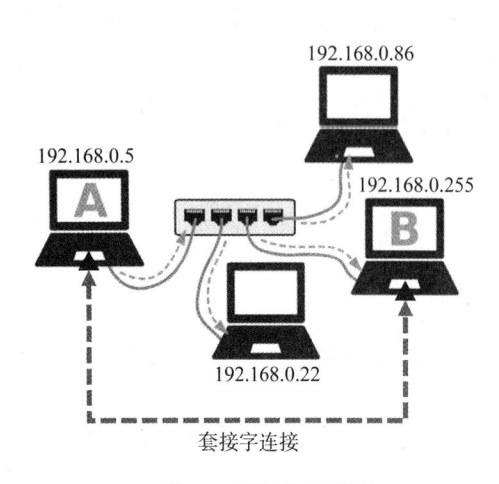

图8.1 简单的局域网

C类网络地址通常都写成点记法形式，比如192.168.0.1。将这些地址拆分后，前三个八位组或者说前24位被看成网络地址（又称为网络标识符，或者NETID）。第四个也就是最后一个八位组或8位被看成本地主机地址（又称为主机标识符或HOSTID）。

```
     192  .168  .0  .1
     网络地址   本地主机地址
```

在本例中，每一个主机、网络设备、路由器、防火墙等，在本地网络中都有相同的网络地址部分（192.168.0），但是都有着独一无二的从0至255的主机地址。这就允许在这个本地环境中可以有256个唯一的IP地址，因此范围就是从192.168.0.0至192.168.0.255。然而实际上只有254个地址可用，这是因为192.168.0.0是网络地址，不能分配给一个本地主机，而192.168.0.255则专门用于广播地址。

基于这些知识，能够使用一些简单的Python内建语言功能，创建一个表示完整范围的IP地址列表。这些语言功能包括一个字符串String、一个列表List、范围函数range以及一个for循环。

```
# Specify the Base Network Address (the first 3 octets)
ipBase = '192.168.0.'

# Next Create an Empty List that will hold the completed
# List of IP Addresses
ipList = []
# Finally, loop through the possible list of local host
# addresses 0-255 using the range function
# Then append each complete address to the ipList
# Notice that I use the str(ip) function in order to
# concatenate the string ipBase with list of numbers 0-255

for ip in range(0,256):
    ipList.append(ipBase+str(ip))
    print ipList.pop()
```

简略的程序输出

192.168.0.0

192.168.0.1

192.168.0.2

192.168.0.3

…… 跳过一些项

192.168.0.252

192.168.0.253

192.168.0.254

192.168.0.255

如你所见，使用标准Python语言元素来生成IP地址非常直接明了。在这一章后面的"ping扫描"一节，将使用这一方法。

8.1.2 最简单使用套接字的网络客户端和服务器连接

作为一种介绍Python提供的套接字API的方法,我会构建客户端与服务器的一个简单网络。为此使用同一个主机(换句话说,客户端与服务器将使用相同的IP地址,且在同一个机器上运行),确定地使用一个特定用途的、保留的本地主机(localhost)回环IP地址127.0.0.1。这个标准的环回IP在几乎所有系统中都是一样的,发送到127.0.0.1的任何消息永远不会到达外部世界,而是被自动地返回到本地主机。当开始尝试网络编程,在完善代码并且做好在真实网络上运行的准备之前,请使用127.0.0.1作为你选择的IP地址(参见图8.2)。

为了实现目标,实际上会创建两个Python程序:(1) server.py 和(2) client.py。为了能够工作,这两个应用程序必须约定一个端口,用来维持通信渠道(已经决定使用本地主机回环IP地址127.0.0.1)。端口号的范围在0至65535之间(基本上是任意的无符号16位整数值)。应该避开小于1024的端口数字,因为它们被分配给标准的网络服务(事实上目前注册端口的数字高达49500,只是没有一个出现在当前的系统中)。在这个应用程序中将使用5555端口,因为它便于记忆。现在已经定义了IP地址和端口号,就拥有了建立一个连接的所有信息。

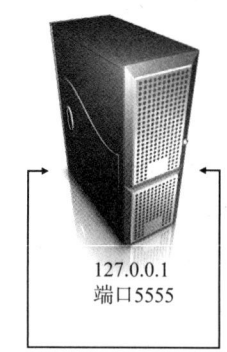

图8.2 独立的本地主机回环

> **IP地址和端口**:换一种更加具体的词汇来理解。将IP地址想象成一个邮局的街道地址,将端口想象成在这个邮局中我想要寄信的特定邮政信箱。

8.1.3 server.py的代码

```python
#
# Server Objective
# 1) Setup a Simple listening Socket
# 2) Wait for a connection request
# 3) Accept a connection on port 5555
# 4) Upon a successful connection send a message to the client
#

import socket        # Standard Library Socket Module

# Create Socket
myServerSocket = socket.socket()

# Get my local host address

localHost = socket.gethostname()

# Specify a local Port to accept connections on

localPort = 5555

# Bind myServerSocket to localHost and the specified Port
# Note the bind call requires one parameter, but that
# parameter is a tuple (notice the parenthesis usage)
```

```python
myServerSocket.bind((localHost, localPort))

# Begin Listening for connections
myServerSocket.listen(1)

# Wait for a connection request
# Note this is a synchronous Call
# meaning the program will halt until a connection is received.
# Once a connection is received
# we will accept the connection and obtain the
# ipAddress of the connector

print 'Python-Forensics .... Waiting for Connection Request'

conn, clientInfo = myServerSocket.accept()

# Print a message to indicate we have received a connection
print 'Connection Received From:', clientInfo

# Send a message to connector using the connection object 'conn'
# that was returned from the myServerSocket.accept() call
# Include the client IP Address and Port used in the response
conn.send('Connection Confirmed:'+'IP:'+ clientInfo[0] +'Port:'+ str(clientInfo[1]))
```

8.1.4　client.py的代码

接下来，客户端代码将会与服务器进行连接。

```python
#
# Client Objective
# 1) Setup a Client Socket
# 2) Attempt a connection to the server on port 5555
# 3) Wait for a reply
# 4) Print out the message received from the server
#

import socket        # Standard Library Socket Module

MAX_BUFFER = 1024    # Set the maximum size to receive

# Create a Socket
myClientSocket = socket.socket()

# Get my local host address
localHost = socket.gethostname()

# Specify a local Port to attempt a connection
localPort = 5555

# Attempt a connection to my localHost and localPort
myClientSocket.connect((localHost, localPort))

# Wait for a reply
# This is a synchronous call, meaning
# that the program will halt until a response is received
```

```
# or the program is terminated
msg = myClientSocket.recv(MAX_BUFFER)
print msg
# Close the Socket, this will terminate the connection
myClientSocket.close()
```

8.1.5　server.py和client.py程序的执行

图8.3描述了程序的执行情况。我创建了两个终端窗口，上面的是server.py的执行情况（它是首先启动的），下面的是client.py的执行情况。请注意，客户端使用源端口59714进行通信，这是由套接字服务自行选定的，而不是在客户端代码中指定的。这个例子中的服务器端口5555是目标端口。

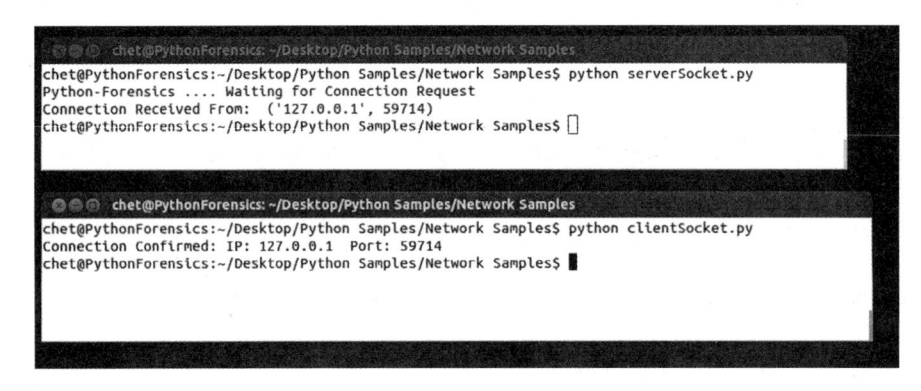

图8.3　server.py/client.py程序运行

我实现的这个例子没有任何调查价值，然而它确实提供了对于网络套接字如何运行的基本认识，并且这是理解一些检验或者调查程序的预备知识。

8.2　队长雷缪斯：再次核实我们到目标的射程…仅需一个PING

你或许还记得这句精彩对白。在名为《猎杀红色十月号》的书及其影片中，由肖恩·康纳利（Sean Connery）扮演的马克·雷缪斯（Marko Ramius）说了这样一句话。当然他们当时使用的是声呐来计算红色十月号与美国潜艇达拉斯号之间的距离（参见图8.4）。

与潜艇大战相似，网络调查的关键因素之一就是发现在一个网络中的所有主机（或者更一般地说，就是终端）。这可以通过向在一个网络中的每一个可能的IP地址发送一个PING（使用"网间控制报文协议"，亦简称ICMP）来完成。那么做出应答的IP地址就会为我们提供两个至关重要的信息：(1)如果它们回应，我们就知道它们是存在的，而且是可应答的；(2)回复应答花费了多长时间。要特别注意的一点是，许多现代的防火墙会阻挡ICMP报文，因

图8.4　洛杉矶级攻击核潜艇达拉斯号的真实照片

为这会被黑客利用来执行网络刺探活动。现代操作系统也是如此，默认情况下它们不会回应ICMP报文。然而在网络内部，它们还是为定位和探测网络上的终端提供了一种有价值的服务。

在接下来这个操作指导性的例子中，会使用Python开发一个PING扫描应用程序，扫描本地网络上可用的IP地址。在这一节会使用几个特殊的模块。首先，使用wxPython为这个PING扫描应用程序建立一个简单的图形用户界面（GUI）。第二，使用一个名为ping.py的第三方模块，它完全由Python语言编写，能处理ICMP协议的主要工作。

在这一章中，之所以选择GUI环境来开发应用程序是因为两个原因，首先是让你接触跨平台的GUI环境wxPython，其二，因为使用命令行选项来执行PING扫描会非常繁琐，但是GUI界面会使互动得到简化。

8.2.1 wxPython

正如在本书中随处可见到的一样，Python的优点之一就是它具备的出色的跨平台能力。秉承Python的这种思想，wxPython也提供了跨平台（Windows、Linux和Mac）的GUI功能。这个库使我们可以建立全功能的基于GUI的应用程序，并且可以直接集成Python的标准语言和结构。本章这个简单的GUI程序仅仅只是对wxPython的一个概要介绍，因为我想让第一个GUI应用程序尽量简单并且尽量容易理解。随着继续深入，在本书的余下章节中还会用到wxPython。

访问http://www.wxPython.org/项目的网页，可以得到更多的有关wxPython的信息以及安装环境。像wxPython这样的第三方库有多个版本来支持不同版本的Python和不同类型的操作系统（即Windows、Mac和Linux）。请确认你选择的安装包与配置是相兼容的。

8.2.2 ping.py

开源的ping.py模块可以在http://www.g-loaded.eu/2009/10/30/Python-ping/页面找到，它是一个完全用Python编写的，专门处理ICMP操作细节的Python模块。因为它是一个开源的模块，所以在此引入其源代码以供参考，以及所有适用的属性与修正。

[PYTHON PING]

```
#!/usr/bin/env Python
"""
A pure Python ping implementation using raw socket.

Note that ICMP messages can only be sent from processes running as root.
Derived from ping.c distributed in Linux's netkit. That code is
copyright (c) 1989 by The Regents of the University of California.
That code is in turn derived from code written by Mike Muuss of the
US Army Ballistic Research Laboratory in December, 1983 and
placed in the public domain. They have my thanks.

Bugs are naturally mine. I'd be glad to hear about them. There are
certainly word - size dependencies here.

Copyright (c) Matthew Dixon Cowles, <http://www.visi.com/mdc/>.
Distributable under the terms of the GNU General Public License
version 2. Provided with no warranties of any sort.
```

```
Original Version from Matthew Dixon Cowles:
-> ftp://ftp.visi.com/users/mdc/ping.py

Rewrite by Jens Diemer:
-> http://www.Python-forum.de/post-69122.html#69122

Rewrite by George Notaras:
-> http://www.g-loaded.eu/2009/10/30/Python-ping/

Revision history
~~~~~~~~~~~~~~~~~~

November 8, 2009
---------------
Improved compatibility with GNU/Linux systems.

Fixes by:
* George Notaras -- http://www.g-loaded.eu
Reported by:
* Chris Hallman -- http://cdhallman.blogspot.com
Changes in this release:
- Re-use time.time() instead of time.clock(). The 2007 implementation
  worked only under Microsoft Windows. Failed on GNU/Linux.
  time.clock() behaves differently under the two OSes[1].

[1] http://docs.Python.org/library/time.html#time.clock

May 30, 2007
-----------
little rewrite by Jens Diemer:
- change socket asterisk import to a normal import
- replace time.time() with time.clock()
- delete "return None" (or change to "return" only)
- in checksum() rename "str" to "source_string"

November 22, 1997
----------------
Initial hack. Doesn't do much, but rather than try to guess
what features I (or others) will want in the future, I've only
put in what I need now.

December 16, 1997
----------------
For some reason, the checksum bytes are in the wrong order when
this is run under Solaris 2.X for SPARC but it works right under
Linux x86. Since I don't know just what's wrong, I'll swap the
bytes always and then do an htons().

December 4, 2000
---------------
Changed the struct.pack() calls to pack the checksum and ID as
unsigned. My thanks to Jerome Poincheval for the fix.

Last commit info:
~~~~~~~~~~~~~~~~~~
$LastChangedDate: $
$Rev: $
$Author: $
"""
```

```python
import os, sys, socket, struct, select, time
# From /usr/include/linux/icmp.h; your mileage may vary.
ICMP_ECHO_REQUEST = 8 # Seems to be the same on Solaris.
def checksum(source_string):
    """
    I'm not too confident that this is right but testing seems
    to suggest that it gives the same answers as in_cksum in ping.c
    """
    sum = 0
    countTo = (len(source_string)/2)*2
    count = 0
    while count<countTo:
        thisVal = ord(source_string[count + 1])*256 + ord
        (source_string[count])
        sum = sum + thisVal
        sum = sum & 0xffffffff # Necessary?
        count = count + 2

    if countTo<len(source_string):
        sum = sum + ord(source_string[len(source_string) - 1])
        sum = sum & 0xffffffff # Necessary?

    sum = (sum >> 16) + (sum & 0xffff)
    sum = sum + (sum >> 16)
    answer = sum
    answer = answer & 0xffff

    # Swap bytes. Bugger me if I know why.
    answer = answer >> 8 | (answer << 8 & 0xff00)

    return answer

def receive_one_ping(my_socket, ID, timeout):
    """
    receive the ping from the socket.
    """
    timeLeft = timeout
    while True:
        startedSelect = time.time()
        whatReady = select.select([my_socket], [], [], timeLeft)
        howLongInSelect = (time.time() - startedSelect)
        if whatReady[0] == []: # Timeout
            return

        timeReceived = time.time()
        recPacket, addr = my_socket.recvfrom(1024)
        icmpHeader = recPacket[20:28]
        type, code, checksum, packetID, sequence = struct.unpack(
            "bbHHh", icmpHeader
        )
        if packetID == ID:
            bytesInDouble = struct.calcsize("d")
            timeSent = struct.unpack("d", recPacket[28:28 +
            bytesInDouble])[0]
```

```python
            return timeReceived - timeSent
        timeLeft = timeLeft - howLongInSelect
        if timeLeft <= 0:
            return
def send_one_ping(my_socket, dest_addr, ID):
    """
    Send one ping to the given >dest_addr<.
    """
    dest_addr = socket.gethostbyname(dest_addr)
    # Header is type (8), code (8), checksum (16), id (16), sequence (16)
    my_checksum = 0

    # Make a dummy header with a 0 checksum.
    header = struct.pack("bbHHh", ICMP_ECHO_REQUEST, 0, my_checksum,
    ID, 1)
    bytesInDouble = struct.calcsize("d")
    data = (192 - bytesInDouble) * "Q"
    data = struct.pack("d", time.time()) + data

    # Calculate the checksum on the data and the dummy header.
    my_checksum = checksum(header + data)

    # Now that we have the right checksum, we put that in. It's just easier
    # to make up a new header than to stuff it into the dummy.
    header = struct.pack(
        "bbHHh", ICMP_ECHO_REQUEST, 0, socket.htons(my_checksum), ID, 1)
    packet = header + data
    my_socket.sendto(packet, (dest_addr, 1)) # Don't know about the 1
def do_one(dest_addr, timeout):
    """
    Returns either the delay (in seconds) or none on timeout.
    """
    icmp = socket.getprotobyname("icmp")
    try:
        my_socket = socket.socket(socket.AF_INET, socket.SOCK_RAW, icmp)
    except socket.error, (errno, msg):
        if errno == 1:
            # Operation not permitted
            msg = msg + (
                " - Note that ICMP messages can only be sent from  
                processes"
                " running as root."
            )
            raise socket.error(msg)
        raise # raise the original error

    my_ID = os.getpid() & 0xFFFF

    send_one_ping(my_socket, dest_addr, my_ID)
    delay = receive_one_ping(my_socket, my_ID, timeout)

    my_socket.close()
    return delay
def verbose_ping(dest_addr, timeout = 2, count = 4):
```

```
"""
Send >count< ping to >dest_addr< with the given >timeout< and
display the result.
"""
for i in xrange(count):
    print "ping %s..." % dest_addr,
    try:
        delay = do_one(dest_addr, timeout)
    except socket.gaierror, e:
        print "failed. (socket error:'%s')" % e[1]
        break

    if delay == None:
        prin t "failed. (timeout within %ssec.)" % timeout
    else:
        delay = delay * 1000
        print "get ping in %0.4fms" % delay
print
if __name__ == '__main__':
    verbose_ping("heise.de")
    verbose_ping("google.com")
    verbose_ping("a-test-url-taht-is-not-available.com")
    verbose_ping("192.168.1.1")
```

我已经随程序提供了详细的文档，因此你可以阅读这些注释来清晰地理解程序。图8.5和图8.6描述了ping扫描程序启动和初始的GUI。注意在图8.5中，在命令行上运用管理员权限来启动这个程序。这是必不可少的，因为ping操作的执行需要管理员权限。在测试代码之前，请先观察程序的整体结构，建议你从考察代码中稍后几页的"Setup the Application Windows"（建立应用程序窗口）部分开始。然后返回到代码的起始点，考察以"def pingScan(event)"开始的pingScan的事件处理器。

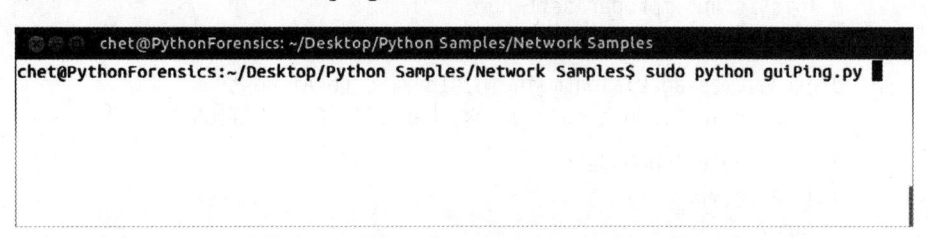

图8.5　以root权限的guiPing.py的命令行启动

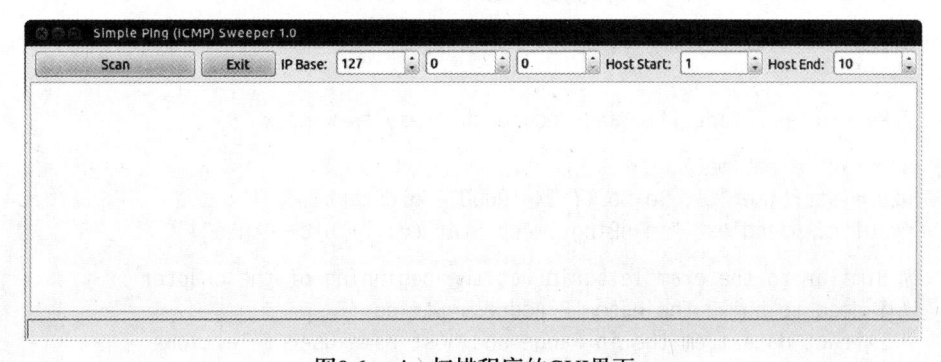

图8.6　ping扫描程序的GUI界面

我选择了一个简单的GUI设计，只有两个按钮Scan和Exit，以及几个数值调节控件，用以指定IP基址和本地主机的范围。

8.2.3　guiPing.py的代码

```
#
# Python Ping Sweep GUI Application
#

import wxversion          # Specify the proper version of wxPython
wxversion.select("2.8")

# Import the necessary modules
import wx                 # Import the GUI module wx
import sys                # Import the standard library module sys
import ping               # Import the ICMP Ping Module
import socket             # Import the standard library module socket

from time import gmtime, strftime # import time functions

#
# Event Handler for the pingScan Button Press
# This is executed each time the Scan Button is pressed on the GUI
#

def pingScan(event):

    # Since the user specifies a range of Hosts to Scan, I need to verify
    # that the startHost value is <= endHost value before scanning
    # this would indicate a valid range
    # If not I need to communicate the error with the user

    if hostEnd.GetValue() < hostStart.GetValue():

        # This is an improper setting
        # Notify the user using a wx.MessageDialog Box

        dlg = wx.MessageDialog(mainWin,"Invalid Local Host
            Selection","Confirm", wx.OK | wx.ICON_EXCLAMATION)

        result = dlg.ShowModal()
        dlg.Destroy()
        return

    # If we have a valid range update the Status Bar

    mainWin.StatusBar.SetStatusText('Executing Ping Sweep .... Please
    Wait'

    # Record the Start Time and Update the results window

    utcStart = gmtime()
    utc = strftime("%a, %d %b %Y %X +0000", utcStart)
    results.AppendText("\n\nPing Sweep Started: "+ utc+ "\n\n")

    # Similar to the example script at the beginning of the chapter
    # I need to build the base IP Address String
    # Extract data from the ip Range and host name user selections
    # Build a Python List of IP Addresses to Sweep
```

```python
        baseIP = str(ipaRange.GetValue())+'.'+str(ipbRange.GetValue())+'.'
        +str(ipcRange.GetValue())+'.'

        ipRange = []

        for i in range(hostStart.GetValue(), (hostEnd.GetValue()+1)):
            ipRange.append(baseIP+str(i))

        # For each of the IP Addresses in the ipRange List, Attempt an PING

        for ipAddress in ipRange:

            try:

                # Report the IP Address to the Window Status Bar
                # Prior to the attempt

                mainWin.StatusBar.SetStatusText('Pinging IP:'+ ipAddress)

                # Perform the Ping
                delay = ping.do_one(ipAddress, timeout=2)

                # Display the IP Address in the Main Window
                results.AppendText(ipAddress+'\t')

                if delay != None:
                    # If Successful (i.e. no timeout) display
                    # the result and response time

                    results.AppendText('Response Success')
                    results.AppendText('Response Time:'+str(delay)+'
                    Seconds')
                    results.AppendText("\n")
                else:
                    # If delay == None, then the request timed out
                    # Report the Response Timeout
                    results.AppendText('Response Timeout')
                    results.AppendText("\n")

            except socket.error, e:

                # If any socket Errors occur Report the offending IP
                # along with any error information provided by the socket

                results.AppendText(ipAddress)
                results.AppendText('Response Failed:')
                results.AppendText(e.message)
                results.AppendText("\n")

        # Once all ipAddresses are processed
        # Record and display the ending time of the sweep

        utcEnd = gmtime()
        utc = strftime("%a, %d %b %Y %X +0000", utcEnd)
        results.AppendText("\nPing Sweep Ended: "+ utc + "\n\n")

        # Clear the Status Bar
        mainWin.StatusBar.SetStatusText(' ')

        return

# End Scan Event Handler ===========================
```

```python
#
# Program Exit Event Handler
# This is executed when the user presses the exit button
# The program is terminated using the sys.exit() method
#

def programExit(event):
    sys.exit()

# End Program Exit Event Handler ==================

#
# Setup the Application Windows ==================
#
# This section of code sets up the GUI environment
#

# Instantiate a wx.App()objet
app = wx.App()

# define the main window including the size and title

mainWin = wx.Frame(None, title="Simple Ping (ICMP) Sweeper 1.0", size
=(1000,600))

# define the action panel, this is the area where the buttons and spinners
# are located

panelAction = wx.Panel(mainWin)
# define action buttons
# I'm creating two buttons, one for Scan and one for Exit
# Notice that each button contains the name of the function that will
# handle the button press event -- pingScan and ProgramExit respectively

scanButton = wx.Button(panelAction, label='Scan')
scanButton.Bind(wx.EVT_BUTTON, pingScan)

exitButton = wx.Button(panelAction, label='Exit')
exitButton.Bind(wx.EVT_BUTTON, programExit)

# define a Text Area where I can display results

Results = wx.TextCtrl(panelAction, style = wx.TE_MULTILINE | wx.
HSCROLL)

# Base Network for Class C IP Addresses have 3 components
# For class C addresses, the first 3 octets (24 bits) define the network
# e.g., 127.0.0
# the last octet (8 bits) defines the host i.e., 0-255
# Thus I setup 3 spin controls one for each of the 3 network octets
# I also set the default value to 127.0.0 for convenience

ipaRange = wx.SpinCtrl(panelAction, -1,'')
ipaRange.SetRange(0, 255)
ipaRange.SetValue(127)

ipbRange = wx.SpinCtrl(panelAction, -1,'')
ipbRange.SetRange(0, 255)
ipbRange.SetValue(0)
```

```
ipcRange = wx.SpinCtrl(panelAction, -1,'')
ipcRange.SetRange(0, 255)
ipcRange.SetValue(0)

# Also, I'm adding a label for the user
ipLabel = wx.StaticText(panelAction, label="IP Base: ")

# Next, I want to provide the user with the ability to set the host range
# they wish to scan. Range is 0 - 255
hostStart = wx.SpinCtrl(panelAction, -1,'')
hostStart.SetRange(0, 255)
hostStart.SetValue(1)

hostEnd = wx.SpinCtrl(panelAction, -1,'')
hostEnd.SetRange(0, 255)
hostEnd.SetValue(10)

HostStartLabel = wx.StaticText(panelAction, label="Host Start: ")
HostEndLabel   = wx.StaticText(panelAction, label="Host End: ")

# Now I create BoxSizer to automatically align the different components
# neatly within the panel
# First, I create a horizontal Box
# I'm adding the buttons, ip Range and Host Spin Controls
actionBox = wx.BoxSizer()
actionBox.Add(scanButton, proportion=1, flag=wx.LEFT, border=5)
actionBox.Add(exitButton, proportion=0, flag=wx.LEFT, border=5)

actionBox.Add(ipLabel, proportion=0, flag=wx.LEFT, border=5)

actionBox.Add(ipaRange, proportion=0, flag=wx.LEFT, border=5)
actionBox.Add(ipbRange, proportion=0, flag=wx.LEFT, border=5)
actionBox.Add(ipcRange, proportion=0, flag=wx.LEFT, border=5)

actionBox.Add(HostStartLabel, proportion=0, flag=wx.LEFT|wx.CENTER, border=5)

actionBox.Add(hostStart, proportion=0, flag=wx.LEFT, border=5)

actionBox.Add(HostEndLabel, proportion=0, flag=wx.LEFT|wx.CENTER, border=5)
actionBox.Add(hostEnd, proportion=0, flag=wx.LEFT, border=5)

# Next I create a Vertical Box that I place the Horizontal Box Inside
# Along with the results text area
vertBox = wx.BoxSizer(wx.VERTICAL)
vertBox.Add(actionBox,proportion=0,flag=wx.EXPAND|wx.ALL,border= 5)
vertBox.Add(results, proportion=1, flag=wx.EXPAND | wx.LEFT | wx.
BOTTOM | wx.RIGHT, border=5)

# I'm adding a status bar to the main windows to display status messages

mainWin.CreateStatusBar()

# Finally, I use the SetSizer function to automatically size the windows
based on the definitions above

panelAction.SetSizer(vertBox)
# Display the main window

mainWin.Show()
```

```
# Enter the Applications Main Loop
# Awaiting User Actions
app.MainLoop()
```

8.2.4 ping扫描的执行

图8.7给出了ping扫描程序的两次运行情况的概要图。在第一次运行中，使用的IP基址是127.0.0.，选择主机号是1~5，并显示了运行的结果。在第二次运行中，选择了我所在的局域网192.168.0.的基址，扫描了1~7的主机号，每一次ping的结果都被记录下来。在这两次运行中，如果主机有响应，那么其时间（或者延迟）也会被记录。

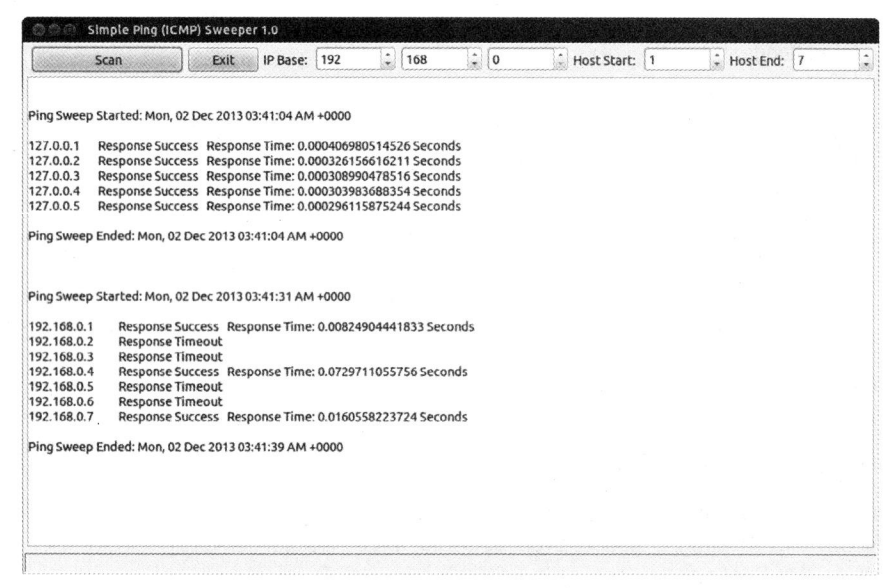

图8.7　ping扫描程序的运行

在图8.8中，有意错误地设定主机选择范围为无效（作为起点的主机号比作为结尾的主机号要大）。正如所预计的一样，出错对话框显示了出来。可以检验pingScan事件处理器中显示此对话框的代码。

> 正如同你看到的那样，大部分的工作都与建立应用程序的GUI、创建需要扫描的IP列表有关。一旦此工作完成，利用ping.py模块执行ping并取得结果的代码仅有一行，就是发送一个，且只有一个ping，代码如下：
>
> ```
> # Perform the Ping
> delay = ping.do_one(ipAddress, timeout = 2)
> ```

图8.8　误设主机范围的错误处理

在执行ping扫描来发现终端主机时，必须牢记于心的一件事就是要进行多次扫描，因为在第一次扫描时，一些终端由于关机或者通信失效而未被识别出。在"问题小结"中将会提出一个挑战性的任务，以改进这个应用并解决问题。

8.3 端口扫描

一旦识别出了局域网中的终端,接下来就是进行端口扫描。到底什么是端口扫描,或者更具体地说,什么是TCP/IP端口扫描?支持通信协议的计算机都使用端口与其他设备连接。为了支持与多个设备的不同会话,我们使用端口来区分不同的通信。例如,Web服务器用超文本传输协议(HTTP)提供网页访问,它默认使用TCP端口号80。简单邮件传送协议或者称为SMTP使用端口号25来发送或传输邮件消息。对于每一个不同的IP地址,协议端口号由一个16位的数字来区分,亦即大家熟知的0~65535间的端口数字。端口号与IP地址相结合就可以得到一个完整的通信地址。通信的各方都必须有一个IP地址和端口号。根据通信方向的不同,源地址和目标地址(IP地址与端口的结合)都是需要的。

在表8.1中,端口被划分为了三种基本类别。

表8.1 网络端口分类

类别	端口范围	用途
公认端口	0~1023	这些端口被系统进程使用,提供广泛应用的网络服务
注册端口	1024~49151	互联网名称与数字地址分配机构(ICANN)管理注册工作,或者更具体地说,由现在被ICANN接管的互联网号码分配当局(IANA)管理
动态端口	49152~65535	本质上,这些端口通常是短暂(或短生命期)的,由操作系统在预定范围内自动按需分配。在服务器上,这些端口被用做与客户端的持续通信连接,这些客户端本来是要连接到公认端口的,如文件传输协议或FTP端口

8.3.1 公认端口的例子

在表8.2中给出了一些你可能熟悉的公认端口(注意这只是全部列表的一部分)。

表8.2 已知端口的例子

服务名	端口号	传输协议	描述
echo	7	tcp	Echo
echo	7	udp	Echo
ftp	21	tcp	文件传输(File Transfer)
ftp	21	udp	文件传输(File Transfer)
ssh	22	tcp	The Secure Shell(SSH)协议
ssh	22	udp	The Secure Shell(SSH)协议
telnet	23	tcp	Telnet
telnet	23	udp	Telnet
smtp	25	tcp	简单邮件传输(Simple Mail Transfer)
smtp	25	udp	简单邮件传输(Simple Mail Transfer)
nameserver	42	tcp	主机命名服务(Host Name Serve)
nameserver	42	udp	主机命名服务(Host Name Serve)
http	80	tcp	万维网超文本传输协议(World Wide Web HTTP)
http	80	udp	万维网超文本传输协议(World Wide Web HTTP)
nntp	119	tcp	网络新闻传输协议(Network News Transfer Protocol)
nntp	119	udp	网络新闻传输协议(Network News Transfer Protocol)
ntp	123	tcp	网络时间协议(Network Time Protocol)

（续表）

服务名	端口号	传输协议	描述
ntp	123	udp	网络时间协议（Network Time Protocol）
netbios-ns	137	tcp	NETBIOS Name Service
netbios-ns	137	udp	NETBIOS Name Service
snmp	161	tcp	简单网络管理协议（SNMP）
snmp	161	udp	简单网络管理协议（SNMP）

8.3.2 注册端口的例子

在表8.3中给出了一些你可能熟悉的注册端口（注意这只是全部列表的一部分）。

表8.3 注册端口的例子

服务名	端口号	传输协议	描述
nlogin	758	tcp	nlogin服务
nlogin	758	udp	nlogin服务
telnets	992	tcp	telnet protocol over TLS/SSL
telnets	992	udp	telnet protocol over TLS/SSL
pop3s	995	tcp	pop3 protocol over TLS/SSL (过去的spop3)
pop3s	995	udp	pop3 protocol over TLS/SSL (过去的spop3)

对于开发最简单的Python端口扫描器程序，需要知道的事情只有几件：

(1) 目标IP地址是哪些？

(2) 应扫描的端口范围是什么？

(3) 是否应当显示端口扫描的所有结果？或者只显示找到的打开的端口，也就是能成功连接的端口。

图8.9描述的是简单端口扫描器的GUI界面。GUI界面允许用户指定扫描的IP地址和端口范围。GUI也包含了一个复选框，它允许用户指定显示所有结果还是只显示成功的结果。

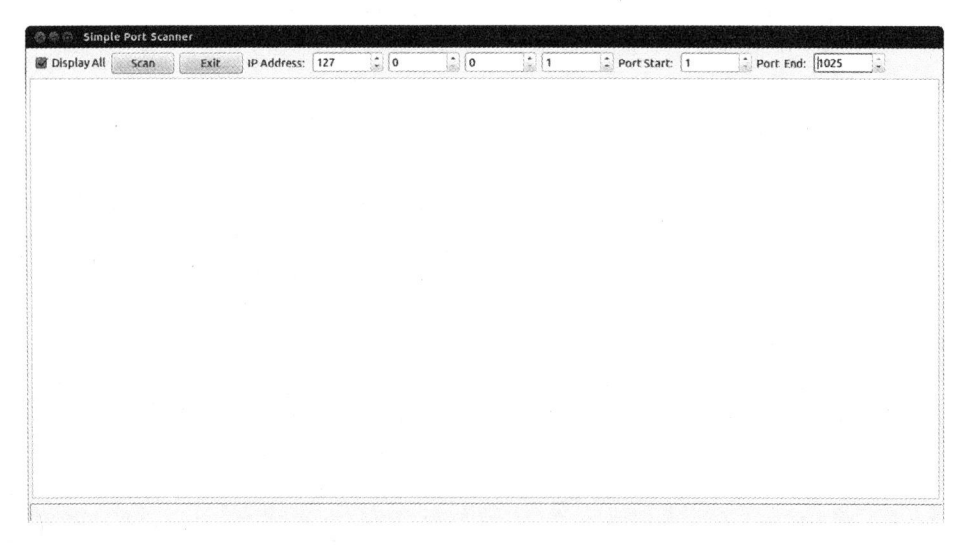

图8.9 端口扫描器的运行界面

我已经随程序提供了详细的文档，因此你可以阅读这些注释来清晰地理解程序。图8.10描述了端口扫描器器GUI的启动界面。正如在图8.10看到的那样，使用管理员权限从命令行启动这个程序。这是必不可少的，因为执行端口扫描的网络操作需要管理员权限。

```
chet@PythonForensics:~/Desktop/Python Samples/Network Samples$ sudo python portScanner.py
[sudo] password for chet:
```

图8.10　端口扫描器的程序启动

在深入代码之前，请先审视程序的整体结构。建议你从考察代码中稍后几页的"Setup the Application Windows"（建立应用程序窗口）部分开始。然后返回到代码的起始点，考察以"def portScan(event)"开始的portScan的事件处理器。

如你所见，大部分的工作都与建立应用程序的GUI、创建需要扫描的主机端口列表有关。一旦此工作完成，真正扫描每一个端口并且检查结果的代码就只需要几行。代码如下：

```
# open a socket
reqSocket = socket(AF_INET, SOCK_STREAM)
# Try Connecting to the specified IP, Port
response = reqSocket.connect_ex((baseIP, port))
```

```python
#
# Python Port Scanner
#
import wxversion
wxversion.select("2.8")

import wx              # Import the GUI module wx
import sys             # Import the standard library module sys
import ping            # Import the ICMP Ping Module
from socket import *   # Import the standard library module socket

from time import gmtime, strftime # import time functions

#
# Event Handler for the portScan Button Press
#

def portScan(event):

    # First, I need to check that the starting port is <= ending port value

    if portEnd.GetValue() < portStart.GetValue():

        # This is an improper setting
        # Notify the user and return
```

```python
            dlg = wx.MessageDialog(mainWin,"Invalid Host Port Selection",
            "Confirm", wx.OK | wx.ICON_EXCLAMATION)

            result = dlg.ShowModal()
            dlg.Destroy()
            return

    # Update the Status Bar
    mainWin.StatusBar.SetStatusText('Executing Port Scan .... Please
    Wait')

    # Record the Start Time
    utcStart = gmtime()
    utc = strftime("%a, %d %b %Y %X +0000", utcStart)
    results.AppendText("\n\nPort Scan Started: "+ utc+ "\n\n")

    # Build the base IP Address String
    # Extract data from the ip Range and host name user selections
    # Build a Python List of IP Addresses to Sweep

    baseIP = str(ipaRange.GetValue())+ \
             '.'+str(ipbRange.GetValue())+ \
             '.'+str(ipcRange.GetValue())+ \
             '.'+str(ipdRange.GetValue())

    # For the IP Addresses Specified, Scan the Ports Specified

    for port in range(portStart.GetValue(), portEnd.GetValue()+1):

        try:

            # Report the IP Address to the Window Status Bar
            mainWin.StatusBar.SetStatusText('Scanning:'+ baseIP+' Port:'+str(port))

            # open a socket
            reqSocket = socket(AF_INET, SOCK_STREAM)

            # Try Connecting to the specified IP, Port

            response = reqSocket.connect_ex((baseIP, port))

            # if we receive a proper response from the port
            # then display the results received

            if(response == 0) :
                # Display the ipAddress and Port
                results.AppendText(baseIP+'\t'+str(port)+'\t')
                results.AppendText('Open')
                results.AppendText("\n")
            else:
                # if the result failed, only display the result
                # when the user has selected the "Display All" check box
                if displayAll.GetValue() == True:
                    results.AppendText(baseIP+'\t'+str(port)+'\t')
                    results.AppendText('Closed')
                    results.AppendText("\n")

            # Close the socket
            reqSocket.close()
```

```
            except socket.error, e:
                # for socket Errors Report the offending IP
                results.AppendText(baseIP+'\t'+str(port)+'\t')
                results.AppendText('Failed:')
                results.AppendText(e.message)
                results.AppendText("\n")

        # Record and display the ending time of the sweep
        utcEnd = gmtime()
        utc = strftime("%a, %d %b %Y %X +0000", utcEnd)
        results.AppendText("\nPort Scan Ended: "+ utc + "\n\n")

        # Clear the Status Bar
        mainWin.StatusBar.SetStatusText('')

# End Scan Event Handler ===========================


#
# Program Exit Event Handler
#
def programExit(event):
    sys.exit()

# End Program Exit Event Handler ==================

#
# Setup the Application Windows ==================
#

app = wx.App()

# define window
mainWin = wx.Frame(None, title="Simple Port Scanner", size=(1200,600))

#define the action panel

panelAction = wx.Panel(mainWin)

# define action buttons
# I'm creating two buttons, one for Scan and one for Exit
# Notice that each button contains the name of the function that will
# handle the button press event. Port Scan and ProgramExit respectively

displayAll = wx.CheckBox(panelAction, -1,'Display All', (10, 10))
displayAll.SetValue(True)

scanButton = wx.Button(panelAction, label='Scan')
scanButton.Bind(wx.EVT_BUTTON, portScan)

exitButton = wx.Button(panelAction, label='Exit')
exitButton.Bind(wx.EVT_BUTTON, programExit)

# define a Text Area where I can display results

results = wx.TextCtrl(panelAction, style = wx.TE_MULTILINE | wx.HSCROLL)

# Base Network for Class C IP Addresses has 3 components
# For class C addresses, the first 3 octets define the network i.e 127.0.0
```

```python
# the last 8 bits define the host i.e. 0-255
# Thus I setup 3 spin controls one for each of the 4 network octets
# I also, set the default value to 127.0.0.0 for convenience
ipaRange = wx.SpinCtrl(panelAction, -1,'')
ipaRange.SetRange(0, 255)
ipaRange.SetValue(127)

ipbRange = wx.SpinCtrl(panelAction, -1,'')
ipbRange.SetRange(0, 255)
ipbRange.SetValue(0)

ipcRange = wx.SpinCtrl(panelAction, -1,'')
ipcRange.SetRange(0, 255)
ipcRange.SetValue(0)

ipdRange = wx.SpinCtrl(panelAction, -1,'')
ipdRange.SetRange(0, 255)
ipdRange.SetValue(1)

# Add a label for clarity
ipLabel = wx.StaticText(panelAction, label="IP Address: ")

# Next, I want to provide the user with the ability to set the port range
# they wish to scan. Maximum is 20 - 1025
portStart = wx.SpinCtrl(panelAction, -1,'')
portStart.SetRange(1, 1025)
portStart.SetValue(1)

portEnd = wx.SpinCtrl(panelAction, -1,'')
portEnd.SetRange(1, 1025)
portEnd.SetValue(5)

PortStartLabel = wx.StaticText(panelAction, label="Port Start: ")
PortEndLabel = wx.StaticText(panelAction, label="Port End: ")

# Now I create BoxSizer to automatically align the different components neatly
# First, I create a horizontal Box
# I'm adding the buttons, ip Range and Host Spin Controls

actionBox = wx.BoxSizer()

actionBox.Add(displayAll, proportion=0, flag=wx.LEFT|wx.CENTER, border=5)
actionBox.Add(scanButton, proportion=0, flag=wx.LEFT, border=5)
actionBox.Add(exitButton, proportion=0, flag=wx.LEFT, border=5)

actionBox.Add(ipLabel, proportion=0, flag=wx.LEFT|wx.CENTER, border=5)

actionBox.Add(ipaRange, proportion=0, flag=wx.LEFT, border=5)
actionBox.Add(ipbRange, proportion=0, flag=wx.LEFT, border=5)
actionBox.Add(ipcRange, proportion=0, flag=wx.LEFT, border=5)
actionBox.Add(ipdRange, proportion=0, flag=wx.LEFT, border=5)

actionBox.Add(PortStartLabel, proportion=0, flag=wx.LEFT|wx.CENTER, border=5)
actionBox.Add(portStart, proportion=0, flag=wx.LEFT, border=5)

actionBox.Add(PortEndLabel, proportion=0, flag=wx.LEFT|wx.CENTER, border=5)
actionBox.Add(portEnd, proportion=0, flag=wx.LEFT, border=5)
```

```
# Next I create a Vertical Box that I place the Horizontal Box components
# inside along with the results text area
vertBox = wx.BoxSizer(wx.VERTICAL)
vertBox.Add(actionBox,proportion=0,flag=wx.EXPAND|wx.ALL,border= 5)
vertBox.Add(results, proportion=1, flag=wx.EXPAND | wx.LEFT | wx.BOTTOM | wx.RIGHT,
border=5)

# I'm adding a menu and status bar to the main window
mainWin.CreateStatusBar()

# Finally, I use the SetSizer function to automatically size the windows
# based on the definitions above
panelAction.SetSizer(vertBox)

# Display the main window
mainWin.Show()

# Enter the Applications Main Loop
# Awaiting User Actions
app.MainLoop
```

现在你阅读完了代码，看一看图8.11和图8.12描述的程序的运行情况。这两幅图唯一的区别就是复选框"Display All"的设置不同。

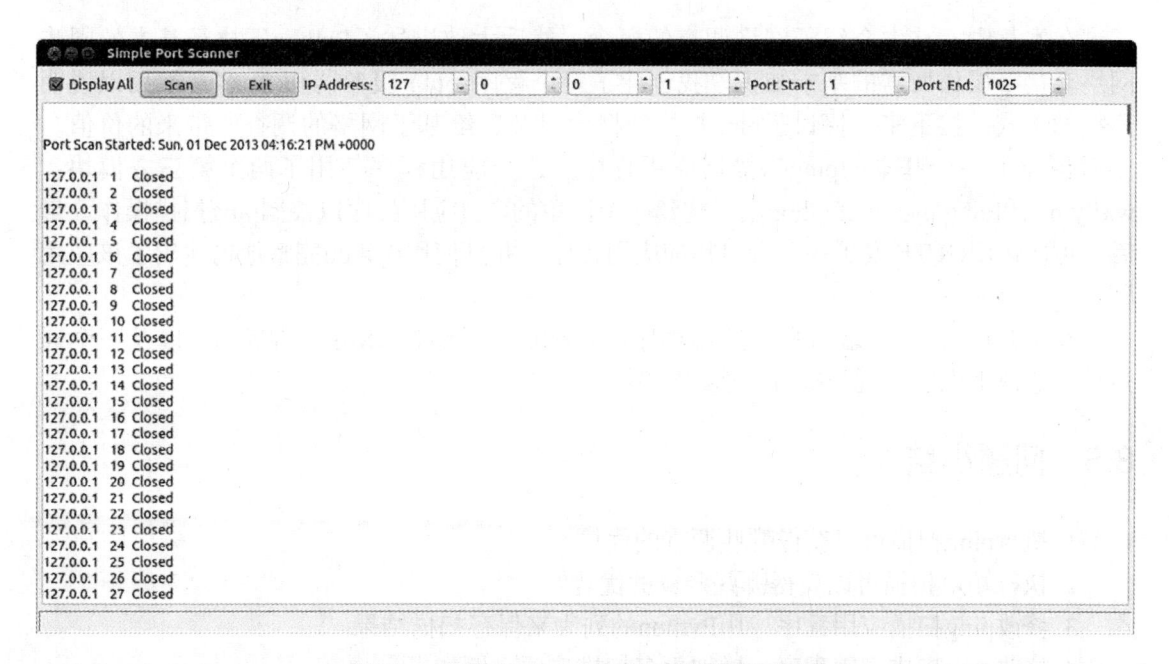

图8.11　选择Display All的端口器扫描运行情况

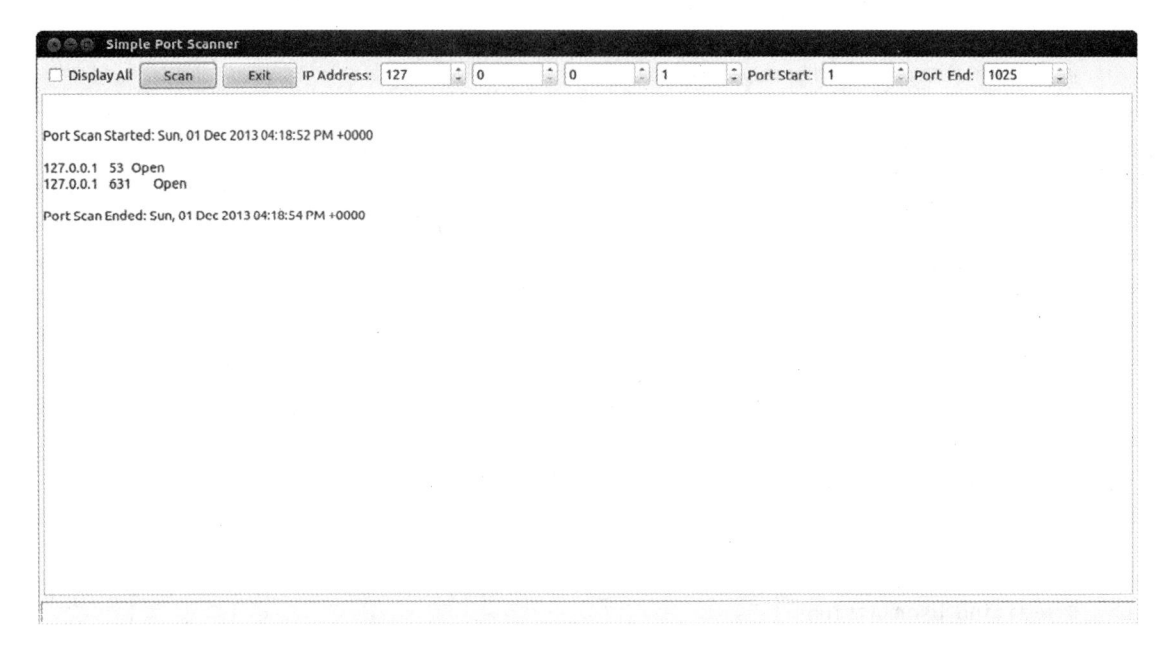

图8.12　未选择Display All的端口器扫描运行情况

8.4　章节回顾

在本章中，首先介绍了网络调查的概念。然后大致讲述了Python下执行基本的同步网络套接字操作所需的基本知识。我创建了三个程序：(1) 服务器和(2) 客户端用以说明连接的方式。接下来，探讨了ping扫描的概念以及它给基于网络的调查所带来的价值。然后创建了一个基本的ping扫描器应用程序。这个应用程序使用了两个第三方模块：wxPython和ping.py。wxPython用以构建一个简单的GUI应用程序以控制ping扫描操作。最后，再次运用GUI开发了一个端口扫描应用程序，并且使用Python完整地构建出了该应用程序。

在第9章中，会对端口扫描应用程序进行拓展，并给出OS指纹的实例，以及一个通过被动监视来识别主机和端口用途的实例。

8.5　问题小结

1. 执行ping扫描可以获得哪些调查的优势？
2. 执行端口扫描可以获得哪些调查的优势？
3. 修改ping扫描应用程序，用Python的列表来保存扫描结果。
4. 修改ping扫描应用程序，增加更多扫描选项，例如：
   a. 设定扫描程序，让它自动并重复地以预先定义的时间间隔运行，以识别大范围的终端。在列表中保留识别出的IP地址的踪迹（对于本操作，也许可以选择使用集合，Python集合有什么优势？）。
   b. 创建一种隐秘模式，以若干天为周期，这个模块会给在指定的IP地址范围内的主机随机发送ping。

5. 修改端口扫描应用程序，扩展可允许的端口范围。
6. 将端口扫描和ping扫描应用用一种方式整合起来，这种方式能让端口扫描自动对响应ping的主机执行并忽略掉没有回应的主机。

8.6 补充资料

1. 互联网名称与数字地址分配机构，网址http://www.icann.org/
2. 猎杀红色十月号，网址http://www.tomclancy.com/book_display.php?isbn13=9780425240335
3. Python Ping 模块，网址https://pypi.Python.org/pypi/ping
4. wxPython GUI 环境，网址www.wxPython.org

第9章 网络取证：第2部分

9.1 本章简介

正如在第8章中所发现的，Python具有一系列功能丰富的标准库，能执行网络交互、探测及分析。一旦熟悉了底层库和模块，ping扫描与端口扫描应用程序将是十分直观的。然而，交互式的扫描和探测存在几个关键的局限性：

1. 为了使得扫描有效，目标（主机、路由器、交换机、打印机、服务器）必须处于开启状态并正常工作，才能与程序相互作用。
2. 你的工作环境必须能容忍这些扫描活动带来的"噪音"。实际上大多数入侵防御系统（IPS）都会精准无误地找到此类扫描活动，将其归入攻击类型，并做出相应的反应，除非它们被设置为忽略这些扫描活动。完成这种设置比想象的要更难，大部分的网络安全人士不倾向于对其IPS的设置进行变更。
3. 当拥有这些端口的终端，如预期的那样对探测进行回应时，端口扫描程序才起作用。我们有意搜索的恶意终端不一定对此进行充分配合，并且不会对这些初级的查询做出回应。
4. 许多恶意服务利用用户报文协议（UDP）与操作者进行通信，即使利用漏洞评估技术去探测，它们也能隐蔽地运行而不被发现。
5. 最后，在关键基础设施环境中，运营者往往不允许对网络进行主动扫描和探测，因为在许多情况下，探测活动可能会导致操作中断，或者系统崩溃。如果这种情况发生在一个监控和数据采集环境中，操作中断和系统崩溃可能会影响成千上万的客户，或者出现更糟的后果。

9.2 数据包嗅探

网络（或者数据包）嗅探是另外一种可以使用的方法，若是使用得当，可以提供更加深入的细节。如果做得好，网络嗅探相较于端口扫描，具有三个重要的优势：

1. 嗅探器是完全隐蔽的，不会在网络上发出任何一个数据包，可以确保对网络操作没有影响。
2. 嗅探器是一个观测器，可以几小时、几天、几周甚至几个月地运行，不间断地收集信息。这些信息能更为全面地描述本地主机、服务器、网络设备，甚至是先前未被发现的恶意设备的活动。
3. 最后，它可以捕获到各种隐蔽的、周期出现，亦或偶尔发生的活动。

第 9 章 网络取证：第 2 部分

在最初的方式中，数据包嗅探器（也称为网络嗅探器）捕获的是通过某个指定网络接口的所有数据包。为了捕获到这些包，其网络接口必须处于混杂模式，并且必须连接到一个能"看到"到所有数据包的端口上。例如，如果对某个特定的子网感兴趣，就要把嗅探器连接到该子网的交换机或集线器上。如今很多现代的交换机通过可交换端口分析器（SPAN）或远程可交换端口分析器支持端口映射，如图9.1和图9.2所示。这些端口通常连接到IPS、网络监控设备，或者能够探测网络负载性能的测量设备上。

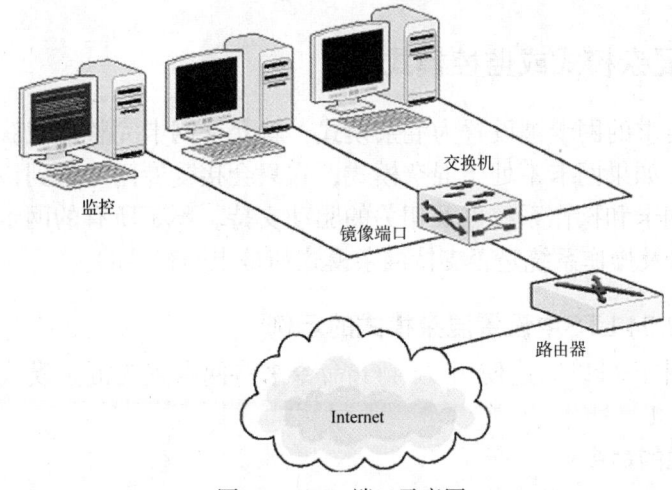

图9.1 SPAN端口示意图

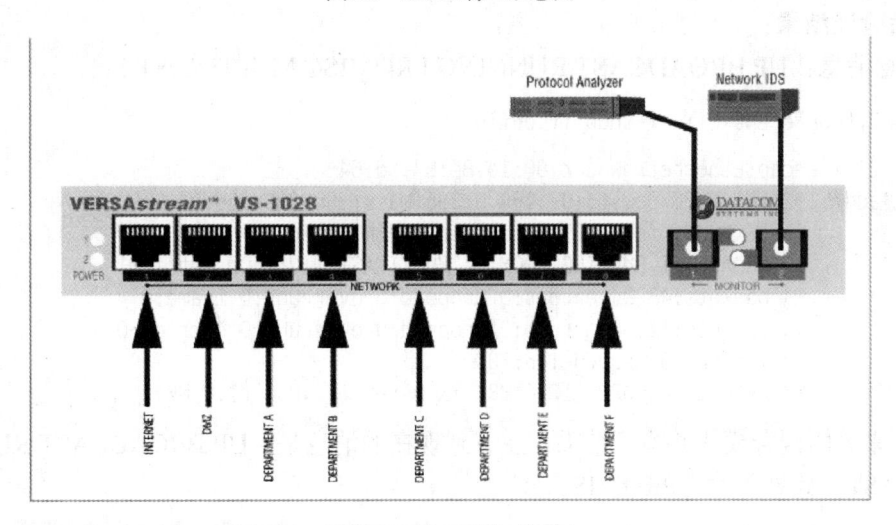

图9.2 SPAN端口连接

> SPAN端口通常要归功于思科公司（最初称之为端口映射）。现代交换机可以被配置为将特定的网络端口映射到一个公共端口，用于进行网络监管，以及与各种安全设备进行交互。

9.3 Python中的原始套接字

为了在Python中进行数据包嗅探，我们将需要以下这些条件：

1. 必须使用具有可运行于混杂模式功能的网卡（NIC）。
2. 一些现代的操作系统，即Windows，Linux，Mac OS X，还必须具有管理员权限。
3. 一旦满足了1和2，就可以创建一个原始套接字。

9.3.1 什么是混杂模式或监控模式

当一个满足要求的网卡被设置为混杂模式，就允许网卡完整地截获并读取每一个抵达的网络数据包。如果网卡不处于混杂模式，它只会接受专门发送到该网卡的数据包。混杂模式必须由网卡和操作系统以及相关的驱动支持。不是所有的网卡支持混杂模式，但确认你的网卡以及操作系统是否支持混杂模式却是十分容易的。

在Ubuntu 12.04 LTS中设置混杂模式的示例

在Linux系统中，可以通过使用`ifconfig`命令来将网卡置为混杂模式（注意需要管理员权限）。

启用混杂模式的命令：

chet@PythonForensics: ~$ sudo ifconfig eth0 promisc

随后验证结果：

（注意消息：UP BROADCAST RUNNING PROMISC MULTICAST）

```
chet@PythonForensics: ~$ sudo ifconfig

eth0 Link encap:Ethernet HWaddr 00:1e:8c:b7:6d:64
inet addr:192.168.0.25 Bcast:192.168.0.255 Mask:255.255.255.0
        inet6 addr: fe80::21e:8cff:feb7:6d64/64 Scope:Link
        UP BROADCAST RUNNING PROMISC MULTICAST MTU:1500 Metric:1
        RX packets:43284 errors:0 dropped:0 overruns:0 frame:0
        TX packets:11338 errors:0 dropped:0 overruns:0 carrier:0
        collisions:0 txqueuelen:1000
        RX bytes:17659022 (17.6 MB) TX bytes:1824060 (1.8 MB)
```

接下来关闭混杂模式并验证结果，注意到现在的消息是：UP BROADCAST RUNNING MULTICAST，此处并没有PROMISC。

```
chet@PythonForensics: ~$ sudo ifconfig eth0 -promisc

chet@PythonForensics: ~

eth0 Link encap:Ethernet HWaddr 00:1e:8c:b7:6d:64

inet addr:192.168.0.25 Bcast:192.168.0.255 Mask:255.255.255.0
        inet6 addr: fe80::21e:8cff:feb7:6d64/64 Scope:Link
        UP BROADCAST RUNNING MULTICAST MTU:1500 Metric:1
        RX packets:43381 errors:0 dropped:0 overruns:0 frame:0
        TX packets:11350 errors:0 dropped:0 overruns:0 carrier:0
        collisions:0 txqueuelen:1000
        RX bytes:17668285 (17.6 MB) TX bytes:1827000 (1.8 MB)
```

第9章 网络取证：第2部分

一旦确认了有一个可进入混杂模式的网卡，就为我们在Python中使用原始套接字做好了准备。

9.3.2 Linux下Python中的原始套接字

特别注意： 在本章的其余部分中，将使用Linux环境。由于处理原始套接字的代码在不同操作系统之间不相同，所以与原始套接字通信的代码需经过修改后才能支持Windows。

用Python创建原始套接字十分简单，如下面的代码所示。该代码完成以下任务：

(1) 启用网卡混杂模式
(2) 创建一个原始套接字
(3) 捕获下一个通过该网卡的TCP数据包
(4) 打印数据包的内容
(5) 禁用网卡混杂模式
(6) 关闭原始套接字

```
# Note: Script must be run with admin privledge

# import the socket and os libraries
import socket
import os

# issue the command to place the adapter in promiscious mode
ret = os.system("ifconfig eth0 promisc")

# if the command was successful continue
if ret == 0:

    # Create a Raw Socket in Linux
    # AF_INET specifies ipv4 packets
    # SOCK_RAW specifies a raw protocol at the network layer
    # IPPROTO_TCP specifies the protocol to capture

    mySocket = socket.socket(socket.AF_INET, socket.SOCK_RAW,
    socket.IPPROTO_TCP)

    # Receive the next packet up to 255 bytes
    # Note this is a synchronous call and will wait until
    # a packet is received

    recvBuffer, addr = mySocket.recvfrom(255)

    # Print out the contents of the buffer

    print recvBuffer
    ret = os.system("ifconfig eth0 -promisc")

else:
    # if the system command fails print out a message
    print 'Promiscious Mode not Set'
```

该代码产生如图9.3所示的输出。如你所见，数据包内容的输出看起来相当神秘。

E\000\0004 ýê\000@ACK2Å \000\000SOH \000\000SOHAPCSÇP%CSI2ÈnµRI jPADDLESOH\000þ(\000\000SOHSOHBS
\000[&ó\000[&é

图9.3 原始TCP/IP包的内容

9.3.3 对缓冲区进行解包

从这样的缓冲区中提取信息可能显得较为繁琐，因为我们必须从缓冲区中解析出相关信息。为了能处理这种结构明确的缓冲数据，Python提供了unpack()函数。

网上有许多这类解包实例和应用程序，可以用来解析各种已知的数据结构。但弄清楚这个函数是如何工作的，通常留给读者自己去想象，或至少需要进一步的研究。

为了便于说明，可以在网上找到类似的例子，从IPv4报头中提取出信息。

```
ipHeader = packet[0:20]
buffer = unpack('!BBHHHBBH4 s4 s', ipHeader)
```

对于这本书的所有章节，都需要深刻理解函数是如何工作的，这样就可以把它们应用到眼下以及未来的其他问题。unpack()函数接受两个参数，第一个是一个字符串，定义保存在缓冲区中的数据格式，第二个即为需要解析的缓冲区。该函数返回一个可以像列表（list）那样处理的元组（tulple）。

为了搞清楚这一点，必须首先研究IPv4数据包的头结构，如图9.4所示，并将其与格式字符串"!BBHHHBBH4 s4 s"做比较。

Offsets	Bytes	0								1								2								3						
Octet	Bit	0	1	2	3	4	5	6	7	8	9	10	11	12	13	14	15	16	17	18	19	20	21	22	23	24	25	26	27	28	29	30	31
0	0	Version				IHL				DSCP						ECN		Total Length															
4	32	Identification																Flags			Fragment Offset												
8	64	Time To Live								Protocol								Header Checksum															
12	96	Source IP Address																															
16	128	Destination IP Address																															
20	160	Options (if IHL > 5)																															

图9.4 典型的Ipv4数据包头

格式字符串中的每一个字符都有特定的意义，规定了unpack()函数的处理方式。如果你的格式字符串有误，那么所得到的将是毫无用处的数据，或者如果作为第二个参数传递的缓冲区与你要求的格式不符，那么结果也会出错。

让我们考察一下格式字符串"!BBHHHBBH4 s4 s"中每一个字符的意义，参见表9.1。注意还有其他的格式规范，并被记录在标准库文档中。

表9.1 格式字符串字符的意义

格式	Python类型	字节长度
!	Big Endian	
B	整数	1
H	整数	2
s	字符串	n

格式字符串中的第一个字符代表数据的字节序，对于网络数据包是大端（big endian）格式，用位于格式规范中首字符的感叹号表示。也可以使用大于标志">"来表示big endian格式，但感叹号是对于那些永远都记不清常用的网络数据字节序的人而准备的。实际上使用感叹号有好处，因为这能帮助我们立即识别出该格式字符串与网络数据包有关。

下表给出了与IPv4报头有关的每种格式串的详细说明，参见表9.2。

```
"!BBHHHBBH4s4s"
```

表9.2 IPv4报头格式串说明

格式	大小（字节）	映射到Ipv4	定义
B	1	版本和IHL	4位的
B	1	DSCP和ECN	
H	2	总长度	
H	2	标识符	
H	2		
B	1	存活时间（TTL）	
B	1	协议	
H	2	头检验和值	16位用于错误检测的检验和
4s	4	源IP地址	4字节源IP地址
4s	4	目的IP地址	4字节源目的地址

现在你理解了格式字符串的含义和基本的解包函数unpack()。下面的代码将对一个IPv4报头进行解包，然后将每个域提取为变量以方便处理。在此还提供了相关代码，使用内建的套接字方法将源地址与目标地址转化为易于阅读的形式。

```
# unpack an IPv4 packet
# note the packet variable is a buffer returned from
# a socket.recvfrom() method that was illustrated in Figure 9.3.
ipHeaderTuple = unpack('!BBHHHBBH4s4s', packet)
# Field Contents
verLen         = ipHeaderTuple[0]     # Field 0: Version and Length
dscpECN        = ipHeaderTuple[1]     # Field 1: DSCP and ECN
packetLength   = ipHeaderTuple[2]     # Field 2: Packet Length
packetID       = ipHeaderTuple[3]     # Field 3: Identification
flagFrag       = ipHeaderTuple[4]     # Field 4: Flags/Frag Offset
timeToLive     = ipHeaderTuple[5]     # Field 5: Time to Live (TTL)
protocol       = ipHeaderTuple[6]     # Field 6: Protocol Number
checkSum       = ipHeaderTuple[7]     # Field 7: Header Checksum
sourceIP       = ipHeaderTuple[8]     # Field 8: Source IP
destIP         = ipHeaderTuple[9]     # Field 9: Destination IP
# Convert the sourceIP and destIP into a
# standard dotted-quad string representation for example '192.168.0.5'
sourceAddress = socket.inet_ntoa(sourceIP);
destAddress = socket.inet_ntoa(destIP);
```

```
# Extract the version and header size, this will give
# us the offset to the data portion of the packet

version      = verLen >> 4 # get upper nibble version
length       = verLen & 0x0F # get lower nibble header length
ipHdrLength  = length * 4 # calculate the hdr size in bytes
fragOffset   = flagFrag & 0x1FFF # get lower 13 bits ...
fragment     = fragOffset * 8 # calculate start of fragment
```

接下来我们使用相同的方法，从包的数据片段提取域，在这里就是TCP报头。你可以通过检查协议域，以确定数据包中数据片段的类型。图9.5描述了一个典型的TCP报头。利用格式字符串"!HHLLBBHHH"及unpack()函数，就可以用来提取TCP报头的每一个域。

Offsets	Bytes	\multicolumn{8}{c}{TCP Header}								
		0	1	2	3
Octet	BITS	0 1 2 3 4 5 6 7	8 9 10 11 12 13 14 15	16 17 18 19 20 21 22 23	24 25 26 27 28 29 30 31
0	0	Source port		Destination port	
4	32	Sequence number			
8	64	Acknowledgment number (if ACK set)			
12	96	Data offset	Reserved 0 0 0	N S	C W R	E C E	U R G	A C K	P S H	R S T	S Y N	F I N	Window Size
16	128	Checksum		Urgent pointer (if URG set)	
20 ...	160 ...	Options (if data offset > 5. Padded at the end with "0" bytes if necessary.)			

图9.5 典型的TCP数据包头

```
# By using the results of the IPv4 header unpacking, we can
# strip the TCP Header from the original packet

# Note the ipHdrLength is the offset from the beginning of
# the buffer. The standard length of a TCP packet is 20
# bytes. For our purposes these 20 bytes contain the
# the pertinent information we are looking for

stripTCPHeader = packet[ipHdrLength:ipHdrLength+20]

# unpack returns a tuple, for illustration I will extract
# each individual values using the unpack() function

tcpHeaderBuffer = unpack('!HHLLBBHHH', stripTCPHeader)

sourcePort            = tcpHeaderBuffer[0]
destinationPort       = tcpHeaderBuffer[1]
sequenceNumber        = tcpHeaderBuffer[2]
acknowledgement       = tcpHeaderBuffer[3]
dataOffsetandReserve  = tcpHeaderBuffer[4]
tcpHeaderLength       = (dataOffsetandReserve >> 4) * 4
flags                 = tcpHeaderBuffer[5]
FIN                   = flags & 0x01
SYN                   = (flags >> 1) & 0x01
```

```
RST                     = (flags >> 2) & 0x01
PSH                     = (flags >> 3) & 0x01
ACK                     = (flags >> 4) & 0x01
URG                     = (flags >> 5) & 0x01
ECE                     = (flags >> 6) & 0x01
CWR                     = (flags >> 7) & 0x01
windowSize              = tcpHeaderBuffer[6]
tcpChecksum             = tcpHeaderBuffer[7]
urgentPointer           = tcpHeaderBuffer[8]
```

现在我们已经掌握了这些基本要素，让我们看看：

1. 如何把网卡设置为混杂模式
2. 如何在Linux中创建一个原始套接字
3. 如何拆解数据包以获得每个域

我们已经准备好建立一个可以捕获网络数据包和提取信息的应用程序，它将使我们能够对网络流进行监控。

9.4 Python隐蔽式网络映射工具（PSNMT）

现在我们已经拥有了嗅探网络数据包的基本方法，我需要对这些数据进行解析，并提取所需信息。对于此例，我对收集数据包和单纯地打印结果并不感兴趣，我有意达到下面的目的：

(1) 收集正在进行监控的网络上活跃的IP地址（我决定把监听器放在某个地方一段时间，以捕捉到那些定期或者偶尔打开的网络设备）。
(2) 收集与我的本地网络交互的远程计算机的IP地址。这些可能是网站、邮件，或各式的云服务。
(3) 收集本地以及/或者远程计算机使用的服务端口。我尤为感兴趣的是那些位于0~1023范围内的"公认端口"，以及位于1024~49151范围内的"注册端口"。
(4) 接下来希望报告的记录是唯一的。换言之，如果发现了本地主机是192.168.0.5，且使用端口号80，我只想看见这个记录出现一次，而不是每一次发现时都记录。
(5) 最后，为了限制程序的范围，只需收集IPv4的环境中的TCP或UDP数据包。以后，这个程序可以轻易地被扩展，用于处理其他协议和IPv6。

为了满足以上所述要求，仅需从报头中提取以下域：

(1) 协议
(2) 源IP地址
(3) 目标IP地址
(4) 源端口
(5) 目标端口

考察图9.4和图9.5，协议域、源和目标IP地址位于IPV4报头中，而源和目标端口则存在于TCP报头中。这意味着我不得不对两个报头都进行解析以获得必要的信息。还应考虑到图9.6描述的UDP报头，这也将用于处理UDP数据包的提取。

UDP Header																																		
Offsets	Bytes	0								1								2								3							
Octet	BITS	0	1	2	3	4	5	6	7	8	9	10	11	12	13	14	15	16	17	18	19	20	21	22	23	24	25	26	27	28	29	30	31
0	0	Source port																Destination port															
4	32	Length																Checksum															

图9.6 典型的UDP数据包头

这里存在着几个需要解决的技术问题，以及高层次的要求：

(1) 该使用什么类型的数据元素来存储所收集到的信息？

 a. 我准备用一个简单的列表来存储从数据包中收集到的数据，并对每一个收到的数据包，将数据附加到列表中。

```
ipObservations = []
```

(2) 由于socket.recvfrom()方法是同步的，当要停止收集的时候要怎样发出信号呢？将会怎样限制收集活动的时间呢？

 a. 将使用Python标准库中的signal模块，并将其集成到收集循环中。为此，首先要创建一个myTimeout类，当指定的时间到达时，该类将会被一个处理器所触发。然后将myTimeout的异常处理器集成到接收数据包循环的try/except处理器中。

```
class myTimeout(Exception):
    pass
def handler(signum, frame):
    print'timeout received', signum
    raise myTimeout()

# Set the signal handler
signal.signal(signal.SIGALRM, handler)

# set the signal to expire in n seconds
signal.alarm(n)
...
...
try:

    while True:
        recvBuffer, addr = mySocket.recvfrom(65535)

        src,dst = decoder.PacketExtractor(recvBuffer,\ False)
        sourceIPObservations.append(src)
        destinationIPObservations.append(dst)

except myTimeout:
    pass
```

(3) 该怎样使创建的记录是唯一的呢？

　　a. 上面的代码将记录每一对源IP/端口和目标IP/端口，其结果是一个未经排序的，包含重复记录的列表。为解决这个问题，收集一旦完成，将利用一些Python数据类型的知识获得帮助。一旦收集完成（对于整个时间框架），首先将列表转换成集合，这将立即消除任何重复（这是集合的基本属性之一）。然后将集合转换回列表，然后将列表排序。

```
uniqueSrc = set(map(tuple, ipObservations))
finalList = list(uniqueSrc)
finalList.sort()
```

(4) 应该怎样输出结果呢？

　　a. 为了得到一个可操作的列表，程序将生成一个逗号分隔值（CSV）文件，它可进一步在工作表中（excel）进行处理和检查。

9.5　PSNMT源代码

源代码被分成以下5个源文件（参见表9.3），每个文件包含了程序各个方面的详细注释。图9.7描述的是此应用程序的WingIDE环境。

表9.3　源代码被分成5个源文件

源代码文件	用途
psnmt.py	Main 程序建立和循环
decoder.py	原始数据包解析
_commandparser.py	用户命令行解析
_csvHandler.py	创建/写csv文件输出的处理器
_classLogging.py	处理取证日志的类

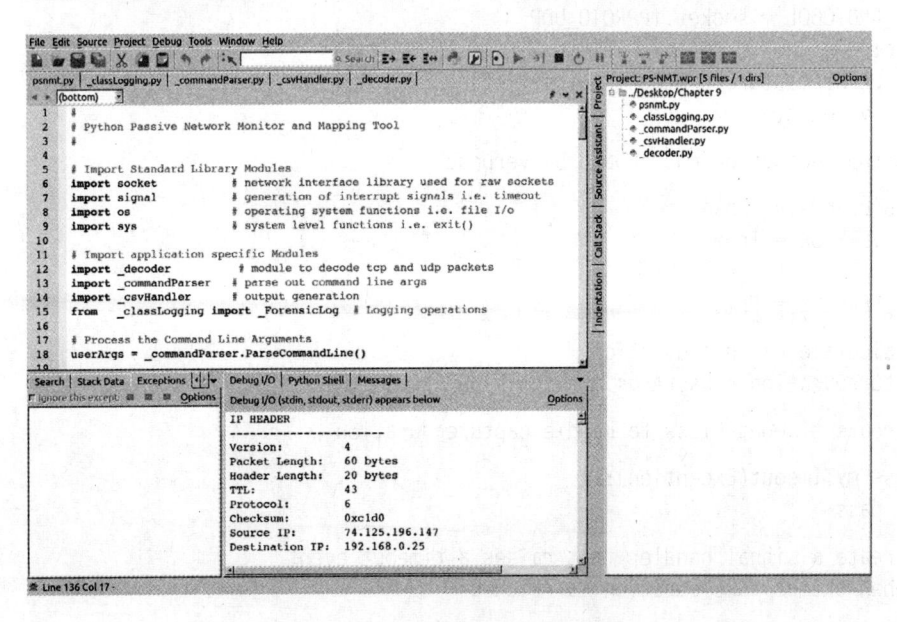

图9.7　PSNMT程序的WingIDE环境

9.5.1 psnmt.py 源代码

```python
#
# Python Passive Network Monitor and Mapping Tool
#

# Import Standard Library Modules
import socket          # network interface library used for raw sockets
import signal          # generation of interrupt signals i.e. timeout
import os              # operating system functions i.e. file I/o
import sys             # system level functions i.e. exit()

# Import application specific Modules
import decoder         # module to decode tcp and udp packets
import _commandParser  # parse out command line args
import _csvHandler     # output generation
from _classLogging import _ForensicLog # Logging operations

# Process the Command Line Arguments
userArgs = _commandParser.ParseCommandLine()

# create a log object
logPath = os.path.join(userArgs.outPath,"ForensicLog.txt")
oLog = _ForensicLog(logPath)

oLog.writeLog("INFO", "PS-NMT Started")

csvPath = os.path.join(userArgs.outPath,"ps-nmtResults.csv")
oCSV = _csvHandler._CSVWriter(csvPath)

# Setup the protocol to capture

if userArgs.TCP:
    PROTOCOL = socket.IPPROTO_TCP
elif userArgs.UDP:
    PROTOCOL = socket.IPPROTO_UDP
else:
    print'Capture protocol not selected'
    sys.exit()

# Setup whether output should be verbose

if userArgs.verbose:
    VERBOSE = True
else:
    VERBOSE = False

# Calculate capture duration
captureDuration = userArgs.minutes * 60

# Create timeout class to handle capture duration

class myTimeout(Exception):
    pass

# Create a signal handler that raises a timeout event
# when the capture duration is reached

def handler(signum, frame):
    print'timeout received', signum
```

```python
        raise myTimeout()

# Enable Promiscious Mode on the NIC

ret = os.system("ifconfig eth0 promisc")

if ret == 0:

    oLog.writeLog("INFO",'Promiscious Mode Enabled')
    # create an INET, raw socket
    # AF_INET specifies         ipv4
    # SOCK_RAW specifies        a raw protocol at the network layer
    # IPPROTO_TCP or UDP        Specifies the protocol to capture
    try:
        mySocket = socket.socket(socket.AF_INET, socket.SOCK_RAW, PROTOCOL)
        oLog.writeLog("INFO",'Raw Socket Open')
    except:
        # if socket open fails
        oLog.writeLog("ERROR",'Raw Socket Open Failed')
        del oLog
        if VERBOSE:
            print'Error Opening Raw Socket'
        sys.exit()

# Set the signal handler to the duraton specified by the user

signal.signal(signal.SIGALRM, handler)
signal.alarm(captureDuration)

# create a list to hold the results from the packet capture
# I'm only interested in Protocol Source IP, Source Port, Destination
IP, Destination Port

ipObservations=[]

# Begin receiving packets until duration is received
# the inner while loop will execute until the timeout

try:

    while True:

            # attempt recieve (this call will wait)
            recvBuffer, addr = mySocket.recvfrom(255)

            # decode the received packet
            content = decoder.PacketExtractor(recvBuffer, VERBOSE)

            # append the results to our list
            ipObservations.append(content)

            # write details to the forensic log file
            oLog.writeLog('INFO', \
                        'RECV:'þcontent[0]þ \
                        'SRC :'þ content[1]þ \
                        'DST :'þ content[3])

except myTimeout:
    pass

# Once time has expired disable Promiscous Mode
```

```python
        ret = os.system("ifconfig eth0 -promisc")
        oLog.writeLog("INFO",'Promiscious Mode Diabled')

        # Close the Raw Socket
        mySocket.close()
        oLog.writeLog("INFO",'Raw Socket Closed')

        # Create unique sorted list
        uniqueSrc = set(map(tuple, ipObservations))
        finalList = list(uniqueSrc)
        finalList.sort()
            # Write each unique sorted packet to the csv file
            for packet in finalList:
                oCSV.writeCSVRow(packet)

            oLog.writeLog('INFO','Program End')

            # Close the Log and CSV objects
            del oLog
            del oCSV

    else:
        print'Promiscious Mode not Set
```

9.5.2　decoder.py 源代码

```python
# Packet Extractor / Decoder Module
#
import socket, sys
from struct import *

# Constants
PROTOCOL_TCP=6
PROTOCOL_UDP=17

# PacketExtractor
#
# Purpose: Extracts fields from the IP, TCP and UDP Header
#
# Input: packet: buffer from socket.recvfrom() method
#        displaySwitch: True: Display the details, False omits
# Output: result list containing
#                   protocol, srcIP, srcPort, dstIP, dstPort
#
def PacketExtractor(packet, displaySwitch):

    # Strip off the first 20 characters for the ip header
    stripPacket= packet[0:20]

    # now unpack them
    ipHeaderTuple=unpack('!BBHHHBBH4s4s', stripPacket)

    # unpack returns a tuple, for illustration I will extract
    # each individual values
                                        # Field Contents
    verLen      = ipHeaderTuple[0]      # Field 0: Version and Length
```

```
    dscpECN        = ipHeaderTuple[1]        # Field 1: DSCP and ECN
    packetLength   = ipHeaderTuple[2]        # Field 2: Packet Length
    packetID       = ipHeaderTuple[3]        # Field 3: Identification
    flagFrag       = ipHeaderTuple[4]        # Field 4: Flags and Fragment Offset
    timeToLive     = ipHeaderTuple[5]        # Field 5: Time to Live (TTL)
    protocol       = ipHeaderTuple[6]        # Field 6: Protocol Number
    checkSum       = ipHeaderTuple[7]        # Field 7: Header Checksum
    sourceIP       = ipHeaderTuple[8]        # Field 8: Source IP
    destIP         = ipHeaderTuple[9]        # Field 9: Destination IP

    # Calculate / Convert extracted values
    version        = verLen >> 4             # Upper Nibble is the versionc
                                               Number
    length         = verLen & 0x0F           # Lower Nibble represents the
                                               size
    ipHdrLength    = length * 4              # Calculate the header length
                                               in bytes

# covert the source and destination address to typical dotted notation strings

    sourceAddress = socket.inet_ntoa(sourceIP);
    destinationAddress = socket.inet_ntoa(destIP);

    if displaySwitch:
        print'========================'
        print'IP HEADER'
        print'_____'
        print'Version:'         + str(version)
        print'Packet Length:' + str(packetLength)þ'bytes'
        print'Header Length:' + str(ipHdrLength) þ'bytes'
        print'TTL:'            + str(timeToLive)
        print'Protocol:'       + str(protocol)
        print'Checksum:'       + hex(checkSum)
        print'Source IP:'      + str(sourceAddress)
        print'Destination IP:'+ str(destinationAddress)

#  _____
    if protocol == PROTOCOL_TCP:

        stripTCPHeader = packet[ipHdrLength:ipHdrLength +20]

        # unpack returns a tuple, for illustration I will extract
        # each individual values using the unpack() function

        tcpHeaderBuffer = unpack('!HHLLBBHHH', stripTCPHeader)

        sourcePort             = tcpHeaderBuffer[0]
        destinationPort        = tcpHeaderBuffer[1]
        sequenceNumber         = tcpHeaderBuffer[2]
        acknowledgement        = tcpHeaderBuffer[3]
        dataOffsetandReserve   = tcpHeaderBuffer[4]
        tcpHeaderLength        = (dataOffsetandReserve >> 4) * 4
        tcpChecksum            = tcpHeaderBuffer[7]

        if displaySwitch:
            print
            print'TCP Header'
```

```
                print'_____'
                print'Source Port:        '+ str(sourcePort)
                print'Destination Port : '+ str(destinationPort)
                print'Sequence Number :   '+ str(sequenceNumber)
                print'Acknowledgement :   '+ str(acknowledgement)
                print'TCP Header Length: '+ str(tcpHeaderLength)+
                                            'bytes '
                print'TCP Checksum:'+ hex(tcpChecksum)
                print

            return(['TCP', sourceAddress, sourcePort, destinationAddress,
            destinationPort])
        elif protocol == PROTOCOL_UDP:
            stripUDPHeader = packet[ipHdrLength:ipHdrLength+8]
            # unpack returns a tuple, for illustration I will extract
            # each individual values using the unpack() function
            udpHeaderBuffer = unpack('!HHHH', stripUDPHeader)
            sourcePort       = udpHeaderBuffer[0]
            destinationPort  = udpHeaderBuffer[1]
            udpLength        = udpHeaderBuffer[2]
            udpChecksum      = udpHeaderBuffer[3]
            if displaySwitch:
                print
                print'UDP Header'
                print'_____'
                print'Source Port:         '+ str(sourcePort)
                print'Destination Port :'+ str(destinationPort)
                print'UDP Length:          '+ str(udpLength)+'bytes'
                print'UDP Checksum:        '+ hex(udpChecksum)
                print

            return(['UDP', sourceAddress, sourcePort, destinationAddress,
            destinationPort])
        else:
            # For expansion protocol support
            if displaySwitch:
                print'Found Protocol :'+ str(protocol)
        return(['Unsupported',sourceAddress,0, \ destinationAddress,0])
```

9.5.3 commandParser.py源代码

```
#
# PSNMT Argument Parser
#
import argparse        # Python Standard Library - Parser for command-line
                      options, arguments
import os              # Standard Library OS functions
# Name: ParseCommand() Function
```

```
#
# Desc: Process and Validate the command line arguments
#          use Python Standard Library module argparse
#
# Input: none
#
# Actions:
#          Uses the Standard Library argparse to process the command line
#
def ParseCommandLine():

    parser= argparse.ArgumentParser('PS-NMT')

    parser.add_argument('-v', '--verbose', help="Display packet details", action='store_true')

    # setup a group where the selection is mutually exclusive and required.
    group= parser.add_mutually_exclusive_group(required=True)
    group.add_argument('--TCP', help = 'TCP   Packet   Capture', action = 'store_true')
    group.add_argument('--UDP', help = 'UDP   Packet   Capture', action = 'store_true')
    parser.add_argument('-m','--minutes', help ='Capture Duration in minutes',type = int)
    parser.add_argument('-p', '--outPath', type = ValidateDirectory, required = True, help = "Output Directory")

    theArgs = parser.parse_args()

    return theArgs

# End Parse Command Line ============================

def ValidateDirectory(theDir):

    # Validate the path is a directory
    if not os.path.isdir(theDir):
        raise argparse.ArgumentTypeError('Directory does not exist')

    # Validate the path is writable
    if os.access(theDir, os.W_OK):
        return theDir
    else:
        raise argparse.ArgumentTypeError('Directory is not writable')
# End ValidateDirectory ============================
```

9.5.4　classLogging.py源代码

```
import logging
#
# Class: _ForensicLog
#
# Desc: Handles Forensic Logging Operations
#
# Methods constructor: Initializes the Logger
#         writeLog:    Writes a record to the log
```

```
#         destructor: Writes message and shutsdown the logger
class _ForensicLog:
    def __init__(self, logName):
        try:
            # Turn on Logging
            logging.basicConfig(filename = logName,level = logging.
            DEBUG,format = '%(asctime)s %(message)s')
        except:
            print "Forensic Log Initialization Failure ... Aborting"
            exit(0)
    def writeLog(self, logType, logMessage):
        if logType == "INFO":
            logging.info(logMessage)
        elif logType == "ERROR":
            logging.error(logMessage)
        elif logType == "WARNING":
            logging.warning(logMessage)
        else:
            logging.error(logMessage)
        return

    def __del__(self):
        logging.info("Logging Shutdown")
        logging.shutdown()
```

9.5.5　csvHandler.py源代码

```
import csv #Python Standard Library - for csv files
#
# Class: _CSVWriter
#
# Desc: Handles all methods related to comma separated value operations
#
# Methods constructor: Initializes the CSV File
#         writeCVSRow: Writes a single row to the csv file
#         writerClose: Closes the CSV File

class _CSVWriter:
    def __init__(self, fileName):
        try:
            # create a writer object and then write the header row
            self.csvFile= open(fileName,'wb')
            self.writer= csv.writer(self.csvFile,       delimiter=',',
            quoting=csv.QUOTE_ALL)
            self.writer.writerow( ('Protocol','Source IP','Source Port',
            'Destination IP','Destination Port') )
        except:
            log.error('CSV File Failure')

    def writeCSVRow(self, row):
```

```
        self.writer.writerow( (row[0], row[1], str(row[2]), row
    [3], str(row[4]) ) )

def __del__(self):
    self.csvFile.close()
```

9.6 程序的执行和输出

如你所见，Python应用程序psnmt被构建为一个命令行应用程序。这种类型的应用程序是有意义的，因为它可以作为一个cron作业而执行（如在特定时间计划运行）。

命令行具有以下参数，参见表9.4。

表9.4 命令行参数

参数	目的和用途
-v	详细模式：当指定时，输出中间结果到标准输出设备
-m	分钟：执行收集活动持续的分钟
-TCP|-UDP	协议：指定捕获的应用程序的协议
-p	产品：定义取证日志和CSV文件的输出路径

命令行示例：

```
sudo Python psnmt -v -TCP -m 60 -p /home/chet/Desktop
```

注意：sudo（用于强制执行管理权限的命令，这是必需的）。这个命令将持续捕获TCP数据包达60分钟，生成详细输出，在用户桌面中生成日志和CSV文件。

图9.8和图9.9显示的是执行TCP和UDP捕获的示例。

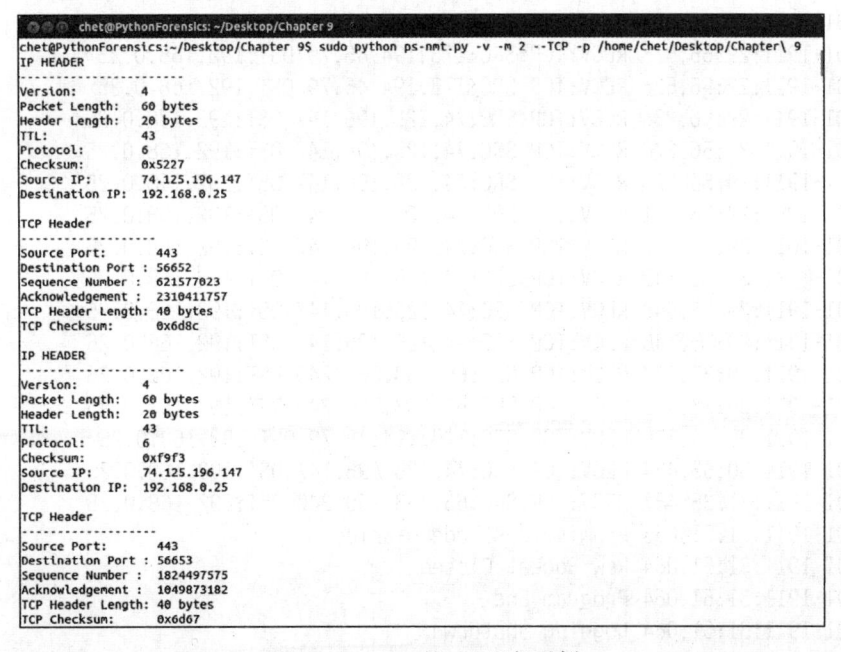

图9.8 PSNMT的TCP运行示例

```
chet@PythonForensics:~/Desktop/Chapter 9$ sudo python psnmt.py -v -m 2 --UDP -p '/home/chet/Desktop/Chapter 9'
IP HEADER
--------------------
Version:            4
Packet Length:      61 bytes
Header Length:      20 bytes
TTL:                64
Protocol:           17
Checksum:           0x98fe
Source IP:          127.0.0.1
Destination IP:     127.0.0.1

UDP Header
--------------------
Source Port:        52309
Destination Port :  53
UDP Length:         41 bytes
UDP Checksum:       0xfe3c

IP HEADER
--------------------
Version:            4
Packet Length:      121 bytes
Header Length:      20 bytes
TTL:                58
Protocol:           17
Checksum:           0x86f7
Source IP:          66.153.128.98
Destination IP:     192.168.0.25

UDP Header
--------------------
Source Port:        53
Destination Port :  23992
UDP Length:         101 bytes
UDP Checksum:       0x474f

IP HEADER
```

图9.9　PSNMT的UDP运行示例

9.6.1　取证日志

TCP 捕获的实例

```
2014-01-1911:29:51,050 PS-NMT Started
2014-01-1911:29:51,057 Promiscious Mode Enabled
2014-01-1911:29:51,057 Raw Socket Open
2014-01-1911:29:55,525 RECV:TCP SRC:173.194.45.79 DST:192.168.0.25
2014-01-1911:29:55,526 RECV:TCP SRC:173.194.45.79 DST:192.168.0.25
2014-01-1911:29:56,236 RECV:TCP SRC:74.125.196.147 DST:192.168.0.25
2014-01-1911:29:56,270 RECV:TCP SRC:74.125.196.147 DST:192.168.0.25
2014-01-1911:29:56,270 RECV:TCP SRC:74.125.196.147 DST:192.168.0.25
2014-01-1911:29:56,271 RECV:TCP SRC:74.125.196.147 DST:192.168.0.25
2014-01-1911:29:56,527 RECV:TCP SRC:74.125.196.147 DST:192.168.0.25
2014-01-1911:29:56,543 RECV:TCP SRC:74.125.196.147 DST:192.168.0.25
2014-01-1911:29:56,544 RECV:TCP SRC:74.125.196.147 DST:192.168.0.25
2014-01-1911:29:56,546 RECV:TCP SRC:74.125.196.147 DST:192.168.0.25
2014-01-1911:30:37,437 RECV:TCP SRC:66.153.250.240 DST:192.168.0.25
2014-01-1911:30:37,449 RECV:TCP SRC:66.153.250.240 DST:192.168.0.25
2014-01-1911:30:54,546 RECV:TCP SRC:173.194.45.79 DST:192.168.0.25
2014-01-1911:30:55,454 RECV:TCP SRC:74.125.196.147 DST:192.168.0.25
2014-01-1911:31:35,487 RECV:TCP SRC:66.153.250.240 DST:192.168.0.25
2014-01-1911:31:51,063 Promiscious Mode Diabled
2014-01-1911:31:51,064 Raw Socket Closed
2014-01-1911:31:51,064 Program End
2014-01-1911:31:51,064 Logging Shutdown
```

UDP捕获的实例

```
2014-01-1913:27:09,366 PS-NMT Started
2014-01-1913:27:09,371 Promiscious Mode Enabled
```

```
2014-01-1913:27:09,372 Raw Socket Open
2014-01-1913:27:09,528 Logging Shutdown
2014-01-1913:36:33,472 PS-NMT Started
2014-01-1913:36:33,477 Promiscious Mode Enabled
2014-01-1913:36:33,477 Raw Socket Open
2014-01-1913:36:45,234 Logging Shutdown
2014-01-1913:37:51,748 PS-NMT Started
2014-01-1913:37:51,754 Promiscious Mode Enabled
2014-01-1913:37:51,754 Raw Socket Open
2014-01-1913:37:59,534 RECV:UDP SRC:127.0.0.1 DST:127.0.0.1
2014-01-1913:37:59,546 RECV:UDP SRC:66.153.128.98 DST:192.168.0.25
2014-01-1913:37:59,546 RECV:UDP SRC:127.0.0.1 DST:127.0.0.1
2014-01-1913:37:59,549 RECV:UDP SRC:66.153.162.98 DST:192.168.0.25
2014-01-1913:38:09,724 RECV:UDP SRC:127.0.0.1 DST:127.0.0.1
2014-01-1913:38:09,879 RECV:UDP SRC:66.153.128.98 DST:192.168.0.25
2014-01-1913:38:09,880 RECV:UDP SRC:127.0.0.1 DST:127.0.0.1
2014-01-1913:38:10,387 RECV:UDP SRC:127.0.0.1 DST:127.0.0.1
2014-01-1913:38:10,551 RECV:UDP SRC:66.153.128.98 DST:192.168.0.25
2014-01-1913:38:10,551 RECV:UDP SRC:127.0.0.1DST:127.0.0.1
2014-01-1913:38:45,114 RECV:UDP SRC:66.153.128.98 DST:192.168.0.25
2014-01-1913:38:46,112 RECV:UDP SRC:66.153.128.98 DST:192.168.0.25
2014-01-1913:39:45,410 RECV:UDP SRC:66.153.128.98 DST:192.168.0.25
2014-01-1913:39:51,760 Promiscious Mode Diabled
2014-01-1913:39:51,761 Raw Socket Closed
2014-01-1913:39:51,761 Program End
2014-01-1913:39:51,761 Logging Shutdown
```

9.6.2 CSV文件输出实例

这些执行过程生成了CSV和取证日志文件及记录。

图9.10和9.11描述的是一个由PSNMT生成的CSV文件示例输出。

	A	B	C	D	E
1	Protocol	Source IP	Source Port	Destination IP	Destination Port
2	TCP	127.0.0.1	36480	127.0.0.1	54792
3	TCP	127.0.0.1	54792	127.0.0.1	36480
4	TCP	66.153.25(	443	192.168.0.25	35027
5	TCP	74.125.19(	443	192.168.0.25	56580
6	TCP	74.125.19(	443	192.168.0.25	56581

图9.10　Excel中展示的TCP输出文件

	A	B	C	D	E
1	Protocol	Source IP	Source Port	Destination IP	Destination Port
2	UDP	127.0.0.1	53	127.0.0.1	35633
3	UDP	127.0.0.1	53	127.0.0.1	51420
4	UDP	127.0.0.1	53	127.0.0.1	52309
5	UDP	127.0.0.1	35633	127.0.0.1	53
6	UDP	127.0.0.1	51420	127.0.0.1	53
7	UDP	127.0.0.1	52309	127.0.0.1	53
8	UDP	66.153.12{	53	192.168.0.25	11303
9	UDP	66.153.12{	53	192.168.0.25	23992
10	UDP	66.153.12{	53	192.168.0.25	35021
11	UDP	66.153.12{	53	192.168.0.25	43421
12	UDP	66.153.12{	53	192.168.0.25	56857
13	UDP	66.153.12{	53	192.168.0.25	58487
14	UDP	66.153.16.	53	192.168.0.25	23992

图9.11　Excel中展示的UDP输出文件

9.7 章节回顾

在本章中介绍了原始套接字，以及如何利用它们来捕获网络数据包。为此，我对现代网络适配器的混杂模式进行了说明，演示了如何对一张网卡进行配置以进行此操作。我还讨论了网络嗅探的重要性，以便更彻底地对网络活动进行映射及监控。用 `unpack()` 函数从IPv4的TCP和UDP数据包中提取出所有域，详细描述了怎样把它运用到缓冲的数据。最后，建立了一个应用程序，可以收集和记录来自不同的源IP、源端口、目标IP和目标端口的TCP或UDP的数据流。该Python应用程序可以通过命令行参数控制，以方便地集成到cron作业或其他计划任务机制。作为命令行的一部分，使用了一个信号机制，以便在指定时间过后停止数据包的收集。

9.8 问题小结

本章仅提出一个问题，但实际上是一个更具有挑战性的问题，并会使PSNMT应用程序到达新的层次。

为使得当前的应用程序更加实用，将端口号解释为公认的服务是必不可少的，可以确定从捕获数据包中提取的每一个IP地址的可能用途。通过使用Internet Engineering Task Force [IETF]（或者阅览 /etc/sevices）所给出的保留及通用端口占用的情况说明，对PSNMT应用程序进行拓展，以分离每一个本地的IP地址并分别列出其可能运行的服务。如果可能的话，尝试通过对端口占用情况的分析，粗略地分辨出每一个IP地址上的操作系统（至少每一个IP地址是Windows、Linux或者其他操作系统）。

9.9 补充资料

1. http://docs.Python.org/2/library/struct.html?highlight=unpack#struct.unpack.
2. http://www.ietf.org/assignments/service-names-port-numbers/service-names-port-numbers.txt.

第10章 多进程的取证应用

10.1 本章简介

随着数字证据和数字犯罪的出现越来越常见，我们进行快速和及时调查的能力显得相当捉襟见肘。根据DFI的报道，"在世界各地，执法机构的待处理案件所积压的工作量已经由最初的几周增长到了几个月，数字取证专业人员无法尽快得到培训，而且分析堆积如山的普通案件中的数字证据所需的专业人员的数量，就已经超出了预算限制"（DFI, 2003）。如今，很多数字取证工具是单线程的，这意味着在同一时刻，软件只能执行一个命令。在多核处理器普及之前，这些工具以最初的方式开发。在本章中将介绍一些常见的、与取证需求有关的Python多进程能力。在第11章中，还会将这些应用程序迁移至云，并展示如何通过扩展使用额外的核，以及让取证操作运行在云平台上来增强其性能。

10.2 何谓多进程

简单地说，多进程是程序在两个或更多的核或CPU上的并行执行。为了得到较为明显的性能改善，取证应用程序的开发者必须使得其代码具有以下特性：

1. 代码是处理器密集型的。
2. 将代码分离为能并发执行的相互独立的处理线程，这是可能的。
3. 线程之间的任务处理能够负载均衡，换言之，其目的就是分配处理任务，使得每一个线程几乎可以同时完成。

可以猜想到，对于一般用途的取证工具，问题在于：若在最初的工程设计中，它们没有满足上述的要求，那么要将其改变以适应现代的多核架构，可能困难重重。而且这些并发运行于多核或者云平台上的技术的许可也许代价高昂。最后，很多在Windows平台上使用得最为广泛的取证工具，理论上并不适合并发地在数以千计的核上运行。

10.3 Python多进程支持

Python标准库中包含了多进程处理包（Python的multiprocessing模块）。使用Python标准库着手多进程处理是一个极为理想的多线程方法，还能确保跨多种计算平台，并且包括云的兼容性。通过导入多进程处理包，我们以一种典型的方式开始使用多进程包。在导入包后，执行help(multiprocessing)函数显示相关细节。在此略去了一些由help命令所带来的无关紧要的内容，并且高亮显示了将用来开发一些多进程例子的函数和类。

```
import multiprocessing

help(multiprocessing)

# NOTE this is only a partial excerpt from the output
# of the Help command

Help on package multiprocessing:

NAME
    multiprocessing

PACKAGE CONTENTS
    connection
    dummy (package)
    forking
    heap
    managers
    pool
    process
    queues
    reduction
    sharedctypes
    synchronize
    util

CLASSES
    class Process(__builtin__.object)
     |  Process objects represent activity that is run in a separate process
     |
     |  The class is analagous to 'threading.Thread'
     |
     |  Methods defined here:
     |
     |  __init__(self, group=None, target=None, name=None, args=(), kwargs={})
     |
     |  __repr__(self)
     |
     |  is_alive(self)
     |      Return whether process is alive
     |
     |  join(self, timeout=None)
     |      Wait until child process terminates
     |
     |  run(self)
     |      Method to be run in sub-process; can be overridden in  sub-class
     |
     |  start(self)
     |      Start child process
     |
     |  terminate(self)
     |      Terminate process; sends SIGTERM signal or uses TerminateProcess()
     |
FUNCTIONS
    Array(typecode_or_type, size_or_initializer, **kwds)
```

> Returns a synchronized shared array

BoundedSemaphore(value = 1)
> Returns a bounded semaphore object

Condition(lock = None)
> Returns a condition object

Event()
> Returns an event object

JoinableQueue(maxsize = 0)
> Returns a queue object

Lock()
> Returns a non-recursive lock object

Manager()
> Returns a manager associated with a running server process
>
> The managers methods such as 'Lock()', 'Condition()' and 'Queue()' can be used to create shared objects.

Pipe(duplex = True)
> Returns two connection object connected by a pipe

Pool(processes = None, initializer = None, initargs = (), maxtasksperchild=None) Returns a process pool object

Queue(maxsize = 0)
> **Returns a queue object**

RLock()
> Returns a recursive lock object

RawArray(typecode_or_type, size_or_initializer)
> Returns a shared array

RawValue(typecode_or_type, *args)
> Returns a shared object

Semaphore(value=1)
> Returns a semaphore object

Value(typecode_or_type, *args, **kwds)
> Returns a synchronized shared object

active_children()
> Return list of process objects corresponding to live child processes

allow_connection_pickling()
> Install support for sending connections and sockets between processes

cpu_count()
> **Returns the number of CPUs in the system**

current_process()
> Return process object representing the current process

freeze_support()
> Check whether this is a fake forked process in a frozen

```
                executable. If so then run code specified by commandline and exit.
VERSION
    0.70a1
AUTHOR
    R. Oudkerk (r.m.oudkerk@gmail.com)
```

在这个多进程处理包中,首先可能感兴趣的是cpu_count()函数。在能够将处理任务在多个核之间分配之前,必须知道有多少个核可以使用。

```
import multiprocessing
multiprocessing.cpu_count()
4
```

如你所见,在我的Windows笔记本上,有四个核可用。若是代码仅运行于其中之一,会是一件惭愧的事情。如果不使用多进程处理,不在算法中设计多核处理方法,我的代码将只能运行于单核上。

让我们开始第一个例子,它是一个利用多进程的Python程序,并具有取证价值和意义。

10.4 最简单的多进程例子

在这第一个实例中,选择了一个最简单,并且能充分发挥我的笔记本电脑上四个核的潜力的多进程例子。这个程序仅有一个函数命名为SearchFile(),这个函数接受两个参数:

(1)一个文件名
(2)希望在此文件中搜寻的字符串

我将使用一个简单的文本文件作为搜索目标,该文件包含一个由单词组成的字典。这个文件有170 MB,这个大小即使在现代的系统上,也可能会产生一些输入和输出(I/O)延迟。我提供了两个实例,第一个实例并未使用多进程,只是单纯地对SearchFile函数连续调用四次。第二个实例创建了四个进程,并将处理任务均衡地分配于四个核上。

10.4.1 单核的文件搜索方案

```
# Simple Files Search Single Core Processing
    import time
    def SearchFile(theFile, theString):
        try:
            fp = open(theFile,'r')
            buffer = fp.read()
            fp.close()
            if theString in buffer:
                print'File:', theFile,'String:',\
                    theString,'\t','Found'
            else:
                print'File:', theFile,'String:', \
                    theString,'\t','Not Found'
```

```
    except:
        J208print'File processing error'
    startTime = time.time()

    SearchFile('c:\\TESTDIR\\Dictionary.txt','thought')
    SearchFile('c:\\TESTDIR\\Dictionary.txt','exile')
    SearchFile('c:\\TESTDIR\\Dictionary.txt','xavier')
    SearchFile('c:\\TESTDIR\\Dictionary.txt','$Slllb!')

    elapsedTime = time.time() - startTime
    print'Duration:', elapsedTime

    # Program Output

    File: c:\TESTDIR\Dictionary.txt String: thought    Found
    File: c:\TESTDIR\Dictionary.txt String: exile      Found
    File: c:\TESTDIR\Dictionary.txt String: xavier     Found
    File: c:\TESTDIR\Dictionary.txt String: $Slllb!    Not Found
    Duration: 4.3140001297 Seconds
```

10.4.2 多进程的文件搜索方法

多进程的方法详情如下。如你所见，即使考虑了相关文件的屡次打开、读取、关闭这些I/O方面上的因素，比较之下其性能表现依然有着明显的提升。

```
# Simple Files Search MultiProcessing

from multiprocessing import Process
import time

def SearchFile(theFile, theString):
    try:
        fp = open(theFile,'r')
        buffer = fp.read()
        fp.close()
        if theString in buffer:
            print 'File:', theFile,'String:', theString, '\t','Found'
        else:
            print 'File: ', theFile, 'String: ', theString, '\t', 'Not Found'
    except:
        print 'File processing error'
#
# Create Main Function
#
if __name__ == '__main__':

    startTime = time.time()

    p1 = Process(target = SearchFile,\
        args = ('c:\\TESTDIR\\Dictionary.txt','thought') )
    p1.start()

    p2 = Process(target = SearchFile, \
        args = ('c:\\TESTDIR\\Dictionary.txt','exile') )
    p2.start()
```

```
        p3 = Process(target = SearchFile,\
            args = ('c:\\TESTDIR\\Dictionary.txt','xavier') )
        p3.start()

        p4 = Process(target = SearchFile,\
            args = ('c:\\TESTDIR\\Dictionary.txt','$Slllb') )
        p4.start()

        # Next we use the join to wait for all processes to complete
        p1.join()
        p2.join()
        p3.join()
        p4.join()

        elapsedTime = time.time() - startTime
        print'Duration:', elapsedTime

# Program Output

File: c:\TESTDIR\Dictionary.txt String:      thought      Found
File: c:\TESTDIR\Dictionary.txt String:      exile        Found
File: c:\TESTDIR\Dictionary.txt String:      xavier       Found
File: c:\TESTDIR\Dictionary.txt String:      $Slllb       Not Found
Duration: 1.80399990082
```

10.5 多进程文件哈希

单向密码学哈希自然是使用最为频繁的取证工具之一。正如读者所知道的,作为标准库的一部分,Python包含一个hashing库。作为一个实验,我准备使用非多进程的方法,对相同文件的四个单独实例执行SHA512哈希计算。我还会设立一个时钟,计算出执行单进程方法所花费的时间。

10.5.1 单核方案

```
# Single Threaded File Hasher

    import hashlib
    import os
    import sys
    import time

    # Create a constant for the local directory
    HASHDIR = 'c:\\HASHTEST\\'
    # Create an empty list to hold the resulting hash results
    results = []
    try:
        # Obtain the list of files in the HASHDIR
        listOfFiles = os.listdir(HASHDIR)

        # Mark the starting time of the main loop
        startTime = time.time()

        for eachFile in listOfFiles:
```

```python
        # Attempt File Open
        fp = open(HASHDIR+eachFile,'rb')

        # Then Read the contents into a buffer
        fileContents = fp.read()

        # Close the File
        fp.close()

        # Create a hasher object of type sha256
        hasher = hashlib.sha256()

        # Hash the contents of the buffer
        hasher.update(fileContents)

        # Store the results in the results list
        results.append([eachFile, hasher.hexdigest()])

        # delete the hasher object
        del hasher

    # Once all the files have been hashed calculate the elapsed time
    elapsedTime = time.time() - startTime

except:

    # If any exceptions occur notify the user and exit
    print('File Processing Error')
    sys.exit(0)

# Print out the results
# Elapsed Time in Seconds and the Filename / Hash Results
print('Elapsed Time:', elapsedTime)
for eachItem in results:
    print eachItem

# Program Output
# Note: Each File Processed is identical with a Size: 249 MB
```

Elapsed Time: 27.8510000705719 Seconds
['image0.raw',
'41ad70ff71407eae7466eef403cb20100771ca7499cbf1504f8ed67e6d869e5b']
['image1.raw',
'41ad70ff71407eae7466eef403cb20100771ca7499cbf1504f8ed67e6d869e5b']
['image2.raw',
'41ad70ff71407eae7466eef403cb20100771ca7499cbf1504f8ed67e6d869e5b']
['image3.raw',
'41ad70ff71407eae7466eef403cb20100771ca7499cbf1504f8ed67e6d869e5b']

10.5.2 多核方案 A

多进程的关键技巧是将问题分解为可以并发运行在多核上的任务片段。一旦每个任务片段完成，来自于各个任务片段的结果将被合并为最终的结果。通常易犯的最大错误便是缺少对这两点的充分考虑。相较于单核的方案，购置多核系统并仅仅简单地将所有方案运行于其上，并不一定会为你带来明显的回报。

下面以单核方案作为基础，创建一个多核方案，该方案能够充分利用笔记本电脑上的四个可用核。对于这第一个例子，将对每一个核实例化一个Process对象。当创建每一个Process对象时仅需提供两个参数。

(1) target=　在此例中就是要调用的函数的名称，在object.start()方法被调用时该函数被调用。

(2) args=　被传递给该函数的参数元组。在本例中仅有一个参数被传递，即所要进行哈希的文件名。

一旦实例化了一个对象，将执行object.start()方法去启动一个进程，最后对每个对象使用object.join()方法，这就使得main()进程中指令的运行停止下来，直到所有的进程都执行完成。同时也可以向object.join()方法中传入一个参数作为该进程的超时值。例如object.join(20)将会限制该进程在20秒内完成。

```python
# Multiprocessing File Hasher A

import hashlib
import os
import sys
import time
import multiprocessing

# Create a constant for the local directory
HASHDIR = 'c:\\HASHTEST\\'

#
# hashFile Function, designed for multiprocessing
#
# Input: Full Pathname of the file to hash
#
#
def hashFile(fileName):
    try:
        fp = open(fileName,'rb')

        # Then Read the contents into a buffer
        fileContents = fp.read()

        # Close the File
        fp.close()

        # Create a hasher object of type sha256
        hasher = hashlib.sha256()

        # Hash the contents of the buffer
        hasher.update(fileContents)

        print(fileName, hasher.hexdigest())

        # delete the hasher object
        del hasher

    except:

        # If any exceptions occur notify the user and exit
```

```
            print('File Processing Error')
            sys.exit(0)
        
    return True
#
# Create Main Function
#
if __name__ == '__main__':

    # Obtain the list of files in the HASHDIR
    listOfFiles = os.listdir(HASHDIR)

    # Mark the starting time of the main loop
    startTime = time.time()

    # create 4 sub-processes to do the work
    # one of each core in this test
    # Each Process contains:
    #           Target function hashFile() it this example
    #           Filename: picked from the list generated
    #                     by os.listdir()
    #                     once again an instance of the
    #                     249 MB file is used
    #
    # Next we start each of the processes

    coreOne = multiprocessing.Process(target = hashFile,
                        args = (HASHDIR+listOfFiles[0],) )
    coreOne.start()

    coreTwo = multiprocessing.Process(target = hashFile,
                        args = (HASHDIR+listOfFiles[1],) )
    coreTwo.start()

    coreThree = multiprocessing.Process(target = hashFile,
                        args = (HASHDIR+listOfFiles[2],) )
    coreThree.start()

    coreFour = multiprocessing.Process(target = hashFile,
                        args = (HASHDIR+listOfFiles[3],) )
    coreFour.start()
```

在本例中应用了对运行应用程序的硬件的了解，以尽可能地分配进程任务。根据核的可用情况，Python的多进程处理库会自动处理进程的分配。另外，由于可以通过使用 `multiprocessing.cpu_count()` 方法获得可用核的数量信息，也可以据此自行分配处理任务。

```
    # Next we use join to wait for all processes to complete

    coreOne.join()
    coreTwo.join()
    coreThree.join()
    coreFour.join()

    # Once all the processes have completed and files have been
    # hashed and results printed
    # I calculate the elapsed time
```

```
        elapsedTime = time.time() - startTime
        print('Elapsed Time:', elapsedTime)
# Program Output
# Note: Each File Processed is identical with a Size: 249 MB
c:\\HASHTEST\\image2.raw 41ad70ff71407eae7466eef403cb20100771ca7499cbf1504f8ed67e6d869e5b
c:\\HASHTEST\\image1.raw 41ad70ff71407eae7466eef403cb20100771ca7499cbf1504f8ed67e6d869e5b
c:\\HASHTEST\\image3.raw 41ad70ff71407eae7466eef403cb20100771ca7499cbf1504f8ed67e6d869e5b
c:\\HASHTEST\\image0.raw 41ad70ff71407eae7466eef403cb20100771ca7499cbf1504f8ed67e6d869e5b
Elapsed Time: 8.40999984741211 Seconds
```

正如所看到的，将处理任务分配于四个核产生了期望的结果，明显地提升了哈希操作的性能。

10.5.3 多核方案 B

这是另一个在多个核之间分配处理任务的可选方案，相较于方案A，还有一些小的性能提升。并且当想使用不同的参数调用相同的函数时，它还提供一种更加简洁的实现方式，这是你在设计取证应用程序时可能会考虑的情况。另外，这种方法仅仅需要使用一个类，即pool，该类能够在单行代码中处理一个完整的多核进程操作。在下面的代码中，高亮显示了简化后的方法。

```
# Multiprocessing File Hasher B
import hashlib
import os
import sys
import time
import multiprocessing
# Create a constant for the local directory
HASHDIR = 'c:\\HASHTEST\\'
#
# hashFile Function, designed for multiprocessing
#
# Input: Full Pathname of the file to hash
#
#
def hashFile(fileName):
    try:
        fp = open(fileName,'rb')
        # Then Read the contents into a buffer
        fileContents = fp.read()
        # Close the File
        fp.close()
```

```python
            # Create a hasher object of type sha256
            hasher = hashlib.sha256()

            # Hash the contents of the buffer
            hasher.update(fileContents)
            print(fileName, hasher.hexdigest())

            # delete the hasher object
            del hasher

        except:
            # If any exceptions occur notify the user and exit
            print('File Processing Error')
            sys.exit(0)

        return True

#
# Create Main Function
#

if __name__ == '__main__':

    # Obtain the list of files in the HASHDIR
    listOfFiles = os.listdir(HASHDIR)

    # Mark the starting time of the main loop
    startTime = time.time()

    # Create a process Pool with 4 processes mapping to
    # the 4 cores on my laptop

    corePool = multiprocessing.Pool(processes = 4)

    # Map the corePool to the hashFile function
    results = corePool.map(hashFile, (HASHDIR+listOfFiles[0],\
                                     HASHDIR+listOfFiles[1],\
                                     HASHDIR+listOfFiles[2],\
                                     HASHDIR+listOfFiles[3],))

    # Once all the files have been hashed and results printed
    # I calculate the elapsed time

    elapsedTime = time.time() - startTime

    print('Elapsed Time:', elapsedTime,'Seconds')

# Program Output
# Note: Each File Processed is identical with a Size: 249 MB

Elapsed Time: , 8.138000085830688, Seconds
c:\\HASHTEST\\image0.raw, 41ad70ff71407eae7466eef403cb20100771ca7499cbf1504f8ed67e6d869e5b
c:\\HASHTEST\\image2.raw, 41ad70ff71407eae7466eef403cb20100771ca7499cbf1504f8ed67e6d869e5b
c:\\HASHTEST\\image1.raw, 41ad70ff71407eae7466eef403cb20100771ca7499cbf1504f8ed67e6d869e5b
c:\\HASHTEST\\image3.raw, 41ad70ff71407eae7466eef403cb20100771ca7499cbf1504f8ed67e6d869e5b
```

回顾这三种实现方法，结果如表10.1所示。

表10.1 三种实现方法的结果

实现方式	处理时间（s）	速度（MB/s）	备注
单核方案	27.851	35.76	现在常见的实现方法，依次处理每个文件
多核方案A	8.409	118.44	使用Process类及start和join方法
多核方案B	8.138	122.39	使用Pool类简化相同功能的实现，表现出稍好些的性能

10.6 多进程哈希表生成

彩虹表的出现已经有相当长一段时间了，它提供了一种方式，将已知的哈希值转化为可能与之对应的口令。换言之，其给出了一种通过查询哈希值，然后与生成该哈希值的字符串关联起来的方法。由于哈希算法是单向的，对所有的实践用途来说，两个不同的字符串将不会产生相同的哈希值，它具有高度的抗碰撞性。彩虹表被用于破解口令，如针对操作系统、受保护文档以及网络用户登录等。

近年来，向哈希值中加盐这一手段使得彩虹表的有效性有所下降，因为随着盐的改变，不得不需要生成新的表。彩虹表之所以有效，是因为所有的口令都是通过相同的方法进行哈希，换言之，两个相同的口令所产生的哈希值也是相同的。

如今利用随机的哈希口令，彩虹表失去了作用。也就是说，即使两个用户使用相同的口令，其生成的哈希值并不会相同。这通常是通过在哈希运算之前，在口令中加入随机字符串，亦称盐来实现的。

密码："letMeIn"
盐："&*6542JK"
将要哈希的合并后的数据："&*6542JKletMeIn"

盐值并不需要保密，因为其用途是挫败彩虹表或者查询表的使用。

这就意味着我们需要一个更快速的方式，生成更多的动态查询表，这便是多进程技术可以效劳的地方了。实际上Python具有独特的内置语言机制，支持生成排列和组合，这将有助于开发者。我将使用itertools标准库（Python的迭代工具模块）来创建需要的暴力攻击（brute force）的口令集合。通过使用高性能且内存优化的工具包，迭代工具模块提供了一些迭代类型的构件。无须自己开发排列、组合或者产品定制的代数算法，该库已为你提供了这些。

首先，下文将创建一个使用单核方案的简单彩虹表生成器。

10.6.1 单核口令生成器代码

```
# Single Core Password Table Generator

# import standard libraries

import hashlib         # Hashing the results
import time            # Timing the operation
import itertools       # Creating controled combinations
```

```python
#
# Create a list of lower case, upper case, numbers
# and special characters to include in the password table
#

lowerCase = ['a', 'b', 'c', 'd', 'e', 'f', 'g', 'h']
upperCase = ['G', 'H', 'I', 'J', 'K', 'L']
numbers = ['0', '1', '2', '3']
special = ['!', '@', '#', '$']

# combine to create a final list
allCharacters = []
allCharacters = lowerCase + upperCase + numbers + special

# Define Directory Path for the password file

DIR = 'C:\\PW\\'

# Define a hypothetical SALT value
SALT = ''&45Bvx9''

# Define the allowable range of password length
PW_LOW = 2
PW_HIGH = 6

# Mark the start time
startTime = time.time()

# Create an empty list to hold the final passwords
pwList = []

# create a loop to include all passwords
# within the allowable range

for r in range(PW_LOW, PW_HIGH):
    # Apply the standard library interator
    # The product interator will generate the cartesian product for
    # allCharacters repeating for the range of
    # PW_LOW to PW_HIGH
    for s in itertools.product(allCharacters, repeat = r):
        # append each generated password to the final list
        pwList.append(''.join(s))

# For each password in the list generate
# a file containing the hash,
# password pairs
# one per line

try:
    # Open the output file
    fp = open(DIR+'all','w')

    # process each generated password

    for pw in pwList:
        # Perform hashing of the password
        md5Hash = hashlib.md5()
        md5Hash.update(SALT+pw)
        md5Digest = md5Hash.hexdigest()
```

```
            # Write the hash, password pair to the file
            fp.write(md5Digest +''+ pw +'\n')
            del md5Hash
except:
    print'File Processing Error'
    fp.close()

# Now create a dictionary to hold the
# Hash, password pairs for easy lookup

pwDict = {}

try:
    # Open each of the output file
    fp = open(DIR+'all','r')
    # Process each line in the file which
    # contains key, value pairs
    for line in fp:
        # extract the key value pairs
        # and update the dictionary
        pairs = line.split()
        pwDict.update({pairs[0] : pairs[1]})
    fp.close()
except:
    print'File Handling Error'
    fp.close()

# When complete calculate the elapsed time

elapsedTime = time.time() - startTime
print 'Elapsed Time:', elapsedTime
print 'Passwords Generated:', len(pwDict)
print

# print out a few of the dictionary entries
# as an example
cnt = 0
for key,value in (pwDict.items()):
    print key, value
    cnt + = 1
    if cnt > 10:
        break;

print

# Demonstrate the use of the Dictionary to Lookup a password using a known hash
# Lookup a Hash Value

pw = pwDict.get('c6f1d6b1d33bcc787c2385c19c29c208')
print 'Hash Value Tested = c6f1d6b1d33bcc787c2385c19c29c208'
print 'Associated Password = '+ pw

# Program Output

Elapsed Time: 89.117000103
Passwords Generated: 5399020
```

```
3e47ac3f51daffdbe46ab671c76b44fb    K23IH
a5a3614f49da18486c900bd04675d7bc    $@fL1
372da5744b1ab1f99376f8d726cd2b7c    hGfdd
aa0865a47331df5de01296bbaaf4996a    21ILG
c6f1d6b1d33bcc787c2385c19c29c208    #I#$$
c3c4246114ee80e9c454603645c9a416    #$b$g
6ca0e4d8f183c6c8b0a032b09861c95a    L1H21
fd86ec2191f415cdb6c305da5e59eb7a    HJg@h
335ef773e663807eb21d100e06b8c53e    a$HbH
d1bae7cd5ae09903886d413884e22628    ba21H
a2a53248ed641bbd22af9bf36b422321    GHcda

Hash Value Tested = 2bca9b23eb8419728fdeca3345b344fc
Associated Password = #I#$$
```

如你所见,上述代码相当简洁而直观,其利用itertools和哈希库生成了一个暴力攻击列表,结果是在不到90秒的时间内,程序产生了一个超过530万个加盐口令的可查询的列表。

10.6.2 多核口令生成器

现在我为生成口令的组合创建了一个成功的模型,并且还使用生成的键/值对建立了一个字典,这里特意再次使用多进程技术,使得解决方案变得更加具备伸缩性。从单核方案中可以看到,只需要不到90秒的时间便能生成超过530万个键/值对。因为在生成过程中,扩展了包含的字符数量,并且允许的口令长度也超过了5,所以产生的组合的数量也呈指数增长。之前所提到建立支持多线程的方法是关键。现在通过回顾之前的多核例子,让我们来测试一下其性能提升究竟有多么明显。

10.6.3 多核口令生成器代码

```
# Multi-Core Password Table Generator

    # import standard libraries

    import hashlib              # Hashing the results
    import time                 # Timing the operation
    import itertools            # Creating controled combinations
    import multiprocessing      # Multiprocessing Library
    #
    # Create a list of lower case, upper case, numbers
    # and special characters to include in the password table
    #
    lowerCase = ['a','b','c','d','e','f','g','h']
    upperCase = ['G','H','I','J','K','L']
    numbers = ['0','1','2','3']
    special = ['!','@','#','$']

    # combine to create a final list
    allCharacters = []
    allCharacters = lowerCase + upperCase + numbers + special
```

```python
# Define Directory Path for the password files
DIR = 'C:\\PW\\'

# Define a hypothetical SALT value
SALT = ''&45Bvx9''

# Define the allowable range of password length
PW_LOW = 2
PW_HIGH = 6

def pwGenerator(size):

    pwList = []

    # create a loop to include all passwords
    # with a length of 3-5 characters

    for r in range(size, size+1):
        # Apply the standard library interator
        for s in itertools.product(allCharacters, repeat = r):
            # append each generated password to the final list
            pwList.append(''.join(s))

    # For each password in the list generate
    # an associated md5 hash and utilize the
    # hash as the key

    try:
        # Open the output file
        fp = open(DIR+str(size),'w')

        # process each generated password

        for pw in pwList:
            # Perform hashing of the password
            md5Hash = hashlib.md5()
            md5Hash.update(SALT+pw)
            md5Digest = md5Hash.hexdigest()
            # Write the hash, password pair to the file
            fp.write(md5Digest +''+ pw +'\n')
            del md5Hash

    except:
        print'File Processing Error'

    finally:
        fp.close()

#
# Create Main Function
#

if __name__ == '__main__':

    # Mark the starting time of the main loop
    startTime = time.time()

    # create a process Pool with 4 processes
    corePool = multiprocessing.Pool(processes = 4)

    # map corePool to the Pool processes
```

```
        results = corePool.map(pwGenerator, (2, 3, 4, 5))

        # Create a dictionary for easy lookups
        pwDict = {}

        # For each file

        for i in range(PW_LOW, PW_HIGH):
            try:
                # Open each of the output files
                fp = open(DIR+str(i),'r')
                # Process each line in the file which
                # contains key, value pairs
                for line in fp:
                    # extract the key value pairs
                    # and update the dictionary
                    pairs = line.split()
                    pwDict.update({pairs[0] : pairs[1]})
                fp.close()
            except:
                print'File Handling Error'
                fp.close()

        # Once all the files have been hashed
        # I calculate the elapsed time

        elapsedTime = time.time() - startTime
        print 'Elapsed Time:', elapsedTime, 'Seconds'

        # print out a few of the dictionary entries
        # as an example
        print'Passwords Generated:', len(pwDict)
        print
        cnt = 0
        for key,value in (pwDict.items()):
            print key, value
            cnt += 1
            if cnt > 10:
                break;

    print

    # Demonstrate the use of the Dictionary to Lookup
    # a password using a known hash value

    pw = pwDict.get('c6f1d6b1d33bcc787c2385c19c29c208')
    print 'Hash Value Tested = 2bca9b23eb8419728fdeca3345b344fc'

    print 'Associated Password = '+ pw

# Program Output

Elapsed Time: 50.504999876 Seconds
Passwords Generated: 5399020

3e47ac3f51daffdbe46ab671c76b44fb  K23IH
a5a3614f49da18486c900bd04675d7bc  $@fL1
372da5744b1ab1f99376f8d726cd2b7c  hGfdd
aa0865a47331df5de01296bbaaf4996a  21ILG
```

```
c6f1d6b1d33bcc787c2385c19c29c208  #I#$$
c3c4246114ee80e9c454603645c9a416  #$b$g
6ca0e4d8f183c6c8b0a032b09861c95a  L1H21
fd86ec2191f415cdb6c305da5e59eb7a  HJg@h
335ef773e663807eb21d100e06b8c53e  a$HbH
d1bae7cd5ae09903886d413884e22628  ba21H
a2a53248ed641bbd22af9bf36b422321  GHcda

Hash Value Tested = 2bca9b23eb8419728fdeca3345b344fc
Associated Password = #I#$$
```

正如预期的那样，多核的方法提升了性能，并且这个方法依然是很直观易读的。

回顾彩虹表中单核以及多核方法的不同实现方法，我们得到以下的结果，如表10.2所示。

表10.2 彩虹表生成器的实现方式对比

实现方式	处理时间(s)	每秒生成口令数	备注
单核方案	89.11	约60 K	现在常见的实现方法，使用单核进行处理
多核方案	50.50	约106 K	使用Pool类以简化实现

除了执行的结果，生成的键/值对（MD5哈希及其对应的口令被写入一个文件）的输出，能够在以后用于更大的资源库的一部分。因为输出仅是单纯的文本文件，如图10.1所示，所以非常易读。

```
SALTED Password MD5 HASH            Associated Password
17ae80e34251ad4e2a61bc81d28b5a09    aa
9e6e21b8664f1590323ecaae3447ebae    ab
e708b3b343cfbc6b0104c60597fff773    ac
dcea12b90e71b523db8929cf6d86e39d    ad
70a3c3c78c79437dfc626ff12605ccb3    ae
41afc8d925b0b94996035b4ef25346ec    af
14b45c3a22caf6c2d5ed2e3daae152ee    ag
3c4493267b90a86303c1d30784b8f33b    ah
5cbba376bbb10688ece346cbfa9b8c28    aG
ffad7a79a9b2c646ef440d1447e18ebe    aH
…
…
eba8905561738d699d47bd6f62e3341c    eeg2
13605b276258b214fdafccac0835fc67    eeg3
0e3a4e8aded5858c94997d9f593c4fa3    eeg!
a6ab3da0c0cc7dc22d2a4cfe629ba0f2    eeg@
8f005cf0ea4b2bf064da85e1b2405c00    eeg#
60c797433e1f1ff9175a93373cf1a6ff    eeg$
e847612d8cab3184caa4d120c212afec    eeha
75cc13015bd40e2a6da4609458bfbe01    eehb
```

图10.1 明文彩虹表输出（有删减）

10.7 章节回顾

在本章中，借助笔记本或台式机系统上可用的核，开始解决使用Python的多核处理问题。我介绍了几个多进程处理的不同方法，概述了Python标准库multiprocessing。还测试了能从多进程处理获益的两个常用的数字调查功能，即1文件哈希和2彩虹表生成。

在第11章中，还会演示如何将这种方法迁移到云上，利用云服务将多进程的范围由桌面扩充至云，这些云服务能提供10个，50个，100个，甚至1000个核。

10.8 问题小结

1. 还有哪些电子调查或者取证应用可以受益于多进程？
2. 当设计多进程解决方案时有哪些要素？
3. 目前对付基于彩虹表的口令攻击，最好的方式是什么？
4. 彩虹表的例子受限于资源，当内存溢出时程序运行会崩溃。在内存受限情况下，如何修改程序，使得它能持续生成口令与哈希的组合？

10.9 补充资料

1. http://www.net-security.org/article.php?id = 1932&p = 1.
2. http://docs.python.org/2/library/itertools.html#module-itertools.
3. http://docs.python.org/3.4/library/multiprocessing.html#module-multiprocessing.

第11章 云中的彩虹表

11.1 本章简介

利用Python创建应用程序的一个显著优势是能在几乎任何平台上部署应用程序的能力，这些平台当然也包括了云（参见图11.1）。这不仅意味着可以在云服务器上执行Python，还可以在任何拥有的手持设备、桌面机、笔记本、平板或者智能手机上启动这些应用程序。

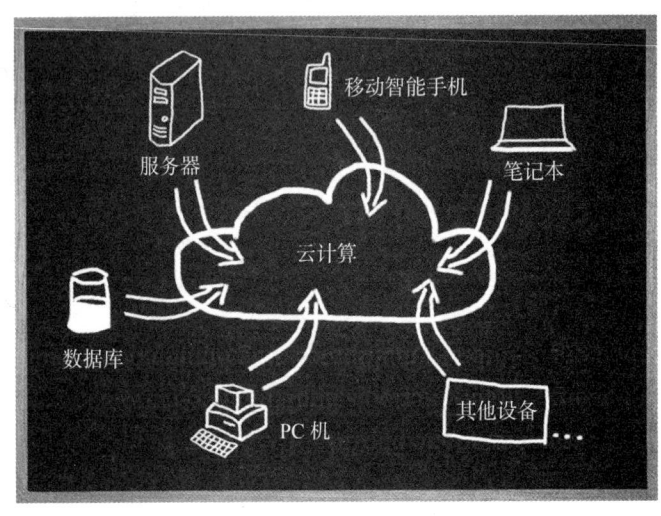

图11.1 典型的云结构

11.2 在云端工作

在第10章中，创建了一个简单的在字典中搜索特定词的应用程序，接着建立了一个单核应用程序，然后建立了一个多核的应用程序。

如图11.2所示，运行这两个执行简单字典搜索的应用程序。从iPad上启动运行在云端的这些程序。与在第10章中的版本相比，代码并没有改变。

sp.py是单进程版本

mp.py是多进程版本

在图11.3中，在桌面浏览器执行简单单核和多核这两个应用程序。正如你看到的那样，通过Python Anywhere，即使在双核云计算机上运行这个多进程应用程序，多核的版本也要运行得快一点。

图11.2 从 iPad 运行云端程序

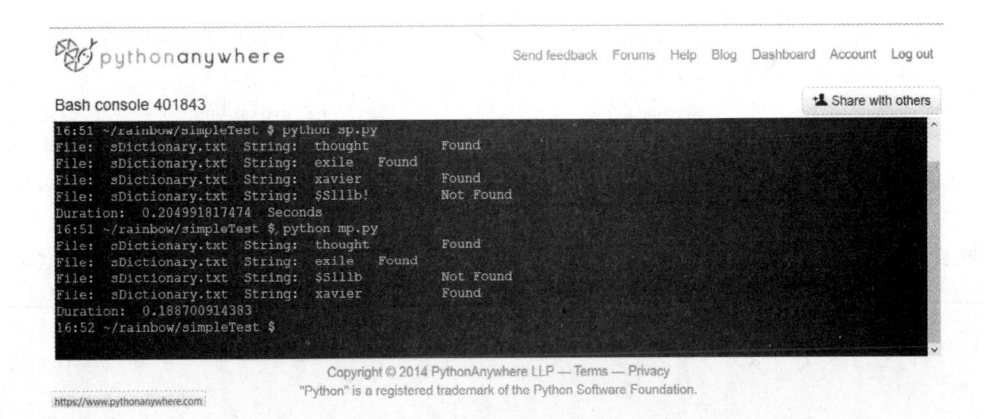

图11.3 从桌面执行云端的简单和多进程应用程序

要注意的是，在这些例子中，并没有对运行于云端的Python程序做哪怕一行代码的修改。因为代码由标准Python解释器执行，而我使用了Python标准库，所以代码就会执行。如果使用第三方库，就需要将其加入基于云的Python安装中（并不是不能做到），如果你坚持使用标准库，事情就会简单得多。如图11.4所示，使用了云服务Python Anywhere，或者网站www.pythonanywhere.com。Python Anywhere是一个在云端开启Python应用程序实验的极好的地方。最小限度账户的注册是免费的，给你的程序提供使用一些核和存储空间。我有一个12美元每月的账户，这种账户给予我500 GB的存储和每天20000个CPU秒。CPU秒是指CPU时间，亦即花费在运行代码上的时间，在内部是用纳秒（nanosecond）来测量的。大部分的在线云服务参考了Amazon的CPU秒的定义："等价于64位的1.0~1.2 GHz 2007皓龙（Opteron）或者2007至强（Xeon）处理器的能力。"

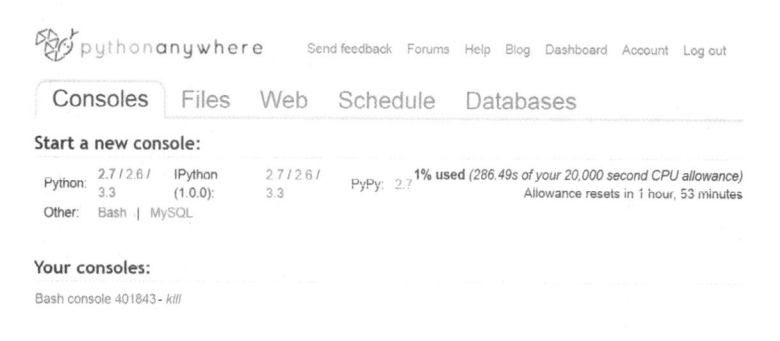

图11.4 pythonanywhere主页

11.3 云端服务的可选资源

很多现有的云服务提供了访问少则2~3个，多则1000个的核来运行程序。表11.1提供了一部分资源列表，你以后或许要用到（注意，有一些已经可以执行Python代码，而其他的则要求你自己安装Python环境）。另外，有一些已经有了定制的客户应用程序界面或称为API，可以应用于多进程，而另外一些则要使用原生的方法。

表11.1 一些云服务的特点

云服务	URL	说明
[PythonAnywhere]	pythonanywhere.com	运行2.6, 2.7, 3.3版本的原生Python代码，如图11.5所示
[PiCloud]	picloud.com	运行原生的Python代码，但需要导入其多进程处理的云模块，如图11.6和图11.7所示
[Digital Ocean]	digitalocean.com	需要安装一个该环境的Python包，以及应用程序，如图11.8和图11.9所示
Others	Amazon、Google、ATT、IBM、Rackspace等	当扩展应用程序时，这些服务为你提供各种解决方案

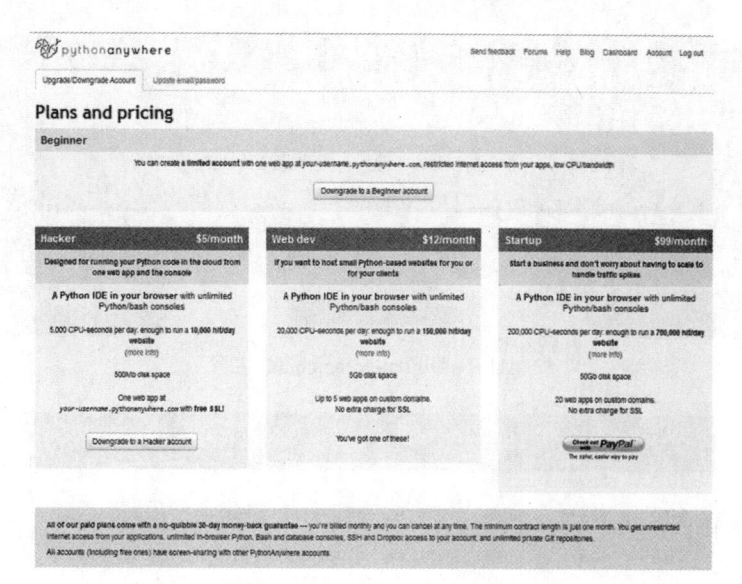

图11.5 pythonanywhere方案

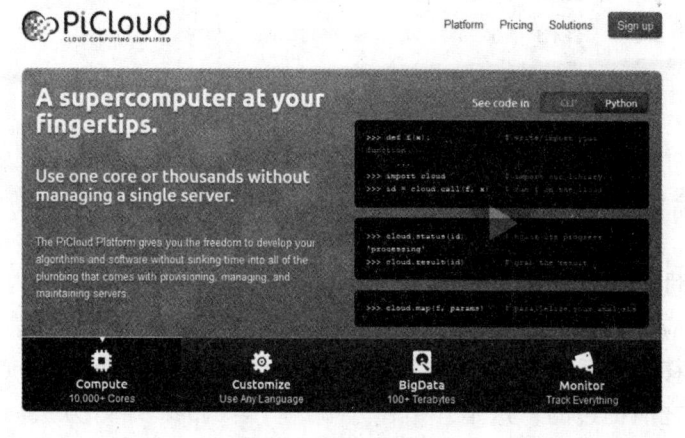

图11.6 PiCloud的主页

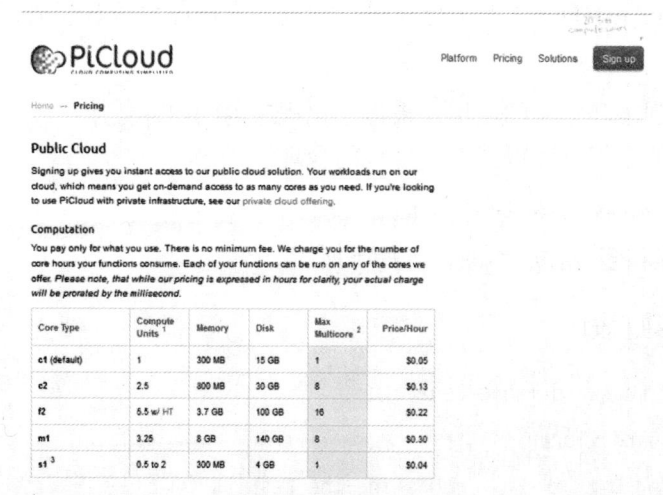

图11.7 PiCloud的方案

图11.8　DigitalOcean.com的主页

Monthly	Hourly	Memory	CPU	Storage	Transfer	Get Started
$160	$0.238	16GB	8 Cores	160GB SSD	6TB	Sign Up
$320	$0.476	32GB	12 Cores	320GB SSD	7TB	Sign Up
$480	$0.705	48GB	16 Cores	480GB SSD	8TB	Sign Up
$640	$0.941	64GB	20 Cores	640GB SSD	9TB	Sign Up
$960	$1.411	96GB	24 Cores	960GB SSD	10TB	Sign Up

图11.9　DigitalOcean.com的方案

11.4　在云端创建彩虹表

为了创建高性能的基于Python的调查平台，有一些权衡和选项值得考虑。适合于云端运行的有趣的应用程序之一就是在第10章讨论并实验过的生成彩虹表。将单进程和多进程版本的应用移动到云端，有一些需要注意的地方。首先，使用Python Anywhere来展示这项能力。如之前提过的，这是开始在云端进行尝试的一个好方法，因为这个环境可以执行2.6、2.7和3.3版本的原生Python应用。由于我确认仅使用标准库模块和核心语言元素，移植到Python Anywhere云就十分简单。但是，我准备对第10章开发的实验代码做一些重大的修改：

(1) 通过消除列表和字典的使用，来最小化程序内的内存使用
(2) 简化使用的字符，以保持口令生成的合理性
(3) 扩展生成的口令长度达到4~8个字符

生成的单线程和多线程版本的代码如下所示。

11.4.1　单核彩虹表

```
# Single Core Password Table Generator

# import standard libraries

import hashlib                    # Hashing the results
import time                       # Timing the operation
import sys
```

```python
import os
import itertools              # Creating controled combinations
#
# Create a list of characters to include in the password generation
#
chars = ['a','b','c','d','e','f','g','h']
# Define a hypothetical SALT value
SALT = "&45Bvx9"
# Define the allowable range of password length
PW_LOW = 4
PW_HIGH = 8
print 'Processing Single Core'
print os.getcwd()
print 'Password Character Set:', chars
print 'Password Lenghts:', str(PW_LOW),'-', str(PW_HIGH)

# Mark the start time
startTime = time.time()

# Open a File for writing the results

try:
    # Open the output file
    fp = open('PW-ALL','w')
except:
    print 'File Processing Error'
    sys.exit(0)

# create a loop to include all passwords within the allowable range

pwCount = 0

for r in range(PW_LOW, PW_HIGH+1):

    # Apply the standard library interator
    for s in itertools.product(chars, repeat = r):

    # Hash each new password as they are generated

        pw = ' '.join(s)
        try:

            md5Hash = hashlib.md5()
            md5Hash.update(SALT+pw)
            md5Digest = md5Hash.hexdigest()

            # Write the hash, password pair to the file
            fp.write(md5Digest+' '+pw+'\n')
            pwCount+ = 1
            del md5Hash
        except:
            print'File Processing Error'

# Close the output file when complete
fp.close()

# When complete calculate the elapsed time
```

```
    elapsedTime = time.time() - startTime
    print 'Single Core Rainbow Complete'
    print 'Elapsed Time:', elapsedTime
    print 'Passwords Generated:', pwCount
    print
```

11.4.2 多核彩虹表

```
# Multi-Core Password Table Generator

    # import standard libraries

    import hashlib          # Hashing the results
    import time             # Timing the operation
    import os
    import itertools        # Creating controled combinations
    import multiprocessing  # Multiprocessing Library

#
# Create a list of characters to include in the password generation
#

chars = ['a','b','c','d','e','f','g','h']

# Define a hypothetical SALT value
SALT = "&45Bvx9"

# Define the allowable range of password length

PW_LOW = 4
PW_HIGH = 8

def pwGenerator(size):

    pwCount = 0
    # create a loop to include all passwords within range specified

    try:

        # Open a File for writing the results
        fp = open('PW-'+str(size),'w')

        for r in range(size, size+1):

            # Apply the standard library interator

            for s in itertools.product(chars, repeat = r):
                # Process each password as they are generated
                pw = ''.join(s)

                # Perform hashing of the password
                md5Hash = hashlib.md5()
                md5Hash.update(SALT+pw)
                md5Digest = md5Hash.hexdigest()

                # Write the hash, password pair to the file
                fp.write(md5Digest+' '+pw+'\n')
                pwCount+ = 1
                del md5Hash

    except:
```

```
            print'File/Hash Processing Error'
        finally:
            fp.close()
            print str(size),'Passwords Processed = ', pwCount
#
# Create Main Function
#
if __name__ == '__main__':

    print'Processing Multi-Core'
    print os.getcwd()
    print'Password string:', chars
    print'Password Lengths:', str(PW_LOW),'-', str(PW_HIGH)

    # Mark the starting time of the main loop
    startTime = time.time()

    # create a process Pool with 5 processes
    corePool = multiprocessing.Pool(processes = 5)

    # map corePool to the Pool processes
    results = corePool.map(pwGenerator, (4, 5, 6, 7, 8))

    elapsedTime = time.time() - startTime

    # When complete calculate the elapsed time

    elapsedTime = time.time() - startTime
    print'Multi-Core Rainbow Complete'
    print'Elapsed Time:', elapsedTime
    print'Passwords Generated:', pwCount
    print
```

可以看到，在Python Anywhere中的单核和多核解决方案的两个执行结果，分别参见图11.10和图11.11。我还显示了在Linux环境中的执行结果，如图11.12所示。实际的性能基于许多因素，当然会有所不同。因为我的Linux是专用的并且运行在3.0 GHz的四核处理器上，所以其性能优于此处的云服务。单核和多核的解决方案显示了一个与单核和多核性能成比例的结果，正如我们预期的那样（参见表11.2）。

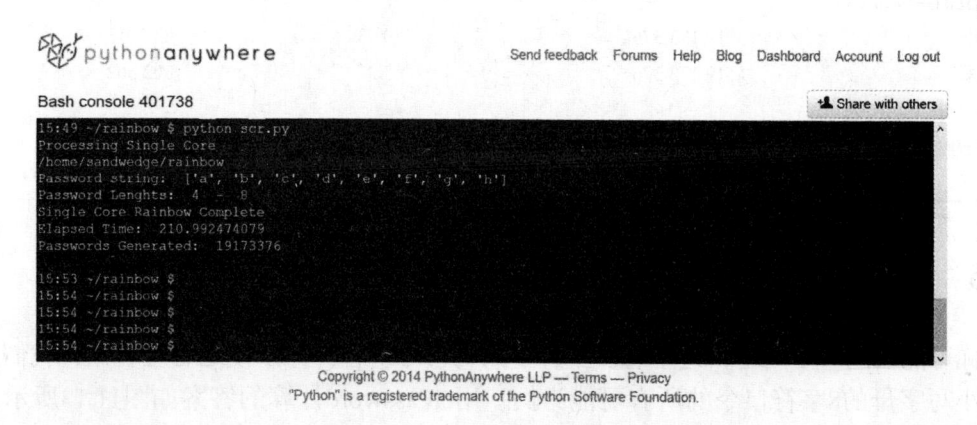

图11.10　pythonanywhere单核执行结果

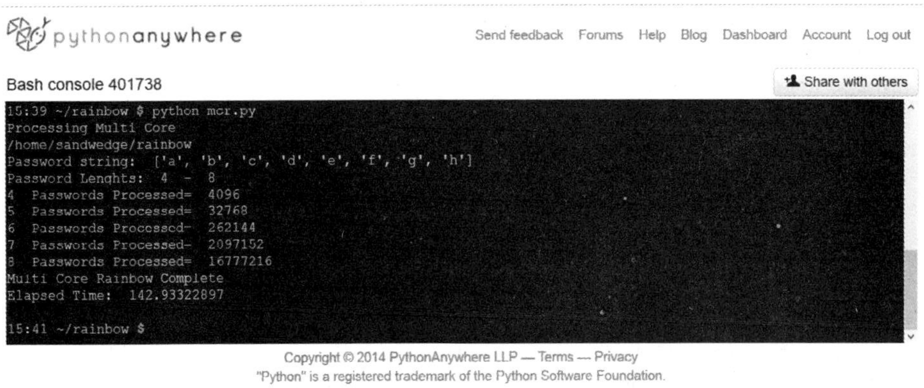

图11.11　pythonanywhere多核执行结果

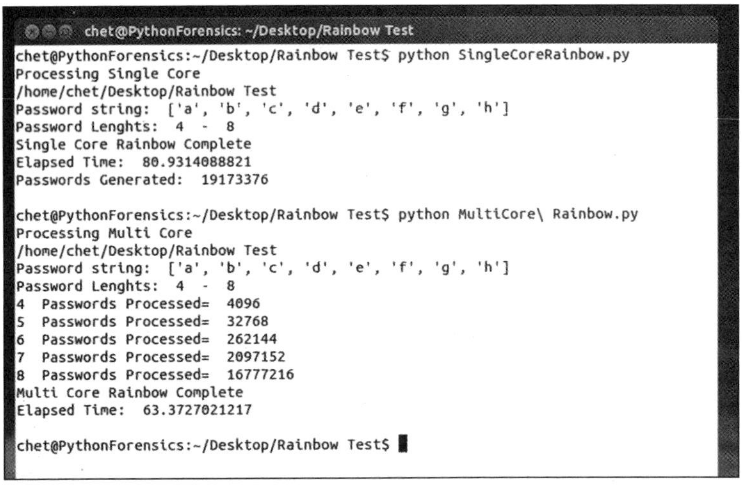

图11.12　独立的Linux单核/多核执行结果

表11.2　运行结果小结

运行的环境	生成和处理的口令数	花费的时间	每秒产生的口令
独立的四核Linux			
单核	19 173 376	80.93	236 913
多核	19 173 376	63.37	302 562
Python Anywhere			
单核	19 173 376	210.99	90 873
多核	19 173 376	142.93	134 145

11.5　口令生成计算

你可能会问一个问题，这里有多少种不同的口令组合？为了使之有理有据，我们以只使用小写字母的8字符口令的所有可能为例。用elPassword计算的答案如图11.13所示。在图11.14中，elPassword计算的答案则是利用了大小写字母、数字以及特殊符号的8字符口令组合。

图11.13　elPassword上的小写字母的8字符组合

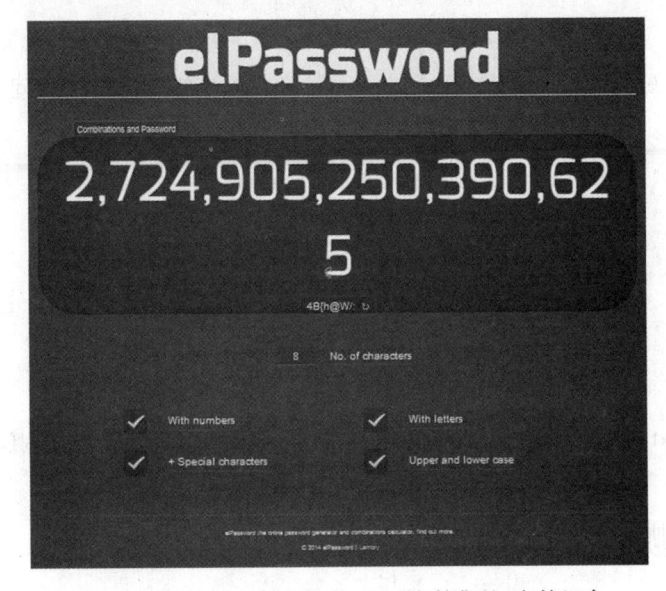

图11.14　elPassword上的全ASCII字符集的8字符组合

使用LastBit的在线资源，按照每秒302 000条口令的最高性能，可以计算暴力攻击所需要的时间长度。在图11.15至图11.18中，执行了4个单独的运行。前2个是分别在1台和100台计算机上使用所有的小写字母，而后2个则分别是在100台和10000台计算机上使用所有的ASCII字符集。自己动手试试看。

图11.15　LastBit使用1台计算机计算小写字母所需要的时间

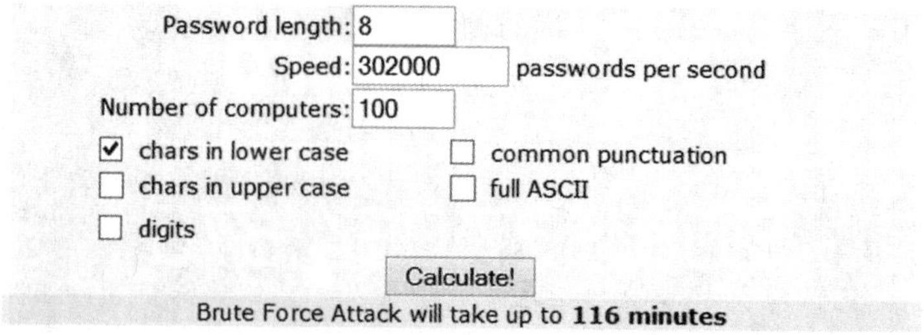

图11.16　LastBit使用100台计算机计算小写字母所需要的时间

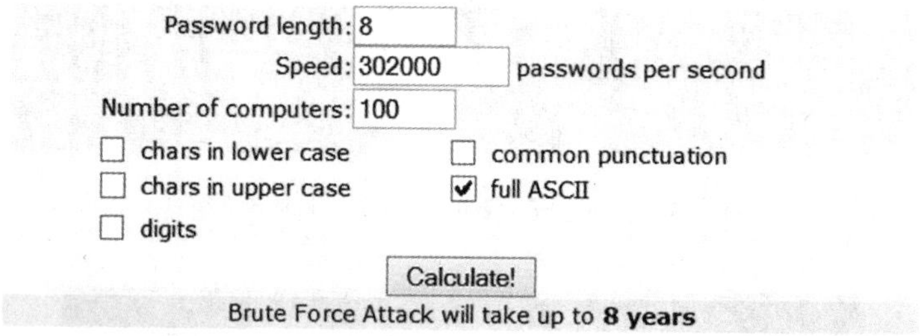

图11.17　LastBit使用100台计算机计算ASCII字符集所需要的时间

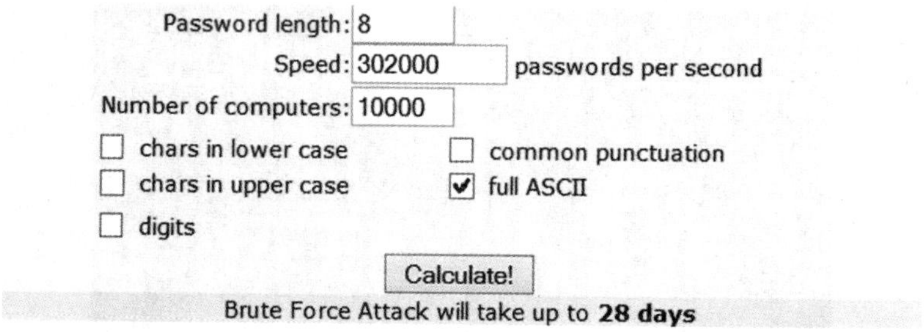

图11.18　Last Bit使用10 000台计算机计算ASCII字符集所需要的时间

11.6　章节回顾

在这一章中介绍了Python Anywhere，一款在云端执行原生Python代码的云服务。从多个平台演示了在云端执行原生Python代码有多么简单。接着，修改了彩虹表口令生成器来最小化内存使用，减少字符，并扩展这一生成过程，以实现达到4~8个字符长度的解决方法。然后，检测了每一个结果的性能，以确定高性能Linux平台和在云端都需要花费多长时间。找获得这些结果，并对破解8字符的口令需要的时间和计算机数量做出了合理的推测。

11.7　问题小结

1. 还有其他哪些程序能受益于云环境的执行，并对取证和调查社区有帮助？
2. 在撰写本文的时候，Intel和AMD都在试验具有16，32，64甚至96个核的处理器，如果我们推测在未来的几年，期望能够得到1000个核的CPU，并不是没有道理的。这将如何改变我们生成或哈希口令、破解加密或搜索数据的能力？

3. 在桌面环境开发和测试你的多核方案。设计并让它能够很容易地部署到云平台，如Python Anywhere。在Python Anywhere建立你的免费账户并用单核和多核方案进行实验。

11.8 补充资料

1. http://www.pythonanywhere.com
2. http://www.picloud.com
3. http://www.digitalocean.com
4. http://projects.lambry.com/elpassword/
5. http://lastbit.com/pswcalc.asp

第12章 展　　望

12.1 本章简介

数字调查和计算机取证领域即将迎来25年。我曾有机会与来自美国纽约州警察局的Stevens共事，他是早期的先驱者之一，也是国内最早一批的（数字）警察之一，这批警察成功地从计算机中收集证据并以此将涉嫌计算机犯罪的人定罪。"作为最早应对由科技犯罪带来威胁的执法部门之一，纽约州警察局在1992年建立了计算机犯罪部门（the Computer Crime Unit）"（Stevens，2001）。

我也曾有机会作为主要调查员服务于第一个数字取证研究项目，此项目由空军研究实验室（Air Force Research Laboratory）于1998年发起。该项目的构思源自两位本领域的先驱者Joe Giordano和John Feldman，他们也都供职于该实验室。项目的名称是"取证信息战争需求"，成果是一个内容全面的报告，描绘了本领域向前发展的一系列需求的轮廓。

然而，认为数字调查、网络空间调查，亦或计算机取证是当今的一门成熟的科学或者学科的想法是错误的。以下摘录自2001年我在第一届数字取证研究研讨会上的演讲（DFRWS，2001）。

电子取证基本原则
- 数字证据范围广大，错综复杂，且易被操纵、隐藏、删除或者发现不了。
- 将重点相互联系起来可能是一件充满不确定性的，且多是无从定论的费力过程。
- 网络空间犯罪和网络空间恐怖主义的分布式特性使得追踪罪犯和受害人，以及打击犯罪的技术变得困难重重。
- 我们的成果可能将受到挑战，被否决，被无视，被误解，被不断地怀疑。

网络空间取证技术的必备特点
- 可靠的
- 精准的
- 不可否认性的
- 易于使用的
- 简单的
- 安全的
- 灵活的
- 异构的
- 分布式

- 自动化
- 免费，或者至少是便宜的

基本问题——网络空间取证技术
- 谁收集数字证据？
- 使用什么工具或者技术？
- 基于什么样的标准和实践？
- 谁审查并验证这种实践？
- 哪一些人具有与数据证据有关的数字探员身份？
- 证据一旦被识别后，是如何处理的？
- 证据是怎样被验证的，通过谁？
- 其有效时间多长？
- 其是如何被存储并被保管的？
- 如何确保数字证据的完整性？
- 使用什么技术来确保证据？
- 为何相信这种工具或技术？
  - 谁开发了它？
  - 它是在何地，何种条件下被开发出来的？
  - 该种技术背后所依赖的软件和硬件有哪些？
  - 谁验证并认可了该技术和该处理过程？
  - 被认可的版本是哪一个（或者哪些）？
  - 谁培训并认可了使用者？
- 这种证据是否有其独特性？
- 这种证据是否是更优先的？
- 这种证据是否坚实？
  - 文件是何时被创建，修改或者销毁的？
  - 处理事务是何时被执行的？
  - 信息是何时发出或接收的？
  - 病毒或者蠕虫是何时植入的？
  - 网络攻击是何时开始的？
  - 在勘察阶段完成多久后，攻击开始？
  - 在哪一个时区？
- 在哪一个点，系统日志依然有效？
- 嫌疑人是否具有犯罪的契机？
- 在网络空间，嫌疑人在哪里？
- 如何才能追踪其足迹？
  - 技术上
  - 法律上

- 他们接下来可能会攻击哪里？
- 他们有同谋吗？抑或是内部人员？
- 他们的能力如何？
    - 带宽
    - 运算能力
    - 水平如何
    - 资源
- 我们之前是否见到过他们？
    - 他们是否比之前更老练？
- 他们的同谋是谁？

小结
- 我们应将精力集中在识别并解决数字取证和数字证据的关键基本要素上。
- 我们应齐心协力，建立能够解决涉及这些基本要素的技术。
- 我们要研究，使用法庭科学来解答有关网络犯罪和恐怖分子问题的目标在哪里？
    - 他们的位置，狡诈程度，可能的下一个目标。
    - 应该怎样做才能阻止他们？
    - 应该如何加强防卫以应对他们？

沿着这个短暂的思路走下去，将是我今天做出这样一个演讲的可怕之处，还有很多相关的部分也是如此。最大的问题便是我们该由此走向何方，Python取证将扮演一个怎样的角色？

12.2 由此我们将走向何方

本书已经指出了关键所在，当把核心问题与Python语言相结合，新的解决方案研发的可能性在哪里。当然可能有所争议的是，其他的语言也能够创造出应对这些问题的可行方案。然而问题在于：

- 这些其他的解决方案是开源并且免费的吗？
- 它们是否可以跨平台呢（包括Windows、Mac、Linux、移动平台和云）？
- 它们是否可以被任何人使用和阅读呢？
- 它们是否具有全球性的支持呢？
- 它们是否营造了一个为计算机科学家、社会学家、执法人员和刚踏上这个领域的学生们能够快速进入的合作性环境呢？

在我看来，紧接着的重大阶段如下：

(1) 构建一个真实的合作性环境，人们可以分享信息（难题、想法和解决方案）。
(2) 获得友好的支持，因为在解决新的调查困难方面，技术是不断进步的。
(3) 开发一个程序和脚本的库，可供下载、扩展和改进，且可被应用于实际问题。
(4) 与按需培训课程集成，深入Python和取证的核心领域。

(5) 一个验证/证明流程，允许第三方组织（如NIST）对用于执法部门，利用Python开发的解决方案进行验证。一旦这个流程建立好，大多数验证工作可以自动完成，并通过使用标准化的取证测试镜像加速验证过程。

(6) 厂商们可以提供应用程序接口，开放集成基于Python的解决方案到已有的取证技术中的可能性。实际上这也可以完善厂商方案的功能，允许他们在更短时间内解决新问题，并且使得他们的产品在市场中更有价值。

(7) 构建有几百个（甚至几千）的处理器核，PB字节级存储和TB字节级内存的基于云的实验平台，以解决运算方面的难题。而且该环境可对学术界和学生开放，以快速地提升课堂教学，推进大学、学院、从业者、厂商和研究者之间的合作，以解决真正的难题。该环境还能为创新提供一个竞赛形式，参赛团队可以来自国内或全球。还能创建针对特定解决方案类型的基准测试（Benchmark），以了解各种方案的性能表现。

(8) 值得考虑的关键问题如下所述。

贯穿本书，提供了几个重要领域的基于Python的实例。这些例子只是基础，尚需要更多工作。我已经指出了一些需要进一步研究和关注的重要问题：

a. **高级搜索和索引**　搜索和索引肯定是所有调查中的核心元素。然而，提高速度和准确度，以及结果与搜索及索引的相关度是必需的。调查员需要能快速提供下列特性的解决方案：

　i. 搜索和索引的结果可以呈现出与案件相关的信息。这种功能强大的搜索/索引必须能揭示出不明显或者被当前技术遗漏的信息。例如，搜索结果能够将时间与空间之间的联系包含到一个直观的视图中。

　ii. 搜索和索引结果能够将多个案件中的信息联系起来，发现之前未曾关联过的同伙、网络、电话、时间、位置以及行为分析的相互联系。

b. **元数据提取**　图像和多媒体的内容包含了相当多的元数据，包括但不限于时间、日期、创建的设备、位置信息、主体内容等。如今这些信息的提取、关联和推理的任务留给了调查员。新的方法给快速提取、关联这些信息，为犯罪现场提供一个更全面和综合的视图带来了希望。

c. **事件同步**　根据2013年的Statistic Brain（2014），6.45亿个注册的推特用户平均每天产生5800万的推文，而且还有每天59亿次的Google搜索，2013年有超过2万亿次的搜索被记录。这仅是每时每刻发生在互联网事件中的一小部分。不管是来自互联网、公司网络，甚至是个人桌面的事件，我们对其同步和推断的能力似乎已经不可接受。我们需要开发出新的可行方法，能够使得这些孤立的行为和事件有意义，并提供确定性的证据。

d. **自然语言**　互联网已经毫无疑问地打破了边境线，带来了全球范围的即时互动和交流。在第7章中已初步涉及了自然语言处理，你已经看到了能够进行语言处理的潜在力量。用于提取语义、确定作者身份、解释意图的自然语言处理应用程序都尽在我们的掌握中。拓展这些技术用以处理更为广泛的各种语言，改进演绎推理，提取人物、地点和物品，评估过去、现在和将来可能的活动等，都是可能的。

e. **Python的发展** 本书提供的展示实例和源代码都是针对Python 2.7.x开发的，旨在确保其跨平台的最佳兼容性。然而，针对2.7.x和3.3.x版本的所有实例将来都能在网络上下载。

Python和第三方的Python库随着网络的发展而继续拓展着。有人甚至声称Python将是最后一门你不得不学的编程语言。我认为这略显夸大，但是这门语言的一些特性是未来语言的根基。在本书写作期间，确切地说是2014年2月9日，Python Version 3.4发布了。根据Python编程语言官方网站（www.python.org）的介绍，主要的语言改进包括：

1. 一个pathlib模块，提供了面向对象方式的文件系统路径。
2. 一个标准化的enum模块。
3. 帮助生成内建类型的内省信息的构造增强。
4. 改进了对象析构的语义。
5. 向标准库中增加了单调度通用函数。
6. 一个新的CAPI，可用于实现定制的内存分配器。
7. 改变了文件的描述符，防止在子进程中被默认继承。
8. 新的statistics模块。
9. 对Python的模块导入系统的模块元数据进行标准化。
10. 与pip包管理器捆绑的安装器。
11. 一个用于跟踪Python内存分配的新的tracemalloc模块。
12. 针对Python字符串和二进制数据的新哈希算法。
13. 针对序列化（pickled，一种对象持久化方法）对象新改进的协议。
14. 一个asyncio的模块，一个新的异步IO框架。

正如你看到的，这种语言以充满活力的节奏不断地演化，同时新改进的第三方Python库也不停地研发出来，推动着取证和数字调查工具的发展。第三方库和工具实在是数不胜数，我决定列出我心目中的前十个。

1. Pillow，一个代替传统的Python Image Library（PIL）的库，用于处理和检查数字图像。
2. wxPython，对于那些需要构建跨平台GUI（图形用户界面）的读者，这个工具包是我所推崇的。
3. Requests，最好的http接口库。
4. Scrapy，如果你的取证调查要求进行Web数据爬取，这个库能帮你创建新颖且极具创意的方法。
5. Twsited，这是为那些需要开发异步网络应用程序的人而准备的。
6. Scapy，对于那些有意进行数据包嗅探和分析的人，Scrapy提供了丰富的功能。
7. NLTK，自然语言工具包。这个工具包涉及广泛，对于调查文本和语言结构必不可少。
8. IPython，当体验新的语言元素，库亦或是模块时，这个高级的Python Shell在你工作和努力的每一个方面都有帮助。
9. WingIDE，这并不是一个库，但我认为这个集成开发环境是最佳的IDE，即使对于最为老练的研究人员，专业版也提供了他们所需要的一切。

10. Googlemaps，许多取证应用程序收集地理标签信息，这个库允许你轻松地与Google地图系统集成。

  f. **多进程** 为了更加有效地深入这些领域，我们使用最新处理器和云解决方案的本领不可或缺。"国际半导体技术路线图"，这是一个由来自世界范围内的半导体公司的专家描绘的，用来展望半导体发展的路线图。它预测到2015年，将会出现搭载了450个处理核心的电子产品，到2020年上升至1500个核心。

  如今，在两个主要处理器生产商的产品中，有哪些可利用的呢？Intel和AMD的CPU参见图12.2和图12.3。不到1000美元就可以拥有这些处理器，不到3000美元便可以组建一个有2个处理器，20至32个核，64 GB内存，数TB级的存储的系统。这肯定是迈向多核和多进程解决方案必需的一步。当其与设计优良的多核Python应用程序搭配，就能向最新的技术迈出一大步。一旦我们见到能够在一个处理器上制造出64、128、256和1024个核心的产品出现，世界将再次发生变化。

图12.1 云端的多进程

图12.2 AMD的6300系列16核处理器

图12.3 Intel的Xeon E7系列10核20线程处理器

12.3 结束语

  将Python语言应用到数字调查和取证应用有着强大的前途。需要的是一个合作社区，这个社区包括：从业者、研究者、开发者、教授、学生、调查员、检查员、警察、律师、检察官、法官、厂商、政府和科研机构等。而且，有着数以千计的核，PB级的存储，TB级的内存的云计算平台也是必需的。

  我向你发出参与的挑战，如果阅读本书的每个人都能贡献出一个点子、挑战性的问题或解决方法，那将会是一个怎样惊人的开始。请从访问Python-Forensics.Org开始吧，我将十分乐意听见你的声音！

12.4 补充资料

1. 司法委员会犯罪分委会打击网络犯罪听证会，网址http://commdocs.house.gov/committees/judiciary/hju72616.000/hju72616_0f.htm; 2001

2. 信息战取证需求研究F30602-98-C-0243. 最终技术报告, 1999.2.2, WetStone Technologies, Inc.提供
3. 一种数字取证研究路线图, 尤蒂卡, 纽约, 网址http://www.dfrws.org/2001/dfrwsrm-final.pdf; 2001.8.7-8
4. 2014.1.1, 网址http://www.statisticbrain.com/twitter-statistics/
5. 破解1000核处理器性能难题. Nick Heath, 网址http://www.zdnet.com/cracking-the-1000-core-processor-power-challenge-7000015554/